DUTCH-ASIATIC TRADE 1620-1740

KRISTOF GLAMANN

DUTCH-ASIATIC TRADE

1620 1740

1981

MARTINUS NIJHOFF
'S-GRAVENHAGE

First published in 1958 by Danish Science Press, Copenhagen and Martinus Nijhoff, 's-Gravenhage

ISBN 90 247 9050 6

Contents

Preface

The present monograph has grown out of a good many years of study of the history of the European trade to the East Indies. The starting-point actually was Danish. Having treated the history of the Danish Asiatic Company during the period 1732–1772 I went abroad in order to familiarize myself with the background to the reorganization of Danish trade about 1732. It was especially the possible connexion with the dissolved Ostend Company and the counter-measures, diplomatic as well as economic, of the Dutch, English, and French companies that interested me. Through these investigations I got acquainted with the various Northwest European company records and soon realized that the Dutch archives offered a rich material, especially as regards quantities and prices. A study on the Dutch Company's trade in Japanese copper, a subject which had previously occupied Scandinavian historians in connexion with the question of the status of Swedish copper on the European market in the 17th century, amplified my knowledge of the archives in the Hague to such a degree that I dared to tackle the greater object of giving a description of the Company's trade as a whole during its heyday. On various points it proved to be necessary to make comparative investigations, especially in the English East India Company's archives in London.

It has not only been an interest in economic history in general and the wealth of the archives of the Dutch Company in special which has made light work of it. The connexion of the subject with the history of the Asiatic countries has been a very strong incentive, too; not least the renaissance which informs historical research in many of the Asiatic countries in the present day and the consequent interest among Asiatic scholars, also in the European sources of their own history, in my view must sooner or later result in a general revaluation of the history of the companies. The fertility of a discussion of the Vasco da Gama epoch was evident at the conference concerning historical writing on the peoples of Asia at the London School of Oriental and African Studies in August 1956. My study is also intended to offer modest contributions to this discussion. The evaluation of the European activities in Asia seems an extraordinarily suitable subject of research athwart tradional national barriers.

My studies have benefited by the helpfulness of the staffs of archives and libraries. First of all I want to express my gratitude to the kind and competent staff of the Algemeen Rijksarchief of the Hague. I direct my thanks to the Keeper of the Archives, Dr. E. Hardenberg, and want especially to mention Mrs. Roelofsz-Meilink, Keeper of the East India documents of the Archives. Furthermore I am indebted to the staffs of the Royal Library of the Hague and of the Gemeente-Archief Amsterdam for facilities. In the latter place Dr. Simon Hart in this case as well as in the case of my other studies in the Archives has readily placed his great knowledge at my disposal, just as he has done me the friendly turn of reading the Dutch quotations in my manuscript. Furthermore, I am much obliged to the staffs of the pleasant Commonwealth Relations Office, London, where the records of the East India Company are kept, and of the British Museum and the Belgian Stadsarchief Antwerpen, Antwerp, where I had facilities for the study of the documents of the Ostend Company, furthermore to the staffs of the French Archives Municipales de Nantes, the Archives Départementales de la Loire-Inférieure at Nantes, and the Archives Nationales in Paris. Finally I offer my best thanks to the staffs of the Swedish Riksarkivet in Stockholm and of the Danish Rigsarkiv and the Royal Library in Copenhagen. Everywhere I have been met with great obligingness and helpfulness.

The manuscript for this work was finished in October 1956. The translation into English has been made by Mr. Niels Haislund, M.A., whom I offer my best thanks.

My visits to archives and libraries abroad were possible only by virtue of good support from home. I must point out the interest which my investigations have been met with at the University of Copenhagen. I am highly indebted to all the professors at the Department of History, Dr. Astrid Friis, Dr. Aksel E. Christensen, Dr. Povl Bagge, and Dr. Sven Henningsen. I owe a special debt of gratitude to Professor Astrid Friis, in whom I have as a Research Fellow found a never failing interest in my work coupled with very great sympathy. Finally, it is my pleasant duty to conclude this preface by offering my respectful thanks to *Den Hielmstierne-Rosencroneske Stiftelse, Statens Almindelige Videnskabsfond*, and *Tuborgfondet* for financial support towards my studies.

Copenhagen, October 1956 and February 1958.

K. G.

Introduction to the second edition

Since I wrote *Dutch-Asiatic Trade* nearly 25 years ago many important studies have appeared, too many for renumeration. Let me therefore confine myself to the tying of a small bouquet of titles to be presented to the prospective reader, and accompanied by a few additional observations of my own, as an introductory supplement to this reprint of my dissertation from 1958. The titles all represent contributions of much relevance to my topic and of stimulating qualities.

Comprehensive bibliographies do exist. In 1960 Professor W. Ph. Coolhaas published *A Critical Survey of Studies on Dutch Colonial History* [1] of which a revised edition is in print. Bibliographical lists are abundant in Frédéric Mauro's *L'expansion européenne 1600–1870* (1964).[2] Attention should also be called to the Center for the History of European Expansion, founded in 1975 by the Faculty of the School of Humanities of the University of Leyden, and its newsletter, now being issued under the title of *Itinerario*, with current bibliographical information. F. S. Gaastra, a member of the Center, has recently written two excellent short accounts of the Dutch company's history down to c. 1800 for volumes VII and VIII of the *Algemene Geschiedenis der Nederlanden* (1980/81) with a selected bibliography accompanying his chapters.

The richly faceted history of Dutch-Asian trade is proceeding within a wide time horizon and with activities spanning half the world. The unfolding of a company of almost global dimensions testifies to the vitality of Dutch commercial enterprise and its example must be of interest to any analysis and discussion of the nature of Dutch capitalism during the early modern epoch.

Overseas ventures set men and matter in motion on a grand scale. The dispatch of the fleets as well as the sales of the returning cargoes were part of the fluctuations of the economies, nationally and internationally. Asian goods figured prominently on the widely circulating and leading Amsterdam price lists. Politically and culturally the Dutch company put its mark on the Netherlands. The foundation of the com-

[1] Koninklijk Instituut voor Taal-, Land- en Volkenkunde. Bibliographical Series No. 4, ('s-Gravenhage, 1960).

[2] Nouvelle Clio No. 27, (Paris, 1964).

pany was an inseparable part of the genesis of the State; close personal links connected the management with members of the ruling class (the so-called *regenten*), although the company not always acted as an extension of the government. The VOC constituted the main channel through which Asian things reached the Netherlands and from there radiated over Europe and beyond. Furthermore, company operations implied a substantial volume of know-how and managerial skills. The feeding of its complicated machinery was a question of logistics and organization. The collection and processing of data engaged people far and wide; even in the field of international relations and diplomacy the company relied upon its own hand-picking of emissaries and contacts who operated side by side with the official representatives of the Dutch government. Cargoes of documents were a regular part of the home going fleet (stowed on board the so-called "bookships") including the account-books and the mandatory diaries that were so meticulously kept by the company servants at all overseas places.

The Dutch East India Company has been termed a state-within-the state or a state-outside-the state. It is tempting to apply a modern analogy, namely that of a multi-national corporation. However, we do not yet possess any study of the company in this capacity. A good many questions assert themselves, some of them intriguing. Did the company adhere to specific principles of commerce? did it work out strategies? what kind of relationship did the *Heeren XVII* have with the company's shareholders and customers? how was the management recruited? how professional was it for the time? etc., etc. On the other hand, the present revival of interest in expansion history, especially among Dutch scholars, means that the prerequisites for such a study are rapidly building up. It may well be that *L'appétit vient en mangeant*.

Turning then to the literature, let me first mention the growing interest in the history of inter-continental trade and development of early modern capitalism, a theme to which the East India companies have lent material. Among the many quests for general syntheses recently published those by Immanuel Wallerstein[3] and Fernand Braudel[4] figure prominently. More directly related to the economic history of the Netherlands and the affairs of the Dutch company are the works of J. G. van Dillen and P. W. Klein. I am especially referring to the posthumus *magnum opus* of Professor van Dillen, *Van Rijkdom en Regenten* (1970),[5] and to Pro-

[3] *The Modern World-System*, I–II, (Academic Press Inc., 1974–80).

[4] *Civilisation Matérielle et Capitalism*, I–III, (Armand Collin, 1967–80).

[5] *Van Rijkdom en Regenten, Handboek tot de Economische en Sociale Geschiedenis van Nederland tijdens de Republiek*, (Martinus Nijhoff, 1970).

fessor Klein's remarkable monograph, *De Trippen in de 17de eeuw* (1965).[6] Not least Pieter Klein's work throws new light on the structure and fluctuations of the Dutch and European markets by studying and analyzing the transactions of the Trip family that was closely connected with the management of the Dutch East India Company. I have benefited by his study in an attempt of my own at interpreting the intricate manoeuvres of Dutch and Swedish copper cartels operating on the European scene during the stormy 1620's when Japanese copper was introduced by the VOC. My study is published in *Schwerpunkte der Kupferproduktion und des Kupferhandels in Europa 1500–1650*, (ed. H. Kellenbenz, 1977).[7] Perhaps it is not too impertinent, neither, to mention my interpretation of the activities of the Dutch company in a broader European context to be found in my contributions to *The Fontana Economic History of Europe*, vol. 2 (ed. Carlo Cipolla, 1971 and 1974)[8] and to *The Cambridge Economic History of Europe*, vol. V (ed. E. E. Rich & C. H. Wilson, 1977).[9]

The maritime and social history of the VOC has been subject to impressive new treatment applying the technique of modern data research upon the masses of material contained in the ledgers and journals, muster rolls and shipping records of the Dutch company. The fate of the individual soldier or sailor will remain in the dark forever, but we are now familar with *Jan Compagnie* as a prototype thanks to a plentitude of demographic and dietetic studies, health statistics and quantitative evidence on sailing routes, passages, etc. A fine example of this research is Professor J. R. Bruijn's study on *Dutch-Asiatic Shipping in the 17th and 18th Centuries* (1979).[10] The former tales of spectacular and adventurous sea voyages must now be supplemented with what is beneath the surface of the iceberg, namely a most solid basis of information that testifies to the regularity and uneventful way in which trade with Asia was carried out. It may be less entertaining and it certainly is detrimental to myth, but the newly collected material undoubtedly brings us into closer contact with historical reality.

One of the basic assumptions of my *Dutch-Asiatic Trade* was an appraisal of the VOC as a going concern to be undertaken from a central point of view, namely that of its headquarters in the Netherlands, the

[6] *De Trippen in de 17e Eeuw. Een Studie over het Ondernemersgedrag op de Hollandse Stapelmarkt*, (Assen, 1965).

[7] Kristof Glamann, "Japanese Copper on the European Market in the 17th Century", *op. cit.* pp. 280–9.

[8] "European Trade, 1500–1750", *op. cit.* pp. 427–526.

[9] "The Changing Pattern of Trade", *op. cit.* pp. 185–289, 645–51.

[10] *Rijks Geschiedkundige Publicatien*, Nos. 166–7. Vol. 165 will be published in 1982.

seat of its management. In this setting the primary aim of the *Heeren XVII* was not to find new markets for Dutch or European products in Asia but to supply the Netherlands and Europe with Asian goods. The home market was of course important; the company's trade policy, however, was not determined by local factors alone but depended in large measure upon fairly precise assessments of the state of the European market as a whole. The company was not instrumental in the re-exportation business; this was left to the merchant-houses who were the main customers of the auction sales. In this the Dutch concern resembled the policy and practice of the other European companies. They all conducted business with a keen view to that part of Europe which was unable to perform direct trade with Asia. No wonder that the competition between the companies was very hard.

These fundamentals call for comparative studies. On a limited scale I did try to include information about the other European companies when I collected material for my book, especially for the chapter on the tea trade. The introduction of the direct traffic to China was in my opinion a crucial and trendsetting event in the relations between Europe and Asia, therefore additional material on the beginning of this process was a must, but it also meant laborious digging in the archives. Today we are much better off. Information about the activities of the competitors of the VOC is now to be found in plenty in the works of an almost cosmopolitan group of scholars.

The English East India Company has got itself an eminent historian, K. N. Chaudhuri, who has dedicated his research to the study of the trade with India in the 17th and 18th centuries by making extensive use of quantitative data systematically extracted from English company records. The results are presented and interpreted in two impressive volumes, *The English East India Company 1600–1640*, (1965) and *The Trading World of Asia and the English East India Company, 1600–1760*, (1978). Another monumental work is due to the late French historian, Professor Louis Dermigny, *La Chine et l'Occident* (1964),[11] focusing on the Canton trade during the 18th and early 19th centuries. The history of the East India companies in general has been discussed on a comparative basis by Louis Dermigny, Holden Furber and myself at the 8th International Colloquium on Maritime History in Beyrouth 1966 and published in the proceedings ed. by Michel Mollet.[12] The Danish example has recently been analyzed by dr. Ole Feldbæk.[13] A voluminous

[11] *La Chine et l'Occident. Le Commerce à Canton au XVIIIe Siècle, 1719–1833*, tome I–III + album, in the Series Ports-Routes-Trafics, École Pratique des Hautes Études, VIe Section, (S.E.V.P.E.N., 1964).

monograph on the activities of the Swedish East India Company during the years 1731–1766 is now at our disposal thanks to the Belgian historian, Dr. C. Koninckx. His study also contains valuable information on the Ostende Company and especially on relations between the Austrian Netherlands and Scandinavia.[14] The study of the European competitors of the VOC has thus advanced far and wide.

But also the Dutch part of European trade to Asia is now being surveyed much more thoroughly than before. Bruijn's e.a. tables over Dutch-Asiatic shipping have been mentioned above. Of equal importance is F. S. Gaastra's study of the exportation of bullion and coins via the VOC.[15] The precious metals were instrumental in financing the imports to Europe and they played a crucial role in the build-up of international trade. Gaastra has presented us with basic information on the provision of the metals and on the composition of the cargoes.

These data can be put together with others in an effort to further the understanding of the complicated pattern of early modern monetary history.[16] Gold, silver and copper were globetrotters, they knew no frontiers and flowed all around the world. Again, the comparative approach is imperative. Japan is of special importance as a major source of bullion and coins for international trade, including the European companies trading to and within Asia. Japanese scholarship has provided us with ample evidence of the country's mining and trade in metals during the Tokugawa Shogunate. The study of Professor Seeichi Iwao and Atsushi Kobata has demonstrated that at its peak Japan's output of precious metals parallelled and even surpassed the production figures of the New World.[17] Through the commercial intercourse with Japan, these metals were instrumental in the offsetting of the trade balances of many

[12] *Sociétés et Compagnies de Commerce en Orient et dans l'Océan Indien*, in the Series Bibliothèque Générale de l'École des Hautes Études, VIe Section, (S.E.V.P.E.N., 1970). Holden Furber, "The History of the East India Companies: General Problems" (pp. 415–8); L. Dermigny, "L'Organisation et le Rôle des Compagnies", + "East India Company et Compagnie des Indes" (pp. 443–69); K. Glamann, "The Danish East India Compagny" (pp. 471–9).

[13] To be published in the series *Comparatives Studies in Overseas History*, vol. III (ed. J. L. Blussé & F. S. Gaastra) by the Leyden Center.

[14] *The First and Second Charter of the Swedish East India Company (1731–1766). A Contribution to the Maritime, Economic and Social History of North-Western Europe in its Relationships with the Far East. With a Preface by Professor K. Glamann*, (Van Ghemmert Pubishing Co., 1980).

[15] "De VOC in de 17e en 18e eeuw; de groei van een bedrijf Geld tegen goederen. Een structurele verandering in het Nederlands-Aziatisch handelsverkeer", *Bijdragen en Mededelingen betreffende de Geschiedenis der Nederlanden*, No. 91:2, (1976).

[16] For the International History Congress in San Francisco 1975 I convened a colloquium on the production of precious metals in early modern history; these papers are being edited by my colleague, Professor Hermann Kellenbenz. In 1977 the History Department of the University of Wisconsin organized an international workshop in "Pre-Modern Monetary History"; these papers are also in print.

regions within maritime Asia. Furthermore, in several areas domestic monetary circulation depended on the imports from Japan. European shipments of gold and silver were consequently influenced by the Japanese bullion flows.

It has generally been assumed (by Adam Smith and others) that the exportation of silver from Europe to Asia was due to a marked and wide disparity in the value of gold and silver in terms of commodities and labour in the two continents. New regional studies on South Asia as well as new data from Japan do not, however, support the ratio-argument. I have recently questioned the ratio-theory by pointing out that these advantages were often eliminated by the imperfect and very costly exchange mechanisms that prevailed at many Asian market places during the 17th and 18th centuries. Company trade in precious metals should therefore be regarded mostly as a cost factor closely connected with the acquisition of Asian commodities for Europe rather than with profitmaking by exportation from Europe.[18]

Historiography has changed the concept of Asia, too. It has broken down our notion of that vast scene from something vague and fluid into more concrete and useful concepts. A picture is on the point of emerging, as colorful and well composed as that which research into commercial history has drawn of Europe. In both cases it would be prudent not to apply too simplified or too general models of explanation. Asian trade structures varied greatly over time and from area to area.

Studies on Asian trade are abundant, not least on Dutch activities. Since 1960 Professor Coolhaas has edited the famous general letters of the governor-generals and council at Batavia to the *Heeren XVII*.[19] Another Dutch scholar, Professor M. A. P. Meilink-Roelofsz has especially dealt with the European imprint on Asia, first and foremost in an original study, *Asian Trade and European Influence in the Indonesian Archipelago between 1500 and about 1630* (1962). *De VOC in Asia* (1976) contains interesting studies by several Asian and European scholars on a broader scale and recently Professor Meilink-Roelofsz

[17] Seeichi Iwao, "Japanese Foreign Trade in the 16th and 17th Centuries", *Acta Asiatica*, Bulletin of the Institute of Eastern Studies, No. 30 (1976), pp. 1–18; Atsushi Kobata, "The Production and Uses of Gold and Silver in Sixteenth and Seventeenth Century Japan", *Economic History* Review, 2nd Ser. XVIII:2 (1965), pp. 245–66.

[18] Kristof Glamann, "Kinsei no kokusai bōeki to kikinzoku no ryūtsū ni kan-suru ichi-kōsatsu", *Tōhōgaku* vol. 56, (Tokyo, 1978), pp. 93–102. Kristof Glamann, "Ædelmetalstrømme og verdenshandel i 16.–18. århundrede, Nogle Synspunkter", *Historisk Tidsskrift*, vol. 80:1, (København, 1980), pp. 69–80.

[19] *Generale Missiven van Gouverneurs-Generaal en Raden aan Heeren XVII der Vereenigde Oost-Indische Compagnie*, R.G.P.-series, vols. 104, 112, 125, 134, 150 and 159. At present Professor Coolhaas' edition covers the period down to the year 1713.

has given a critical appraisal[20] of Professor Niels Steensgaard's dissertation on the structural crises in the European-Asian trade in the early 17th century that was published in 1975 under the title of *Carracks, Caravans and Companies*,[21] an indispensable study on the development in Western Asia using Ormuz as a focal point.

To the same group of subjects belong Professor S. Arasaratnam's ground breaking work from 1958 on *Dutch Power in Ceylon 1658–1687*, and Professor K. W. Goonewardena's *The Foundation of Dutch Power in Ceylon, 1638–1658* (1958). So does *Jan Company in Coromandel, 1605–1690* (1962)[22] by the Indian historian Professor T. Raychaudhuri.

A whole series of studies testify to the interest Indian scholarschip has taken in these matters, some of them being doctoral thesis from the Delhi School of Economics. Let me mention at random Professor Ashin Das Gupta, *Malabar in Asian Trade, 1740–1800* (1967), Indira Anand (née Narang) *Indias Overseas Trade, 1715–1725* (1969), Susil Chaudhuri, *Trade and Commercial Organization in Bengal 1650–1750* (1975), Om Prakash, *The Dutch East India Company and the Economy of Bengal, 1650–1717* (1967) and the same author, *Bullion for Goods: International Trade and the Economy of Early Eighteenth Century Bengal* (1976).[23] A Dutch contribution to the flow of regional studies on India is H. K. 's Jacob, *De Nederlanders in Kerala, 1663–1701* (1976).[24]

Regarding Eastern Asia suffice it to mention two recent studies: dr. Jörg's on the Dutch trade in China[25] and *Pepper, Guns and Parleys: The Dutch East India Company and China, 1662–1681* (1974), an excellent work by the American scholar Dr. J. C. Wills jr.

Finally, two admirable general surveys as a culminating treat: *The Dutch Seaborn Empire, 1600–1800* (1965) by Professor C. R. Boxer and *Rival Empires of Trade in the Orient, 1600–1800* (1976) by Professor Holden Furber, our *Altmeister* of European expansion history.[26]

Economic and social structures figure prominently in modern research,

[20] *Mare Luso-Indicum*, vol. IV, (Paris, 1980), pp. 1–43, "The Structures of Trade in Asia in the Sixteenth and Seventeenth Centuries. Niels Steengaard's "Carracks, caravans and companies". The Asian trade revolutions. A critical appraisal".

[21] American edition under the title *The Asian Trade Revolution of the Seventeenth Century. The East India Companies and the Decline of the Caravan Trade* (1975).

[22] *Verhandelingen van het Koninklijk Instituut voor Taal-, Land- en Volkenkunde*, deel 38 ('s-Gravenhage, 1962).

[23] *The Indian Economic and Social History Review* vol. XIII No. 2 (April-June 1976).

[24] R.G.P. series. Kleine Serie. Vol. 43 ('s-Gravenhage, 1978).

[25] C. J. A. Jörg, *Porselein als handelswaar. De porseleinhandel als onderdeel van de China handel van de V.O.C., 1729–1794*, (Groningen, 1978). English edition to be published in 1981.

[26] In the series *Europe and the World in the Age of Expansion*, (ed. by Boyd C. Shafer), Volume 2, (University of Minnesota Press, 1976).

in contrast with former generations' preoccupation in the politico-military complex. The Europeans in Asia are looked on as being primarily traders and rivals in a foreign sea. It should always be kept in mind that during this period the larger part of the Asian production resources was still in the subsistence economy and that trade only moved marginal quantities of produce from one continent to another. The main bulk of Asia imports to Europe were of agrarian origin, such as pepper and spices, tea and coffee; regarding these products we may assume with Adam Smith that "in agriculture the labour of the rich country is not always much more productive than that of the poor";[27] incidentally Smith considered the Asian trading partners to be belonging to the 'opulent' part of the nations. They were rich countries to him. Any explanation following a modern north-south model is therefore probably not very fertile. Or to use Professor Furber's words: "Cows were kept in the heart of London just as they were in the Center of Delhi and other great Asian cities".[28]

Copenhagen August 1980

Kristof Glamann

[27] *The Wealth of Nations*, (Everyman's Library, ed. London, 1947), p. 6.
[28] *Rival Empires of Trade*, p. 7.

List of Tables

APPENDICES

CHAPTER I

Introduction

Considering that the Dutch East India Company through a number of years undoubtedly was the greatest trading company of the world, it is surprising that its commercial history has never been written. Its activities have been considered from many different angles: political, organisatory, financial, naval, military, colonial, religious, as well as from the point of view of the history of science. The economic, let alone the business economic aspect, has only been commented on in passing, – and still commerce was the basis of the Company. Its founders were merchants, and the commercial character never passed off, the dividends were the final aim of its activities.[1] The studies submitted here are intended to shed some light on this extensive *terra incognita*. The investigations have been made on the general assumption that at the appraisal of a commercial concern it must be considered as a whole and from a central point of view.[2] As starting-point of the description the Company's office in the Netherlands has been chosen, which was the seat of the Court of Directors, the so-called *Heeren XVII*. If one concentrates upon the records of the Heeren XVII, it is evident that the general view is realistic and therefore necessary when attempting an account of the commercial policy of the management. The Company was an organism whose European and Asiatic organs cannot be separated. The interplay between the two large areas is one of the leitmotifs of the present study, and as it is to a wide extent an economic affair, it must be expressed in quantities like supply, demand, costs, profits, etc. The wish for following trade through a century or more has made it necessary to select series of sources, as will be understood from a quick glance at the masses of archives of the Company. The selection has been combined by a critical

[1] H. Terpstra, "Enige opmerkingen over het bedrijf der Oostindische Compagnie", *Tijdschrift voor Geschiedenis*, 57. jaargang (Groningen, 1942), p. 1.

[2] W. M. F. Mansvelt, *Rechtsvorm en geldelijk beheer bij de Oost-Indische Compagnie* (Amsterdam, 1922) pp. 1 ff.

analysis, not least as regards quantitative statistics and the setting up of series of prices. For practical reasons the critical and statistical apparatus has been placed as an appendix. In spite of their obvious shortcomings the investigations through a prolonged period have been preferred to investigations more limited in time, as they open up new vistas in the discussion about the bankruptcy of the Company towards the end of the 18th century, and in a still wider connexion they touch on the topical problem of the expansion of the Europeans in Asia. The period selected – the years from about 1620 to about 1740 – includes the expansive phase of the Dutch Company as well as the culmination of its power in the East. About 1620 we dimly discern the contours of the Dutch empire in Southeast Asia, "commercial at the outset like Śrivijaya and Malacca, but gradually becoming predominantly territorial; yet not in the true line of succession to either since the centre of control lay thousands of miles away," as an English historian recently has put it.[3] When we proceed to the beginning of the 18th century, the Company appears as a giant, in its exterior a well-equipped and rich business concern, the activities of which yield annual dividends in the Netherlands of normally 25–40 per cent. during the years from 1700 to the middle of the 1730's. It looks like a golden age. Within the walls the outlook is not quite so bright. Gradually a descending curve is recognized, demands for reforms become urgent and manifest themselves during the years about 1740 by a number of the proposals and reports which were to be so characteristic of the rest of the life-time of the Company.

Properly, it is not due to any specific Dutch defect that the commercial history of the East India Company has never been written. Professor Tawney's comment still applies to the major part of literature concerning the companies of the 17th and 18th centuries, that the interest has been greater in "the externals of company organization – the rules and regulations – than in the economic realities behind it."[4] First of all it has concentrated on the similarities and dissimilarities of the companies with the modern joint-stock company. Jurists and historians have studied the companies as institutional manifestations of capitalism. From an economic point of view these investigations are decidedly valuable, indeed indispensable, since the knowledge of the legal and administrative structure of the companies is a necessary basis of a description of their trade. This does not least apply to the Dutch East India Company,

[3] D. G. E. Hall, *A History of South-East Asia* (London, 1955), p. 251.
[4] *Economic History Review*, vol. IV (London, 1933), p. 344.

the structure of which is so singular that a number of authors have just denied the unity directed from a centre which we have taken for granted above. Therefore a brief discussion of the organization will be necessary.[5]

The constitution of the Company was embodied in the charter adopted by the States General on 20 March 1602, and by virtue of which the Company came into existence. The previously existing companies in Amsterdam, Hoorn, Enkhuizen, Rotterdam, Delft, and Middelburg became chambers in the United East India Company. The central management of the Company was assigned to the Court of Directors – Heeren XVII – consisting of 17 delegates from the chambers: 8 from Amsterdam, 4 from Zeeland (Middelburg), 1 from each of the others, and a seventeenth person, who was elected either by Zeeland or by one of the small chambers. The Heeren XVII normally held meetings twice a year, in the spring and in the autumn. If further negotiations were urgent, they might take place in a subcommittee, the so-called *Kleine Zeventien*. The local affairs were attended to by the *bewindhebbers* or directors in the various chambers. At the foundation of the Company it was decided that the *bewindhebbers* in the local companies should also be *bewindhebbers* in the United Company; furthermore, it was decided that vacant seats of the *bewindhebbers* should be filled in such a way that the other *bewindhebbers* in the chamber in which a seat was vacant drew up a list of three candidates, among whom the mayors in the town of the chamber in question nominated the new *bewindhebber*. This decision secured for the ruling families of the towns an influence which became traditional.[6] At the renewal of the charter in 1623 the *bewindhebbers*' term of office was restricted to three years; they could only be re-elected after a three-year interval. This rule, however, was of no practical importance in the long run, it was only a result of dissatisfaction among the stockholders with the dividend policy of the Company. In 1647 the so-called *extra-*

[5] A short and able discussion of the Dutch Company's organization is found in C. de Heer, *Bijdrage tot de financiëele geschiedenis der Oost-Indische Compagnie* ('s-Gravenhage, 1929). The standard work on the subject is G. C. Klerk de Reus, *Geschichtlicher Ueberblick der administrativen, rechtlichen und finanziellen Entwicklung der niederländisch-ostindischen Compagnie* (Verhandelingen van het Bataviaasch Genootschap van Kunsten en Wetenschappen, deel XLVII, Batavia-Solo-'s Hage, 1894).

[6] de Heer has adduced a few exceptions which confirm this rule, viz. an attempt at having effected that only persons not entrusted with a public charge should be elected *bewindhebbers* because of the great commercial burden resting on these; de Heer, *op cit.* p. 7, Note 5. In his otherwise reliable account of the history of the Company Charles de Lannoy states that in his opinion the Company about the middle of the 17th century changed its character – from at first being directed by merchants to being directed by "des hommes exerçant de fonctions publiques" – thus identifying the opposition of the shareholders in the 1620's with the commercial aspect, which is hardly correct; Charles de Lannoy & Herman van der Linden, *Histoire de l'Expansion Coloniale des Peuples Européens* (Bruxelles, 1911), p. 172 *et seq.*

ordinaire bewindhebbers were added to the ordinary ones. In this way some of the towns in the province of Holland and the landed aristocracy in the provinces of Holland, Gelderland, Utrecht, Friesland, Overijsel, and Groningen got an opportunity of getting representatives in the management of the Company. Another result of the stockholders' dissatisfaction with the management was the introduction into the charter of 1623 of sworn principal stockholders (in Dutch *beëdigde hoofdparticipanten*). These were to act as supervisors of the discharge of the official duties of the *bewindhebbers*, and they were also admitted to discuss proposals for new candidates for the *bewindhebber*ship. Every fourth year a complete account of the state of affairs of the Company should be submitted to the principal stockholders. They were elected by holders with the same number of shares as necessary to become a *bewindhebber* – 6,000 and 3,000 fl., respectively – to a number of 9, viz. 4 from Kamer Amsterdam, 2 from Kamer Zeeland, and 3 from the small chambers together. The Heeren XVII should consult the principal stockholders in all important matters. This institution, however, does not seem in the long run to have been of any appreciable importance either. Finally it may be added that Willem IV, the Stadholder, in 1747 was appointed *Opperbewindhebber*, a rank which was also held by Willem V. The *Opperbewindhebber* appointed *bewindhebbers* and formally had the power of appointment to the higher offices in the Company, but did not in person attend the meetings of the Heeren XVII, at which he was represented by a deputy.

That the Heeren XVII by nature must be considered the actual management of the Company, its central organ, appears from the mere fact that its decisions were binding for the chambers. True, it is evident that during the first years it was difficult for the Heeren XVII to assert their authority as long as the directors in the chambers were identical with those of the previous local companies. But gradually the Board gained ground and strengthened its authority. The procedure at the meetings was in advance announced to the chambers by the so-called presidial chamber, i.e. the chamber in which the Heeren XVII held their meeting and from where their president was elected. Only Amsterdam and Zeeland could function as presidial chambers, Amsterdam for six years and Zeeland for two years. Items outside the order of the day might be advanced. According to the charter of 1602 it was a rule that if the assembly did not come to an agreement as to a question, this was to be decided by the States General. Soon a division of labour developed, committees were appointed for treatment of the various spheres. Thus four departments were distinguished: one for receipts, a second for equipment of ships, a third for accountancy, and a fourth for commerce. During the second half of the 17th century the work had become so comprehensive that the management tried to find means for a relief, especially of the very time-consuming and important task of reading and answering reports and letters from India. About 1650 it was decided to transfer this activity to a committee apart – outside the Seventeen – consisting of two *bewindhebbers* from Amsterdam, one from each of the other chambers, and one principal stockholder. The committee was named *Haagsche Besognes*. Later it was enlarged.

Each chamber managed the equipment of its ships, and its *bewindhebbers* were personally responsible for it with their shares. In agreement with this arrangement the return cargoes were addressed to the local authorities. But it was the Heeren XVII that decided the total extent of the equipments and their distribution, just as the import commodities could only be sold by the Heeren XVII. It was also the Heeren XVII who demanded supervision of the borrowing by the chambers, and all chambers were jointly and severally responsible for the debt. It might happen that a chamber possessed idle working capital, while another was in need of money. Then a loan was arranged from one chamber to the other. Similarly, a chamber that was heavily encumbered with debts, might be relieved by chambers that were less heavily encumbered and that had a possibility of raising loans at cheaper interest. As regards assets as well as liabilities a principle of equality was in force, i.e. each chamber administered an amount which relatively was to correspond to the portion the chamber possessed of the total capital of the United Company (viz. $\frac{1}{2}$, $\frac{1}{4}$, and $4 \times {}^{1}/_{16}$). The Heeren XVII made a survey of the degree to which the distributional instalments corresponded to reality, by means of annual or bi-annual so-called *liquidatien*, a kind of balance-sheets which showed the distribution of cargoes, equipages, ship-building, debts, bills of exchange, stock in bank, cash balances, etc.

In appearance the Dutch Company thus might very well seem to have been a conglomerate of different units, but on closer examination it appears that it was not without a management. The organization in chambers was partly conditioned by practical considerations – it was considered most expedient for the selling of commodities and for the borrowing – partly historically conditioned. "It was a truly remarkable piece of amalgamation, in which local interests and central direction were harmonized in such a way as to provide for the utmost concentration of the national effort" (D.G.E. Hall). Another piece of evidence of this concentration was the share capital of about 6.5 million fl., which was practically ten times the amount with which the English started in 1600.[7] At the end of the 17th century Pieter van Dam, the famous historian of the Company, was indefatigable in emphasizing that the genesis of the Company was not due to the subscribers' wish for it, but to the interference of the Government. The States General had use for a financially strong central organism which might divert the war of Spain against the Netherlands and wage the war in India without any expenses on the part of the Government.[8]

Also in the European theatre the Company on several occasions had to aid the Government with ships, men, ammunition, etc. This was done more or less volunterily in accordance with Article 39 in the charter, which said that the Government could only with the Company's approval requisition ordnance and ammuniation. In 1605–06 the Company contributed 250,000 fl. towards the expedition of the Netherlands to Portugal, in 1639 it equipped four ships for the hard pressed Admiral Tromp, thus also during the first war with England. The greatest sacrifices were required during the second war with England, when the Company bound itself to aid the Government with 20 war ships, which in money corresponded to nearly 5 million fl. While the Government, although with great delay, repaid the previous outlay to the Company, the expenses during the second war with England were considered a compensation for the renewal of the charter, which took place in 1672. In the same year the Company aided in the action against the enclosed Groningen with military forces, ammunition, and money to an amount of about 2.2 million fl., but this aid was immediately repaid in 4 per cent. stocks which the shareholders got as dividend, – for that matter to the detriment of their own interests. The first charter of 1602 was granted for a period of 21 years and paid by the modest amount of 25,000 fl., which the Government contributed to the assets of the Company. In 1623 it was renewed for another 21 years, for which nothing was paid, but the result of the negotiations about the charter in the middle of the 1640's was that the charter in 1647 was renewed for 25 years against payment of 1.5 million fl., and in 1696 it was renewed for 40 years (the period of 1701 to 1740), which cost 3 million fl. While the amounts paid at the renewals of the charter were to be considered the price for the

[7] D.G.E.Hall, *op. cit.* p. 233 *et seq.*

[8] Pieter van Dam, *Beschryvinge van de Oostindische Compagnie*, 1:II (ed. F.W. Stapel, Rijks Geschiedkundige Publicatiën, No. 68, 's-Gravenhage, 1929), p. 484. For the following, see G.E.Klerk de Reus, *op. cit.* p. 275; F.W. Stapel, *De Vereenigde Oostindische Compagnie in de groote orlogen der XVIIde eeuw* (Den Haag-Batavia, 1932); Kol. Arch. No. 8396, "Oktroyen".

monopoly of the East India trade, the Company paid an annual amount to the Government in the form of convoy and licence money for the protection it enjoyed in times of war by convoying. The money was paid to the Admiralty according to the value of the cargoes brought home. As a registration of the cargoes took some time, an arrangement was made in 1683 in such a way that the Company paid 360,000 fl. a year, from 1701 increased to 364,000 fl. a year.

The interest of the States General in making the Dutch Company a strong military power endowed it from its very foundation with a distinctive feature which was never obliterated. The Company was a "staat-buiten-de-staat"[9] with its own administration, own jurisdiction, and finally also a right to make agreements with the foreign, Asiatic powers. During the first decades the military apparatus was rather onerous. The dividends were as might be expected. There was no lack of complaints on the part of dissatisfied stockholders, among whom there were a few who for religious reasons opposed the use of force. An interesting and instructive document is a declaration signed in Amsterdam on 4 December 1608 from the four merchants Simon Jansz: Fortuyn, Syvert Pietersz: Sem, Jacob Thomasz: van Dalen, and Cornelis van Campen. Since 1597 they had invested in the voyages from Amsterdam under Jacob van Neck, Steven van Hagen, Jacob Wilckens, Wolfert Harmens, and Jacob van Heemskerck, all their ships having been equipped with instructions to carry on honest trade as merchants without soldiers and warriors, without any orders to build forts or capture Portuguese and Spanish caracks. Even a strong pressure on the part of the Amsterdam mayors to have soldiers sent by the ships under Wolfert Harmens for use by the King of Ternate and the Dutchmen on the Moluccas they had resisted, "overmits zij als coopluyden die compagnie uyt haer selffs hadden opgerecht, alleenlijk om eerlijck te negotieren ende in vrundtschappe te handelen ende niet om eenige hostiliteijt oft offensie te gebruycken, dewijle onder alsulcke conditien, veele van de perticipanten haer gelt hadden ingeleijt ende die liever uyte compagnie wilden scheijden, dan sulcx in te willigen."[10] The four merchants concluded their declaration by stating that the foundation of the United Company meant a decision to act offensively, for which reason they had withdrawn from commerce. By the Company's charter the stockholders got a right to withdraw their capital at the end of each decade, but when the first

[9] H. Terpstra, "Enige opmerkingen", p. 1.

[10] Gemeente-Archief Amsterdam, Not. Arch. No. 196 (Not. J. F. Bruyningh), fos. 140a–142a, 4 December 1608. I am indebted to Dr. Simon Hart, Amsterdam, for his references to this and the following examples.

decade was closing the Court of Directors repudiated this provision. Dissatisfied investors were told to get their money back by selling their shares. Consequently a disbursement of capital never took place and so the Company in fact had a permanent joint stock from the beginning.[11] Against this state of things another group of Amsterdam merchants protested in 1613. They maintained that they had contributed large amounts in the first 10-year stock, complained of the modest dividends and the increasing debt of the Company. The *bewindhebbers* sinned against the rules laid down in the charter by using the receipts of the import goods for new payments towards the continuation of the war. With reference to the increasing English commercial activities in the East it was said straight out that if the States General would not pay the expenses of the war directly, the Government would have to subsidize the Company. The task of the East India Company ought to be that of carrying on trade, i.e. sending out ships and carrying goods home.[12] The dissatisfaction of the shareholders with the policy of dividends lasted for still more years, but it could not change the militant policy. On the contrary, we may say. In 1614 Jan Pietersz: Coen submitted his very expansive programme for the East to the directors, aiming at territorial conquests and colonization at the expense of the Iberians, combined with annihilation of competing European shipping, especially the English trade to the Moluccas. Parts of this programme were implemented by Coen's appointment in 1618 to the post of Governor General. The history of this and of the fights during the following decades is well-known. It is also well-known that the home directors of the Company itself were sometimes shocked at the arrangements of the Governors General and tried to restrain them with reference to the interests of trade. It seems that the Heeren XVII on the whole were more peaceful in their attitude than the Governor General and Council at Batavia. However, it was hardly considerations for the dividends that carried the greatest weight. It is true that the Heeren XVII were shareholders, but to them the possession of the shares meant first of all admission to the directors' chairs. The dividend was of less interest to them, partly because as directors they may have been supposed to have identified themselves with the prosperity of the Company, partly because as great merchants and mayors they were otherwise economically engaged in the management of the Company, viz. as buyers and sellers. We shall later return to this last matter.

[11] Herbert Heaton, *Economic History of Europe* (New York, 1948), p. 362.

[12] Gemeente-Archief Amsterdam, Not. Arch. No. 133 (Not. J. F. Bruyningh), fo. 113a, 16 December 1613.

The charter gave the Company a monopoly of trade east of the Cape of Good Hope. It must be assumed that this monopoly was actually enforced. The phenomenon of "interloping" hardly played any appreciable part in the Netherlands themselves, in contrast to England. What commodities were carried to the Netherlands behind the back of the Company, was smuggled in beside the regular cargoes in the ships of the Company.[13] Of course this means a factor of uncertainty at the appraisal of the Dutch imports from the East, but this margin means nothing as compared with the "interloping" that included whole shiploads which e.g. took place in England and occasionally made the monopoly of the English East India Company illusory. In return there are numerous examples of Dutchmen's participation in trade to the East Indies outside the Netherlands. The procedure, indeed, was prohibited by the States General by a Placard of the 9 September 1606, and the Company was very attentive, too, thus by collecting information through the Dutch envoys and consuls in the neighbouring countries in Europe, but it was not possible to prevent the investment of Dutch capital and the placement of Dutchmen in the foreign companies.[14] Thus there were Dutchmen behind the plans for East India trade from Tuscany in 1608, three years later the *bewindhebbers* in Kamer Amsterdam charged Gerhardt de Roy with having bought ships in Flushing and Medemblink for the purpose of fitting them out for voyages to the East Indies from France or elsewhere,[15] which expeditions were made with support from the great speculator Isaac le Maire, and in 1614 the Dutchman Pieter Hoote wanted to subscribe to the first English joint-stock company. The participation of the Dutch in the Danish East India Company established in 1616 is obvious; here, too, the rebel Le Maire offered himself with his Amsterdam partners in 1621. Examples are found throughout the 17th century: the project for the Scottish company in 1622, the plans for trade from Friedrichstadt in Holstein by way of Russia to Persia in the middle of the 1630's, Richelieu's general trading company, which also was to trade to the East, the French China Company 1660, Colbert's *Compagnie des Indes* founded four years later, the reorganization of the Danish company in 1670, the Brandenburg company in 1681. The 18th century did not become any quieter. Great anxiety was

[13] Further particulars of this question are given below in the chapter on the Company's trade in tea, see pp. 237 ff.

[14] Violet Barbour, *Capitalism in Amsterdam in the Seventeenth Century* (The Johns Hopkins University Studies in Historical and Political Science, Series LXVII, No. 1, Baltimore, 1950), *passim.*

[15] Gemeente-Archief Amsterdam, Not. Arch. No. 124 (Not. J. F. Bruyningh), fos. 90a–90b, 1 June 1611.

aroused by the comprehensive "interloping" which during the second decade developed from Ostend in the Austrian Netherlands and in which Dutchmen participated, too. The situation was aggravated when the Emperor Charles VI in 1720 legalized this trade by founding the Imperial East India Company of Ostend. After joint Dutch-English-French pressure it was in 1727 contrived to have the Ostend company suspended, which, however, caused a great trading capital to be liberated and to seek other spheres of activity. Projectors were in clover. The Amsterdam citizen Josias van Asperen at the end of the year 1727 proposed to the Danish company, then inactive, that it should open a branch office in Altona on the Elbe; the dethroned mountebank Pieter Backer – previously in the service of the President of the Dutch Company – presented himself in Copenhagen with plans for direct trade to China, and one of the contacts of the Ostend company in Amsterdam, Charles Pike, was active in the Swedish East India Company in Gothenburg founded in 1731.[16]

"Interloping" was an evasion of the monopoly of the Company and tantamount to competition. It may be termed illegal as distinct from the legal competition which existed between the national and legal companies. Whereas the competitive feature has been generally recognized in the relations between the companies in Asia, it is as if scholars at the treatment of the European activities have become hypnotized by the privileges of monopoly given in the charter. The liberalist criticism at the end of the 18th and the beginning of the 19th centuries had a sure hold of many of the later historians of the Company. Not least considering the appreciable part played by re-exportation in the sale of Indian goods, however, it comes natural to consider the market internationally and view e.g. Northwestern Europe as a unit. If so, it is a question of a limited number of great sellers alongside of each other. Futhermore, there is another feature of a still greater scope. The bulk of the East India commodities had a "milieu" in Europe. To Northwestern Europe the intercourse with the Iberian peninsula and the trade to the Levant meant an indirect line to Asia, as did the connexion with Eastern Europe by land. To a higher degree determinative of the "milieu" were the related European and other commodities in the European market, e.g. cloths, silks, dye-stuffs, saltpetre, sugar, metals, etc. Thus there are in advance several reasons to question the monopoly and investigate its

[16] Kristof Glamann, "Hollandske Indberetninger om Altona-projektet 1728–1729", *Danske Magazin*, 7th ser., vol. V (København, 1953), pp. 263 ff; by the same, "En ostindisk Rejse eller Thomas Thomsen på Galejen", *Sjöhistorisk Årsbok 1953–1954* (Stockholm, 1954), p. 19 *et seq.*

character in practice, remembering the investigations in our own times of the many stages between complete monopoly and complete competition. This, again, involves a contestation of the current view, based on the monopoly, of the Dutch company as a being which is commercially without history.[17] In fairness it should be added that the monopoly or the "buy cheap, sell dear" system is very conspicuous when one studies the production- or plantation-policy of the Company in Indonesia and Ceylon. But can this characterization without further circumstances be transferred to the Dutch-Asiatic trade in the period of 1620–1740? It should also be mentioned that the idea has just crossed the minds of several authors that the monopoly of the Company has been over-dimensioned. Both H. Terpstra and B. Vlekke have called attention to the fact that the Company dealt in other commodities than spices and pepper, and that this trade was not protected by the monopoly,[18] just as Professor I. J. Brugmans has raised objections to Werner Sombart's exaggerated idea of the contribution of the Company to the welfare of the Netherlands in the 17th and 18th centuries.[19] The profit by the Dutch-Asiatic trade was moderate as compared with the receipts won by the Dutch by shipping and commerce in Europe.

[17] The monopolistic interpretation e.g. by G. Gonggrijp, *Schets eener economische geschiedenis van Nederlandsch-Indië* (Haarlem, 1928), p. 29 ["Een schrijver over de Compagnie heeft gezegd dat dit handelslichaam geen geschiedenis heeft. Dit is in economischen zin waar. De uitspraak karakteriseert treffend het feit, dat de bestuurders der O.I.C. den ganschen duur van haar bestaan op een en dezelfde manier hebben gestreefd naar de bereiking van het doel, het maken van handelswinst, nl. door angstvallig vast te houden aan het monopolie"].

[18] H. Terpstra, "Enige opmerkingen", p. 1; B. Vlekke, *Geschiedenis van den Indischen Archipel* (1947), pp. 177 ff.

[19] I. J. Brugmans, "De Oost-Indische Compagnie en de weelvaart in de Republiek", *Tijdschrift voor Geschiedenis*, 61. jaargang (Groningen, 1948), p. 231.

CHAPTER II

The Factory "Nederland"

In order to tackle at once the myth about the stable character of the East India trade, marked by the Company's monopoly, the constant structure of the trade, we shall select the factory *Nederland* as our starting-point and investigate what commodities were carried to Europe from the East by the Company, and what the proportions were between the various products. It will be expedient for the sake of clarity to divide the variegated multitude of goods into groups and take either the cost-price value or the sales value as the standard of the proportions. By means of the cost-price value the proportions are mainly illuminated from an "investment point of view", as in this manner we can obtain a general view of the way in which the invoices intended for Nederland were composed. The sales value, on the other hand, tells us about the capacity of the commodities carried home for being converted into cash, the sales value being identical with the auction sale turnover. It is based solely on the volume realized at the auction sales and does not consider surplus and stock. The two points of view are not identical, although closely connected. On the long view possible essential displacements of the proportions between the groups of commodities will be registered with both standards. Together they constitute the very nerve of the activities of the Company. They form the basis of the simple calculation of profit, at which the gross profit appears as the difference between auction price and invoice price. Add to this the quantities realized as a decisive and necessary supplement. In order to eliminate more accidental fluctuations from year to year or, rather, from season to season, the analyses are based on triennial averages.

The existing material allows us to carry the analyses of the cost-price values farthest back in time, so we shall begin with these. The first section is from 1619–1621, the next is made about the middle of the 17th century, the years 1648–50, the third includes the years 1668–70, and the fourth the triennium 1698–1700. It has been endeavoured to select a term of years when there was no war between the Northwest European competitors, as the observation of the structure of commerce in this way can be disturbed by more superficial interventions in the form of attacks on the returning fleets and the like. Not least because the Company during these wars called off a number of important commodities, e.g. spices, in the return cargoes, such a selection is necessary. It is more difficult – and hardly so decisive either – to demand corresponding peaceful conditions in the Asiatic existence of the Company. There conditions constantly were influenced by displacements of power which it will be artificial to leave out, to which must be added the fact that trade as a rule flowed on more or less peacefully in spite of the wars. The analyses yielded the following result:[1]

Table 1. *Invoice Value of the Patria Cargoes on the Departure from the East in Selected Triennial Periods.*

	1619–21	1648–50	1668–70*	1698–1700
1. Spices	17.55	17.85	12.05	11.70
2. Pepper	56.45	50.34	30.53	11.23
3. Sugar	—	6.39	4.24	0.24
4. Tea and coffee	—	—	—	4.24
5. Drugs, dye-stuffs, etc.	9.84	8.52	5.84	8.29
6. Saltpetre	—	2.07	5.08	3.92
7. Metals	0.10	0.50	5.74	5.26
8. Textiles, silk, cotton, etc.	16.06	14.16	36.46	54.73
9. Sundries	—	0.17	0.06	0.39
In all %	100.00	100.00	100.00	100.00
1,000 fl.	2,943	6,257	10,813	15,026

* Ex Ceylon.

It is evident from this table that a thorough change of the structure of the Patria cargoes takes place during the second half of the 17th century. The change is relative, for the values of the total number of cargoes are doubled from Section 1 to Section 2 and again from Section 2 to Section 4. The displacements between Sections 1 and 2 are small and suggest that the East Indian imports to Nederland were of a fairly unchanged

[1] Reference should be made to the statistical appendix for a detailed mention of the material, see below pp. 269 ff. The invoices for the Ceylon ships apparently have not been preserved for the triennium 1668–1670. Parts of the Ceylon cargoes may be reconstructed from the statements in the *Hollantse Mercurius*. Hence it must be supposed that the share of pepper in the total number of return cargoes must have been a few per cent. higher.

character. More than half of the invoice amount intended for Nederland was placed in pepper, while the spices and the textile group hold the second and third place, respectively. How very different at the end of the 17th century! There the textile group has grown into a dominant quantity, which in fact has occupied the place of pepper. Almost 55 per cent. of the capital invested has been placed in textiles, silk, cotton, etc. Pepper as well as spices has lost ground considerably. Each of them only occupied about 11 per cent. of the purchases. At the same time a number of the small groups have gained ground, among them coffee and tea, which did not previously play a part worth mentioning.

The displacements in the trade are also reflected in the analyses of the auction sales in Nederland, which in the case of Kamer Amsterdam can be traced back to the middle of the 17th century. Below, corresponding sections of the auction material will be given, this material, however, being followed into the 18th century, thus besides the above-mentioned triennia also including the triennia 1738–40 and 1778–80. Comparative material shows that the Amsterdam figures are representative, which is conditioned by the fact that more than half of the Company's turnover originated from the chamber in Amsterdam.[2]

Table 2. *Analyses of Sales at Kamer Amsterdam in Triennial Periods.*

	1648–50	1668–70	1698–1700	1738–40	1778–80
1. Spices	26.36	28.43	24.78	23.63	24.43
2. Pepper	32.89	28.99	13.31	11.43	11.03
3. Sugar	8.80	2.02	0.20	3.00	0.61
4. Tea and coffee	—	0.03	4.10	24.92	22.92
5. Drugs, dye-stuffs, etc.	7.35	5.86	6.57	2.70	2.29
6. Saltpetre	4.30	7.63	4.00	3.54	2.79
7. Metals	0.70	2.99	2.94	0.58	1.37
8. Textiles, silk, cotton, etc.	17.54	23.77	43.45	28.27	32.66
9. Sundries	2.06	0.28	0.65	1.93	1.90
In all %	100.00	100.00	100.00	100.00	100.00
1,000 fl.	8,771	17,760	21,032	23,195	28,137

It appears from the analyses that the new feature in the 18th century (a feature which is brought out clearly in the section 1738–40) is the placing of coffee and tea among the chief groups of commodities. At the sales in Amsterdam in 1738–40 almost one fourth of the gross receipts

[2] In the case of this material reference is also made to the statistical appendix for details, see below pp. 272 ff. Profits on bank money, etc., are not included in the sale figures.

originates from tea and coffee. The decline of pepper continues, while the placing of spices is almost constant. The textile group during the first four decades of the 18th century shows a distinct decline, after which the group again gains a little ground. Here, too, the relative character of the figures must be stressed.

If we compare the sections common to the two series of analyses, it is seen that the movements on the whole are the same. About the middle of the 17th century pepper was the chief article of the Company, both as regards purchase and sale, as seen from the factory Nederland and in the sense that most money was invested in pepper and that pepper at the sales gave the greatest receipts. During the following 50 years this fact was changed. While pepper about 1670 was still the article which at the sales gave the largest gross amount, it was the textile group which from the point of view of investment swallowed up most money, and about 1700 the textile group was clearly at the head both in purchases and in sales. It also appears from the figures that spices constituted a group which yielded a constant and great profit, their share in the sales constantly being at a higher level than their share in the purchases. We shall not otherwise discuss the question of profits in this place, but shall preliminarily content ourselves by stating that the result of the investigations mentioned above shows that the imports from the East to Europe during the 17th and 18th centuries underwent considerable changes in composition, so that we already on this basis must abandon the view that the commercial history of the Company is without epoch-making features. The picture is rather one of a pulsatory undertaking, changeable and animate. There is special reason to fix one's attention on the last decades of the 17th century and the first decades of the 18th century, in which the displacements are striking. During these years a considerable increase in the total volume of the trade takes place, as appears from the table below, which shows the values of cargoes received and the sales in Nederland from decade to decade during the period from 1639/40 to 1738/39.[3] Trade is in the melting-pot, it is a period of transition in which features develop which – if you want to look at it that way – separate the 17th from the 18th century. The change in the interest in the various groups of commodities and the increase in the volume of trade involves changed circumstances of purchase and sale. Below, an attempt will be made at studying this problem by a treatment in more detail of the various elements. Provisionally the contents of the groups of commodities must be specified.

[3] On the authorities for these figures, see Appendix 1, p. 312 *et seq.*

Table 3. *Returns Received and Sales in Nederland from 1639/40 to 1738/39. Fl.*

	Returns	Sales
1639/40–1648/49	26,389,832	72,910,888
1649/50–1658/59	25,301,001	81,813,724
1659/60–1668/69	25,748,676	89,524,017
1669/70–1678/79	34,106,828	92,906,604
1679/80–1688/89	45,077,635	101,635,295
1689/90–1698/99	40,952,476	124,484,392
1699/00–1708/09	48,611,379	137,904,774
1709/10–1718/19	63,061,511	159,166,522
1719/20–1728/29	84,541,672	188,587,834
1729/30–1738/39	70,211,726	167,869,650

In the comprehensive instructions for the government in the East of 26 April 1650 the Heeren XVII wrote that "the peaceful trade throughout the whole of the Indies the kitchen at home must smoke of."[4] There were a good number of commodities that belonged to the kitchen regions, first of all the famous spices, which are so well-known that a further presentation is really superfluous. We shall still mention the various sorts in order in this way to point out that here as well as in the case of many other East India commodities there is often a large number of qualities.[5] Nutmeg (*muskaatnoten*) was specified into four main qualities by the Company, viz. (i) the fat nuts (*vette* or *gave noten*), (ii) the so-called *rompen*, which were unripe nutmegs that dropped to the ground as a consequence of kerang mould infection, and which were subdivided into two subqualities, whole *rompen* and pieces of *rompen*, furthermore (iii) the worm-eaten nutmegs (*vermijterde noten*), and finally (iv) *foelie* or *macis*, i.e. the red, reticular chip which covered the shell of the nutmeg. *Foelie* was the most expensive of the four qualities mentioned. A special term was *foelie-noten*, which denoted very small nutmegs the size of peppercorns and covered with a particularly thick layer of hard *foelie* (the *palla radja* of the natives). Another special sort was *mannetjesnoten*, nutmegs with little fragrance. The Company also divided cloves (*kruidnagelen*) into four qualities, viz. (i) *nagelen* or *giroffelen*, which were whole cloves, (ii) *capletten*, i.e. the round heads of the clove, (iii) *antoffelen*, the stems without the head, and (iv) *blom* or *poeier*, i.e. ground clove. If the fruit of clove was allowed to develop fully, it became an olive-like fruit, *moernagel*,

[4] J. C. van Leur, *Indonesian Trade and Society*, Essays in Asian Social and Economic History (Selected Studies on Indonesia by Dutch Scholars, vol. I, The Hague-Bandung, 1955), p. 243.

[5] Concerning the knowledge of commodities, see the glossaries by Dr. Stapel in his edition of Pieter van Dam, *Beschryvinge van de Oostindische Compagnie*, 1. boek, deel I–II, 2. boek, deel I–III, 3. boek (Rijks Geschiedkundige Publicatiën, Nos. 63, 68, 74, 76, 83, and 87, 's-Gravenhage, 1927–43).

which was used either for sowing or was sold preserved in sugar or wine (*geconfijte nagelen*). All these qualities, apart from the candied ones, like cinnamon, were placed in the first group in the analyses recorded above. They all appear from the very beginning, but cinnamon does not become important until the Company gained a foothold in Ceylon. During the first decades of the 17th century cinnamon was carried home from Formosa, China, and Tongking. These sorts (*cassia lignea*) were considered to be inferior to Ceylon cinnamon.[6] The group corresponds to what in Dutch is understood by the term *specerijen*.

As to Group 2 in the analyses, pepper, the question of quality is different. In the beginning of the 17th century we find pepper named in the invoices after the various areas of production, e. g. Achin, Jambi, Bantam, and Priaman. There are differences in the prices, which suggests a certain difference in quality. Fairly soon, however, the Company adopted the practice of mixing the various sorts in Batavia and sending the mixture to Nederland under one name, black or brown pepper, and at one price. This was the case as early as the end of the 1620's. Even after the Company had obtained firm control over the Malabar Coast and from there fetched large amounts of pepper, the practice mentioned was mostly retained. When the *bewindhebbers* in the 1650's discovered that the English successfully introduced white pepper, they ordered this new sort from India. In the auction sales at Kamer Amsterdam, the first named parcel of white pepper appeared in 1655–56, and from the beginning of the 1670's white pepper was sold regularly in Amsterdam.[7] White pepper was manufactured of black or brown pepper, the preparation taking almost a month, and the losses connected with the process on an average amounted to 38–40 per cent. of the weight of ordinary pepper, for which reason white pepper automatically became more expensive than black pepper.[8]

On the other hand the so-called long pepper has been placed in the group including drugs, dye-stuffs, etc., Group 5. This group is very comprehensive and besides the drugs and dye-stuffs proper also includes those commodities which by the Dutch are covered by the term *kruide-*

[6] *Pieter van Dam* 1:II, p. 146 Note 4; Dr. Stapel's glossary in the same volume.

[7] See Kol. Arch. Nos. 10,234 ff. The sale in 1655/56 comprises a modest 1,986 ponds. In the season of 1658/59 27,133 ponds were sold, then again there was a sale in 1660/61 of 2,800 ponds, etc. It is not correct, as maintained by W. A. Horst, that white pepper was not received in Holland until 1669. W. A. Horst, "De peperhandel van de Vereenigde Oostindische Compagnie" in *Bijdragen voor Vaderlandsche Geschiedenis en Oudheidkunde*, VIIIe reeks, deel III ('s-Gravenhage, 1941), pp. 95–103. For that matter, the English company had already previously imported pepper to Europe.

[8] On the making of white pepper at Palembang, see *Pieter van Dam* 2:I, p. 305 *et seq.*

rijen and the obsolete term *kruidenierijen.*[9] It applies to several of the East India specialties that they may be used in cooking as well as for dyeing and the manufacture of medicaments. If only for this reason they are difficult to place in definite classifications. The fine furniture timbers, such as ebony and others, have also been placed here, as related to certain of the dye-stuffs and lakes, forming the Asiatic contribution to the materials for European applied art. Finally Group 5 also includes jewels and diamonds. Thus it is a medley of products ranging from such delicacies as preserved ginger, anise, and rice, typical dye-stuffs such as indigo, sappan-wood,[10] and caliatour-wood, drugs such as cardamom, borax, camphor, sal-ammoniac, myrrh, benzoin, ambergris, bezoar, musk, etc., to such materials for applied art as ebony and pearls. In this variety indigo was one of the most important articles from the point of view of sale and purchase. A distinction was made between three sorts, named after the places of production in India, viz. *indigo circhees* (from Sarkhej), *indigo biana* (from Biana), and *indigo lauro* (from Lahore). Later on indigo came from other areas of production, e.g. Java. Sappan-wood and caliatour-wood were also solid items in the group throughout the period. Diamonds and jewels were weighty items during the first period, but later on lost interest. Group 5 grew during the 17th century. About the middle of the century it included about 15–20 different products and by the year 1700 was of more than 30 units. Especially in the lively decades towards the end of the 17th and in the beginning of the 18th century the Company was inventive as regards carrying new specialties to Europe, though mostly without this being of any appreciable economic significance. At the auction-sales in Amsterdam thus a small quantity of marmalade was sold in 1690/91, in 1693/94 a modest quantity of "Schiocolade", and in the years 1700/01 to 1702/03 small amounts of birds' nests.

Tea and coffee have been set up as an independent category. They turned up at the auction sales in Amsterdam in the second half of the 17th century, tea in 1651/52 and coffee in 1661/62. Tea appeared in two sorts, viz. "Chiaa" and Japanese tea. Coffee was "cauwa de Mocha". Java coffee belonged to the 18th century. It was first sold at the sales in 1712. The special questions of quality concerning tea and coffee will be discussed in the chapters on these articles.

[9] Cf. the headings of the price lists of Amsterdam, N. W. Posthumus, *Nederlandsche Prijsgeschiedenis* (Leiden, 1943).

[10] Sappan-wood, or redwood, resembles Brazil-wood in colour and properties, *Pieter van Dam* 1:II, p. 158 Note 2.

Sugar has been sorted out as a group apart, although it might as well be placed in Group 5. This is due to the special interest attached to sugar in connexion with trade in the East and the plantations in Java. In the first section from 1619–21 there is no sugar, which, however, does not mean that this article was not known. As early as 1616 the Heeren XVII recommended the factors of the Company in India to send home sugar by the ships which had been scrapped and were to return to Nederland.[11] Among the ships sent from the East to Nederland in 1622 was the "Schoonhoven", who carried 796 piculs Chinese *poeder* sugar (powdered sugar) and 14 piculs 62 catti *kandij* sugar (sugar-candy).[12] These two sorts were the most important ones. Both sorts were found in a brown and a white type. The white type was the finest one. As in the case of so many other commodities the area of production also here implied a certain description: China, Siam, Bengal, and Java.

Nor does saltpetre appear in the first section, 1619–21, but like sugar it was known by the Company, thus the ships "Hollandia" and "Middelburgh", who left Batavia in November 1621, had just under 39,000 ponds and well over 39,000 ponds saltpetre, respectively, onboard. The saltpetre came from the Coromandel Coast.[13] In the first section the metal group includes lead and copper. The lead must be considered European lead, which had been returned to Nederland, whereas the copper was Asiatic, from Japan. It was found in the cargo of the "Leyden", who had left Batavia in April 1621, and it comprised nine small cases as a trial consignment. The contents consisted of four parcels: (i) *fijn koper in staefkens*, (ii) *bladt koper*, (iii) *root koper in broden*, and (iv) *rouwe koper*.[14] Of these qualities the refined bars of copper (parcel No. i) soon became the dominant sort of copper in the exports of the Company to Nederland. In the later sections lead has disappeared. In return tin – *tin malacx*, i.e. from Malacca – turned up at the auction-sales in Amsterdam in 1667/68, and in the following year steel as well. Steel was not a stable commodity. As a rule only diminutive quantities of it were carried home,[15] but during the last decades of the 17th century tin became a constant article, which during periods of the 18th century was imported in larger quantities than the Japanese copper in bars. As a rule it was named after the

[11] J. J. Reesse, *De Suikerhandel van Amsterdam* (Haarlem, 1908), p. 160.
[12] Kol. Arch. No. 987, fo. 176 *et seq.*
[13] Kol. Arch. No. 986, fos. 234, 235, and 239.
[14] Kol. Arch. No. 985, fo. 15 *et seq.*
[15] Iron and steel from Japan and the Coromandel Coast already in the beginning of the 17th century circulated in the Company's Asiatic trade; see *Jan Pietersz: Coen, Bescheiden omtrent zijn bedrijf in Indië*, vol. 7:11, ed. W. Ph. Coolhaas ('s-Gravenhage, 1953), p. 1064, letter dated at Masulipatam 15 January 1623.

areas of production: Malacca, Siam, Tongking, etc. Among the metals we should also mention *spiauter*, which was carried home now and then during the whole period. *Spiauter* or *tutenage* was an alloy of zinc obtained from China.[16]

Group 8 is the most comprehensive of all and the one which is actually most difficult to probe to the bottom as regards a description of quality and goods. It included partly fabrics, partly the raw products silk, cotton, and wool. In the invoices and accounts of the Company the fabrics are mainly termed *lijwaten* or *lijnwaten*. It is the famous materials of India. Their name is legion, the various qualities or varieties were determined by texture, dyeing, patterns, etc. Often the same sort varied from one locality to another. Among *lijnwaten* in the first section the so-called *guinees* were dominant; through the whole existence of the Company they continued being a great article. The name was derived from Guinea in Africa, and they were also called *cambaijen* or *negroskleeden*, being chequered cotton materials important for the purchase in Africa of slaves by the West India trade and the African trade altogether. In the invoice of the "Leyden" from April 1621 there are a parcel of cloth with patterns "voor Guinea van Suratte" and three parcels with patterns "voor Patria van Suratte".[17] These were not expensive materials, on the contrary they probably belonged to the simplest ones among the cotton materials. *Gingans* also appears in the section from 1619 to 1621, also a coarse cotton product, chequered and a little stiff. A third important cotton was *salempouris*, a kind of chintz,[18] which among other things was used as bedspreads and often was of one colour, white with a red stripe woven in the edge. It was named after Salemporis on the Coromandel Coast. *Salempouris* occurs in large quantities in the following analyses. *Mouris*, blue cloths in one colour, also originated from Coromandel. Among the piece-goods we should furthermore mention *bethilles*, which were very fine, muslin cloths, and the white-and-black *baftas*, the best of which came from Broach in Gujarat.[19] Of the smaller fabrics we may specially mention the so-called *parcallen*, which, if anything, must be described as densely woven cotton patches, and *roemaals*,

[16] J. de Hullu, "Over den Chinaschen handel der Oost-Indische Compagnie in de eerste dertig jaar van de 18e eeuw", *Bijdragen tot de Taal-, Land- en Volkenkunde van Nederlandsch Indië*, deel 73 ('s-Gravenhage, 1917), p. 37.

[17] Kol. Arch. No. 985, fo. 15 *et seq.* In the demands made in September, 1642, the Court of Directors grouped an assortment of goods under the heading "Voor de Westindische Compagnie", namely: "Bougis [see below], Suratse cleeden met blau en witte streepen, roode & blauwe geschilderde cattoene negros cleeden van de Cust off Suratte, witte fijne cattoene lijwaten met cleyne blauwe ruytgens", Kol. Arch. No. 250, 22 September 1642.

[18] H. Yule & A. C. Burnell (W. Crooke), *Hobson-Jobson* (London, 1903).

[19] Dr. Stapel's glossary in *Pieter van Dam* 1:I.

which were small cloths that were used as towels and pocket handkerchiefs.[20] How comprehensive the category of *lijnwaten* was, appears i.a. from a survey of the auction-sale at Kamer Delft from 1700/01, in which between 30 and 40 different sorts of cotton materials were enumerated.

The silks, too, were numerous. Already in the invoices from the first section the most important make their appearance, viz. *armozijnen*, a thin, satin-like material named after the town Ormuz and much used for linings, and *atlassen*, which were both a fine silk and a kind of piece-goods made of the same material. *Allegiassen* were brilliant, multicoloured silk cloths, *gilams* were cloths woven of Persian silk, but the Company also bought *gilams* from China. *Pansjes* was the name of a small-size cotton material which was re-exported to Africa, where it was used by the Africans as a loin-cloth, as well as a white silk material bought by the Company in China.[21] Articles which should not be forgotten were the *damasten*, the white, heavy silks, and the famous Japanese silk-dresses or kimonos. As in the case of the cottons, the silks also included artistically painted specialties which it would take us too far to discuss.

As regards the raw materials, we shall first mention cotton, cotton yarn, and silk. Here silk is the absolutely decisive article, one og the most important of the Company's commodities. It was mainly obtained from three areas, Persia, Bengal, and China. The numerous names found in the records of the Company refer to the degree of working-up of the silk, to its quality, and to its origin. Thus Persian silk was several different things: *ardasse* was a coarse quality from the district of Shirwan, *ardassina* was pearl silk of the best quality, *canary* was silk with white spots, *gilam* was silk from the province of Gilan on the Caspian Sea (a similar sort from China, of which the Dutch sold much in Japan, was also called *gilam*), *legi* or *legia* was the best quality from the district of Lahidja or Laidsjan. Bengali silk mostly was characterized by the three descriptions *cabessa*, *bariga*, and *pee*, which simply means "first, second, and third quality" (from Portuguese "head", "stomach", and "foot"). As to the Chinese silks we often in the first section find the names *rouwe zijde*, i.e. "raw silk", *poolzijde*, which is silk with plush-shaped threads (it was used for the weaving of velvet), *getweernde zijde*, i.e. spun silk, and *floszijde*, i.e. coarse, unspun silk (amongst other things used for the so-called *florette garens*). Of other sorts of silk we should finally mention *moghta*, which was a wild and therefore cheap silk. Wool does not appear until

[20] *Ibid.*

[21] Dr. Stapel's glossary in *Pieter van Dam* 1:II; Kol. Arch. No. 10,239, the auction sales at Delft in the financial year 1700/01.

the section about the turn of the century. Through the trade to Persia and Gujarat the Company, indeed, at an early stage became acquainted with Persian wool, but only in the 1680's it is possible from the orders of the Heeren XVII for return goods to Europe to note an incipient interest in wool; it is, however, only a modest article in the textile group. It was especially the so-called *Kirmanse* wool which was carried to Nederland. This sort was considered a finer and better quality than the ordinary Persian wool. The wool has disappeared in the last auction-sale section from 1778–80.

It may seem very prosaic to try to convert these the most beautiful of the fabrics and materials, colours and forms into dry figures, but this is necessary if we want to entangle the great medley of the textile group and find our way to the economically most essential constituents.

The last group in the main analyses contains all kinds of Indian curiosities, left-over, dispatched, or discarded materials which were returned, besides two permanent or regular kinds of returns, viz. cowries and porcelain. They do not appear in the first section, but porcelain was among the commodities which were wanted for Nederland already in the early days of the Company. In an existing request for return cargoes from April 1622, fl. 300,000 were set aside for "Chormandelsche waren, allerleij rariteijten, geeijschte droguen, fijn porcelijn."[22] Indeed, porcelain is found in several invoices from the 1620's. Cowries, on the other hand, must be considered a regular article only from about the middle of the 17th century.[23] They occur in the section of 1648–50. Cowries or *cauris* were fine, white shells of a mussel which mainly was fished from the Maladives in the Indian Ocean. The Dutch company secured a supply of cowries from Coromandel, Bengal, and Ceylon. The shells were used as a medium of exchange in Siam and Southeast Asia, where they occasionally appear in the documents under the name of *beas* or *bougis*. In India and in Africa, too, they were used locally as money by the natives. Especially the fact that the Africans highly appreciated them, made cowries a commodity which the Company found it advantageous to carry to Nederland, where they were mainly sold to the West India companies for the purchase of slaves. Amsterdam in the 18th century was considered the chief market of cowries, where English buyers also provided themselves with the shells. The commodity occurred in two

[22] Kol. Arch. No. 4409, "Extract uyt missive van de mayores in data 14de April Ao. 1622 pr. "Erasmus" ges: daer by dat van Indien jaerlijcx int gros eyschen dese naer volgende retouren."

[23] *Cauris* are mentioned in the demands made in September, 1642, see above p. 20 Note 17.

qualities, sorted and unsorted cowries.[24] In the sections from the 18th century some commodities turn up which have been placed in the groups of sundries, thus whalebone, which the Company obtained from Japan and tentatively dealt in during the 1730's and the 1740's, but then abandoned amongst other things because of protests in Nederland from the merchants of the Arctic trade. In the section of 1778–80 we furthermore find arrack and some wines from Cape Colony, thus muscatel and Madeira. From Cape Colony wheat was also sent to Nederland during these years. *Rottingen*, i.e. rattan or bamboo canes, were entered as an independent article in the auction-sale accounts from the 18th century. They have also been included under sundries.

A great knowledge of commodities in the people of the Company was needed in order to buy all this in the right qualities, a point which should not be overlooked. Later, we shall adduce a number of examples of the troubles given to the Company by the qualities.[25] Knowledge was also needed to have the commodities placed properly onboard the ships; not all products could equally well bear being placed side by side. Furthermore, there was the purely technical problem of having the ships loaded correctly. This technical question should also be emphasized, as it, so to say, conditioned certain relations between a number of different products. Actually the imports of the Company might be divided into categories determined by the placing onboard the ships. By way of illustration we shall adduce the following concrete example: the homeward bound East Indiaman "Ceulen", leaving Batavia in January 1697.[26] The "Ceulen" was of 160 lasts, had an armament of 40 guns and a crew of 105 sailors, 30 military men, 5 artificers, and 10 sick people in the service of the Company, in all 150 men, to which should be added officers and repatriated officials. At the very bottom of the "Ceulen" there were in the middle, under the main hatch, 8 old iron anchors and along the garboard forward to the bulkhead at the waterway (in Dutch *watergat*) 400 chests of Japanese copper in bars besides 134 pieces of Siamese tin. Furthermore, 50,000 ponds sappan-wood was placed as lining between the ribs and the knee braces. This constituted the ballast and the so-called *garnier* which protected the other commodities and permitted firm stowage. 580,281 ponds black pepper was also included in

[24] Dr. Stapel's glossary in *Pieter van Dam* 2:I; Kol. Arch. No. 201, 5 September 1730; Kol. Arch. No. 202, 24 August 1731 (on the sorting of *cauris* "in die maniere als door de Kamer van Amsterdam werd gepractiseert"); Collectie van Ghesel No. 152, "Aanteekening over de prijzen van niet-gegarbuleerde cauris in de jaaren 1742–1755".

[25] Dr. Terpstra has called attention to the responsibility of the servants for selecting qualities and patterns properly, "Enige opmerkingen", *passim*.

[26] Kol. Arch. No. 1463, fos. 379 ff.

the *garnier* or was placed in the so-called "koebrug", which was an extra flooring to make the ship strong. The dunnage part of the cargo consisted of 1400 bags of saltpetre and 100 pieces of Siamese tin. The latter were placed in the front of the waterway "om't schip bij sijn last te brengen." In the water space 32 whole ahms of candied ginger and 16 whole ahms of nutmeg were placed. Against the bulkhead at the waterway there was space for 6,000 ponds tainted nutmegs, and at the after hatchway a bulkhead was set up, where 312 bags of cloves and 20 bags of Javanese cardamom were stowed in bulk. This was followed by six layers of commodities. The first "smooth" layer – as it was called – from the bulkhead in front of the cabins to the main mast consisted of 75 chests of Radix China, 36 bags of white pepper, and 52 chests of benzoin, and from the main mast to the bulkhead at the waterway of 47 parcels of cottons, 2 cases of *atlassen* materials, 2 bales of Javanese cotton yarn, and 8 parcels of silk yarn, furthermore various chests and bags of drugs, and 36 bags of white pepper. The second smooth layer chiefly consisted of textiles, but like the first layer had bags with white pepper along the shipboard. The third layer also contained a number of parcels and cases of textiles, besides bales of Persian and Bengali silk and 35 bales of cinnamon. The fourth, fifth, and sixth layer mainly consisted of cinnamon. Finally there were the commodities in the cabins. In the foremost cabin aport they had placed 17,272 ponds of nutmegs, the best of them in chests, while the rest had been in bulk. The aftermost chamber to starboard at the sails was filled with Chinese silk and expensive silks besides 3 rolls of Bengali canvas and 11 cases of indigo. In the constable's cabin there were amongst other things a chest of nutmeg cakes (pressed oil cakes), 2 small cases of bird's nests, 1 pot of civet, and 15 bales of Chinese tea. Finally the responsibility for a chest of pearls had been assigned to Vice-Commander Hendrik van Buytenhan, who was to go home to Nederland by the "Ceulen".

The cargo of the "Ceulen" is one example among many. It is typical of a large number of the annually returning ships, even though the cargo does not include all the commodities which the Company carried home at the time in question. There were also cargoes which were more uniform or special, e.g. those of the so-called sugar ships and the later tea ships. To illustrate how a special ship was loaded we may mention the sugar flutes which the Company had built in 1715 and 1718. Their task was that of carrying large supplies of sugar from Batavia to Nederland, i.a. in an attempt at checking the country trade with Javanese sugar in Asia. They were of 130 feet (width 36 feet, depth 15 feet) and were to have a crew of 76 men on the outward passage, but only 66 men on the home passage. The armament consisted of 16 iron guns and 4 metal swivel guns. According to the instructions of the maritime experts the *garnier* was to consist of 7 inches of sappan-wood and 5 inches of pepper, which would give a weight of 36,000 ponds. The dunnage consisted of nearly 500 chests of sugar or 135,000 ponds. It was placed in a layer 4 feet high before the mast and a layer 3 feet high behind the mast. Then the hold might be filled with *canassers* of sugar, viz. 11 feet before and 12 feet behind the mast. The cargo thus must be calculated at 550,000–600,000 ponds. The maritime experts added that it was necessary to place something heavy between the waterway "om het schip bij zijn last te krijgen."[27]

Actually nearly all ships, irrespective of the character of the cargo, must have a ballast. For this such coarse commodities as copper, tin, spelter, saltpetre, and sugar were used. These decided ballast goods actually did not occupy any space in the ships, but filled the same function as old iron anchors, stones, and other heavy things. As a rule the Dutch company did not charter its ships, but built them itself. Thus it had not got the freightage immediately to indicate the utilization of the tonnage. The Court of Directors, however, continually supervised the effective use of the tonnage, not least the ballast, and made complaints when the Batavian government e.g. used old iron instead of merchandise. The Heeren XVII generally considered saltpetre to be the most advantageous ballast commodity, which was succeeded by sugar, copper, and tin; but of course this depended on the prices. Thus it is remarkable that the importation of copper by the Company was great during the years in which the prices of saltpetre in Europe showed a falling tendency. From the point of view of transport the ballast commodities are secondary; their total volume is decided by the tonnage determined by the primary products. An extension beyond this would lead to the building of special ships. Their volume must also be considered in relation to some of the primary commodities, especially that of pepper and later coffee and tea.

Another technical factor should be mentioned. This is the duration of the voyage. Normally it was about nine months. The return cargoes from Batavia, from where the main part of the products destined for Nederland was sent from the wide-spread factories, started in October-November in a joint fleet, while the ships from Ceylon started in November-December. During the months of February-March, the so-called "after-ships" were sent from Batavia to Nederland. At the end of the 17th and

[27] Kol. Arch. No. 464, 15 July 1718 (section on Batavia).

in the beginning of the 18th centuries, when the number of ships was very great, the ships from Batavia were sent in several groups during the period from October to March. The returning East Indiamen arrived in Nederland during the summer, and part of the cargoes was offered at auction-sales in the autumn, about one year after they had left the East. The equipment of the ships from Nederland normally took place during late summer and the autumn until the New Year, with arrival at Batavia in August-September. The extent to which the ships sailed in fleets or only a few together was conditioned by war and peace. In spite of a number of attempts, especially in the 1730's and the 1740's it proved impossible in the period considered here to reduce the duration of the voyages appreciably, the consequence being that the Heeren XVII, when submitting their orders for return commodities, always had to make the necessary arrangements two years ahead. Thus also in the case of the direct trade to China in the 1720's and 1730's, where the time of the voyage was shortest in relation to the distance. The considerable distance in time between demand and supply gave the East India trade its special character. The farther away the factories were from Batavia, the more effective was the time factor. Below a survey will be given of the distance by sea from headquarters at Batavia to some of the most important places.[28]

Table 4. *Distance from Batavia to Some Important Trading Stations and Possessions.*

EASTWARDS:		
Cheribon	38	miles
Tagal	45	-
Samarang	58	-
Japara	67	-
Surabaya	96	-
Macassar	180	-
Timor	225	-
Amboyna	300	-
Banda	325	-
Ternate	350	-
NORTHWARDS:		
Palembang	82	-
Jambi	123	-
Malacca	160	-
Ligor	248	-
Siam	328	miles
Japan	738	-
WESTWARDS:		
Bantam	13	-
Princen Eyland	36	-
Padang	120	-
Gale (Ceylon)	410	-
Colombo	430	-
Negapatam (Coromandel)	466	-
Cochin (Malabar)	496	-
Bengal	600	-
Surat	692	-
Persia	900	-
Mocha	970	-
Cape of Good Hope	1483	-
The Channel	3432	-

[28] Collectie van Vredenburch No. 8.

The survey of the distances ought to be supplemented by a map of the monsoons, for after all they indicated the rhythm of the Asiatic trade. They limited the traffic between the factories to annual or bi-annual voyages – if the passage was lost, there was only one thing to do, viz. waiting – and they restricted the shipping routes.[29]

A great scene unfolded itself at the arrival of the returning fleet from the East.[30] The prelude took place at sea. The Company had ships cruising in the European waters, and a prize was offered to the captain who first sighted the East Indiamen. In times of peace ships were often hired in the English Channel ports for this task, in years of war, on the other hand, the arrival home was a secret and exciting affair. The navigation route then was laid round the north of Scotland. The navy of the States General had orders of convoying. A well-known incident was the dramatic arrival home in 1653, when some of the units of the returning fleet had to go to Bergen in Norway, while others went down into the Sound until Admiral Witte de With got them safely to port together with 400 Dutch vessels. Or the analogous situation in 1665 during the second English war, when the ships were convoyed to Nederland, this time accompanied by the Levant fleet and 70 vessels. At the first reliable news of the appearance of the fleet in the home waters, a number of *bewindhebbers* constituted themselves as a committee for the reception of the returning ships. At the head of a band of garblers and lumpers onboard a fleet of lighters provided with a store of bags they went to Texel at the Zuider Zee in order to supervise and conduct the unloading. When the ships had safely got inside the bar they dropped anchor at de Vlieter. The committee at once went alongside the flagship in order to receive a short report from the commander about the voyage, then distributed themselves to the various ships, where officers and crew were bid welcome on the *kuyl*-deck. After the garblers had been placed onboard to guard the cargo, the *bewindhebber* sat down in the cabin in order to get detailed information about the ship. Amongst other things he was to investigate whether, when crossing the bar, there had been any strange vessels alongside the ship. From the shipmaster he received the costly leather bags with jewels and diamonds and other valuables, which were sent onboard the *bewindhebbers*' own sloop. Furthermore the keys to the

[29] C. Northcote Parkinson, *Trade in the Eastern Seas 1793–1813* (Cambridge, 1937), pp. 98 ff.

[30] The following picture is based on Kol. Arch. No. 4409, "Memorie voor de gecommitteerde bewindhebberen tot het ontfangen en lossen van Comp:s retournerende schepen", and Holl. Zeeuwsche Staatscommissie, No. 5, Litra P, "Notitie van de wijze op welke alle betalingen in de respective kameren van d'Oost Indische Compagnie werden geboekt" (section on *Ongelden retour*).

hold as well as the list of the cargo, and the books, charts, and log of the ship were handed over to the *bewindhebber*. Then inspection on deck followed. Each single officer and sailor had his venture or "privilege tonnage" noted on the muster-roll. Orders were given to take out the kitbags from the berths. They were searched. A lighter came alongside the ship, crew and kitbags were placed there, shipmaster and mates were asked whether they had anything to say against the crew, and the crew, whether they had any complaints against the officers; then the *bewindhebber* released all of them from their oath, and they left. Another lighter appeared, and the lumpers came onboard. In this lighter prisoners were placed, besides venture goods, log-books, and the chests with seamen's clothes, boots, and other equipment. The busy *bewindhebber* inspected guns and ammunition. The guns were discharged, locked, and a flat-bottomed sloop came for the powder. Finally the time had come to open the hold and start the unloading. One lighter after the other went alongside the ships, each with a sworn "lighterman" as foreman. In the hold the lumpers handled bales and bags, ropes were cut, bulkheads broken down, the spices were chuted. They were dusty and burnt the throat, and so, in the intervals, the men got a small ration of gin with sugared pretzels. The hatches of the heavily loaded lighters slammed to, a solid bar was pushed in place over it, and the sworn "lighterman" got from the *bewindhebber* a list of his cargo together with a letter to the chamber for which the lighter was intended. The ships had been unloaded down to the ballast goods. The *bewindhebbers* climbed out of the holds, handed over the command to the pilots, and then left in their sloop. By the Dutch waterways the rich return goods were distributed to Enkhuizen, Hoorn, Amsterdam, farther into the country, through the customs at Gouda to Delft, Rotterdam, and as far as Middelburg in Zeeland. In the warehouses they were ready with scales and measures for the registration of qualities and quantities. They garbled and sorted out. In Amsterdam the spices, the silk, and the finest textiles stored in the very *Oost-Indische Huys*, a previous town warehouse in Colveniersburgwal, which in 1605 had been converted into headquarters. The bulky goods such as pepper, sugar, saltpetre, indigo, the timbers, camphor, copper, etc., were placed in other stores and warehouses in the town, e.g. in Y-graft or in the large *Zee-Magazijn*, which in 1660/61 was built in Oostenburg. The lists of invoices were studied and surveys were made of loss and shrinkage. In the presidial chamber the Heeren XVII assembled in order to open the brown leather bags together.

Already before the goods were unloaded, the great work of arranging the sale was started, which was an international event. All over Europe merchant's houses waited for bulletins from Amsterdam. Their Netherlands correspondents sent advance reports about the expected offer and the state of the market. Printed lists of different provenience of the cargoes were dispersed in the main languages, but the decisive announcement, of course, was the Heeren XVII's notice of the sales. Below, in connexion with the discussion of the various commodities we shall try to elucidate the conditions of the market in more detail. Here we shall consider the auction sales more generally and ask: under what forms was the offer made? Or formulated more directly: who bought the return commodities of the Company?

The question is difficult to answer. For a great part of the 17th century the information is defective, and passing on to the accounts kept from the beginning of the 18th century is like jumping out of the frying-pan into the fire: the material from that time is so comprehensive that going through it takes much time and taxes the strength to such a degree that it must almost be characterized as a study apart. What follows is therefore rather some instructive examples and random samples than an exhaustive treatment of an interesting and unheeded aspect of the history of the East India companies. While the relation between shareholders and directors has been discussed by others, thus in respect of the speculative trade and the policy of profits, just as in the case of the English company the shipping interest has been touched on, the purchasers and for that matter the suppliers of the goods of the companies have on the whole remained unknown factors.[31]

In the small companies of the 18th century the interests of purchasers and suppliers are so pronounced that they cannot be neglected if we want an all-round description of these companies. Thus the example of the Danish Asiatic Company shows that the management of the company comprised merchants who at the same time were ardent suppliers of equipment goods and great buyers at the auction sales on their own and other merchants' account. A proposal made in the beginning of the 1750's to reduce the influence of these merchants, amongst other things by demanding that no director might be a supplier to the company, was flatly rejected on the grounds that Copenhagen did not harbour so

[31] Cf. the fact that in the editions of the English East India Company's records the names of the buyers at the auctions have been cut out, interesting information about e.g. the quotas of the Levant trade and the trade to the West Indies in the imports from the East Indies, and about the spheres of activity of the individual commercial houses thus being withheld from the readers.

great capitalists and well-to-do merchants that they could be made to enter the board of directors of the Asiatic Company without at the same time offering them a possibility of supplies, commissions, and trade in Asiatic commodities.[32] These merchants also represented connexions with foreign countries. They probably attended to the greater part of the re-exports, but just this many-sided activity meant that they first of all considered the company as part of their own business rather than a company whose welfare they were to serve for the company's own sake. Trade to them was the central aspect. In the beginning they needed state aid. The privileges were beneficial, but by the growing importance of the trade to China they felt their obligations towards the state to maintain the Indian forts and trading stations to be hampering, and the same circles more and more intensely maintained their demands for a free trade.

Of course, it is not possible without further circumstances to transfer this characterization to Dutch conditions. The Amsterdam capitalism was too fully developed for that. An analysis of some of the auction sales of the Dutch East India Company in the 18th century shows a fairly great specialization among the buyers and no immediate connexion between the great buyers and the Directors of the Company, the Heeren XVII. There does not seem to have been any direct connexion between these groups and the group of suppliers. But it is a feature common to both companies that it is possible to distinguish between a category of great buyers and a category of small ones. If we go back to the beginning of the 17th century, the Dutch Company's great buyers stand out very clearly, indeed, it is difficult to catch sight of the small buyers. In this period there are a good number examples of the same buyers asserting themselves in the chief groups of the imports, and it is not difficult to spot the connexion with the Directors.

Let us illustrate this, beginning with the most important of all imports in the first half of the 17th century, viz. pepper. On 12 September 1620 a syndicate consisting of Messrs. Elias Trip, Gerrit van Schoonhoven, Jeronimus de Haze, and Philippe Calandrini bought "alle den peper die tegenwoordich onder de Comp.[e] hier te lande is berustende."[33] The same Trip and Calandrini at the end of April the following year secured all the pepper arriving by the ships "Witten Beer" and "De Vrede".[34] In 1622 it was another syndicate that acquired the pepper of the Company,

[32] Kristof Glamann, "Studie i Asiatisk Kompagnis økonomiske Historie, 1732–1772", *Historisk Tidsskrift*, 11th ser., vol. II (København, 1949), pp. 52 ff.

[33] Kol. Arch. No. 249, 12 September 1620.

[34] *Ibid.* 29 April 1621.

viz. Messrs. Gert Dircksz: Raedt, Cornelis van Campen, Hans Broers & Co. They bought nearly 10,000 bales, which was the complete stock in hand in the respective chambers. At the sale the Company entered into the obligation not to offer pepper for one year.[35] As to other spices, Gerrit van Schoonhoven and Cornelis Bicker in January 1621 bought "alle de macis die tegenwoordich onder all de respective Cameren is,"[36] and barely two months later these two gentlemen together with Elias Trip and Hans van Loon contracted for the *macis* which had arrived by the sloop "De Vrede". This contract also included all imports of *macis* by the English company during the calender year, for it should be kept in mind that the agreement of 1619 between the two companies as to the imports of spices was still in force.[37] By a contract of April 2, the same year, Gerrit van Schoonhoven, Hans van Loon, and Cornelis Bicker secured the corresponding Dutch imports in 1621.[38] A similar contract for the Dutch imports of 1623 was made with Hans Broers and Hubrecht de Haze.[39] As to nutmeg, it should be stated that the cargo of the "Walcheren" in July 1621 was sold to Cornelis van Campen and Elias Trip,[40] while the stocks of the respective chambers in September 1622 were sold to the constellation of Elias Trip, Hans van Loon, Cornelis Bicker & Co.,[41] and in August 1623 to the syndicate Cornelis van Campen, Hans Broers, Cornelis Bicker, Hans van Loon, and Godert Kerckrinck.[42] As appears, the factors are the same, but their combination varies. It all reminds of French governments of the present time. In the case of some of the other – less important – commodities we find these acquaintances again. Elias Trip and Hubrecht de Haze in 1623 took part in the purchase of the Company's stock of indigo.[43] Cornelis Bicker, Hans van Loon, Godert Kerckrinck, and Rogier Alewijn in the same year contracted for all the *guinees* textiles,[44] while Hans van Loon and Melchior van Hoorn bought the stock of *salempouris* and *parcallen*,[45] and Cornelis Bicker in his capacity of *bewindhebber* in the West India Company together with his partner Elias Pels contracted for a quantity of *armozijnen*.[46] It should, however, be added that other names also appear in connexion with these categories of commodities.

For the period ten years later we may take raw silk, which then played a great role in the sales of the Company. In 1631 the Company sold all the Chinese silk brought home by the ships to Andries Pels, Jan van Wickevoort & Co., while Jacob Pietersz: Hooghkamer & Co. bought

[35] *Ibid.* 1 June 1622.
[36] *Ibid.* 15 January 1621.
[37] *Ibid.* 4 March 1621.
[38] *Ibid.* 2 April 1621.
[39] *Ibid.* 8 August 1623.
[40] *Ibid.* July 1621.
[41] *Ibid.* 7 September 1622.
[42] *Ibid.* 8 August 1623.
[43] *Ibid.* 9 August 1623.
[44] *Ibid.* 9 August 1623.
[45] *Ibid.* 10 August 1623.
[46] *Ibid.* 6 May 1623.

the cargo of Persian silk.[47] In the following year it was the constellation Jacob Pietersz: Hooghkamer, Godert Kerckrinck, Cornelius Spiering & Co. who bought the Chinese silk, while Paulus Timmermann bought the Chinese "getweernde zijde", and Gommer Spranger "alle de geele rouwe Chinesche zijde."[48] In July 1633 a lot of Persian silk was offered for general sale at fixed minimum prices subject to the proviso that the smallest sale should comprise one bale,[49] but at the normal great sale in the autumn the Persian silk brought home was sold by contract to Jacob Pietersz: Hooghkamer & Co.[50] In the same autumn a contract for the Chinese silk was made with Hooghkamer, van Loon & Co., while Andries Pels and Paulus Timmermann bought the inferior sorts of silks.[51] In 1634 it was Cornelis Bicker & Co. who bought the Persian silk and Gillis Puts who bought the Chinese silk,[52] while the following year it was Cornelis Bicker, Godert Kerckrinck, Gysbert Tholincx & Co. who contracted for the Chinese silk and Hooghkamer, Cornelis and Jacob Bicker & Co. who bought the Persian silk.[53] Finally it may be mentioned that in the year 1636 two contracts were made for the Persian silk, one in September with Carel Quina, Jacques and Guillaume van Hoorn, Willem van Dael, and Cornelis Gysbertz: van Goor, the other in November with Hooghkamer, Jacob Bicker, Gysbert Tholincx, Godert Kerckrinck, and Hans van Loon.[54] In September the Chinese silk was sold to Gommer Spranger, Rombout Jacobsz:, Jan de Raedt & Co.,[55] while a lot of Bengali silk in the same month was sold to Carel Quina & Co.[56] The inferior silks were sold by contracts to Andries Pels and to Philips & Gilbert de Flines.[57] As to the other commodities there were also, in the 1630's, great buyers by contract, and we find here again several of the names mentioned in connexion with the silk. Thus in October 1632 all pepper was sold to Gommer Spranger, Jan de Raedt, Carel Looten, Jan Cort, Hubrecht de Haze, Cornelis Spieringh, Godert Kerckrinck & Co.[58] In July 1633 Gommer Spranger & Co. bought a lot of pepper,[59] and in September of the same year Messrs. Jacob Bicker, Gommer Spranger, Jan de Raedt, Carel Looten & Co. bought another lot, this time subject to the proviso that the Company during the whole of the year 1634 must not sell or distribute pepper.[60] In agreement with this arrangement we

[47] Kol. Arch. No. 250, 14 November 1631.
[48] *Ibid.* 29 September 1632.
[49] *Ibid.* 7 July 1633.
[50] *Ibid.* 17 September 1633.
[51] *Ibid.* 13, 14, and 17 September 1633.
[52] *Ibid.* 16 and 17 August 1634.
[53] *Ibid.* 7 and 10 September 1635.
[54] Kol. Arch. No. 251, 17 September and 21 November 1636.
[55] *Ibid.* 19 September 1636.
[56] *Ibid.* 18 September 1636.
[57] *Ibid.* 18 September 1636.
[58] Kol. Arch. No. 250, 1 October 1632.
[59] *Ibid.* 5 July 1633.
[60] *Ibid.* 15 September 1633.

find the following pepper contract in February 1635. It was made with Symon van der Oors, David Fransz:, Jean Duyts, Claes Claesz: Ansloo & Co.[61] In September of the same year Jean Duyts, Hendrick de Haze, Jan Wisser, Samuel Timmermanns, and Jan Coymans bought another lot.[62] Finally, in 1636, too, we find two contracts for pepper: one from September with Daniel Godijn & Co. and the other from November with Daniel Godijn, George Everhard Klenck, David Fransz: & Co.[63]

These examples from the 1620's and the 1630's would seem to be sufficient to show that the sale by contract – the so-called *verkoop bij contractatie* – may be characterized as the conspicuous form of sale. The Heeren XVII entered into a contract with a group of merchants – a "bourse" – for the whole stock or a lot of a commodity at a pre-arranged price. The contract generally was subject to the proviso that the Company for a definite space of time committed itself to refraining from selling more of its supplies, new or old, of the commodity in question. This time-limit was called *stilstand*. It gave the buyer a security that the market would not be supplied with new quantities by the Company, after which he might arrange his price policy. However, we also find another form of sale during these years. It is especially distinct as regards spices. It was the sale of the goods at fixed prices, i.e. prices fixed by the Directors, the so-called *prijseeringh* or *prijsstellinge*. As appears from the chapter on the spices, sale at fixed prices became typical of this group of commodities during long periods of the lifetime of the Company. On the other hand, during the first period we find few traces of the third way of selling, that of free sale to the highest bidder. In Dutch this form of sale was called *op stock*, cf. the term *bij de stok verkoopen*. This auction sale during the 17th century was to gain ground more and more. However, let us examine the early predominant form of sale, the contract, and the buyers in more detail.

How comprehensive a single contract sale might be appears from the deal on 19 October 1623 between the Company and a syndicate consisting of Gert Dircksz: Raedt, Cornelis van Campen, and Hans Broers of all pepper in stock and brought home before 1 May 1624.[64] The contract promised the buyers a *stilstand* of 24 months, and they were allowed to have 5000 to 6000 bales of pepper stored in the Amsterdam warehouses for five or six months at their own risk. This sale meant gross proceeds of about 4 million fl. to the Company. The size of the

[61] *Ibid.* 3 February 1635. [62] *Ibid.* 7 September 1635.
[63] Kol. Arch. No. 251, 17 September and 20 November 1636.
[64] Kol. Arch. No. 249, 19 October 1623.

amount perhaps is best felt when it is remembered that the share capital of the Company was well over 6 million fl., and that its debts – *penningen à deposito* – at the time of the contract constituted about 8 million fl. The Heeren XVII for that matter wanted the total proceeds from the sale to be used for reducing these oppressive debts by half.[65] The contract is evidence of the calibre of the Dutch capitalists, not least considering that the same merchants were also active in other fields. As mentioned above, this does not only apply to the East India goods, but also to the great products of European trade. Thus Cornelis van Campen was well-known for his trade in Russian grain,[66] i.a. under the style of Pieter Bas & Cornelis van Campen. Or we may mention the first ancestor of the Bicker family, Gerrit Bicker Pietersz:, who was active at the foundation of the Company in 1602, *bewindhebber* in Kamer Amsterdam, and participant in the syndicate of 17 distinguished Dutch merchants which shortly before his death in 1604 was established for trade to the White Sea.[67] His son Cornelis Bicker from 1622 was *bewindhebber* in the West India Company, while another son, Jacob Bicker, from 1618 was *bewindhebber* in the East India Company. The de Haze family, whose name also appears among the buyers of the Company, and who later in the 17th and 18th centuries belonged to the leading *bewindhebbers*, were active in the trade to Spain, Italy, and the Levant. Elias Trip, from 1614 a resident of Amsterdam and East India *bewindhebber*, carried on an extensive trade in iron, arms, and ammunition. About 1626 he established contact with Sweden, where he collaborated with his brother-in-law, Louis de Geer, in the latter's endeavours to utilize the wealth of minerals in Sweden by founding mines and ironworks. The previous year he had become manager of the Levant trade.[68] In this way we might continue. It is also possible to point out family ties which connected a long series of names of buyers, such as Trip, Coymans, de Haze, van Schoonhoven, Bicker; but it is more relevant to consider the relations between the buyers and the Court of Directors.

We have already mentioned several examples of *bewindhebbers* being partners in syndicates to which the Heeren XVII sold commodities. About 1629–30 this gave rise to a violent conflict within the Company. This conflict broke out in the autumn of 1629 with the criticism by Kamer Zeeland of the sale of pepper and raw silk by the Heeren XVII.

[65] Kol. Arch. No. 184, October 1623.
[66] J. E. Elias, *De Vroedschap van Amsterdam, 1578–1795* (Haarlem, 1903–05), vol. I, p. 85.
[67] *Ibid.* vol. I, pp. 173 ff.
[68] *Ibid.* vol. II, p. 551; J. G. van Dillen, "Amsterdamsche notarieele acten betreffende den koperhandel en de uitoefening van mijnbouw en metaalindustrie in Zweden", *Bijdragen en Mededeelingen van het Historisch Genootschap,* deel 58 (Utrecht, 1937), pp. 220 ff.

It was not stated what contracts were referred to, but it may be mentioned that the Heeren XVII in July 1628 sold all pepper to the syndicate of Cornelis Bicker, Pieter Bas, Hillebrant den Otter, Hans van Loon & Hubrecht de Haze,[69] and that the Court of Directors in August 1629 sold the complete cargoes of pepper of six ships to Messrs. Cornelis Bicker, Hans Broers & Godert Kerckrinck.[70] As to the silk the Amsterdam silk-mercer Jacob Pietersz: Hooghkamer & Co. in August 1627 had proposed to the Heeren XVII an arrangement according to which he should have an option of the Chinese silk for a number of years,[71] but the proposal was not accepted. In October 1628 all the Chinese silk of the Company was sold to Cornelis Bicker, Pieter Bas & Co., and in August 1629 to Cornelis Bicker & Godert Kerckrinck.[72] Of the Persian silk the Heeren XVII in July 1628 had sold 300 bales to the above-mentioned Hooghkamer and 301 bales to the syndicate of Pieter Seulijns, Jan van de Wouwer, Andries Pels & Geraldo de la Troys,[73] furthermore in November of the same year the cargoes of three ships to Cornelis Bicker, Pieter Bas, Hans van Loon & Co., and finally in August 1629 the cargoes of four ships to Cornelis Bicker & Godert Kerckrinck.[74] Parts of the lots of silk and pepper contracted for were stored at Middelburg. In 1629 the representatives of Kamer Zeeland in the Heeren XVII stated that according to the decision of the Zeeland States they had been ordered not to assist in any deal concerning lots of goods arriving at Kamer Zeeland. The chamber refused handing over what had already been sold.[75] The case was brought before the States General by the delegates of the province of Zeeland. At the contract sale, it said in the indictment, the commodities of the Company only fell into the hands of a very small number of persons, mainly living in Amsterdam. These people controlled the market and could at pleasure force others to buy from them. Among the contracting parties there were *bewindhebbers* who were among the Heeren XVII, which gave the Zeeland delegates occasion to assume that neither the interests of the shareholders nor those of the Company were looked after. The inner circle was acquainted with the stores in all chambers; when giving the orders to the East they determined the composition of

[69] Kol. Arch. No. 184, 21 July 1628.

[70] *Ibid.* 25 August 1629. Furthermore, in March, 1629, the pepper cargo of a single ship, the "Vianen", was sold to Hendrick Broers, Philip Pelt & Co., *ibid.* 17 March 1629.

[71] *Ibid.* 10 August 1627.

[72] *Ibid.* 31 October 1628 and 22 August 1629. The Chinese silk of the "Vianen" was sold to Christoffel Roephoen & Co. in March, 1629, *ibid.* 19 March 1629.

[73] *Ibid.* 21 July 1628.

[74] *Ibid.* 1 November 1628 and 23 August 1629.

[75] *Ibid.* 27 August 1629 and March 1630, Item 5.

the returns and they fixed the terms at the sales. Therefore *bewindhebbers* should neither directly nor indirectly be allowed to share in contracts on the buying side. Besides, the delegates of Zeeland referred to the provision of the charter of 1602 that each chamber had the administration of its own ships and commodities. In cases in which a chamber had not received returns from India, it was reasonable that commodities were made over from the other chambers, but it should never be so that the chambers were to make over everything, amongst other things because the various provinces in this way were deprived of the duties from the re-exports.[76] The complaint was followed by a remonstrance from the principal shareholders in Zeeland, in which they demanded that a right be secured for the merchants in Zeeland to participate in contracts by up to one fourth, and furthermore they proposed that the chambers and the sworn principal stockholders should be invited to discuss the question whether it was better to sell the commodities of the Company by auction sale or at fixed prices.[77] The Heeren XVII replied that the latter question belonged to their assembly only, where, for that matter, it had already been discussed together with the principal stockholders and decided by a majority of votes. This reply referred to the session of August 1629 when the first item on the agenda had been the sale of the commodities. There it had been decided to continue the sales "nae den ouden voet", i.e. on the line that the important commodities should be sold by contract to the highest bidders, whereas "de cleijnicheden als porceleijnen & andere" should be sold "bij den stock". If it was not possible by contracts to obtain a satisfactory price, the commodities ought to be offered at fixed prices.[78] The Heeren XVII also rejected the proposal for the right of the Zeeland merchants to participate by one fourth, declaring that the Zeeland merchants singly or jointly were more than welcome to buy whole lots if so desired. The lots would always be sold to the highest bidders, regardless of locality.[79] The actual point of the conflict – the refusal of Kamer Zeeland to hand over the lots of pepper and silk sold – was decided by the States General on 3 November 1629. The contracts should remain in force and the lots consequently be handed over. At the same time the States General made the fundamental decision that *bewindhebbers* who got a seat among the Heeren XVII, in future should neither directly nor indirectly be allowed to participate in the purchase of commodities by contract.[80] There the matter rested. It is

[76] Kol. Arch. No. 501, 30 October 1629.
[77] Kol. Arch. No. 184, 9 March 1630.
[78] *Ibid.* August 1629, Item 1.
[79] *Ibid.* 9 March 1630.
[80] Kol. Arch. No. 501, 3 November 1629.

true that the matter remained pending for several months and cost the Company a compensation to the buyers of the disputed lots. Thus Zeeland tried to take up the question of the access of other *bewindhebbers* not among the Heeren XVII to make purchases by contract. Pieter van Dam appointed the two Zeeland principal stockholders Blasius Naghtegaal and Lucas Schorer to be leaders of the action,[81] which, however, came to nothing. Neither the States General nor the Heeren XVII would shake the private *bewindhebbers'* access to buying the commodities whether by contract or otherwise.[82]

We have from these years a few interesting examples of the degree to which the goods of the Company could fall into the hands of a small number of merchants. In the autumn of 1628 the Company wanted to sell some of its stock of cloves, but neither found sale by contract nor offer at a fixed price suitable. The reason was that various "perticuliere noch veele quarteelen in handen hebben die altijt voor de Comp.[e] onder de prijs derselver sullen vercoopen."[83] After an appointed committee had presented a report, the following solution was worked out: an alliance was made with the latest customer as regards cloves, the syndicate of Joan van der Straten, Casper van Wickevoort, David de Weert & Co.,[84] who agreed to offer their whole stock together with a corresponding lot of the cloves of the Company. The two contracting parties offered their cloves together at a common, fixed price, and the Company bound itself to sell no other lots of cloves before the pooled lot had been sold. Such an arrangement presupposed that the parties involved thought that they together controlled the market. It is probable that it was a successful speculation. A similar arrangement for *macis* was made in the autumn of 1629.[85] In this case the customer was the omnipresent Cornelis Bicker & Co.[86] The Heeren XVII straightforwardly recognized that Bicker's syndicate had at their disposal twice as much *macis* as the Company,[87] and it was agreed to offer the article jointly at fixed prices. In an example from 1634 it was the buyers who wanted an article to be offered jointly. It was the parties that had contracted for pepper.[88] They proposed "een

[81] *Pieter van Dam* 1:II, pp. 179 and 290 ff.

[82] In the years down to 1633 inclusive the Heeren XVII and the sworn principal stockholders at the beginning of the season promised to refrain from sharing in contracts. Then this ceremony was discontinued. *Pieter van Dam* 1:II, p. 183.

[83] Kol. Arch. No. 184, 1 November 1628.

[84] Their contract for all cloves in the Company's stock was dated at 30 October 1626, *ibid.*

[85] *Ibid.* 27 August 1629.

[86] In July, 1628, Cornelis Bicker & Hans van Loon bought all the mace of the returning ships, *ibid.* 15 June 1628.

[87] *Ibid.* 25 August 1629.

[88] Jacob Bicker, Gommer Spranger, Jan de Raedt, Carel Looten & Co, contract dated at 15 September 1633, Kol. Arch. No. 250.

combinatie van peper", but the Heeren XVII refused.[89] Just in pepper a menacing speculation developed towards the end of the 1630's – we shall deal with this in a different connexion – which shook the contract system to its foundations. To this was added the ascertainment of different terms from chamber to chamber in the case of the other forms of sale. The old particularism raised its head. In September 1638 the Heeren XVII enjoined on those concerned that all sales should be made as homogeneously as possible. No merchant should have any advantage over any other, as this would only injure and impede the sale as a whole. Therefore it was requested that the *bewindhebbers* from the respective chambers should every spring appear before the Heeren XVII with a declaration that they had precisely followed the order of the Court concerning the terms of sale, especially concerning the delivery of the commodities and the credit. Furthermore it was proposed that the chambers should exchange information about inferior debtors.[90] It was a still more serious affair that the Heeren XVII had ascertained that some persons under the pretext of being different buyers had tried to secure all lots of a commodity "zijnde notoire collusie en monopolie."[91] A general debate followed. The result was that the Company in 1642 gave up the sale by contract and decided on auction sales as the safest means against speculation. The commodities were in this way distributed among a larger number of buyers. In the case of spices the auction sale was not, however, the form preferred in the long run. A sequence of the auctions was worked out by the chambers between them, and a standing committee was appointed for the task of attending the auctions in the various chambers. It came to consist of five members, one from Kamer Amsterdam, one from Kamer Zeeland, one from Zuyderquartier, one from Noorderquartier, and finally one principal stockholder.[92]

It applied to all forms of sale that payment within 1–2 months after the date of the sale was considered cash payment and remunerated by a discount, e.g. 6 per cent.[93] Otherwise a period was stipulated within which payment was to take place. This credit might vary from e.g. 6 to 12 months.[94] The prices listed in our tables are, for the time after 1649/50, averages based on the statements of sales in the accounts from Kamer

[89] *Pieter van Dam* 1:II, p. 185.

[90] Kol. Arch. No. 251, 10 September 1638.

[91] *Ibid.*

[92] *Pieter van Dam* 1:II, p. 190 *et seq.*

[93] This cash period was also called *stilstand*. If the buyer paid before the expiry of the cash period, it was a case of the so-called *voorbetaling*, for which an extra discount was given. Inversely, it was a case of *nabetaling*, if the buyer paying cash after the expiry of the *stilstand* had not yet paid. In the latter case he had to pay a kind of interest to the Company. Combinations of these two forms also occur.

[94] On the different terms of sale, see Dr. Stapel's glossary in *Pieter van Dam* 1:II.

Amsterdam. The averages are based on the mixture of discount and non-discount (cash and credit) sales appearing in fact, and thus correspond to the net proceeds of the Company. The prices which we have found for the first half of the 17th century, on the other hand, originate from information in the papers of the Court of Directors concerning contracts, fixed prices, or references to the predominant prices at the preceding sales. As the periods of credit are not stated in all cases, some uncertainty is involved in these prices. For that matter, we can in the case of the spices during the period after 1649/50 make an estimate of the extent to which cash payment occurred, viz. by comparing the fixed prices with the actual averages. Let us as an example of such analyses take the beginning of the 1650's, when the Heeren XVII offered *noten* at 54 *stuivers* per pond on 9 months' credit.[95] Kamer Amsterdam shows the following averages during the years 1649/50–1655/56:

1649/50	50.40	*stuivers* per pond
1650/51	50.40	- - -
1651/52	50.40	- - -
1652/53	50.40	- - -
1653/54	49.20	- - -
1654/55	49.00	- - -
1655/56	49.40	- - -

This suggests pronounced cash payment during these years. It is, however, only in the case of the fixed prices that investigations of the practice of payment can be carried out.

In the course of years the clientèle of buyers increased and became more specialized. This can only be established exactly from the beginning of the 18th century, from which time the general commerce journals of the Company have been preserved, i.e. from a time when the free auction sale must be assumed to have long been predominant. As an example of this type of sale we may take the pepper auction sale in Amsterdam in May 1714,[96] when 2,210 bales of black pepper to a net weight of 955,733 ponds were sold, the proceeds being about 882,000 fl. There were 66 buyers in all, 16 of whom bought more than the average. The 9 greatest buyers bought more than half of the pepper. Among the greatest buyers we find such names as Isaac Cossart, Pierre Testas, and Jeronimo de Haze de Giorgio.[97] Some of these names of buyers are found in the same year's sale of spices, but if we take the auction sale of cinna-

[95] *Pieter van Dam* 1:II, p. 204. [96] Kol. Arch. No. 10.412, pp. 393 ff.
[97] Jeronimo de Haze de Giorgio was from 1716 President of the *Heeren XVII*

mon, there are other names at the head: Joan Schutt, Nutges & de Certt, Joan Blom, and Jan Scherenberg. If in this year we pass on to saltpetre, there are other buyers again: Nicolaes & Hendrick van Hoorn,[98] Jacob & Jan Balde, de Wed^ve Abraham Kroock & Zoonen, Jan Braams, etc., and in the case of such an important article as Bengali silk we find the family Verhammen, David van Mollem, Simon Bevel, Anthony Laars, and others. The above characterization is based on such random samples. It should, however, be added that pepper is one of those commodities which shows the greatest difference between great and small buyers. Finally it should be noted that among the fairly great buyers of coffee in the 1720's we find the book-keeper of the Company, Hendrick van Bronkhorst.[99] Also in the case of the other chambers we find some of these traits, but there it is to a much greater extent a question of great buyers who assert themselves within many categories of commodities. As in Amsterdam, the sales were free, but the type was more old-fashioned. In e.g. Kamer Zeeland in the 1720's and the 1730's[100] it is seen that 5 or 6 names figure as great buyers of such varied commodities as pepper, cinnamon, sugar, tea, coffee, saltpetre, and cottons, viz. Casparus Ribaut, Bourssen & Grimalla, Isaac Tulleken, Pieter Six,[101] and Jan Beukelaar. A typical sale was e.g. the sale in October 1727 of about 600,000 ponds mainly Java coffee to a value of half a million fl. The sale was distributed to 38 buyers, 4 of whom bought more than the average. The three greatest buyers were Casparus Ribaut, Bourssen & Grimalla, and Jan Beukelaar.[102]

The receipts of the goods from the East and the sale of them were one beat in the pulse of the factory Nederland, the sending of ships and cargoes the other. If the variegated splendour of Asia is reflected in the analyses of the invoices, the fertile wealth of Europe is reviewed in the lists of the equipments. There are the substantial products from the north, Riga hemp and the hemp from Königsberg, canvas from St. Petersburg, Stockholm pitch, Viborg tar, Norwegian timber, train-oil from the Arctic Sea, and the indispensable Dutch *haring*. Furthermore, Setubal salt, brandy from Bourdeaux and Conjacque, the French, Spanish, and German wines, soap from Marseilles, English leather and lead, Newcastle coals, Hamburg leaf copper, Delft ware, Edam cheese, and butter

[98] Nicolaes van Hoorn was a member of the Seventeen.
[99] E.g. Kol. Arch. No. 10,417, pp. 314 ff.
[100] Kol. Arch. No. 8335, "Versamelingh van de verkoopinghen".
[101] Isaac Tulleken and Pieter Six were members of the Seventeen.
[102] Kol. Arch. No. 8335, "Versamelingh van de verkoopinghen".

from Friesland. One might continue like this. When the Heeren XVII in the beginning of the 18th century carried into effect that the chambers should send information about their purchases of equipment goods, forms were printed including more than 220 different articles.[103] At the top we find precious metals, uncoined and coined, African gold, American silver, *mexicanen*, Spanish piasters, Dutch *schellingen*. The dispatch was not only a question of commodities, it was also the work at timber-yards, along ropewalks, in smithies, in the shops of coopers, tailors, shoemakers, bakers, in breweries, the callous business of hiring sailors and soldiers, the drawing-up of instructions, and the clergymen's prayers for blessing. The equipment as a rule took place during the summer so that the ships were ready to sail in the autumn. It was important to have the ships sent off so early that they might arrive at Batavia in time for their European cargoes of cash and goods to pass on without any appreciable delay due to the Asiatic trade winds.[104]

The equipments by the Company as made up in *florins* from decade to decade during the period from 1639 to 1740 appear from the following survey:[105]

Table 5. *Equipments by the Company from 1639/40 to 1738/39. Fl.*

1639/40–1648/49	42,681,165
1649/50–1658/59	71,073,234
1659/60–1668/69	80,367,268
1669/70–1678/79	76,990,165
1679/80–1688/89	87,568,699
1689/90–1698/99	106,879,160
1699/00–1708/09	122,558,389
1709/10–1718/19	135,182,897
1719/20–1728/29	172,859,243
1729/30–1738/39	158,955,936

The table broadly shows the same movement as the above surveys of returns and sales, the expenditure on the equipments all along being at a level below the proceeds from the sales. While the receipts of the Company in Nederland, apart from loans, consist of the proceeds from the sales only, the question arises to what degree the expenditure of the factory Nederland was included in the equipment figures above. In brief, what is covered by the figures?

[103] E.g. Collectie Radermacher No. 121, "Rooster van de prijzen der goederen by de Kamer Zeeland ingekogt".

[104] *Pieter van Dam* 1:I, p. 665; see also the Company's *uitloopsboeken*.

[105] On the authorities for these figures, see Appendix I.

The Dutch term for the equipments is *equipagien.* The term is ambiguous. If e.g. we take a balance as on ultimo April 1654 on the basis of the ledgers of Kamer Amsterdam, *equipagien* appears as an item of expenditure among other items of expenditure, as follows:[106]

Table 6. *Kamer Amsterdam, Balance on ultimo April 1654.*

DEBIT		*CREDIT*	
Proceeds from sale 1653/54	5,903,366 fl.	Balance carried forward	19,770,140 fl.
Sundries	625 fl.	Monthly wages of crews	649,909 fl.
Balance	18,080,735 fl.	Other wages and salaries	487,456 fl.
		Equipagien	2,710,838 fl.
		Bills of exchange, India	307,460 fl.
		Bills of exchange, Europe	36,990 fl.
		Interest on *voorbetaling**	16,796 fl.
		Sundries	5,137 fl.
	23,984,726 fl.		23,984,726 fl.

* See above p. 38 Note 93.

The same is the case in another example selected, viz. the cost of equipment of Kamer Zeeland during the season 1679/80,[107] but there the interesting point is that also the total amount of the cost is termed *equipagien,* and that this total enters in the total figure for the six chambers of the Company, which figure is contained in Table 5.

Table 7. *Kamer Zeeland's Equipagie 1679/80.*

Equipagie	£ Flemish		185,018
Tractementen	-	-	6,838
Convoy and octroi money	-	-	14,961
Monthly wages of returning crews	-	-	63,734
Interest on loans	-	-	8,886
Necessaries for India	-	-	3,528
Rent of warehouses	-	-	231
Brokerage	-	-	1,940
Packing	-	-	647
Bills of exchange and costs on the returning ships	-	-	23,803
In all	£ Flemish		309,586

[106] Kol. Arch. No. 10,235, "Staet sommier getrocken uyt de grootboecken van de O.I.C. ter Kamer van Amsterdam onder ultimo April 1654."

[107] Kol. Arch. No. 10,236. The Chamber of Zeeland kept the accounts in Flemish £, 1 Flemish £ of 20 *schellingen* being equivalent to 6 florins.

From this and similar examples it appears that the term *equipagien* partly covers the total working expenses, partly in a strict sense the expenses connected with the dispatch of the ships. The total working expenses were made up annually in connexion with the preparation of the general statement of the Company, from which originates the ten-year equipment figures. If, on the other hand, we want to analyze the individual items, the statements are insufficient, i.a. because *equipagien* in a strict sense, as appears from the two examples selected, are determined by the practice of book-keeping, which varies from chamber to chamber and from time to time. There were a number of items of expenditure which the Company found it natural to split up, but which it may be desirable to assemble. This, e.g., applies to the important item of pay for the crews. It was customary before the departure to give the crew two months' pay in advance, while the remaining pay was not handed over until the ships came home. The Company consequently entered the two months' pay as an immediate item of *equipagie*, and the pay after the arrival home as a cost connected with the returns. The cash sent out by the ships was also entered as expenditure on *equipagie*, while the bills of exchange drawn by the Governor General and the Council on Nederland were entered as expenses apart, although in a certain respect they functioned as capital sent out. If therefore we want to be on firm ground, we must turn to the accounts themselves. These are available from the beginning of the 18th century. Before that time a general analysis of the expenses is not possible. The accounts from Kamer Amsterdam are in the best state of preservation. Below we shall give the result of an analysis of the expenses of this chamber during the period of 15 years from 1714 to 1728 inclusive.[108]

[108] Regarding the material, see Appendix B pp. 272 ff. The analysis is based upon the accounts of "Equipagie" and "Retouren der Vierjarige Reeck:e." The heading of *Cargoes* includes the following items: (i) bullion & money ["Contante Penningen"], (ii) commodities ["Bier tot Koopmanschap", "Laekenen", "Loot", "Verscheyde Behoeften voor Indie", "Diverse Koopmansz: Equipagie", "Zijdenstoffen Equipagie", "Wollenwaren", "Wynen"]; the *Ships* include (i) materials ["Geschut en Ammunitie van Oorlog", "Hout", "Iserwerck", "Seyldoek", "Touwerk", "Verscheyde Materialen", "Stuurmansgeretschappen"], (ii) victualling ["Bier voor de Equipagie", "Boter", "Broot", "Fustagien", "Kaas", "Oly", "Pottagien", "Speck", "Vettewarijen", "Visch", "Vleesch", "Barbiersbehoeften", "Cajuytsbehoeften", "Gemaakte Kleederen", "Scheepsgelt", "Verscheyde Scheepsbehoeften"]; the *Wages* cover (i) crews ["Maanthuren Equipagie", "Maanthuren der wedergekomen Schepen"], (ii) day-labourers ["Arbeydsloonen"], (iii) servants ["Tractementen"]; and finally the group *Other expenses* is made up of (i) embarkation & unloading ["Ongelden Equipagie", "Generale Ongelden op de Retouren"], (ii) buying & sale ["Courtagie van vercochte Retouren", "Voor- en Naarbetalinge"].

Table 8. *Analysis of Working Expenses at Kamer Amsterdam during the Years 1714–1728.*

Cargoes	43.33 %,	viz.	38.92 %	bullion and money
			4.41 %	commodities
Ships	22.89 %,	viz.	15.11 %	materials
			7.78 %	victualling
Wages	26.79 %,	viz.	18.49 %	crews
			6.50 %	day-labourers
			1.80 %	servants
Other expenses	6.99 %,	viz.	5.47 %	embarkation and unloading
			1.52 %	buying and sale
In all 100.00 % or 106,718,143 fl.				

It should first be noted that in the analysis above we have kept out the expenses for interest on borrowed money and for the payment of bills of exchange. These amounts during the 15 years in question came to 3.6 million fl. and 5.2 million fl., respectively,[109] in all 8.8 million fl. If we consider the bills of exchange honoured as an addition to the cash forwarded, the percentage of bullion and money will be a little higher, just as the percentage of the group concerning other expenses will rise if the interest is added there.[110] Next, it should be noted that the distinctions between the various groups are not quite well-defined. In spite of the detailed information it is not possible to dissolve their *equipagie* and return accounts into all the components desired.[111] Thus it may be taken for granted that the group of wages was higher than stated, as a wage factor enters in a number of the elements placed under shipping materials, such as hemp, cordage, oak wood, timber for masts, iron-work, lead, etc., viz. pay for hammering, sawing, etc. The accounts did not enter the expenses for the building or repair of a ship together per ship built or repaired, but split them up into elements as those mentioned. What is entered as wages is day's wages paid by the chamber to unskilled labourers occupied in the warehouses, in the shipyards, and elsewhere. Furthermore, the costs of embarkation and unloading included pay, e.g. to the pilots, towage, etc., which cannot be specified. It necessarily follows from what has been stated above that the percentage of the group con-

[109] Extracted from *Resolutien Heeren XVII* [the Court Minutes].

[110] The interest is in the accounts entered as equipment expenses in a strict sense. We have kept this money and the amounts of bills apart, as they can also be regarded as financial amounts and in this connexion will be made the object of a brief mention in the chapter on Profit and Loss.

[111] Holl. Zeeuwsche Staatscommissie, No. 5, Litra P, "Notitie van de wijze op welke alle betalingen in de respective kameren van d'Oost Indische Compagnie werden geboekt".

cerning shipping materials is too high. This is not only so because of the wage element, but also because some of the materials, just as some of the victualling, were forwarded to the East and therefore strictly belong in the groups of cargo commodities.

Kamer Amsterdam during the 15 years mentioned equipped ships with a total number of lasts of 34,585, while during the same period it built new ships to a total of 6,820 lasts.[112] These lasts must be considered a kind of commercial lasts, as they indicate the carrying capacity of the ships after space for the crew, provisions, and other necessaries of the ship had been deducted. They were made up i. a. out of consideration for certain duties and were determined in the way that a ship of 160 feet was reckoned as equal to 180 lasts, a ship of 145 feet equal to 140 lasts, a ship of 130 feet equal to 100 lasts, and so on.[113] If the total number of lasts equipped is related to the items of expenditure of ship's materials, victualling, and wages for the crew and day-labourers, we get an average cost per last of 1478 fl. As, however, both measures and values are ill-defined, we shall try in a different way to throw light on the transportation costs of the Company.

By good fortune the accounts show a single exception from the general practice of book-keeping sketched above. The matter in question is the direct trade from Amsterdam to Canton in China started in December 1728 and ended in the summer of 1735. A total of 11 ships were equipped in six expeditions, but two of the ships were wrecked at their departure.[114] These expeditions were booked *aparte* with all expenses and receipts specified and with a clearer division of cargo, ship, wages, etc., than previously. In the case of the first three expeditions the value of the ships was booked as an absolute item of expenditure, while in the case of the three last expeditions, they only stated the value of the ships and instead entered the wear and tear of the ships as expenditure. We shall give an abstract of the accounts for the three first expeditions comprising the ships "Coxhorn" (leaving on 5 December 1728 and returning home on 15 July 1730), "Duyfje" (leaving on 11 November 1729 and re-

[112] Extracted from *Resolutien Heeren XVII* [the Court Minutes].

[113] In the 17th century the last figures were put considerably higher. Pieter van Dam mentions that in 1637 a ship of 160 feet was rated at 350 lasts, but later was reduced to 250 lasts and lower when the payment of *last- en veylgelt* was connected with the ship's cargo of merchandise. "Een schip van 160 voeten lang, van hier naar Indiën gaande, ophebbende 275 á 300 koppen, voorzien van vivres en andere scheepsbehoeften, tot soo lange reyse nodigh, sal geen 250 lasten aan koopmanschappen kunnen innemen en op die wyse word het land daarin niet verkort;" *op cit.* 1 :I, p. 480.

[114] The "Buren" was equipped twice, having been both times severely damaged by gales in European waters. On the direct trade to China, which was also carried on from Kamer Zeeland, see further the chapter on Tea.

turning home on 30 July 1731), "Leyduyn" and "Coxhorn" (both leaving on 11 December 1730 and returning home on 7 August 1732). It should be added that the "Leyduyn" was 130 feet long and the two others were 120 feet long.

Table 9. *Expenses for Four Direct China Ships Equipped from Kamer Amsterdam, 1728–1730.*

Cargo in cash	67.14 %
- in commodities	2.32 %
Value of the ships (hull)	15.89 %
Wages	7.34 %
Other costs (victualling, duties, pilotage, etc.)	7.31 %
In all 1,637,135 fl. or	100.00 %

A corresponding abstract of the accounts for the three last expeditions includes the ships "Knappenhof" and "Ypenrode" (both leaving on 2 January 1732 and returning home on 19/20 September 1733), "Leyduyn" and "Voorduyn"[115] (both leaving on 26 November 1732 and returning home on 27 August 1734), and the "Noordwolfsbergen" (leaving on 17 January 1734 and returning home on 23 July 1735), all of them 130 feet long:

Table 10. *Expenses for Five Direct China Ships Equipped from Kamer Amsterdam, 1732–1734.*

Cargo in cash	71.30 %
- in commodities	2.89 %
Wear and tear of the ships*	6.64 %
Wages	9.00 %
Other costs (victualling, duties, pilotage, etc.)	10.17 %
In all 1,878,311 fl. or	100.00 %

* In money wear and tear amounted to 124,668 fl; the value of the ships (hull) was stated to be 393,368 fl.

This last abstract agrees best with a modern arrangement of the working expenses, for which reason we shall keep to that. According to the Company's way of stating the number of lasts the five ships represent a tonnage of 500 "commercial" lasts in all,[116] which gives an item of

[115] The "Voorduyn" at her departure was damaged by a gale – as appears from the dates of departure, the ships bound for China were sent off later than normally — and her cargo was transhipped to the "Sorghwijck", who was renamed the "Voorduyn". This involved that the *Other costs* of the fifth expedition became higher than usual.

[116] 1 ship of 130 feet equal to 100 lasts.

expenditure per last of 970 fl., the cargoes being disregarded.[117] However, in order to get behind the schematic figure of lasts, we may take the volume of the commodities brought home from China. The majority of the return cargoes consisted of tea, 1.35 million ponds net in all. It is not reasonable to charge this quantity with all the costs of transportation as the ships also carried other commodities home. But if, from an estimate of the share of the tea in purchase and sale,[118] we charge the tea with three fourths of the costs of transportation, this will mean that the transportation of a quantity of 1025 ponds tea cost about 275 fl. This quantity corresponds to the freight ton of the English East India Company for Bohea tea, for which the English company in the same year paid 25 pounds sterling, or about 263 fl.[119] If we equalize a last to 2 tons, the figures become 550 fl. and 526 fl., respectively. It is only in this exceptional case that it is possible with some certainty to form an estimate of the Company's costs of transportation.

In the general description of the expenses it was mentioned that there does not for the 17th century exist any material of accounts which allows of comprehensive analyses. A single one of the groups of expenses, however, appears in the balances of the Company before 1700, viz. the pay to the crews. In and after the season of 1676/77 it appears in the balances of all the six chambers. Furthermore, we may form an estimate of the size of the capitals in cash sent to the East, in the surveys running from 1639/40 and worked out on the basis of the resolutions of the Heeren XVII.[120] It appears from these that the share of the cash in the expenses in large parts of the 17th century played a considerably smaller part than in the 18th century. As an example it may be mentioned that the percentage of the cash of the total number of equipments during the

[117] In money wear and tear, pay, and other costs amounted to a total of 484,838 fl.

[118] The sales thus yielded well over 3.2 mill. fl., the share of tea being just under 2.4 mill. fl.

[119] Calculated at an average rate of exchange of 35 *schellingen* per £ sterling; cf. N. W. Posthumus, *Nederlandsche Prijsgeschiedenis* (Leiden, 1943). The weight is converted on the ratio 100 lbs. = 91.50 ponds; cf. Alexander Justice, "A Treatise of the Weights of Holland, and of their Conformity with those of Other Countries, etc." in *General Treatise of Monies & Exchanges* (London, 1707). The English East India Company's rates of freight have been adduced from the Company's general commerce journals, C.R.O., London. From these it appears that the Company reckoned 8 cwt. to 1 ton green tea, and 10 cwt. to 1 ton Bohea tea. Actually the English rate of freight of tea ought to be increased by part of the extra costs incurred, which, however, in the case of normal voyages were small. Only when appreciable delays occurred, e.g. the item of "demurrage" made itself felt decisively (see e.g. the freight account of the "Wyndham" 30 June 1735). As, however, the Dutch voyages considered were normal, it is natural to compare them with corresponding English voyages. If the English rates ought to be increased, the Dutch rates ought to be reduced by the costs of unloading and other expenses which cannot be quite distinctly separated out. The elements of uncertainty mentioned thus decrease the distance between the figures.

[120] See the Appendix for description of the balances and the revision of the tables in Pieter van Dam and Klerk de Reus, besides the origin of the statistics of capitals sent out (D and I).

seven years 1676/77–1682/83 was only 20.53. The wages during the same period amounted to 22.64 per cent. and thus do not show so great a change as the cash. Furthermore it seems to appear from random samples in the invoices of the ships sent out that the low percentage of the cash was not counterbalanced by a correspondingly higher part for the group of commodities in the cargoes. The structure of the cargoes seems rather unchanged.[121] This is all that we dare say about the picture of the Dutch costs of the Company in the 17th century.[122]

Above, the framework of the activities of the factory Nederland has been outlined. The most important quantities among its receipts and expenditure have been described. The figures for returns and sales as well as equipments point towards the last decades of the 17th century and the first decades of the 18th century as a suggestive period, which evinces a high degree of activity. In these years clear displacements in the structure of the cargoes of commodities brought home are observed, just as the composition of the equipments is changed, the precious metals playing a greater and greater part. We shall now look at some of the commodities singly and in this way try to throw light on the interplay between the European and the Asiatic organs of the Company.

[121] Right back to the beginning of the period the cargoes of the ships were dominated by bullion and money; see e.g. the invoices kept in Kol. Arch. Nos. 450 and 451 from the years 1616 to 1620, ships equipped by Kamer Amsterdam. The sector of goods is characterized by the same commodities as later: lead, copper, cloth, wine, corals, small wares, etc. Furthermore of war materials.

[122] From 1636 there is an interesting example of a calculation of transport, Kol. Arch. No. 250, November 1636, "Calculatie wat de equipagie van een fluyt groot 170: à 180 lasten soude comen te costen en wat advance daer mede soude connen werden gedaen." In that year the Seventeen intended to get af flute at a value of 29,000 fl. and a lastage of 170–180 and with a crew of 40 men in all. In 20 months it should go to Batavia and return with a cargo of 450,000 ponds of sugar. The purchase of this cargo would cost 33,750 fl., and allowance was made for a leakage of 15 per cent., so that the cargo would be of 382,500 ponds net in Nederland. On the basis of the calculations of the Court of Directors the costs may be set up as follows:

Value of return cargo (purchase)	33,750 fl.
Wear and tear of the flute	7,380 -
Pay of the crew	13,020 -
Provisions	9,600 -
In all ..	63,750 fl.

Hence, the transport of the sugar can be calculated at about 80 fl. per 1,025 ponds net. This is not, however, an account, but an estimate, and a "pared" one at that. Thus only the provisions have been considered which in the analyses above of the direct trade to China constituted two thirds of the group of *Other costs*. Furthermore, the crew was small, also according to the standard of the 1630's. If the "pared" costs are calculated per month, the ship would cost 1500 fl. during the voyage. According to the calculation the last of sugar would be of 2500–2600 ponds. For comparison it may be stated that the Company according to a survey from August 1630 of the returns calculated the last of saltpetre at 4,000 ponds, that of pepper at 2,400 ponds, and that of cloves at 2,000 ponds, cf. Kol. Arch. No. 184, 26 August 1630, "Memorie van de waeren ende coopmanschappen die bij de Vergadering van XVII goet gevonden werden met de eerste brieven van Indien te ontbieden." Later in the 18th century the last of sugar in the Indies was calculated at 3,000 ponds; cf. Kol. Arch. No. 464, Batavia 15 July 1718.

We shall begin with the precious metals, which were the most important exports of Nederland. Next, we shall take a selection of the imports: pepper, spices, raw silk, textiles, sugar, copper, coffee, and tea. In total this selection must be considered to cover more than 85 per cent. of the Company's imports to Nederland, both as regards purchase and sale. It may be objected that sugar and copper from the point of view of importation might just as well be replaced by such characteristic commodities as saltpetre and indigo. The reason why the articles mentioned have been preferred is partly that as ballast goods they are of the same character as saltpetre and to a certain degree indigo as well, partly that by the place occupied by them in the Asiatic trade of the Company they give occasion for touching on conditions which, not least from a general view, it must be considered valuable to have brought out.

CHAPTER III

Bullion and Money

When the Dutch gained a footing in Java, they there as elsewhere in East Asia met with the Spanish *piastra fuerte* as a current trade coin and unit of account. They called it by many names, thus *reaal van achten* or only *reaal*, which later in Batavia became the name of a unit of silver weight. The English called the coin piece-of-eight or ryall-of-eight and later the Spanish dollar, while the Portuguese talked about *pataca* or *pardas de reales*.[1] The Dutch were very familiar with the Spanish coin from home. Linguistically *reaal van achten* covered a coin of 8 *schellingen*, for which reason the term *stuk van achten*, which also occurs, is actually more correct. It appeared with subdivisions of $^1/_2$, $^1/_4$, $^1/_8$, $^1/_{16}$, and $^1/_{32}$.[2] The rial in 1594 in Nederland was equal to 45 *stuivers*, in 1603 46 st., in 1607 47 st., and in 1622 48 st. The last-mentioned rate of conversion was carried through in the factories of the East India Company, where the rial by a slight over-estimate was considered equivalent to the rix-dollar, i.e. 2 ½ florins.[3] The rial was coined in Mexico and Peru as well as in Seville. After these places of coinage we now and then find the coins to be named *mexicanen*, *peruanen*, and *sivilianen*, they may also be found under the names of *pilaren* and *colonnen* with allusion to the two pillars or columns on the obverse of the coin.[4] A special type among the American rials must be mentioned, the so-called *reaal batoe* or *kantige reaalen*, i.e. square rials, in Spanish called *piastra cuadrada*. These coins which the Portuguese and the Spaniards exported from the Peruvian mints, were just provided with a stamp which indicated their weight. When about the middle of the 17th century they were much debased,

[1] H. W. Codrington, *Ceylon Coins and Currency* (Memoirs of the Colombo Museum, Series A, No. 3, Colombo, 1924), p. 169 *et seq.*

[2] E. Netscher & I. A. van der Chijs, *De munten van Nederlandsch Indië* (Batavia, 1863), p. 3. 1/32 is equivalent to 1 ½ *stuivers*.

[3] Codrington, *op. cit.* p. 107.

[4] J. G. van Dillen, "Amsterdam als wereldmarkt der edele metalen in de 17de en 18de eeuw", *De Economist*, jaargang 1923, p. 586, Note 28.

they got a bad name, and the Peruvian rials or *peruleros* for a certain period were prohibited in the Dutch Company.[5]

It was only natural that the Dutch should try to secure rials for their trade to the East Indies. The war with Spain, indeed, caused difficulties. Thus a momentaneous break in the silver stream from Spain caused that the *Compagnie van Verre* in 1601 had to obtain permission from the State of Holland to coin rials in Nederland.[6] But on the whole it was surprising how they were capable of providing the Spanish money, a piece of evidence among others of the calibre of the Amsterdam market of precious metals and about the rich trade to Spain maintained during the war by way of Hamburg. At the foundation of the Company in 1602 the Heeren XVII established the rule for the equipments that the chambers should exclusively send rials of eight, and if they could not be provided, then, as an alternative, gold. According to Pieter van Dam this was practicable. Not until 1618 gold was sent – intended for the Coromandel Coast – in all 72,000 rials out of a total cargo of money of 612,000 rials. The following year 4000 rose-nobles were sent to Amboyna.[7] An examination of the invoices for the ships which during the years 1616–1620 were sent out by Kamer Amsterdam, affirms van Dam's statement. The invoice price of the rials fluctuated between 48 and 49¾ st. per coin. The silver coins were packed in chests, each chest containing 8000 rials.[8] As a precautionary measure against wreckage and the like the Heeren XVII in 1629 decided that in future only 4000 rials should be packed in each chest.[9] The long conflict with Spain caused another shortage of rials in 1622. In a letter from this year to Batavia the Seventeen explained this situation and mentioned the constantly increasing prices of the Spanish money. The Directors urged the Government in Batavia to attempt having the Dutch coins introduced at the purchases in Amboyna, the Moluccas, Banda, and elsewhere.[10]

It is characteristic of the following decades that Dutch coins to an increasing extent were placed in the exports. The rials of eight were still predominant, and not least in the important trade in pepper they continued being indispensable, but in other fields new coins advanced. The

[5] See also Earl J. Hamilton, *War and Prices in Spain, 1651–1800* (Harvard Economic Studies, vol. LXXXI, Cambridge Mass., 1947), p. 11 *et seq.*

[6] van Dillen, "Amsterdam als wereldmarkt", p. 544.

[7] *Pieter van Dam* 1:I, p. 632 *et seq.*

[8] Kol. Arch. Nos. 450 and 451, *passim.*

[9] Kol. Arch. No. 184, 17 March 1629.

[10] *Pieter van Dam* 1:I, p. 633; H. Dunlop (ed.), *Bronnen tot de geschiedenis der Oostindische Compagnie in Perzië*, 1. deel, 1611–1638 (Rijks Geschiedkundige Publicatiën, No. 72, 's-Gravenhage, 1930), p. 27 *et seq.*, invoice dated at Surat, 10 November 1623, mentions a price of 51 *stuivers* per *real.*

famous Dutch "negotiepenningen", i.e. commercial money, money for exportation, found their way to Asia. The rixdollar in the Asiatic trade became a Northwest European counterpart to the Spanish rial and roamed as widely about.[11] It was followed by the Dutch *silvere leeuwendaalders*, also named *kroonen*, which in a report from 1635 were mentioned as being exported to the Levant and farther to Armenia and Persia.[12] There were, furthermore, the small coins, *schellingen*, *dubbelde* and *enkelde stuivers*. On the other hand, exportation of gold and silver in bullion was strictly prohibited in Nederland during the first half of the 17th century, and the East India Company was no exception from this rule. Towards the end of the Thirty Years' War the prohibition was modified. With a view to the Southern Netherlands the Spanish King in 1647 declared himself willing to send bullion to the ports of the Republic provided that exportation was permitted. The States General decided that two thirds of the silver which was imported on the King's account might be re-exported. At the suggestion of Amsterdam merchants it was added that the origin of the silver might be disregarded, so that in reality the path was free for the exportation of bullion if only one third was sold to the mintmasters or the bank. As early as 1646 we find bar silver among the species which the Heeren XVII decided to send to the East.[13] In 1683 the general masters of the Mint suggested that only half of the silver should be allowed to be exported without being coined. The town of Amsterdam had the matter delayed for seven years. Then they bowed before the rising silver prices and the poor state of the coinage. The restriction was carried through in 1690 and lasted to the beginning of the 18th century. For some time a maximum price was imposed upon the silver, as there had been before 1670. On the other hand the exportation of "negotiepenningen" remained free, as it had been during the whole century. Only in 1701, when it was feared, in connexion with the War of the Spanish Succession, that the supplies of silver would be cut off, the exportation of "negotiepenningen" was prohibited for a short period, but otherwise the 18th century was characterized by a practically unhampered exportation. In 1749 it is found that the trade in precious metals was quite free.[14]

The phenomenon of "negotiepenningen" is not only evidence of the Dutch conditions, which were so unique in a so-called mercantilistic time. It is also expressive of a process common in most European coun-

[11] J. B. Tavernier, *Les Six Voyages, &c.*, 2. partie (Paris, 1678), p. 15.
[12] van Dillen, "Amsterdam als wereldmarkt", p. 586.
[13] Kol. Arch. No. 251, August 1646.
[14] van Dillen, "Amsterdam als wereldmarkt", pp. 589 ff.

tries, the course of which is generally characterized by a reference to Gresham's Law. In Nederland the Dutch coins were superseded by debased, mainly foreign coins. There is a good number of examples that it was tried during the 17th century to succeed in finding a standard coin remaining in circulation. At the great reorganization of the coinage in 1659 it was thus decided to mint two new coins, the *zilveren rijder* or *dukaton* and the *zilveren ducaat* or *rijksdaalder*, as it was also called, the old – and better – rixdollar now, as distinct from it, being called the *bankrijksdaalder*. But these two coins, too, had to share in the fate of their predecessors, i.e. they soon became "negotiepenningen". They were exported in the trade. Conditions only improved by the minting of the *driegulden* and its subdivisions towards the end of the century. It was the State of Holland which took the first step in 1681. Later, in the 1690's, the States General followed suit. At first very small amounts of this piece were coined, as in relation to the price of silver the coinage of it was very unprofitable for the mintmasters. During this period the mintmasters swore by the *schellingen*, which were of lower alloy, and Nederland was worried by *schellingen* during the last two decades of the 17th century. But *dukatons* were also struck in great amounts for exportation and at export prices. In spite of the reintroduction of the maximum price in 1690 the price of silver continued rising. Still, they gradually succeeded in having the *driegulden* placed in the circulation. It became the new "standpenning" of Nederland, and a sharp distinction was made between "standpenningen", which must not be exported, and "negotiepenningen", which might be so.[15]

The East India trade was one of the channels through which the precious metals of the Amsterdam market flowed out.[16] With "negotiepenningen" also the European dilemma of currency was exported. They passed the buck. The Government of Batavia got the same difficulties to contend with as the States General had at home. Soon a problem arose as regards the so-called *payement*, i.e. Dutch small change, which often proved to be clipped pieces or base coins demonetized at home.[17] Such *payement* was packed in small bags – *payement packjes* – with a nominal value of 10 rixdollars. The unequal character of the *payement* caused the larger silver coins of higher value to be driven out. The Government in Batavia tried to detain the larger silver coins by changing their conversion rates. The *leeuwendaalder* or *kroon*, which was equal to 40 st., was

[15] *Ibid.* p. 586 *et seq.*

[16] The English East India Company also provided itself amply with bullion and money in Nederland. Rotterdam was the port of shipment; *ibid.* p. 595 *et seq.*

[17] Codrington, *op. cit.* p. 107.

first raised to 42 st. and in 1639 to 48 st. The following year, 1640, it must be officially recognized that the rial, too, in fact circulated at a higher value than its par of 48 st. It was then fixed at 60 st. The same was the case of the rixdollar, the *provintiedaalder* or the *keizerdaalder*, which in Nederland equalled 50 st. In the accounts of the Company the rial, however, continued being put at 48 st. as a unit of account. The Court of Directors felt hampered by the high rating of the large coins. It gave rise to a confusing picture of the trade profits, as the cargoes exported thus automatically were supplied with an imaginary profit of 20–25 per cent. Inversely the Government in Batavia maintained that the profit was not quite imaginary, as silver was worth more in Asia than in Europe. In 1652 the Seventeen imposed by force a new set of money conversion rates, at which the rixdollar was to be equivalent to only 52 st., the rial to 50 st., and the *leeuwendaalder* or *kroon* to 42 st. The order also mentioned two new coins, the large silver coins the *dukaton*, from the Spanish Netherlands, and the Brabant rixdollar or *kruisdaalder*, which had now begun appearing in the East, and which were fixed at 63 and 50 st., respectively. The decisive question was still the character of the *payement*. Nederland continued sending out the clipped coins. The valuation of the circulating silver coins dictated from home was carried through in May 1652. It meant an undervaluation of the full-bodied, large pieces, which as a consequence were bought up and taken out of the circulation in Batavia. The Chinese merchants in the town as always were greatly interested in buying silver for export. It all happened so rapidly that already towards the end of the month of August the same year it became necessary to put quantities of demonetized coin into circulation.[18] In 1654 the rial was raised to a value of 62 st. and treated as a commodity. The war against England caused interruptions of the supplies of silver from home and threatened to make Batavia a moneyless town.

These events form the background of the adjustment in 1656, when the points of view of the Government in Batavia were victorious. The rial, the rixdollar, and the Brabant *kruisdaalder* were all fixed at 60 st. The *dukaton* remained unchanged 63 st., and the *leeuwendaalder* was raised to its old rate of 48 st. The Heeren XVII, however, enforced that also the *payement* should be adjusted in such a way that the *schelling* at 6 st. should be put at 7 ½ st., the *dubbeltje* at 2 st. should in future be equivalent to 2 ½ st., and the *stuiver* should be worth 1 ¼ st. Under the protest of the Indian Government the new rates of the *payement* were put into force in

[18] *Ibid.* p. 108.

November 1658. The smallest unit in the Batavian monetary system thus became an imaginary, "light" *stuiver* in contrast to the "heavy" *stuiver* coin. The "light" *stuiver* corresponded to $^4/_5$ of the silver *stuiver*. Perhaps, with a view to the transfer of amounts of money from Batavia to Nederland, it was considered that the "light" *stuiver* should represent the clipped small change in the East and the "heavy" *stuiver* the ordinary silver coins in Nederland. In this way the proportion between large coins and small change was maintained, but just by raising the conversion rate of the small change the foundations were laid for a new agio on the large coins. The matter was complicated by the fact that the unit of account, the guilder or florin, which in Nederland was equal to 20 st., also in the East continued being 20 st. The former was heavy, the latter was light.[19] In the new Batavian monetary system, moreover, the rixdollar at 3 fl. now replaced the rial as unit of account. As to the booking in Batavia of the cash sent out, the rule was that the cashier credited the general account by 20 per cent. with the money intended for the daily expenditure at the head office, whereas the money "die als een koopmanschap werden gehouden" and which was forwarded to the factories was entered at the European invoice price. Thus it was the factories which in their accounts were to make the 20 per cent. conversion.[20] From the extant material of accounts from the 18th century it appears, however, that practice was very fluctuating.

Now as before it was the quality of the *payement* which was decisive of the stability or balance of the circulation in Batavia. Nor could the balance be maintained during the following period. The imported silver coins of the Company constantly disappeared. This was not, of course, only a function of statutory, unrealistically established money conversion rates. It was also due to conditions of trade and payment in Batavia, but the rates of conversion in connexion with statements of the stock of coins were the outward criteria first of all fastened upon. The fate of the *dukaton* offers an example of the course of development and shows that the above sketched, conflicting points of view or interests in the monetary policy constantly asserted themselves. This coin, the largest and most distinguished European coin in Indian circulation – the silvery knight – was in 1656 put at 63 st., the same value as in Nederland. Thus there is no doubt that the 63 st. were heavy. As expressed in light *stuivers* its value would have been approximately 79 st. The valuation was too low in

[19] Cf. the fact that Codrington considers the 60 *stuivers* of the rixdollar as "light", while the *Encyclopedie van Ned.-Indië* is of opinion that they are "heavy" and should be compared with 75 "light" *stuivers*.

[20] *Pieter van Dam* 1:I, p. 634.

relation to the intrinsic value of the coin, so in 1676 the *dukaton* was officially raised to the rate of 90 light st. In 1682 a drastic reduction to 75 light st. was attempted, but the experiment failed. In 1686 they had to raise the rate of the coin to 90 st. again, and in a desperate attempt at retaining the *dukaton* they started stamping it with the mark of the Company. In vain. False coins soon turned up in the circulation, and in 1692 the marked *dukatons* were withdrawn. In 1700 the *dukaton* was raised to 97 ½ light st., and when in the beginning of the 18th century the Philippus dollar made its appearance, this was also – officially in 1715 – put at 97 ½ st.[21] A reduction of the *dukaton* in 1719 to 82 ½ light st. lasted until 1727, when the Company's own *dukaton* was put into circulation at 78 heavy or 97 ½ light st.

In order to inquire further into the question of the precious metals, we shall, however, leave the provisions of the decrees concerning the money conversion rates – actually they represent only a single aspect of the matter, viz. the Company's trouble of finding a standard coin in Batavia – and consider what the Governor General and the Council wanted of the various species, the extent to which the Court of Directors in Nederland fulfilled the requests of the Government, and how this important export commodity was placed in the East. Unfortunately we are far from having any complete material at our disposal and we recognize that it will be possible to adduce a good deal more by continued investigations, but we hope that the following section may supplement the information published mainly about Batavia and the numismatics.

As mentioned above, the rial was the most important coin in the Company's exports during the first decades of the 17th century. During the 1620's and 1630's the "negotiepenning" asserted itself, although the rial still was predominant. The changed character can be illustrated by the request of the Batavian Government dated in January 1640. They asked for 100,000–120,000 rials of eight ("in spetie"), which were put at a cost-price of 50–56 st., the item thus being valued at 300,000 fl. Furthermore, the Governor General and the Council asked for *kroonen*, *schellingen*, *dubbelde* and *enkelde stuivers* to an amount of 100,000 fl. The total request for money thus was for 400,000 fl.[22] It is not always possible to see how the Heeren XVII executed the order of the Government in Batavia, thus not in the example adduced. But the total of the annual consignments varied much during the 1640's, from 400,000 fl. to 2.2 mill. fl.[23] In 1646

[21] Netscher & van der Chijs, *op. cit.* p. 55.
[22] Kol. Arch. No. 10,061, January 1640.
[23] The 2.2 mill. fl. were sent in 1642 according to *Pieter van Dam* 1:I, p. 633; but in his table re p. 364 he only states 1.6 mill. fl. for that year.

the Heeren XVII decided to send 600,000 fl. in cash to Batavia, the Government having asked for 1 mill. fl. The composition was as follows: 250,000 fl. rials, 150,000 fl. rixdollars, *dukatons*, and *patacons*, 150,000 fl. bar silver, and 50,000 fl. *payement*. The request of the Batavian Government for 1 mill. fl. had included no less than ½ mill. fl. in gold from the Guinea Coast, which the Heeren XVII thus could not or would not send.[24] The same was repeated the following year. The Government asked for 800,000 fl. in cash, half of it in Guinea gold, but the Heeren XVII decided to send only 400,000 fl. in silver.[25] In silver the Governor General and Council wanted 100,000 fl. *payement*, the greater part of which should be in double *stuivers*, "die door gans India seer courant sijn."[26] In December 1647 the Batavian Government asked for 1 mill. fl. owing to the fact that the China trade was on the eve of a boom. The 700,000 fl. ought to be in rixdollars and *kroonen*, the rest in *payement*. The rial was not mentioned. It was emphasized that the *payement* was indispensable in Batavia as well as in the other Indian quarters. The Heeren XVII found it possible to send 800,000 fl. and decided to send 200,000 fl. silver in bullion, 225,000 fl. in rixdollars, 75,000 fl. in rials, 75,000 fl. in *kroonen* and 225,000 fl. in *payement*.[27] The following two years, i.e. in the requests for 1650 and 1651, it was urged that the Government was in great need of *payement*. The first year they asked for a total of 400,000 fl., 250,000 fl. of which should be in rixdollars and rials for the purchase and payment of pepper, the rest in *payement*, the second year they wanted 200,000 fl. in *payement*, the Government stating that they were well-supplied with other kinds of cash and with gold. In both cases the Heeren XVII decided that the requests should be complied with in full.[28]

The pronounced fluctuations in requests and consignments, both as regards contents and volume, were connected with the changing conditions of the Company's Asiatic trade. The Batavian Government was not exclusively referred to asking for consignments of precious metals from Europe, in Asia, too, they might be obtained. Thus in 1640 the trade to Japan and China was altogether characterized as the most important trade of the Company in the whole of Asia.[29] The reason was that the preceding year 6 ships from Japan had arrived in Formosa (Taiwan)

[24] Kol. Arch. No. 10,061, 31 December 1645; Kol. Arch. No. 251, August 1646.
[25] Kol. Arch. No. 251, September 1647.
[26] Kol. Arch. No. 10,061, 31 December 1646.
[27] Kol. Arch. No. 10,061, 28 December 1647; Kol. Arch. No. 251, September–October 1648, Item 3.
[28] Kol. Arch. No. 10,061, 15 January and 31 December 1649; Kol. Arch. No. 251, September 1649 and August 1650.
[29] Kol. Arch. No. 488, 11 September 1640.

with a total of 3 mill. fl. in silver. Down to 1668 the stream of silver from Japan was an essential factor in the Company's trade in Asia. Another source of precious metals was Manila, the terminus of the Spanish galliots, which carried the American silver from Acapulca by the long route across the Pacific. The Indonesian archipelago, first of all the west coast of Sumatra, and Malacca produced gold. Finally there was in the North-west Indian area the ancient stream of gold and silver from Europe to Asia, the one flowing by way of the Levant and Asia Minor to Arabia and Persia, from where, along the routes of the "Moorish" trade, it flowed on to Gujarat, the Malabar Coast, and Ceylon. Thus there were several possibilities open, and the question arises how dependent on the supplies from Nederland, the Government in Batavia was.

The Company's exports of silver (and later, gold) from Japan appears to have been of an order of magnitude which in some years surpassed the supplies from Nederland. Roughly the quantities were as follows:[30]

Table 11. *The Company's Exports of Silver and Gold from Japan, 1640–1699. Decennial Totals in Fl.*

	Silver	Gold
1640–1649	15,188,713	—
1650–1659	13,151,211	—
1660–1669	10,488,214	4,060,919
1670–1679	—	11,541,481
1680–1689	—	2,983,830
1690–1699	—	2,289,520

In the case of Batavia it is possible to draw up the survey (Table 12) of the supplies of silver and gold during the accounting year 1 September 1652–31 August 1653. The survey has been made on the basis of the general commerce ledger of Batavia, the only one extant from the 17th century.[31]

The ledger shows that the majority of the rials originated from Surat, while a minor portion came from the Moluccas. The "Asiatic" rixdollars had been obtained from Persia, while the "Asiatic" *payement* entered the Company's treasury in Batavia. The Japanese silver, which was the so-called *schuitzilver*, i.e. a kind of bullion, originated partly from Japan, partly from Canton. The gold in bullion was mainly bought for cash in Batavia, while minor amounts had come from Macassar and Jambi.

[30] The figures are based upon the tables of Oskar Nachod, *Die Beziehungen der Niederländischen Ostindischen Kompagnie zu Japan im Siebzehnten Jahrhundert* (Leipzig, 1897), Appendix, supplemented with Kol. Arch. No. 2504, pp. 304 ff., van Imhoff's considerations on the Japan trade containing statistical information extracted from the Company's journals of commerce.

[31] Kol. Arch. No. 10,396.

Table 12. *Supply of Silver and Gold to Batavia 1652/53. Fl.*

		Nederland	Asia	Total
SILVER:	Rials	—	248,400	248,400
	Rixdollars	150,122	6,166	156,288
	Payement	9,000	5,100	14,100
	Japanese silver	—	134,943	134,943
	In all...	159,122	394,609	553,731
GOLD:	Bullion	—	203,991	203,991
	Maas	—	107,741	107,741
	In all...	—	311,732	311,732
SILVER and GOLD:	In all...	159,122	706,341	865,463

The gold coins, *maas*, originated from Macassar and the Moluccas.[32] Hence, the Asiatic sphere was the absolutely greatest supplier to the Company of silver and gold, or, in other words, the Asiatic trade of the Company was to be self-contained, a state which had been one of Jan Pietersz: Coen's wish dreams. It should, however, be emphasized that the survey is based on one single year, which was just abnormal as regards supplies from Nederland. In April 1652 the first English war broke out, and the war risk gave rise to caution as regards consignments of silver. Besides this quite a different fact should be noted, viz. that Batavia, indeed, was the centre of the Company's Asiatic network of trade routes, but during this period by no means the point of passage of all its inter-Asiatic transactions. The general commerce ledger of Batavia therefore does not give a complete picture of the movements of gold and silver.[33] This should be kept in mind at a mention of the places where the gold and the silver were going. The two metals were distributed as follows:

Table 13. *Silver and Gold Sent from Batavia 1652/53. Fl.*

	Rials	Rix-dollars	*Paye-ment*	Japanese Silver	Gold in bullion	*Maas*	In all
Java and Sumatra ..	61,798	206,805	45,000	—	—	—	313,603
The Moluccas	—	33,150	21,100	—	13,310	32,159	99,719
Malacca	—	12,750	—	—	37,236	—	49,986
Arakan	59,653	20,400	18,000	—	—	—	98,053
Coromandel	—	—	—	132,515	153,913	—	286,428
Ceylon............	—	12,750	21,000	—	—	—	33,750
China	—	—	—	2,428	—	—	2,428
	121,451	285,855	105,100	134,943	204,459	32,159	883,967

[32] One *maas* was $^1/_{10}$ *thail*, which in large areas of the Far East and Southeast Asia was a unit of weight as well as a monetary unit.

[33] Supplementary information may be found in the Batavian *Dagh-Registers*. Otherwise we must wait for monographs of the areas of Coromandel, Bengal, and Ceylon.

In the survey Java and Sumatra cover the trade in Batavia, which absorbed the majority of the rixdollars, as well as consignments to the factories on the two large islands. Similarly the Moluccas are taken in the widest sense, including also Amboyna, Banda, Solor, and Macassar.

The requests of the Batavian Government for bullion and specie from Nederland increased in quantity during the following period. From 800,000 fl. in the beginning of the 1650's they passed a million and in 1657 and 1658 (the requests for 1658 and 1659) reached 2 mill. fl., after which they became more modest, viz. for 1.2 mill. fl. for the following three years. Each year the Heeren XVII cut down the requests, but not always equally drastically. The great orders received for the seasons 1658 and 1659, each for 2 mill. fl., were executed by 1.2 and 1.9 mill. fl., respectively.[34] In both cases the main part of the consignment was rials of eight. The Government in Batavia had in the first case suggested that 1.2 mill. fl. should be in rixdollars and *kroonen*, ½ mill. fl. in bar silver, alternatively gold, 100,000 fl. in heavy Spanish rials, and 200,000 in *payement*. The Heeren XVII, however, decided on the following composition: 600,000 fl. in Spanish rials, 300,000 fl. in rixdollars, and 300,000 fl. in bar silver, but no *payement*.[35] The request of the Government for the year 1660 for 1.2 fl. was cut down severely by the Court of Directors in Nederland, who decided to send only 400,000 fl., 375,000 of them in *provintiedaalders*; but the orders for 1661 and 1662 were almost fulfilled, with respectively 1.1 mill. fl.[36] and 1 mill. fl. For the season of 1661 the Batavian Government amongst other things had asked for 25,000 fl. in single *stuivers* and *oortjens*, but the Seventeen would only send 8,000 fl. in single *stuivers* and no *oortjens* "also de tangen ganckbaer sijn."[37] In the request for 1662 the Government asked for 300,000 fl. in gold coins or gold in bullion, with the addition that gold ducats must be considered most suitable as they could be exchanged more advantageously than silver. This was repeated in the request for 1663, when the Government as a substitute for ducats asked for good Spanish rials. From the same request it appears that the previously prohibited Peruvian rials were no longer scorned; they were requested on a line with Mexican rials and "de goede soort mark realen."[38] The Heeren XVII fulfilled the whole

[34] Pieter van Dam writes 1.9 mill. fl., but states only 1.7 mill. fl. in his table.

[35] Kol. Arch. No. 10,061, 18 October 1657 and 28 August 1658.

[36] Pieter van Dam states 1.2 mill. fl. in his table.

[37] Kol. Arch. No. 10,061, 14 December 1658 (2 September 1659), 16 December 1659 (21 August 1660), and 15 December 1660 (20 August 1661). The *tang* was a primitive small coin; see *Begin ende voortgang van de vereenigde Nederlandtsche geoctroyeerde Oost-Indische Compagnie*, 1. deel (1646), on weight, measure, and coins in the East Indies.

[38] Kol. Arch. No. 10,061, 22 December 1661. On the other hand, the Government would not have anything to do with "*plusoulters*", as they had been returned from various places.

section of gold in the request for 1662 and decided that 300,000 fl. should be sent "in goude ducaten ofte ongemunt gout."[39]

The consignments from Nederland to the East during the last part of the 1660's and the beginning of the 1670's were on the whole modest as compared with the period from the middle of the 1650's to the middle of the 1660's. No bullion or money at all was sent in 1673. From about 1674 the consignments again increased and in 1677 reached a temporary culmination, 2.2 mill. fl. being sent. In the case of the following eight years we know, by good fortune, the amounts actually sent, as appear from the following survey:[40]

Table 14. *Analysis of Silver and Gold Received in Batavia from Nederland, 1677/78–1684/85. 1,000 Fl.*

	1677/78	1678/79	1679/80	1680/81	1681/82	1682/83	1683/84	1684/85
SILVER:								
Rials of eight	—	—	—	—	—	—	10	—
Mark rials	786	407	503	889	1,182	337	91	316
Dukatons	101	60	110	36	63	68	—	39
Rixdollars	357	26	44	23	—	—	—	—
Leeuwendaalders	240	109	254	205	108	331	254	53
Silver in bullion	102	93	500	332	236	1,020	649	532
Payement	472	134	58	339	46	183	45	192
GOLD:								
Ducats	—	—	20	—	—	—	—	—
Gold in bullion	165	222	89	—	13	209	305	—
TOTAL in 1,000 fl.	2,223	1,051	1,578	1,824	1,648	2,148	1,354	1,132

The survey shows that rials of eight during this period practically had disappeared from the Company's consignments of bullion and money. In return the so-called *mark realen* played a dominant part. *Mark realen* covers a number of Spanish coins, e.g. Sevillan and Mexican rials, which were sold unsorted by weight, viz. 1 mark. Towards the end of the 1680's

Towards the end of the 1650's a series of rials with the inscription "Plus ultra" was coined by the Mint of Potosi; see Tomás Dasí, *Estudio De Los Reales De A Ocho*, Tome 2 (Valencia, 1950), p. 174 *et seq.* I am indebted to Dr. Rudi Thomsen, Copenhagen, for his reference to this work.

[39] Kol. Arch. No. 10,061, 22 December 1661 (11 September 1662).

[40] Kol. Arch. No. 1297, fo. 871, "Specificatie van de contante capital die zedert ultimo Aug. 1677 tot ultimo Aug. 1685 uyt het Patria jaarlyx alhier sijn aangebragt." If we compare the amounts given in the table with Klerk de Reus, *op. cit.* Supplement V, the column concerning cash or bullion sent out, it appears that for the years 1679, 1680, 1682, 1683, and 1684 there are occasionally considerable deviations, considering the difference between the rates of exchange of Nederland and Batavia. The origin of Klerk de Reus' figures is unknown; so it is difficult to explain how his figures have arisen; this case is one among a good number showing with what care this author's material should be used.

1 mark Sevillan rials was counted as equal to 22 fl. 8 st. and 1 mark Mexican rials equal to 22 fl. 4 st. in Nederland. In order to distinguish these coins sold by weight from the regular pieces of eight, the latter in surveys of accounts, etc., came to be called sorted Spanish rials, presumably because in practice it was possible to sort out the large coins from a parcel of *mark realen* and deal in them apart. The large quantities of *mark realen* for that matter meant that a special conversion rate of 1 rial developed in Batavia – not to be mistaken for the weight of the same name – which in 1686 was 48 light st. or $38^4/_5$ heavy st., the same price as the *kroon* or *leeuwendaalder*.[41] Like the rixdollar in Northern Europe the large Spanish rial during the 17th century became rarer in the increasing stream of debased coins. The shipping of silver in bullion is also an important feature in the analysis above. Furthermore it is seen that *dukatons* and rixdollars were constantly sent to the East, but among the Nederland silver coins the *leeuwendaalders* or *kroonen* took up rather more room. The share of the *payement* varies much from year to year. The average of the total for the eight years is: rials of eight 0.07 per cent., *mark realen* 34.55 per cent., *dukatons* 3.69 per cent., rixdollars 3.49 per cent., *leeuwendaalders* 12.04 per cent., silver in bullion 26.84 per cent., *payement* 11.38 per cent., ducats 0.16 per cent., and gold in bullion 7.78 per cent.

During the same period the value of the consignments of silver and gold sent from Batavia to the various factories in the East was about 19.8 mill. fl. or about 46 per cent. more than the consignments of Nederland sent to Batavia. The Asiatic part, i.e. Asiatic coins proper, of the exports from Batavia amounted to at least about 30 per cent. and especially consisted of Indian silver rupees from Surat and Japanese gold *koubangs*. Furthermore it appears from the evidence that rixdollars and ducats were not sent out, but presumably were exclusively used in the trade in Batavia.[42] For the last five years of the period the destination of parts of the exports is known, information about the lots to Bengal and the Coromandel Coast being given. These two areas absorbed more than half (about 57 per cent.) of the money and bullion, viz. Bengal about 4.51 mill. fl. and the Coromandel Coast about 3.03 mill. fl.[43] The total exports of bar silver and rupees from headquarters in Batavia during the years 1680/81 and 1681/82 went to Bengal, and during the following three years the greater part of the species mentioned was sent up there. Simi-

[41] Kol. Arch. No. 1307, fos. 511–61, "Uytreckeningh van de goude en silvere muntswaardye, inhout der maten, en swaarte der gewichten in de respective gewesten in Indien".

[42] Kol. Arch. No. 1297, fo. 874.

[43] *Ibid.*, fos. 879–80, "Specificatie der contanten 'tsedert den jaere 1680 tot Ao 1685 succesive nae Bengaele gesonden. Ditto naar't Cormandelse gouvernement".

larly the Coromandel Coast received the main part of the gold, as practically all the gold in bullion was exported up there and during the first three years all the Japanese *koubangs* as well. Only in 1681/82 and 1682/83 silver was sent to Coromandel, viz. 3.9 plums and 3.4 plums Spanish rials of eight, respectively.

As mentioned above, the stream of silver from Japan down to 1668 was a principal feature of the Company's Asiatic trade. In this year, however, the Japanese Government issued a decree prohibiting the exportation of silver. The officials of the Dutch Company then directed their attention towards the Japanese gold coins, the *koubangs*. As early as 1665 the Company had obtained the Emperor's permission to export *koubangs*, which could profitably be used on the Coromandel Coast. Till then the Company had mainly obtained gold coins by trade with the Chinese by way of Formosa, but the loss of this important commercial centre as a consequence of Koxinga's conquest of the island in 1662 put an end to this trade. Towards the end of the 1660's great findings of gold were made in Japan, and the Company acquired large quantities of gold at cheap prices. An export boom in gold developed in the years around 1670. In 1670 the Japanese raised the price of *koubangs* from 56 to 58 *maas* and in 1672 from 58 to 68 *maas*. This slowed down the East India Company's export and the quota of gold in the export figures decreased considerably in the years that followed. Furthermore there was a temporary ban on the export of gold in 1685–86. The Japanese feared that the export should cause a shortage of their currency. It should, however, be added that the Company's export of gold from Japan did not cease, even though during the following decades they mainly concentrated on the third coining metal, copper.[44]

The Japanese gold coins also made their entry elsewhere, thus into Batavia. For want of any accounts proper from this period it is difficult to say anything concrete about the money circulation in Batavia, but we get a hint of conditions by casting a glance at the payments made into the treasury of the Company for the purpose of having the amounts transferred to Europe by bill of exchange. It appears that the Spanish rial of eight completely dominated the picture down to about the middle of the 17th century. During the 1650's the rial disappeared and was supplanted by a motley crowd consisting of *provintiedaalders*, *kruysdaalders*, a few *kroonen*, and *payement* in the form of *schellingen* and *dobbelde stuivers*. About 1670 the Brabant *kruysdaalder* was the species of coin occurring

[44] Kristof Glamann, "The Dutch East India Company's Trade in Japanese Copper, 1645–1736", *Scandinavian Economic History Review*, vol. I (1953), p. 45 *et seq.*

most frequently, closely followed by the *provintiedaalders*. Ten years later the *kruysdaalder* practically reigned supreme and thus apparently was disclosed as the heir of the Spanish pieces in Batavia. But it did not hold this position for long. During the 1680's the *koubang* advanced and dominated the situation towards the end of the 1680's, at which time, however, also *dukatons* and *schellingen* appeared in some of the payments. The *kruysdaalder* and the *provintiedaalder*, on the other hand, had completely disappeared. About the turn of the century the Japanese gold coin was dominant.[45]

The fact that the Spanish rial disappeared from the payments hardly means that there were no rials of eight to be had in Batavia. Only, they were worth more than the rate fixed by the Company. The Company itself at intervals bought rials for its consignments to Bengal and elsewhere. During the period 1680–85 thus more than 200,000 pieces of Spanish rials were bought, at a value of about 700,000 fl. The purchases took place during the years 1683, 1684, and 1685, and the Company had to pay an agio of 12 ½ per cent. in 1683, 14 per cent. in 1684, and $17^{11}/_{17}$ per cent. in the spring of 1685. The suppliers were partly Chinese merchants, partly the traders to Manila.[46] The scope still there for the Spanish rial in the Asiatic trade of the Company appears from a manual from about 1686 of the conversion rates of the gold and silver coins at the various factories and trading stations.[47] The Spanish rial was quoted at 60 light st. for the whole archipelago and Malacca: Batavia, Bantam, Japara, Banjermassin, Amboyna, Banda, Ternate, Solor, Timor, Macassar, furthermore Palembang, Jambi, Indragiri, Malacca, Perak, Ligor, Achin, and the stations on the west coast of Sumatra (Padang, the island of Poulo Chinco, Baros, and Priaman). In Taiwan (Formosa) it was quoted at 52 st., on the Coromandel Coast at 54 st., and on Tutucorin at 57 st.[48]

Other coins dominated trade in the various areas of India. It was the rupee in Bengal and the pagoda on the Coromandel Coast. The statement of the consignments from Batavia during the first half of the 1680's

[45] This development has been outlined on the basis of samples from the collection *Overgekomen Papieren*, namely the General Letter's lists of remittances to the Netherlands; the following numbers have been used, Kol. Arch. Nos. 1036 (22 December 1638), 1066 (18 January 1649), 1120 (17 November 1669), 1231 (13 March 1680), 1330 (27 December 1688), 1657 (15 January 1708).

[46] Kol. Arch. No. 1297, fo. 879.

[47] Kol. Arch. No. 1307, fos. 511–61, "Uytreckeningh van de goude en silvere muntswaardye, etc."

[48] The fact that it does not appear elsewhere need not, of course, mean that it was not used, but only that it was of secondary importance in cases of conversion. Thus, it does not figure in the manual under Mocha, but later in the 18th century, when the coffee boom developed, purchases with rials were made to a wide extent. The rate of exchange on Tutucorin was 9½ *fanums* at 6 *stuivers*.

showed that a good portion of the Spanish rials and *mark realen* was shipped to Bengal. Having arrived there they disappeared into the crucibles and were reminted into rupees. About 1686 the East India Company put 1 rupee equal to 28 light st. in its Bengal factory accounts. With this rate of conversion it yielded to the Company a profit of 16–18 per cent. to have the Spanish rials and bar silver reminted in Bengal into sicca rupees.[49] The accounts of such a reminting at the factory at Ragiamahol might be like this:[50]

Bar silver per mark, invoice price	26 fl. 15 st.
Mintage per mark	1 - — -
Loss on refining	15 -
Total expenditure	28 fl. 10 st.

At the reminting 21 ¼–21 ½ sicca rupees were struck, which according to the account above corresponded to 29 fl. 15 st. to 30 fl. 2 st., whereas minting of foil silver from Pegu in Ragiamahol about 1686 involved a loss of 14–14 ½ per cent. An example showing the extent of the Company's activities in Ragiamahol is found in Pieter van Dam, who records a *rendement* dated at 5 January 1687, according to which 637,573 sicca rupees were coined at one minting. The greater part of the material for the minting was bar silver, and there were smaller portions of *kroonen*, *mark realen*, and *dukatons*.[51] The Company's profit by having pagodas minted on the Coromandel Coast was still greater than the profit from the silver in Bengal. The pagoda gold coin in the 1680's was rated at 120 light st., and a statement of a quantity of gold of 189 marks 5 onces 18 engels arriving ultimo January 1687 from Malacca shows that a total of 13,620 pagodas were minted to a value of 81,724 fl., which for the three parcels comprised by the cargo, yielded profits between about 29 and just below 34 per cent.[52]

The salient point in these calculations actually was the very rate between Dutch *stuivers* and e.g. the pagoda. In 1683 the Company had changed the rate of conversion from 105 to 120 light st. for the pagoda, and also the rate of the rupee had been changed repeatedly in the same direction during the 1660's and 1680's. It will be wrong to interpret these changes in the rate of conversion as only expressing the wish for increased profit by the sale. What the Company won by the sales, it lost by the

[49] This was the name of the coins struck by the Company, the "new *ropias*", in contrast to the *ropias piet*, the domestic old *ropias*; see *Pieter van Dam* 1 : II, p. 69, Note 10 (Dr. F. W. Stapel).
[50] Kol. Arch. No. 1307, fos. 511 ff.
[51] *Pieter van Dam* 1 : II, pp. 79–86.
[52] *Ibid.* Appendix IV.

purchases. Only in the case that the main stress lay on the sale, this motive may have come into play. It should, however, be kept in mind, that the Company in its remintings had to do in India as the Indians did. Actually there were many mints, and it is characteristic of the minting policy of the Mogul period that while the Indian coins in the beginning were known for their high standard, this changed completely during the decline of the empire. Parallelly with the disintegration of the empire into independent areas there developed a tendency among the local princes and mintmasters to debase the coins. This resulted in India being encumbered with a confusing multitude of rupees of different values.[53] From this emerged the class of moneychangers, the so-called "sarrafs" or "schroffs", who had a lucrative occupation by speculating in the agio and the rate of exchange. In the business world it was tried to meet the confusion by establishing a "current rupee" – by the Dutch called *bankgeld* – which represented a stabler monetary unit. The newly minted sicca rupee was often launched as *bankgeld*, but it is significant of the monetary circumstances – especially in Bengal – that they were soon depreciated in the circulation, "and a batta or discount was imposed on all coins according to the period of their coming out of the mint, though there might have been no depreciation at all. The older a sicca was, the greater would be the amount of discount chargeable on it" (Dr. Bhattacharya).[54]

If we turn from Bengal and Coromandel to Ceylon, the Malabar Coast and the Gujarat area, where Surat was the most important factory of the Company, and farther north to the Persian sphere, the picture is quite different. The manual from about 1686 shows that there Indian, European, and Arab ("Moorish") coins met in variegated multitudes. The Company's chief coin, from the point of view of accounts and commerce, was probably the rixdollar, which everywhere was quoted at 60 light st. At Surat dealings of course were in rupees, the rates of exchange being: before 1665 24 st., from 1666 28 st., and from 1683 30 st. per Surat rupee. It seems that the rixdollar in the Northwest Indian trade and traffic held the same position as the Spanish rial in the Indonesian archipelago. This impression is corroborated by the French traveller Jean Baptiste Tavernier's descriptions of conditions in Persia and Gujarat after the middle of the 17th century. Tavernier states that the German rixdollars reach these areas i.a. by way of Poland and Russia through the intercourse with the Armenian merchants in the silk trade.[55]

[53] Sukumar Bhattacharya, *The East India Company and the Economy of Bengal*, From 1704 to 1740 (London, 1954), p. 106. [54] *Ibid.* [55] Tavernier, *op. cit.* p. 15.

Also German gold ducats as well as ducats from Scandinavia, Poland, and Hungary according to Tavernier were found in Persia and Gujarat, where gold coins from Venice, Cairo, Sale, and Morocco also made their appearance.[56] The ducat of Venice from early times was in high repute and was the model of the Turkish coins of the same metal. Thus in the first half of the 15th century they circulated in parts of Northwest India, and it is not improbable that the pagoda weight is due to the influence of this widespread coin.[57] Contributory to the wide distribution of the Italian coin in time and place was the stability characterizing it. Its standard was very constant, and it varied but little in design from the 13th century to the end of the republic in 1797.[58]

The importance of the Northwest Indian area as a supplier of precious metals to the Company increased during the last decades of the 17th century. As an example it may be mentioned that the Company's factory at Gamron in Persia during the season of 1697/98 sent cargoes to Ceylon and Surat valued at a total of 980,000 fl., 88.5 per cent. of them being in European gold ducats.[59] It appears from the surveys of the trade to Tutucorin under the Government of Ceylon – later an important centre for the purchase of Malabar pepper – that the profit from the European ducats about the end of the 17th century amounted to 6 – 11 per cent., thus in the season of 1700/1701 there was a turnover of 128,000 coins at a sales value of well over 0.9 mill. fl. with a profit of 9¾ per cent. About 80 per cent. of the receipts originated from the ducats.[60] The factory at Surat, too, sent considerable quantities of precious metals away during these years. The exports from Surat during the period 1699–1702 amounted to a total of about 4.3 mill. fl. in commodities and cash. 1.7 mill. fl. of these were shipped to the various Indian offices, while the rest was intended for the cargoes for Europe. About 0.5 mill. fl. of the Indian cargoes consisted of cash, the greater part of which was silver rupees for Batavia. The rest was Spanish rials and "Moorish" ducats.[61] In a way it was not a sign of particular prosperity or profitable commerce that the Dutch Company secured gold and silver from Persia and Gujarat. As compared with the goods which the Company previously in the 17th century had been able to secure, the money was a modest product from the point of view of profit. The export of gold and

[56] *Ibid.* p. 9.
[57] Codrington, *op. cit.* p. 169.
[58] *Ibid.* The first Dutch price-lists from Surat in the beginning of the 17th century include several examples of commodities the prices of which are quoted in Venetian ducats.
[59] Kol. Arch. No. 1477, fo. 1677 *et seq.*, letter dated at Gamron, 6 May 1698.
[60] Kol. Arch. No. 1536, fo. 932.
[61] *Pieter van Dam* 2:III, p. 213.

silver must be viewed in connexion with the displacements in the Company's other exports, e.g. of Persian silk and Surat calicoes, just as the placing of the Northwest Indian money on the Malabar Coast, in Ceylon and Bengal was dictated by the Company's interest in such commodities as Malabar pepper and Bengali piece goods. In 1693 the Surat rupee was admitted to the Batavian system of money conversion rates within which it was fixed at 35 light st., which rate in 1699 was changed into 37½ light st.[62] The Batavian Government during these years turned to Surat in an emergency, thus in August 1701 they asked by letter for 100,000 pieces of "heele silvere ropias tot den dagelijcxen uytgift alhier," adding that if the factory in Surat could not provide the sum by sale of commodities, it must borrow the money, as the head office would otherwise get into difficulties.[63] During the first decade of the 18th century the Indian silver coin emerged in the payments into the treasury of the Company in Batavia of amounts transferable to Nederland by bill of exchange. The use of rupees at these payments became more frequent. About 1719 it was much in evidence, but the rupee did not remain for long in circulation in Batavia. In the payments for bills of exchange it was supplanted by the *dukaton*.[64]

Still more decisive of the Company's trade in precious metals was the fact that the Japanese in 1696 debased their silver and gold coins. The new gold *koubangs* contained less gold than the old ones, but kept the same weight, and the Company was forced to take them at the same price as previously. This meant that *koubangs*, which had yielded a profit at the sale on the Coromandel Coast, now involved a loss of about 15 per cent.[65] A further debasement of the gold coin in 1720 made the figure rise to 37 or 38 per cent.[66] In spite of the loss the Company still continued the export of *koubangs* from Japan right down to 1752, though with an interruption during the years 1739–42.[67] This occurred partly because the coins meant a supply of cash to Coromandel, partly because the Japanese commercial restrictions did not offer any great possibilities of exportation of other commodities. It should, however, be added that the export figures during the 1730's decreased considerably. During the period

[62] Netscher & van der Chijs, *op. cit.* p. 55.

[63] Kol. Arch. No. 839, letter dated at Batavia, 16 August 1701.

[64] Kol. Arch. No. 1657, fos. 90 ff. (Batavia, 15 January 1708), No. 1807, fos. 484 ff. (Batavia, 30 November 1719), No. 2032, fos. 154 ff. (Batavia, 17 October 1730), and No. 2342, fo. 556 (Batavia, 12 December 1739).

[65] *Pieter van Dam* 2:I, pp. 529, 534, 537, and 540.

[66] J. Feenstra Kuiper, *Japan en de buitenwereld in de achttiende eeuw* (Werken uitgegeven door de vereeniging Het Nederlandsch Economisch-Historisch Archief, vol. 3, 's-Gravenhage, 1921), p. 115.

[67] *Ibid.* Table II.

of 1701–1724 the Dutch Company exported a total of slightly below 300,000 *koubangs* from Japan to the Coromandel Coast and by doing so sustained a total loss of more than 1 ½ mill. fl.[68]

A factor of radical importance also was the displacement in the Company's trade within the bullion and money consuming areas which took place during the Indian civil wars and which were observed during the 1680's: the decline on the Coromandel Coast and the rise in Bengal. The coinage of Bengal was based on a bimetallic system of silver and copper.[69] The displacement therefore meant an increased need of silver and copper. It was possible to provide copper from Japan. The silver – as we have seen – could be obtained in Surat, but the quantities were far from sufficient. The Company gradually got into the situation that it could no longer drain the Asiatic trade of sufficient silver. So the requests for consignments from Europe became the more urgent. The exports of silver and gold from Nederland during the 1680's and 1690's increased from about 2.4 mill. fl. a year to about 3.6 mill. fl. a year. A temporary climax of 5.1 mill. fl. was reached in the year 1700. During the following three decades the exports were no year less than 3 mill. fl. The years from 1722 to 1728 represented a second climax with annual consigments of 6.8–7.9 mill. fl.[70]

One of the silver coins which in great quantities were sent from Nederland to Batavia during the years now under observation was the *dukaton*. In the year 1719 the Heeren XVII discovered that the Company during the period from 1713 to 1718 by reminting of European *dukatons* into rupees in Bengal – nearly 990,000 *dukatons* – had lost nearly 750,000 fl.[71] The cause was that the *dukaton* had been rated too high in the fixation of the conversion rate by the Batavian Government.[72] As mentioned above, the *dukaton* by a Placard of 23 August 1700 had been fixed at 97 ½ light st. or 78 heavy st. The price of *dukatons* in Nederland in the beginning of the 18th century, however, was hardly higher than 60 Dutch st. odd, its face value being 63 st. It was therefore a lucrative business to smuggle out *dukatons* by the Company's ships and pay them into the treasury of the Company for transfer by bills of exchange. The result was lack of *dukatons* in Nederland and loss by the minting in Bengal, where they

[68] Kol. Arch. No. 1931, fos. 2178 ff.

[69] A gold standard was found, but gold coins generally were not circulated, for which reason it is most natural to refer to a bimetallic system of silver and copper. Sukumar Bhattacharya, *op. cit.* p. 104 *et seq.*

[70] See below, the Appendix D.

[71] If the *dukaton* is reckoned at 97½ light *stuivers*, the loss means about 15–16 per cent. of 4.8 mill. fl.

[72] Collectie Radermacher No. 455, "Wegens duyten en ducatons met het marck van de Oostind: Comp: te munten beginnende Ao. 1726".

mainly were sent – to a certain degree under compulsion, as the Company because of the great payments had an abundance of *dukatons* in their treasury. In order to change this lopsidedness the Batavian Government therefore in 1719 was ordered to fix a new conversion rate.[73] The *dukaton* then was rated at 82½ light st. or 66 heavy st. The latter rate fairly corresponded to the value of the coin in Nederland. At the same time shipping of *dukatons* for reminting in Bengal was prohibited. This decree put an end to the smuggling, but also hampered legal transfers of amounts from Batavia to Nederland, as the *dukaton* was the only current coin of any importance. An examination of the general commerce ledgers of Batavia shows that it was really a question of considerable amounts of money that had gone to Bengal. Thus in the season of 1718/19 no less than 3.8 mill. fl. in *dukatons* had been sent, out of a total shipping to Bengal of nearly 5 mill. fl. in silver. Next it will be seen that the *dukatons* received from Nederland before as well as after 1719 were booked at the old price, i.e. at about 80 st.,[74] while the *dukatons* bought at Batavia were booked at 97½ st. Furthermore, it appears that the consignments of *dukatons* intended for Bengal after 1719 ceased and a perceptible decrease occured in the supply of *dukatons* to Batavia. During the years about the decree of 1719 the shippings of *dukatons* from Batavia were as follows:

Table 15. *Dukatons Shipped from Batavia, 1713/14-1723/24. Fl.*

Accounting year	Shipped to Bengal	Shipped Elsewhere	Balance at the end of the year
1713/14	2,354,696	36,000	668,002
1715/16	2,513,625	287,652	751,716
1718/19	3,816,481	221,350	178,884
1721/22	—	532,432	—
1723/24	—	490,778	21,750

The supplies during the same period were as follows:

Table 16. *Dukatons Received in Batavia, 1713/14-1723/24. Fl.*

Accounting year	Turnover (incl. profit and loss)	Stock in hand at the beginning of the year	Received from Europe	Received from Asia
1713/14	3,187,449	571,782	1,853,491	762,276
1715/16	3,552,995	567,579	2,107,916	877,500
1718/19	4,216,716	1,807,784	947,410	1,461,525
1721/22	532,432	—	227,602	255,441
1723/24	512,655	26,968	318,614	113,158

[73] Kol. Arch. No. 199, 27 July 1719.

[74] The "old" price denotes the rate of exchange in the 1700-placard of 78 heavy or 97½ light st.

The analysis suggests that the payment of *dukatons* into the treasury of the Company for transfer by bill of exchange had ceased. The Company, however, continued purchasing *dukatons* in Batavia, and it is remarkable that in spite of the decree the *dukaton* was paid by 97 ½ light st. per coin. In other words, apart from the difference between "light" and "heavy" coins, there was an agio of about 20 per cent. on the *dukaton* as compared with its value in Nederland. The decree thus put an end to the export of *dukatons* to Bengal, which was carried on at a loss, and likewise stopped the traffic of smuggling out the coins and changing them at the rate of 97 ½ stuivers. But Batavia could not change the price at purchases. There they had to pay the discount of the market on the coin.

The situation proved to be precarious. In 1726 *dukatons* minted with the mark of the Company were circulated. This new *dukaton* had a value of 13 *schellingen* or 78 st. Actually they had thus returned to the previous evaluation, 78 Dutch st. corresponding to 97 ½ light st., but the marking of the coins with the insignia of the Company was to prevent smuggling. Soon the new *dukaton* emerged in the transfer by bill of exchange.[75] During the years from 1728 to 1740 *dukatons* to a value of 12 mill. fl. were sent from Nederland to Batavia. During the same period the Company's consignments of *dukatons* sent from Batavia to Bengal amounted to about 14.4 mill. fl., and about 14.3 mill. fl. in *dukatons* at 78 st. were transferred by bills of exchange from Batavia to Nederland, i.e. that from other quarters 16.7 mill. fl. in *dukatons* flowed into the Company's treasury at Batavia. It was calculated that the new *dukaton* reminted in Bengal corresponded to 84 st. 3 penn.[76] As compared with the value of the *dukaton* in Nederland, viz. 63 st., this reminting yielded a profit of about 33 per cent., but in relation to the rate of 78 Dutch st. in Batavia a profit of about 0.8 per cent. and at the rate of 97 ½ light st. a loss of about 15 per cent.[77] From the accounts showing the development immediately after 1726 we obtain the following information:

Table 17. *Turnover of Dukatons in the General Commerce Ledgers of Batavia, 1724/25–1734/35. Fl.*

1724/25	948,739
1726/27	1,716,735
1727/28	1,358,628
1730/31	3,042,927
1732/33	5,969,542
1733/34	7,064,023
1734/35	5,389,323

[75] Kol. Arch. No. 2032, fos. 154 ff. [Batavia, 17 October 1730: "54,027 stucx in nieuwe met Comp:s merk gestempelde silvere ducatons à 13 schellingen of 78 stuivers ider ducaton"].

[76] If 1 rupee is equal to 30 *stuivers*.

[77] Collectie Radermacher No. 35, 22 November 1740, mentions a profit of 33 per cent.

Marking of the new *dukatons* yielded no results in the long run. At their meeting in August 1735 the Seventeen again discussed the problem of smuggling of *dukatons* from Nederland to Batavia with consequent transfer by bill of exchange at a profit of 21–22 per cent., besides the 4 per cent. which the Company from of old used to place to the credit of the receiver of the bill of exchange for interest lost during the period of the transfer from Batavia to Europe. The occasion was an alarming increase in the amounts transferred by bill of exchange. While in the beginning of the 1730's ½ to $^{2}/_{3}$ mill. fl. a year was drawn on the Company – by the Batavian Government and the "country" traders together – the amount in 1733 rose to nearly 2 mill. fl. and in 1735 amounted to no less than 4.4 mill. fl. From the latter amount 1.5 mill. fl. originated from *dukatons*, which were transferred at a rate of exchange of 78 heavy st. or 13 *schellingen* per coin. The Heeren XVII appointed a commission to look into the matter, and this commission in November 1735 presented a report which concluded in a proposal for doing away with the 4 per cent. compensation for the loss of interest on payment in *dukatons*. On the other hand, it was not attempted to change the conversion rates. It was recommended to intensify the control at payment to the treasury in Batavia so that the customers were to document that the money was their own and on what conditions the transfers were based. Finally it was left to the Batavian Government to find out suitable means and inquire into the question whether ducats, pagodas, or rupees could not replace the injurious *dukaton.*[78] Improvement of the perpetual dilemma of finding a standard coin in Batavia occurred when the Soesoehoenan of Surakarta in 1744 declared himself willing to give up his right of coining, and the Company thus got a mint of its own in Java.[79]

[78] Kol. Arch. No. 202, 16 August and 7 November 1735.
[79] *Encyclopædie van Nederlandsch-Indië*, 2. deel, p. 797.

CHAPTER IV

Pepper

As shown by the analyses of the Company's purchases and sales, pepper was decidedly the most important commodity for the factory Nederland during great parts of the 17th century. For periods more than half of the invoice capital for homeward voyages was invested in pepper, and even though the commodity relatively lost ground during the second half of the century, it should be pointed out that the quantities of pepper carried home during this period mostly were considerably greater than the supplies during the first half of the century. The general increase in the trade of the Company in connexion with a lower level of prices, however, caused that the pepper no longer had so great a share in the whole. The dominant position of pepper actually shows the competitive character of the Dutch trade to the East Indies, for presumably the scramble of the European companies for the supplies to Western Europe was in few commodities more intense. In what follows we shall trace the chief phases in this race and see how the prices at intervals gave way to such a degree that they threatened to make the trade in pepper unprofitable and thus gave rise to a more or less voluntary cessation of hostilities. In spite of the fact that the Dutch Company long followed the old custom taken over from Antwerp not to announce the quantities of pepper and spices carried home, it was hardly possible for any prolonged period to conceal how much was available at the sales. Some reserve in the buyers, indeed, in periods with extraordinarily great imports might be obviated by an annual application of the quota system to the sale, as appears from several examples, but this practice could only check a fall in prices, not prevent it. The opposite situation was much more difficult. The rumour of empty warehouses on several occasions made the price of pepper take some violent jumps, and even though the *bewindhebbers* normally were pleased with high selling prices, they did not consider such extremes beneficial: they created unstable marketing conditions and, as it were, invited the competitors to start a new buying offensive.

The stock in hand in connexion with an estimate of the total annual requirements for pepper thus was an essential factor in the European marketing. On two occasions in the 17th century we have records showing the Heeren XVII's judgment of the annual European *débit.* The first estimate dates from 1622. There the total annual consumption of pepper in Europe is estimated at some 7 mill. ponds, of which the Portuguese imported about 1.4 mill. ponds, while the remaining about 5.6 mill. ponds should be distributed between the English and the Dutch.[1] The latter quantity of immediate importance to the Northwest European companies actually comes very close to Thomas Mun's calculation of 1621, in which he compares the expenses connected with the fetching of the European demands of spices, pepper, indigo, and Persian raw silk by way of the Levant (from Aleppo) and direct from the East Indies, respectively. Mun in his estimate reckons with 6 mill. English lbs. of pepper.[2] The other estimate dates from 1688. There the Heeren XVII are of opinion that Europe can consume about 7.2 mill. ponds of pepper annually. It appears from the context that this time the reference is to that European sale which is covered by the supplies of the English and Dutch companies, so that the order of magnitude is to be compared with the about 5.6 mill. ponds from 1622.[3] Hence, the annual European requirements should have risen by about 1.6 mill. ponds. In 1713 the Dutch Company estimated its share in the annual European consumption at 3.87 to 4.30 mill. ponds of pepper.[4] As compared with the examples of the Dutch and English imports adduced below, these estimates do not seem unreasonable. They are undoubtedly expressive of a limit of saturation and thus serve as a background to the demand of the factory Nederland. They provide a standard of the Dutch Company's intentions as regards the trade in pepper. At the same time as the Heeren XVII in 1688 estimated the European sale at 7.2 mill. ponds, they asked for 5.6 to 6 mill. ponds and the following year 6.02 to 6.45 mill. ponds of pepper from the East Indies, i.e. that the Court of Directors of the Dutch East India Company in these years counted on covering the main part of the requirements.

[1] *Pieter van Dam* 1:II, p. 167.
[2] J. R. McCulloch (ed.), *Early English Tracts on Commerce* (London, 1856; reissued Cambridge, 1952), p. 11.
[3] *Pieter van Dam* 1:II, p. 261.
[4] Kol. Arch. No. 264, 8 March 1713.

Such an evaluation of marketing and consumption might suggest a monopoly, but this is out of the question at any time. This was prevented by the Asiatic trade and the wide distribution of the occurrence of pepper in Asia. From of old pepper was one of the chief commodities of Asiatic trade. The pepper which the Dutch primarily came to deal in, grew in Java, Sumatra, Malaya, and Borneo, and was shipped from Bantam, from the ports on the west coast of Sumatra, e.g. Indrapura and Priaman, and from the ports of the east coast, Jambi, Indragiri, Kampar, from Achin, from Patani, Ligor, Sengora, and from Martapura and other ports in southeastern Borneo. J. C. van Leur has estimated the annual production of pepper in these areas for marketing in the beginning of the 17th century at about 9.3 mill. ponds[5] and pointed out that the bulk of the exports of pepper from the archipelago before the arrival of the Dutch had gone to China, while only a small portion had gone to India. The exports of pepper from India originated from the country's own production.[6] The evidence of Chinese influence in the trade in pepper is abundant. On the chief market of pepper, Bantam, the office of the shahbandar was often held by a Chinaman, as a rule a member of the commercial patriciate, which was an important element in the town and among which the Chinese were predominant.[7] In the Dutch invoices from the beginning of the 17th century we now and then come across the term "China peper", which linguistically testifies to the importance of China as buyer of Indonesian pepper.[8] The direct contact established between Northwest Europe and these areas came to transform the old trade in pepper radically. The Indonesian exports in the course of the first decades of the 17th century made a turn from China to Europe.[9] Furthermore, the Europeans also took over part of the Asiatic trade in pepper. The Dutch undoubtedly were very enterprising, but the wide geographical distribution of the pepper meant that the Dutch Company in spite of its increasingly strong position in the archipelago and in spite of its outmanoeuvering of the indigenous trade was unable to appropriate the whole production for export. Until about 1680 the Prince of Bantam kept his sovereignty, and the Chinese, the Indians, the English, the French, the Danes, and other nations could freely secure pepper there. On the other hand, the Dutch benefited by being so close to one of the main markets.

[5] Van Leur, *op. cit.* p. 209. [6] *Ibid.* p. 124. [7] *Ibid.* pp. 137 ff.

[8] E.g. Kol. Arch. No. 979, fo. 176, invoice of the "Thoolen" dated at Jacatra 25 July 1618 ["1296 picol 44 catti China Jambische peper"] and Kol. Arch. No. 980, fo. 212, invoice of the "Zierickzee" dated at Jacatra 28 September 1618 ["239,069 catti China pepper"].

[9] van Leur, *op. cit.* p. 188.

The new European demand produced a rise in the cost price of pepper during the two first decades of the century. About 1600 it was possible to buy 10 Bantam sacks of black pepper (i.e. 600 ponds) at 10 to 12 rials of eight, but in 1618 the prices had risen to some amount between 50 and 60 rials.[10] The race between the Dutch and the English for a short while became so destructive that it was decided to co-ordinate the purchases in order in this way to prevent further rises. According to the famous agreement concluded in the beginning of February 1619 in London a co-operation between the two companies was to be established so that one third of the trade in spices should fall to the English East India Company and two thirds to the Dutch Company. The pepper trade at Bantam was to be shared equally.[11] There was also, however, a European background to the agreement, as the expiry of the Twelve Years Truce compelled the States General to take precautions. The agreement did not function for long, and it was not, for that matter, fully obeyed by the people of the two companies in the East. The execution of 10 Englishmen, 9 Japanese warriors, and the chief of the quarters of the slaves on Amboyna in 1623 brought the "co-operation" to a dramatic conclusion, and competition in the purchases of pepper again became the normal. This also explains why the price of pepper actually never since then fell to the level of about 1600. Through great parts of the 17th century the average price of pepper in the Dutch invoices was comparatively stable – the trade in pepper being to a wide a extent settled by contract – at a level not much below that of 1618, viz. 18 fl. per 100 ponds.

From the point of view of the Company pepper down to the beginning of the 1640's was decidedly a commodity for homeward-bound ships. This does not mean that the Asiatic market was not considered, but that the European demand was the primary feature. During this period prices in Europe, in so far as they are known, in spite of great fluctuations were always above the level of 60 fl. per 100 ponds. During the 1640's a great fall occurred, which brought the prices down to a level below 60 fl. per 100 ponds. During the long period from 1648 to 1732, 84 years in all, we only find 10 years in which the price of pepper was above 60 fl. per 100 ponds. In this period, too, the European demand was something of central importance, but we see that the Directors of the Company in years with greatly declining European prices attached much importance to the market in India. It is hardly wrong to assume that simultaneously with the decreasing relative importance of pepper on the Dutch market its importance increased on the Asiatic market. From about 1712 we

[10] *Ibid.* p. 370, Note 29. [11] *Ibid.* p. 183.

have in the extant material of accounts from Batavia a basis for an estimate of the placing of Indonesian pepper on the various markets, from which it appears that Nederland considered as a factory still received the greatest quantity, but on the whole – during a fairly long series of years – the greater part of the pepper at that time was sold in Asia. It should be added that simultaneously with the decreasing share of Europe, a fall in cost prices appeared, so that the invoice price in the beginning of the 1680's fell to about 11 fl. per 100 ponds, at which level it stayed during the rest of the period treated here. The fall in prices was also conditioned by the conquest of Bantam by the Dutch.

How do the different phases of the European demand appear? From about 1610 to 1616 the price of pepper was increasing highly. The demand is not known, but in 1617, when the price of pepper was very high, it is put at 4.2 to 4.8 mill. ponds, and the Heeren XVII declared themselves willing to receive still more pepper, up to a quantity of 6 mill. ponds.[12] From 1622 another order for return goods is extent,[13] from which it appears that the Seventeen then would be content to get 2.625 mill. ponds of pepper. This guardedness was dictated partly by the prices in Nederland, which had been falling since 1617, partly by the above-mentioned agreement with the English East India Company. An increase in the prices of pepper from 1625 to 1627 is presumably reflected in the order of 1627, in which the Directors asked for 4.2 mill. ponds to be bought at "civil" prices, viz. 20 to 25 rials per 10 sacks,[14] but as the declining tendency continued after 1627 the order was restricted and in 1631 and 1633 was put at 3 mill. ponds a year. In the order of 1631 the Heeren XVII counted on a cost price of 12.5 fl. per 100 ponds,[15] and in 1633 it was added that more than 3 mill. ponds might be shipped "om d'Engelse te prevenieëren."[16] A contributory cause of the declining prices during these years was the Company's occasionally great stock of pepper. Thus in 1625 the stores were of about 3.85 mill. ponds,[17] and the *bewindhebbers* tried to reduce this by annually offering part of it together with the consignments from the ships that had returned from Asia. These

[12] Kol. Arch. No. 450, "Aenwijsinge ende particuliere memorie van de goederen die uyt Oost-Indien komende hier te lande jaerlycx cunnen vertiert ende vercocht werden", dispatched in February 1617.

[13] Kol. Arch. No. 4409, "Extract uyt missive van de mayores in data 14de April Ao. 1622 pr. "Erasmus" ges: daer by dat van Indien jaerlijcx int gros eyschen dese naer volgende retouren".

[14] *Pieter van Dam* 1:II, p. 173.

[15] Kol. Arch. No. 250, "Lijste van retouren ter vergaderinge van de XVII in Nov. 1631 gearresteert, omme van India voor 't Vaderlandt ontboden te werden".

[16] Kol. Arch. No. 250, 17 September 1633.

[17] 11,000 bales at 350 ponds.

consignments in the period from 1620 to 1638 are supposed on an average to have amounted to about 2.5 mill. ponds.[18]

If the price movement and the market in Europe thus in the beginning of the 1630's, if anything, were steady, there was war to the knife in the Asiatic pepper trade.[19] The Government in Batavia was hampered by the English competition in Sumatra and was keen on getting pepper, amongst other things because this might be used in Persia for the very important purchases of raw silk. In several cases pepper consigned for Nederland was kept back and sold in Persia.[20] The activities of the Chinese traders also hampered the Dutch, who wanted themselves to control the exports to China by way of the trade to Taiwan. In its endeavours to provide pepper the Dutch Company directed its attention towards the Malabar Coast controlled by the Portuguese. If it was possible to secure Malabar pepper for Persia, the pepper from the archipelago might be distributed to Nederland, China, and Japan. In 1636 the blockade of Goa was started. As is well-known Antonie van Diemen's campaign against the Portuguese was aimed at the conquest of Malacca, which was achieved in 1641 with very great political consequences for the western part of the Indonesian archipelago. The campaign, however, immediately influenced the supplies of pepper to Europe. For nine years strong fleets sailed from Batavia to the west coast of India and prevented Portuguese vessels with complete cargoes from leaving Goa. At the same time purchases of Malabar pepper were made. In Nederland they realized that the Asiatic market as far as possible should not suffer, not least for the sake of Persian silk; on the other hand, they were anxious about the scant supplies. The English and Portuguese supplies were small as well. The English met with the mishap that a ship with a complete cargo of pepper was wrecked on the Thames, and a Portuguese carrack that had succeeded in leaving Goa suffered the same fate on her way to Lisbon. In December 1637 the Heeren XVII stated[21] that throughout Christendom there were scant supplies of pepper, which was the more embar-

[18] W. A. Horst, "De peperhandel van de Vereenigde Oostindische Compagnie", *Bijdragen voor Vaderlandsche Geschiedenis en Oudheidkunde*, 8:III ('s-Gravenhage, 1941), pp. 95–103; see also Collectie van Ghesel No. 200, "Memorie van peper uyt India voor de Nederlantse O:Ind: Comp: gearriveert," a 1702-copy of a calculation made in February 1658 by the *bewindhebber* Hans van Loon.

[19] M. A. P. Roelofsz, *De vestiging der Nederlanders ter kuste Malabar* (Verhandelingen van het Koninklijk Insituut voor de Taal-, Land- en Volkenkunde van Nederlandsch-Indië, deel 4, 's-Gravenhage, 1943), p. 77.

[20] H. Dunlop, *Bronnen tot de geschiedenis der Oostindische Compagnie in Perzië*, 1. deel 1611–1638 (Rijks Geschiedkundige Publicatiën, No. 72, 's-Gravenhage, 1930), p. 611, order from 1637 to sell the pepper of the homeward-bound cargoes if 50 per cent. can be made on it.

[21] Kol. Arch. No. 250, 3 October 1637; Kol. Arch. No. 454, December 1637.

rassing since the consumption was increasing. Prices rose. In November of the same year the Seventeen had sold a quantity of pepper which had arrived home by two ships – about 263,000 ponds – to a syndicate at a price of 21 st. per pond (105 fl. per 100 ponds), while the prices on the exchange of Amsterdam according to the quotations in 1635 and 1636 had been 11–12 st. per pond (55–60 fl. per 100 ponds).[22] In August the Heeren XVII unanimously decided to offer the pepper that had arrived home at a fixed price instead of selling the whole lot to a single buyer. The price was fixed at 18 ½ st. per pond (92 ½ fl. per 100 ponds), and the intending buyers got 75 per cent. of what they had ordered.[23] This procedure should no doubt be considered a measure against speculation. It was not sufficient. Neither in 1638 nor in 1639 did any carracks arrive in Portugal from India, and this under-supply in connexion with the rumour that the Dutch Company's store rooms for pepper were empty, made the prices rise at a record pace. The rumour was true. A survey of the stocks for all chambers from March 1639 showed that there were only some diminutive quantities of pepper damaged by seawater in the Company's warehouses.[24] During the summer 6,000 bales of pepper arrived from the East, and it was again decided to offer the pepper at a fixed price, viz. 25 st. per pond (125 fl. per 100 ponds). The buyers were to send in their orders in closed envelopes to Amsterdam. The time for entering the orders was the days from the 1 to the 10 September. When the orders were counted up, it appeared that the buyers had asked for 380 mill. ponds of pepper, while the quantity offered amounted to about 2.4 mill. ponds, only. In this situation, which was a mixture of panic and speculation, the price of pepper rose to 35 st. per pond (175 fl. per 100 ponds). The Heeren XVII tried to have the entering of orders annulled. Instead they wanted to offer the pepper at a public sale to the highest bidder, partly because the Company in this way might score the highest profit now that the attempt at checking the boom had failed, partly because in this way it was possible to distribute the quantity offered among the chambers. The latter point was not the least decisive one, as the entering of orders had shown exceedingly large orders from the old circle of Amsterdam contract customers: Cornelis Bicker, Geraldo Welhouck, Jan de Raedt, and others. The disagreement with Kamer Zeeland for this reason had flared up again. The States General, however, did not approve of the annulment of the entering of orders, and the Heeren

[22] Kol. Arch. No. 250, 30 November 1637; Kol. Arch. No. 454, December 1637; Posthumus, *op. cit.* Table 74.

[23] Kol. Arch. No. 250, 30 August and 18 September 1638. [24] *Ibid.* March 1639.

XVII had to start long negotiations, which on the 20 October were concluded by an arrangement with the various groups of buyers.[25]

Under the impression of these events the Heeren XVII increased their annual order to 4.8–6 mill. ponds of pepper and allowed as high a cost price as 25 fl. per 100 ponds.[26] Already in 1640 the Company received 4.24 mill. ponds and immediately offered 3.84 mill. ponds for which orders were to be entered, though, taught by experience, the Heeren XVII now established categories of intending buyers. The price was fixed unchanged at 25 st. per pond (125 fl. per 100 ponds). The smallest quantity for which an intending buyer might enter orders was put at 10 bales of pepper at 400 ponds. It was decided that all buyers of quantities between 10 and 50 bales would have their full quota, while buyers of 50 bales and more would get a proportional share of the rest. When the entering of orders was finished, it appeared that the buyers of 50 bales and more could have 18,250 ponds of pepper per 50 bales.[27] In 1641 the pepper was also sold in this way. 4 mill. ponds were offered at 13 st. per pond (65 fl. per 100 ponds).[28] The peak had been passed. The following year it was, after much discussion, decided to sell the pepper at a public sale to the highest bidders. The discussion turned on the question where the sale was to take place. The struggle was between Amsterdam and the other chambers. By way of compromise it was decided to sell the pepper from the chambers in Amsterdam, Middelburg, and Hoorn.[29]

The average of the 16 years' imports of pepper from 1641 to 1656 was 4.6 mill. ponds a year.[30] In other words, the extreme prices in 1639–40 gave rise to almost a doubling of the imports of pepper to Nederland; in spite of clearly falling prices in the 1640's[31] the Directors did not as

[25] Kol. Arch. No. 250, August, September, October 1639; *Pieter van Dam* 1:II, p. 193. See also W. A. Horst, *op. cit.*, p. 95 ff. – The unrest in those years can also be read from the English prices of pepper. In February 1637 the Court of Sales occupied itself with "the fall of the price of pepper in Holland, which has now risen again", C. R. O. London, Court Book vol. XVI, p. 246. The members of the Court were anxious about speculation and felt that such a one was developing. Thus in the month of May of the same year it was said that pepper in the old days, before English East India trade took shape, cost 3–4 shillings per lb. in England. Later the price had dropped and now was between 18 and 20 pence "but if strangers engross it, the old price (or higher still) will be demanded", *Court Minutes of the East India Company*, vol. I (Oxford, 1907), p. 272. This presentiment came true. During 1639 the East India Company sold its pepper at the previous high prices: in August about 2 shillings 6 pence, in September 3 shillings, and in November 3 shillings 8 pence and 4 shillings per lb., C. R. O. London, Court Book vol. XVII, pp. 25, 47, and 83.

[26] *Pieter van Dam* 1:II, p. 192.

[27] Kol. Arch. No. 250, 8–10 September and 8 October 1640.

[28] *Ibid.* 26 August 1641.

[29] *Ibid.* 17 September 1642.

[30] Collectie van Ghesel No. 200.

[31] Cf. Posthumus, *op. cit.* Table 74.

previously reduce their orders. In the order of 1642 the cost price was reduced to 16.5 fl. per 100 ponds – it appeared that the actual price became higher, viz. about 18 fl. per 100 ponds – but the Directors continually ordered 4.8–6 mill. ponds, though adding that great importance should be attached to the question how much pepper could profitably be sold in Asia.[32] In 1651 the demand was raised to 6 mill. ponds outright.

These large supplies reduced the prices of pepper to another level than the previous ones in Nederland. The element of competition is pronounced. The purchases of the other European companies, especially the English one, was an important stimulus to the Dutch Company, which wanted to keep a leading position. It should be highly emphasized that the very increase in the quantities sold for some time fully made up for the fall in the prices of pepper, indeed, probably yielded an increased profit to the Company. In the beginning of the 1650's, however, the Heeren XVII were tired out. They still wanted great purchases in order in this way to weaken their adversaries, and they stubbornly maintained that the Dutch Company would not give in. But at the same time they requested the Batavian Government not to let pepper occupy room instead of more important return commodities in the ships, and finally in 1652, when the price of pepper had been reduced to about 38 fl. per 100 ponds, orders were given for the Government to hold back. Europe is glutted with pepper, it said in the Seventeen's letter of 27 September 1652, and to such a degree that even if supplies were stopped, it would be possible to manage with the stock in hand for three whole years. The level of prices at that time was characterized as being so low that it did not pay carrying the great quantities to Nederland. The annual orders consequently were reduced to 4.2–4.8 mill. ponds, the Government in Batavia might very well send less than this, even though other European nations bought up a corresponding quantity. The necessity of taking care that cost prices were low was severely enjoined on the Government. In 1652 the trade from Batavia to the Malabar Coast was stopped. The Malabar pepper was too dear, and the warehouses in Batavia were bursting with Indonesian pepper. Large new plantations in the archipelago had given rise to overproduction.[33] About the same time the English company also seems to have very much reduced its imports of pepper to Europe. From having imported between 2.5 and 2.8 mill. ponds a year towards the end of the 1640's, it reduced its imports to well over half a mill.

[32] *Pieter van Dam* 1:II, p. 197.
[33] Roelofsz, *op. cit.* p. 147.

ponds in 1652 and 1653. On an average the English East India Company during the period of 1638–1653 imported about 1.4 mill. ponds a year, which may be paralleled with the Dutch Company's imports mentioned above of 4.6 mill. ponds during the period 1642–1655, as appears from a Dutch survey of the two countries' imports made in the 1650's.[34] If these figures are correct, the Dutch Company held a very secure leading place.[35]

The breathing-space, however, was not to be long. The order for limited supplies, it is true, already in 1653 resulted in an import to Nederland of only about 3.25 mill. ponds of pepper. The same year the price of pepper took a leap to the high level above 60 fl. per 100 ponds, the price at the public sale at Kamer Amsterdam being of no less than 70 fl. per 100 ponds. The proper cause of this sudden increase, however, was not the fall in supplies – the stock in hand was great – but the prospect of an interruption of the supplies from the East Indies as a consequence of the first English-Dutch war, which broke out in April 1652. For the same reason the Heeren XVII in their missive of January 1654 increased their order for pepper to 7.2 mill. ponds or more, dependent on the capacity of the homeward-bound fleet. When the war in the month of April was brought to an end, the Heeren XVII hastened to countermand the order and reduce the quantity wanted to the pre-war level, viz. 4.2–4.8 mill. ponds. However, they had realized that because of the time factor they could not avoid receiving great supplies the following year – in 1655 almost 7 mill. ponds of pepper arrived – and therefore made an arrangement with the buyers for a regulation of the offer during the next period.[36] The supplies during the following years were actually greater than indicated in the orders, but when the prices after having touched rock-bottom in 1656 began climbing slowly, the order in 1658 was raised to 6.4–7.2 mill. ponds and the following year it was revealed that it was intended to create a stock in Nederland of a year's harvest or export of pepper. The importance of this decision was emphasized by the fact that the Company had four flutes built to carry the pepper home.[37] Even though the Batavian Government did not meet the demand completely, the imports were increasing during the first half of the 1660's and in 1664 were at nearly 6.2 mill. ponds. In March 1665 the second English-Dutch war broke out, and the prices of pepper again registered the buyers' misgivings about coming to have empty warehouses because of an interruption of the supplies. At the sales of the 1666/67 season at

[34] Collectie van Ghesel No. 200.

[35] Professor Bal Krishna estimates the English East India Company's imports at 1.5 mill. lbs. in the 1630's and 2 mill. lbs. in the 1660's. *Commercial Relations between India and England, 1601–1757* (Studies in Economics and Political Science, No. 67, London, 1924), p. 148.

[36] *Pieter van Dam* 1:II, p. 208 *et seq.* [37] *Ibid.* p. 212 *et seq.*

Kamer Amsterdam the average price was the highest in the second half of the century, viz. 110 fl. per 100 ponds. The war ended in July 1667, but the Heeren XVII did not hesitate to put the annual demand at 8 mill. ponds of pepper, and the Company actually during the following years received quantities which approached to this large amount, indeed, even surpassed it, thus in 1670, when the homeward bound fleet carried 9.2 mill. ponds of black pepper from Batavia and Ceylon, besides about 134,000 ponds of white pepper, probably the greatest quantity ever carried to Nederland in the 17th century. This record supply produced a reduction of the demand, which was put at 7.2–8 mill. ponds. It was evident that the prices gave way to the great offer. In spite of the wars with France and England from 1672 to 1678 the market had a downward tendency, and the prices at the sales in 1677/78 fell to a new low, the lowest in the 17th century. The Heeren XVII in 1677 reduced their demand to 6–6.4 mill. ponds and two years later to 4–4.8 mill. ponds. The European market was characterized as very flat. At the autumn sale in 1679 and the spring sale in 1680 the Seventeen tried to fix a minimum price of pepper, but as the sales proved to be very small, the limit was cancelled in the autumn of 1680 and the pepper was sold "sonder limitatie van prijs."[38] This was the conclusion of the most intense phase in the Company's trade in pepper.

The reduction of the demand was followed by a request to increase the sales in Asia. It became a set phrase in the missives to the East that the meeting of the demands of Nederland should only be conditioned by the possibility that it was not detrimental to the Asiatic trade. In 1680 it was suggested to the Governor General and the Council that a surplus of pepper be sent to Bengal and other stations in need of capital.[39] At the same time the definite indication of quantity was cancelled and the Heeren XVII only asked for the pepper which could not be sold in India. The Asiatic trade in pepper during the 1660's and 1670's was informed partly by the conquest of the Malabar Coast, which in 1663 was made an independent "commandement", by the Dutch under the leadership of van Goens, partly by conditions in Bantam, where Sultan Ageng Tirtajasi down to 1680 maintained his sovereignty and not least, after Macassar in 1669 had had to recognize the supremacy of the Dutch, tried to form a barrier against the influence of Batavia by attracting the trade of as many foreign nations as possible. It was especially the Portuguese, the English, and the Danes who took advantage of this situation, and the old traffic to Bantam flared up. New factories were established, and large quantities of pepper were shipped to Europe by English and

[38] See Appendix E, p. 298 *et seq.*

[39] Kol. Arch. No. 257, 28 October 1680.

Danish vessels. Thus the Danish King in 1670 made an agreement with the Sultan, and the Danish East India Company, which was reorganized in the same year, in the beginning of the 1670's sent a number of large ships to Bantam. We know the constituents of the cargo of one of the Danish ships, the "Oldenburg", which in 1675 arrived at Copenhagen with more than 4.7 mill. ponds of pepper,[40] which was more than half of the Dutch import in that year. The imports of the English company were also great in these eventful years. The *Hollantse Mercurius* e.g. in July 1669 contained an item of news of ships arrived in England which "brachte mede so veel peper, dat de selve niet boven 15. gros mocht gelden, maer in Seelandt golt sy noch wel 18. gros ende een achste."[41] In 1671 the news-letter mentioned the cargoes of 10 English homeward-bound ships, 4 of which arrived direct from Bantam with 2.3 mill. ponds of pepper.[42]

We can verify the English imports by examining the accounts of the English East India Company and on the basis of them set up the following statistics of imports for the period of 1669–1686:[43]

Table 18. *The English East India Company's Imports of Black Pepper 1669–1686; 1000 lbs. and 1000 ponds.*

Calendar year	Bantam	Surat	Madras	Total
	1000 lbs.	1000 lbs.	1000 lbs.	1000 ponds
1669	2,264	359	—	2,408
1670	2,076	611	—	2,467
1671	3,689	793	—	4,115
1672	4,691	652	—	4,905
1673	2,270	845	—	2,859
1674	—	1,347	—	1,237
1675	4,011	437	—	4,083
1676	3,003	1,554	34	4,214
1677	4,686	1,097	41	5,346
1678	4,046	643	—	4,304
1679	5,798	23	—	5,344
1680	1,738	329	—	1,897
1681	1,536	870	—	2,209
1682	4,031	852	—	4,482
1683	518	1,108	96	1,581
1684	—	1,490	6	1,374
1685	—	1,364	41	1,290
1686	—	886	857	1,600

[40] Henning Henningsen ed., *Dagbog fra en Ostindiefart 1672–75 af J. P. Cortemünde* (Søhistoriske Skrifter, vol. V, Handels- og Søfartsmuseet på Kronborg, 1953), p. 32.
[41] *Hollantse Mercurius* 1669, p. 85 *et seq.* [42] *Ibid.* 1671, p. 157 *et seq.*
[43] C. R. O. London, E. I. C., the General Ledgers, account "Pepper black" (from the English factories at Bantam, Madras, and Surat).

The above-mentioned substantial Dutch supplies of pepper to Europe towards the end of the 1660's and in the 1670's thus were not only conditioned by prices, but equally much due to the wish for hampering the Company's competitors. It was trade war. In February 1679 van Goens wrote from Batavia to the Heeren XVII that "d' vaert der Portugeesen, Engelschen, Deenen, Mooren ende veele andere inlandse natien maeckt Bantam weeligh, rycker ende vermetel stout." The Governor General mentioned how Englishmen and Danes in the year before had eagerly tried to secure pepper for homeward bound ships in Bantam, Jambi, Cheribon, and elsewhere, which had failed in the case of the Danes; but the English had in Bantam collected 1.4 mill. ponds of pepper.[44] In 1680 the Company struck. Bantam was conquered, and thus the race for pepper was brought to a provisional conclusion. The trend of prices in Europe also contributed to damping the companies' interest in pepper.

To the Dutch Company the question then arose how to market the Indonesian pepper in the Asiatic trade. It should be kept in mind that the Company throughout the 17th century had sold pepper from a number of its Asiatic factories. Most profitable was the sales in the most distant areas, i.e. Persia, Taiwan, and Japan.[45] In Surat and Bengal and on the Coromandel Coast as well the Company sold pepper, but the majority of the sales in Northwest India and Persia probably were of Indian pepper from the Malabar Coast. There are some indications that the Company now endeavoured to place the Indonesian pepper also in regions where Indian pepper dominated. In other words, a sales offensive which in many respects reminds of that which was attempted in the case of the Java sugar and which was also successful. Later in the 18th century we find Persia and Surat as good buyers of Indonesian black pepper, each being a greater customer to the Company than Bengal and Coromandel.[46] In the 18th century there was also a direct import of

[44] J.K.J. de Jonge, *De opkomst van het Nederlandsch gezag in Oost-Indie*, 7. deel ('s-Gravenhage-Amsterdam, 1873), p. 8 *et seq.*

[45] Dunlop, *op. cit. passim; Pieter van Dam* 2:I, p. 449 (export to Japan in the year 1674 of 420,625 ponds of pepper).

[46] According to Kol. Arch. No. 1286, fos. 429–437, the sales in Bengal towards the end of the 1670's and in the beginning of the 1680's were as follows (1 *man* = 68 ponds):

	Quantities Sold ponds	Price at Hoogly rupees per *man*		Quantities Sold ponds	Price at Hoogly rupees per *man*
1674	216,920	12	1680	473,106	10¾
1675	115,668	12–11	1681	154,708	11–10
1676	125,518	12–11	1682	457,643	9¾
1677	97,788	11–10	1683	471,743	9½
1678	236,294	11–10	1684	710,773	10
1679	568,864	15–14			

The greater part was sold from the factory at Hoogly, the prices of which are listed in the column on the right. These prices were below those in Europe, which is only natural and which does not mean that it was a bad piece of business to sell the pepper in Asia.

pepper to China from Batavia, while at the same time the old imports by Chinese junks still flourished.

Towards the end of the 1680's the price of pepper rose considerably at the sales in Amsterdam. The Heeren XVII in their missive sent in November 1687 gave orders to stop the sale of pepper from the Asiatic factories where the price did not comparatively correspond to that prevailing in Nederland of 45 fl. per 100 ponds. At the same time the European demand was again fixed, being put at 4–4.8 mill. ponds a year. The order was already the following year raised to 5.6–6 mill. ponds. The Directors in this connexion mentioned that the limited supplies through some years had been a drain on the stocks of the Company, now minimal, which had supported the prices. The changed balance of power in Indonesia caused that the Company at length had most of the pepper in hand. By only carrying moderate quantities to Europe it might therefore enforce still higher prices. The Heeren XVII, however, did not wish to pursue such a policy, because it involved a risk that the high prices would start a new campaign of purchases among their competitors, first of all the English. On this ground the order for pepper was increased. The Batavian Government was warned against selling pepper so cheap in Asia that the other European nations might profit by buying it and sending it to Europe. In 1689 the demand was increased due to the high prices, which then had reached the level above 60 fl. per 100 ponds. The Company's order was put at 6.02–6.45 mill. ponds. The Directors emphasized the necessity of sending pepper to Nederland as stocks were low. Furthermore, the English in the Heeren XVII's opinion had few ships at their disposal in India, for which reason the time was favourable for laying in a fairly great stock of pepper in Nederland. The actual supplies during these years were great. They almost corresponded to the demands apart from the season of 1691, when several thousand bales of pepper were lost by shipwreck and only about 2.76 mill. ponds were received. The warehouses of the Company were full, and in 1694, under the impression of the fall in prices that had occurred, the Directors could reduce their demand to 4.3–5.16 mill. ponds. The state of the market, however, became much unsettled during the years about the turn of the century. The war against France was concluded in September 1697 by the Peace in Rijswijk, then the year of high prices followed in 1698, and in 1702 the War of the Spanish Succession broke out. During the rise in prices in 1696–98, when pepper in one season reached the high level, there was an eager sale from the stock, and great profits were obtained. Then the warehouses were empty or nearly empty, i.e. there was a stock of about 1 mill. ponds, and at the same time it became evident that the dissension in England in connexion with the East India trade would give rise to an intensification of the activities of the English in the East. A new race was brewing. In July 1698 the Heeren XVII wrote to Batavia pressing for pepper. It was important to get Bantam pepper, which was most desired in Europe, on the market "eer het gros van de Interloopers hier kan aankomen."[47] But Batavia failed. The supplies decreased from 6 mill. ponds in 1697 to just under 3 mill. ponds in the year 1700. It was decided to send off flutes immediately to Batavia in order to fetch the Government's whole stock. From 1700 to 1725 the Court of Directors in Nederland every year demanded between 5.16 and 6.45 mill. ponds of brown pepper in homeward bound ships. Then the demand was raised to 6.45–8.60 mill. ponds a year. As distinct from conditions previously this constant demand was not expressive of a stable price level, but conditioned by the fact that the consignments sent by the Batavian Government were very fluctuating and on the whole were of an order of magnitude which did not satisfy the Heeren XVII.

The Batavian Government several times pleaded that they had not sufficient tonnage to send home all the pepper wanted by Nederland. The Heeren XVII were not inclined to swallow that excuse, since, as mentioned above, they had sent flutes to the East for the special purpose of conveying pepper to Europe. On several occasions the Directors pointed out that their stock of pepper was very low, while the stocks in Batavia were abundant. Thus in March 1713 they wrote to the Governor General and Council complaining that a returning fleet of 20 ships had only had about 3 mill. ponds of pepper onboard, whereas there was a stock of almost 9 mill. ponds in Batavia.[48] This subject was discussed in more detail in 1719 in a general missive to the East. The Heeren XVII in this letter called on the Batavian Government and the servants in Ceylon to utilize the tonnage better, illustrating their request by a statement of the returns in 1708 and 1716. The former consisted of about 4.8 mill. ponds of pepper in 16 ships, while the latter had about 4.4 mill. ponds in 27 ships.[49] In the same missive the Heeren XVII also gave an account of their policy in the trade in pepper. It was briefly to the effect that they wished by "alle mercantile middelen" to prevent the competitors' purchases in Asia, while at the same time the Company by laying in a large stock

[47] Kol. Arch. No. 261, 24 July 1698. [48] Kol. Arch. No. 264, 8 March 1713.
[49] Kol. Arch. No. 464, 27 March 1719 (section on Malabar).

in Nederland should be enabled to "de markt daar op so laag te stellen, dat onse competiteuren de peper ... met seer weijnig of geen voordeel konnen overvoeren."[50] The Heeren XVII especially criticized the Asiatic price policy of the Batavian Government. The Directors had several times put a minimum price of 10 rixdollars per picul at sales in Batavia, which at a contracted price of 5 rixdollars per picul meant a minimum gross profit of 100 per cent. This minimum price had not been kept; but the Heeren XVII were especially uneasy about the fact that it had been intended to sell the more expensive Malabar pepper, which was bought by the Company at a cost price of 7 rixdollars per picul, at a 25 per cent. gross profit at a price of 8¾ rixdollars per picul. The gross profit in Nederland being about 300 per cent. it was profitable for the Company's competitors to buy the pepper at second hand and ship it to Europe. In their account the Heeren estimated the annual supplies of pepper to Batavia at about 10 mill. ponds, the greater part of which was sold in Asia.

During those years great efforts were made to increase the purchase of pepper. The Company succeeded in making new contracts with Palembang, from where in 1717 about 5.9 mill. ponds of pepper was received,[51] and in 1720 the supplies from Palembang to Batavia reached the record of 6.3 mill. ponds,[52] while in 1719 they amounted to well over 5 mill. ponds.[53] The Heeren XVII were pleased. In Jambi, too, a special effort was made. The Company requested the Sultan to start new plantations.[54] The first results were disappointing, but the Heeren XVII referred to the fact that as a rule pepper plantations did not yield profits worth mentioning until after five or six years.[55] Supplies from the old pepper district of Bantam also were great. During the years from 1718 to 1723 they were between 3.8 mill. and 5.4 mill. ponds a year, and in 1724 they exceeded 7 mill. ponds.[56] This increase manifested itself in great supplies to Nederland. The highest imports were reached in 1722, when the Court of Directors received more than 9 mill. ponds of pepper.[57] In spite of everything the Heeren XVII were not unconditionally satisfied with the Company's trade. Thus the Court of Directors reproached

[50] *Ibid.* [51] Kol. Arch. No. 464, 27 July 1719 (section on Palembang).
[52] *Ibid.* 30 July 1721 (section on Palembang).
[53] *Ibid.* 17 July 1722 (section on Palembang).
[54] *Ibid.* (section on Jambi). [55] *Ibid.* 21 July 1723 (section on Jambi).
[56] Kol. Arch. No. 2195, fo. 5153, "Samentrecking der quantiteyten witte en swarte peper die ten fortresse Speelwijck in Bantam 't sedert de boekjaren van 1683 to den jare 1734 inclusive van wegen de Generale Nederlandse Maatschappye sijn ontfangen, dan wel in den cours van 51 agter een volgende jaren".
[57] See Appendix E.

the Ceylonese ministers for having sent a ship in ballast to Batavia in 1721 regardless of the fact that there was a stock of 5.3 mill. ponds of pepper in Ceylon, some of which ought to have been transferred to headquarters. The Directors undeniably seem to have been wise after the event, for the reproach was made after the junk traffic between China and Java, which in 1718 had been interrupted, in 1722 had been resumed with the result that a shortage of pepper suddenly arose in Batavia as a consequence of heavy Chinese purchases.[58]

After the middle of the 1720's a perceptible fall in the Company's supplies of pepper occurred. The Palembang district yielded some small quantities, but the Heeren XVII maintained that the English conveyed larger amounts of pepper from there than previously.[59] Supplies from other districts, Bantam, Banjermassin, and Jambi, were also decreasing. The order of magnitude of the supplies to Batavia by the districts towards the end of the 1720's and the beginning of the 1730's appears from the following survey:[60]

Table 19. *Supplies of Brown Pepper to Batavia, 1729/30–1733/34. Ponds.*

Accounting year	Bantam	Palembang	Banjermassin	Jambi
1729/30	2,782,125	1,168,034	574,076	31,964
1730/31	3,066,375	1,128,315	403,151	39,040
1731/32	3,679,875	2,115,237	276,834	35,258
1732/33	2,453,625	1,922,823	—	26,108
1733/34	2,722,125	1,702,101	264,347	12,200
In all	14,704,125	8,036,510	1,518,408	144,570

The figures originate from a survey made in Batavia in the beginning of 1735. It was evident to the Governor General and Council as well as the Heeren XVII that if the Company was again to secure a greater share in the production of pepper in the archipelago, the contracts with the native princes had to be revised. The Heeren XVII proposed a contract with Banjermassin according to which the Dutch as the only Europeans should take the pepper of this area, and the trade of the Chinese in the area should be put at one junk a year. They mentioned a cost price of 4.50 Spanish rials per picul including duty, but they were aware that the Chinese merchants were willing to pay 5.50 rials per picul,

[58] Kol. Arch. No. 464, 21 July 1723 (section on Ceylon).
[59] Kol. Arch. No. 465, 15 March 1728 (section on Palembang).
[60] Based upon Kol. Arch. No. 2195, fos. 5162–5.

for which reason the Government in Batavia was authorized to offer 5 rials, in return demanding from the King that he should forbid the Chinese with their one annual junk to export pepper.[61] The cost price of 5 rials was the same as that paid by the Company in Bantam. As regards the Jambi district, the Company had no contract giving it a monopoly. The importance of this area had increased – which does not appear from the figures above – as the inner tracts of the country had developed a trade with the English in Banculo (Benkulen). The Heeren XVII thought that the English offered higher prices in money and better cottons.[62] In Palembang, too, the Company revised its pepper policy. The price of pepper had been raised from 5 to 6 rixdollars per picul.[63] The results obtained by these efforts belong to the following period. Suffice it to say that they are unmistakable evidence of the competition which from start to finish characterized the Company's trade in pepper, especially the competition with the Chinese and the English. The displacements in the traffic with cottons also influenced the Company's position, not least in Sumatra. Furthermore, it is evident that Batavia in the 18th century had come to depend very much on its Asiatic trade in pepper. The need for cash on several occasions was covered through great sales of pepper at prices under the minimum prices ordered. A great export drive was made in China during the 1730's and the 1740's for the purpose of buying tea by means of pepper. The Heeren XVII never succeeded in realizing the plan of "engrossing" in Asia and moderate "dumping" in Europe. A symptomatic *cri de coeur* slipped in when the Seventeen in the introduction to their order to India in 1736 wrote that the English alone imported as much pepper to Europe as Batavia annually received from all its pepper districts in the archipelago. Furthermore, there were the considerable imports developed by the French and Danish companies.[64]

[61] Kol. Arch. No. 466, 3 September 1735 (section on Banjermassin).
[62] *Ibid.* (section on Jambi).
[63] Kol. Arch. No. 467, 17 September 1737 (section on Palembang).
[64] Kol. Arch. No. 202, 22 March 1736.

CHAPTER V

Spices

To posterity spices have appeared as the most typical group of commodities of the Dutch East India Company, the original motive power behind its interest in the trade to the East. They were monopolized goods, which yielded enormous profits. In a number of cases the trade of the Company has altogether been identified with the trade in spices and its whole activities on this basis been described as monopolistic. It has already been shown that the latter view will not hold water, and we shall here introductorily emphasize that decades passed before spices became real monopolized products, i.e. products the prices of which could be controlled by the Company without any fear of being undersold by others on the Dutch market. But in the course of time the Company succeeded in controlling the trade in nutmeg and cloves (and their subdivisions). The trend of prices of cinnamon also shows that the commodity after the conquest of Ceylon by the Dutch became a monopolized product, only with the slight difference that the prices of cinnamon did not bear quite the same constant stamp as the prices of nutmeg and cloves. It has been said that the Dutch were firmly convinced that the monopoly of spices was of vital national importance to them and that this conviction caused them to apply their greatest effort of empire-building to an object that was only temporarily worth attaining.[1] For by the expansion of world trade the trade in spices became less and less significant so that the futile display of energy in the East contributed to the decline of their national power in the second half of the 17th century.[2] This view must also be modified, partly because the Dutch expansion was not only commercial, but also a political and military action against the Iberians, partly because the Dutch empire in the East in our period is rather characterized by its many-sidedness than by its onesidedness.

[1] J. A. Williamson, *The Ocean in English History* (Oxford, 1941), p. 103.
[2] Hall, *op. cit.* p. 251.

An important incident in the struggle for spices, as is well-known, was the conquest of the Banda Islands in 1621 under Jan Pietersz: Coen, through which the Company secured the supremacy of the chief place of origin of nutmeg and mace. It took thirty years to enforce an effective control system in the vast archipelago. The "spice islands" were groups of small islands spread over eastern Indonesia. While nutmeg was cultivated on the Banda Islands, cloves grew on Amboyna, Ceram, and the northern Moluccas. From Ternate to Amboyna there was a distance of about 375 miles and from Amboyna to Banda another 150 miles.[3] The Dutch proceeded heavy-handedly and cruelly against the populations of these islands, and they were no less warlike in their endeavours through a large system of forts and bases to prevent smuggling. After the last great expeditions (amongst others the so-called *hongitochten*) had been concluded in 1656, the Company had at length succeeded in attaining its object, the control of the eastern archipelago. Still the old hereditary enemy Spain for some years held the west coast of Ternate, where the Spaniards in 1606 had occupied the Portuguese fortress Gama-lama. Not until 1663 did they completely relax their hold of the Moluccas.[4] The monopoly achieved was complete in the case of cloves, as amongst other things appears from the prices, which from 1677 to 1744 were entirely constant, viz. 75 st. per pond at the sales in Europe. The price was fixed by the Heeren XVII, and the reactions of the buyers only manifested itself in the quantities they bought from year to year. The monopoly, however, was only established by a very rigorous check on the areas cultivated. As early as 1613 General Reynst received orders to cut down the crops on the Moluccas and Banda.[5] The increasing power of the Dutch was at times accompanied by drastic campaigns of "extirpation" with the result that the production of cloves after the middle of the century decreased more than calculated. The greatly reduced supplies in the 1660's gave rise to prices so high that the consumption suffered. Thus the monopoly of cloves was introduced to the detriment of the sales, and the Company only succeeded in regaining some of the lost ground during the 18th century. Nutmeg was also fixed at a point determined by the monopoly, from 1702 corresponding to that of cloves, viz. 75 st. per pond. By the conquest of the Banda Islands the Company had already from the end of the 1620's been able to fix the price of nutmeg, but in spite of prolonged periods with fixed prices, thus the years 1626–1643,

[3] van Leur, *op. cit.* pp. 122 and 141. Occasionally a distinction is made in the records between *Molucxse waren* (i.e. nutmeg, mace, etc.) and cloves from Amboyna.

[4] *Pieter van Dam* 1:II, p. 157, Note 3.

[5] *Ibid.* p. 163 *et seq.*

1649–52, and 1685–1696, temporarily great fluctuations in prices could not be avoided. It should be added that fluctuations in selling prices did not necessarily mean contestation of the monopoly, as differences in quality from harvest to harvest might make itself felt – especially during the first decade of the period – and render a comparison difficult from year to year.

By controlling the islands the Company could fix an arbitrary low price of delivery, so that the gross profit from the spices became overwhelming, often more than 1000 per cent. The actual fluctuations in prices ascertained rarely originated from changes in the price of production, but were caused by fluctuations in the supply and demand in Europe. As the spices simultaneously played a role in the Company's Asiatic turnover – especially the sales in Northwestern India, Persia, and Arabia – the price policy as in the case of pepper had to consider the Asiatic as well as the European areas. Generally formulated it was in the opinion of the Company important to find a level in Asia which was sufficiently high to make it unprofitable for others to buy up the spices and send them to Europe by way of the Levant or direct by sea, but also such a level that the sales in Asia were encouraged. A number of authors have pronounced a hard judgment on this policy and reproached the Company for not having chosen lower prices with a correspondingly greater turnover. However, it is evident that the Heeren XVII, indeed, in their price policy were all for monopoly, but this was not identical with the highest price, partly because, as mentioned above, it might be detrimental to the sales, partly because it tempted others to try breaking the monopoly by smuggling or by experimenting with the cultivation of spices outside the areas of the Company. Actually it was no easy matter to fix the point of monopoly for the various sorts of spices and in fact the Company's history includes several examples of the Heeren XVII counteracting extreme prices, also after they had won the mastery of the production. In what follows we shall try to give further particulars of these components of the Company's trade in spices, preferably dealing with cloves and nutmeg.

In the London agreement of 1619 between the English and the Dutch East India Company it was stipulated that the share of the English in the common booty of spices should be one third. About the same time the Heeren XVII estimated the annual sale in Nederland to be between 450,000–500,000 ponds of cloves, 400,000 ponds of nutmeg, and 80,000 ponds of mace.[6] Because of very great supplies and also very great stocks

[6] *Ibid.* p. 163.

the estimate of the sales was reduced during the following years, so that in 1622 it was stated to be 324,000–360,000 ponds of cloves.[7] Actually the stocks were so abundant that the Heeren XVII thought that they were able to supply the whole of Europe with cloves for 7–8 years.[8] This impression corresponds to the few applicable pieces of information about the selling prices. About 1620 they were low. This also agrees with the fact that the Heeren XVII, forced by the shareholders' demand for dividend, in 1623 decided to pay 25 per cent. in cloves at a price – one is tempted to say a rate – of 60 st. per pond.[9] This practice had been introduced at the first dividend of the Company in 1610 and was retained down to 1645.[10] It meant that the shareholders themselves had to see to the further sale of the dividend in kind. At an estimate of the dividend we must therefore consider the market price of the dividend commodity as it was after the dividend had been declared. The actual cause of the dividend in 1623 was that the shareholders from England had had cloves fetched which the English company sold at a price lower than the Dutch one. The English supplies of cloves from the East in this year were estimated at a quantity between 200,000 and 250,000 ponds.[11] The decision of the Court of Directors as to the dividend was dated at October 1623. In the extant Amsterdam price list of February 1624 we find a price of cloves of 2.40 fl. per pond, while the dividend price, as mentioned above, was 3 fl. On the assumption of some months to realize the dividend this means that the dividend calculated in money represented just under 20 per cent., as at the sale of the cloves on the shareholders' account there was also brokerage.

In the beginning of the 1620's the Heeren XVII had kept a fixed price of cloves of 3.30 fl. per pond.[12] As stated above, the dividend price in 1623 was 3 fl., and the market price fell below that. The English cloves were the actual cause of the system of fixed prices being broken up. The fall in prices, however, was checked by not delivering any cloves at all during the following three years, neither at fixed prices nor by contract sales.[13] When in October 1626 it was again decided to open the sales, the price was fixed at 4.80 fl. per pond of cloves, and by contract in the same month the Company sold cloves at 5.10 fl. per pond.[14] By a contract made in the month of August the following year the cloves received by

[7] *Ibid.* [8] *Ibid.*
[9] Kol. Arch. No. 184, 21 October 1623; Mansvelt, *op. cit.* p. 88.
[10] *Pieter van Dam* 1:II, pp. 433 ff. (Table of dividends).
[11] *Pieter van Dam* 1:I, p. 417.
[12] Kol. Arch. No. 249, April 1621, August 1622, and August 1623.
[13] *Ibid.* December 1625, April and August 1626.
[14] Kol. Arch. No. 184, 29–30 October 1626.

the ship "Leyden" were sold at 6.00 fl. per pond.[15] In other words, the Company succeeded in bringing about an appreciable rise in prices by barring the sales for a while. The Heeren XVII, however, did not quite control the market. In July 1628 they fixed the price at 5.40 fl. per pond of cloves.[16] The market price, however, was lower. In September it was 4.65 fl. per pond.[17] It has previously, in a different connexion, been mentioned,[18] that in the month of November in the same year it was necessary to make an arrangement with a syndicate of old customers to offer cloves jointly with the Company. Only in this way the Heeren XVII counted on maintaining the fixed price, 5.40 fl. per pond, which they also succeeded in doing, as appears from the Amsterdam price lists from 1630 to 1635 which quote this price for cloves. In 1635 the Company again declared a dividend in kind. This was followed by annual dividends in kind or combined dividends in kind and money during the period down to 1645, no dividend, however, being paid in 1639. The provisions in each case were cloves. The price of cloves reacted immediately. In 1635 it fell from 5.40 fl. to 3.28 per pond, in 1642 it even fell to 2.41 fl. per pond, and in 1645 it was 2.49 fl. per pond. The dividends in cloves to and including February 1641 were calculated according to a price of 4 fl. per pond. The amount of money to which this was equivalent is illustrated by a discussion between the chambers about the dividend in 1640. The Company on the 1 January 1640 had decided on a dividend of 15 per cent. in cloves at 4 fl. per pond. They were, however, prepared to pay an extra portion during the autumn, and opinions about its size were divergent. What is interesting in this connexion is that Kamer Zeeland proposed either a combined dividend consisting of 25 per cent. in money and 15 per cent. in cloves or a dividend in money only of 30 per cent.,[19] i.e. that a dividend in cloves of 15 per cent. is put equal to a 5 per cent. dividend in money. Kamer Amsterdam, which was always guarded in the policy of dividends, proposed 15 per cent. in money and 15 per cent. in cloves. The final result was that the Heeren XVII declared 25 per cent. in money per 1 November 1640 and 15 per cent. in cloves to be paid by the middle of February 1641. In the case of the following dividend per 1 November 1641 the price of cloves was reduced to 50 st. per pond or 2.50 fl. This price also applied to the following dividends. This was a considerable improvement of the dividend from the point of view of the stockholders. Still, they were not satisfied, as appears from complaints from the principal stockholders of the Company. In 1644

[15] *Ibid.* 6 August 1627. [16] *Ibid.* 20 July 1628. [17] Posthumus, *op. cit.* Table 68.
[18] See above p. 37. [19] *Pieter van Dam* 1 :I, p. 421.

the complaints resulted in a reduction of the price from 50 to 40 st. per pond, the difference being intended to cover expenses at the sale of the commodity. The view of the Heeren XVII of this practice and the ensuing fall in prices appears from their letter to Batavia sent in December 1637. They wrote that cloves "werden by de Comp: tot jaerlijcxse afgifte gebruyct in plaets van gelt, sijn daer door op legen prijs gevallen maer werden te meerder geconsumeert ende door gants Europa verspreijt."[20] Actually it was considerable quantities which the Company "sold" in this way. For instance it may be stated that the distribution per 1 February 1643 of 15 per cent. in cloves at 50 st. per pond was calculated to comprise nearly 390,000 ponds,[21] and the distribution per 1 November 1644 of 25 per cent. at 40 st. per pond of cloves meant a sale of just under 650,000 ponds.[22] By the procedure sketched above some of the reduction of prices fell to the dividend-demanding shareholders, and the Heeren XVII might theoretically pursue a policy of dumping without great detriment to the Company in itself. The competition with the other European companies was again evident during these years. Smuggling of cloves from the spice islands was comprehensive. The Heeren XVII in several cases justified the dividends in kind with a reference to this and mentioned the quantities of cloves which arrived in England and Denmark, thus in 1638.[23] At the payments of dividend in 1640 and 1641 the Company parted with all its cloves in stock.[24]

While the price movement in the case of cloves in Nederland showed great fluctuations, the movement in the case of nutmeg was more steady. In the beginning of the 1620's nutmeg was sold partly at fixed prices, partly by contract. The sale in 1624 was a contract sale at the price of 1.15 fl. per pond. Then offers were closed for three years, and when the sale was opened again in August 1626 a price of 2.50 fl .per pond was fixed.[25] This price was retained until about the middle of the 1640's, when there was a fall in prices for a short period, this fall in 1646 being followed by a rise to 3.30 fl. per pond.[26] In the year 1648 the Heeren XVII tentatively tried to sell 170,000 ponds of nutmeg at a public auction without fixed prices, but in spite of the fact that the prices on the Amsterdam price lists of this year were 3.00 fl. per pond of nutmeg,

[20] Kol. Arch. No. 454, December 1637, "Bevindinge van de coopmanschappen van Batavia, Persie, ende Suratte ... ontfangen ... Ao. 1637, etc."

[21] *Pieter van Dam* 1:II, p. 197. [22] *Ibid.* p. 199. [23] *Pieter van Dam* 1:I, p. 421. [24] *Ibid.*

[25] Kol. Arch. No. 249, September 1620 (fixed price: 1.25 fl. per pond), July 1621 (contract-sale price: 1.82 fl. per pond), March 1622 (fixed price, Amsterdam: 1.65 fl. per pond), September 1622 (contract-sale price: 1.35 fl. per pond), August 1623 (contract-sale price: 1.35 fl. per pond); Kol. Arch. No. 184, October 1624 (contract-sale price: 1.15 fl. per pond), and August 1626 (fixed price: 2.50 fl. per pond). [26] Posthumus, *op. cit.* Table 69.

the Court of Directors confined themselves to the attempt and the following year again made up their minds to fix the price, this time at a level of 2.70 fl.[27] It was hardly accidental that they did not aim higher. They took good care not to challenge their competitors by extreme prices. An interesting and instructive contract for cloves dates from the same year, 1648. In this contract the buyers as regards the Company entered into an obligation not to resell the cloves at prices above 4 fl. per pond.[28] The following year the price of cloves was also fixed. It was put at 3.50 fl. per pond.

The orders of the Company during these years were for 400,000–500,000 ponds of nutmeg and 150,000–180,000 ponds of mace. The orders for cloves as a rule were unspecified, i.e. that the Heeren XVII asked for what could be supplied by the Moluccas and Amboyna. For all the three spices it was a rule that the supplies for Europe should depend on the Asiatic market. To judge from the wording of the letters the Asiatic market was of primary importance. The Governor General and the Council only had to take care that the spices in Asia were not sold at so low prices that it would be profitable for the English and others to buy them up and convey them to Europe. It was for a long time left to the Government in Batavia and the merchants of the various factories to fix these selling prices, but in 1653 the Heeren XVII for the first time felt called upon to fix some minimum prices for the Asiatic factories. Cloves should not be sold at a price below 48 st., i.e. 2.40 fl. per pond (the corresponding price at the factory Nederland was 3.50 fl.), and nutmeg not below a price of 33 st. or 1.65 fl. per pond (fixed price in Nederland 2.70 fl.).[29] This measure was not least intended to secure supplies for the Dutch market, the import figures during the 1640's and the beginning of the 1650's showing that the orders in the minority of cases were fully complied with,[30] even though it was not a question of undersupplies during that period. Furthermore it was desired to have well-stocked warehouses, on the principle that stores should be laid up in years of peace in order that the Company could the better in years of war avoid carrying spices in the homeward bound ships and hence avoid the risk of having the monopolized products fall into the hands of the competitors. The annual sales in Nederland at the same time were estimated at 400,000–425,000 ponds of cloves, 340,000–350,000 ponds of nutmeg and about 120,000 ponds of mace. The actual sales are known from the accounting year 1654/55. They amounted to nearly 2½ mill.

[27] *Pieter van Dam* 1:II, p. 203 *et seq.*
[28] *Ibid.* p. 203.
[29] *Pieter van Dam* 2:III, p. 118.
[30] *Pieter van Dam* 1:II, p. 192.

fl. distributed on about 360,000 ponds of cloves, about 270,000 ponds of nutmeg, and just under 100,000 ponds of mace.[31] The example shows that the sale of nutmeg was somewhat below the requirements estimated. In the opinion of the Heeren XVII this was due to the fact that great supplies of nutmeg and *rompen* by land had weakened the demand, the quantities, which originated from the Company's sales in Surat and elsewhere in Northwestern India, having reached France by way of the Levant. An inquiry showed that in Surat *rompen* had been sold at a price of $9^5/_9$ st. per pond on the pretext that the quality was very poor. Elsewhere the Company's servants had sold *rompen* at 11 ½ st. per pond. In the order about minimum prices these were fixed at 33 st. per pond of nutmeg and 24 st. per pond of *rompen*. This was now supplemented by an order on a Dutch pattern to mix nutmeg and *rompen* and sell the mixture at a minimum price of 30 st. per pond. If this was not practicable the prices first fixed were to remain in force. *Rompen* should rather risk being spoilt in the hot climate than be sold at prices which ruined the very profitable market in Nederland.[32] The Nederland market thus was not in every respect secondary.

The fixed price system established about the middle of the century for cloves and nutmeg was not to be of any long duration. In 1656 symptoms of failing supplies as a consequence of "extirpation" on the Moluccas could be traced. The limitation of the production was especially perceptible in the case of cloves. The supplies of nutmeg, on the other hand, were good and the stock in hand in Nederland was great. The trend of prices took different courses in the case of the two important spices. While the prices of cloves rose due to shortage, the prices of nutmeg were low and the market was depressed. In 1656 the Heeren XVII got wind of the fact that some of the Company's customers after obtaining news of the plans for "extirpation" counted on increasing prices of cloves and for that purpose provided themselves with abundant cloves at the fixed price, 3.50 fl. per pond.[33] A few customers bought 480,000 ponds of cloves, and the total sale in 1656 rose to 600,000 ponds. The Company's stores, however, were great. In April 1657 they were stated to be 1.2 mill. ponds of cloves, which corresponded to well over three years' consumption. The Court of Directors were firmly determined to prevent speculation. They wrote to the Governor General and the Council in Batavia that the Government at the sales in India should pursue the old policy of selling cloves at prices which made resale for Europe unprofitable, but

[31] *Ibid.* p. 204 *et seq.* [32] *Ibid.* p. 207.

[33] Here and in what precedes the price has all along been stated at a respite of 9 months. The cash price corresponding to 3.50 fl. was 3.30 fl. per pond.

at the same time avoid too high prices. Neither in Nederland nor in Asia the prices might be forced up. This would rouse the neighbours and make them try again to force their way into the trade in spices.[34] The Heeren XVII wanted to keep the price of 3.50 fl. in Nederland. At the statement of ultimo April 1659 it appeared that the stores had been reduced to about 750,000 ponds of cloves. At the Heeren XVII's meeting on the 25 August it was decided to suspend the current sales, as they had learnt that a speculation was developing. As no very great quantities could be expected from India, the Heeren XVII wanted to discuss with the chambers the question whether "de Compagnie selfs niet eenige voordeelen daar uyt soude cunnen trecken 't sij dat deselve in prijs werden verhoogt, of dat daar van een gedeelte publeijckelijcq aen de meestbiedende werde vercocht, om daar door d'selve noch vooreerst in ons gewelt te blijven houden."[35] In the evening express messages were sent to the chambers about it. On the 28 August it was decided to offer 250,000 ponds of cloves at a public sale with a *stilstand* until the 1 August 1660. Through Thomas Broers – one of the Heeren XVII – an offer was made by a syndicate to buy the whole lot at a price of 75 st., i.e. 3.75 fl. per pond, which was 5 st. more than the price previously fixed. Broers, however, was refused; the Court of Directors stuck to their decision that the cloves should be sold at a public sale to the highest bidders.[36] Thus the fixed price of cloves was abolished – the same, for that matter, also happened to nutmeg and the following year to mace.[37] Theoretically the road was clear for a rise in prices. The central feature of the new arrangement, however, was rather that by the public sales the cloves were distributed among a number of buyers, and thus it was tried to oppose the speculation. The offers in the following years fluctuated between 250,000 and 300,000 ponds of cloves.[38] The stocks were conserved as much as possibile. It appears from the statement of the total stock by ultimo April 1662 that the Company only had a stock of 200,245 ponds of cloves.[39] With a reserve like this the Company carried on for a couple of years.[40] In 1666 it was evident that the supplies from the East had

[34] *Pieter van Dam* 1:II, p. 213 *et seq.*

[35] Kol. Arch. No. 253, 25 August 1659.

[36] *Ibid.* 28 August 1659; *Pieter van Dam* 1:II, p. 215 *et seq.*

[37] Kol. Arch. No. 254, 11 August 1660.

[38] Kol. Arch. No. 254, Resolutions on the following offers: 11 August 1660: 300,000 ponds; 16 August 1661: 250,000 ponds; 5 September 1662: 275,000 ponds; 13 August 1663: 300,000 ponds; 23 September 1664: 270,000 ponds, which were to be offered in the spring of 1665 with *stilstand* until 1 March 1666. At the same time it was decided to sell 63,000 ponds of *poeder van nagelen* – the whole stock – at 6 years' *stilstand.*

[39] Kol. Arch. No. 10,235. The stock mainly consisted of cloves received in 1660 and 1661.

[40] The statement at the end of April 1666 showed 205,603 ponds. The chamber of Enkhuizen is not known from this year. Kol. Arch. No. 10,235.

decreased so much that the Heeren XVII had to restrict the offer to 200,000 ponds of cloves.[41] Indeed, the following year they even were only able to offer 150,000 ponds at the public sale.[42] In this way a rise in prices occurred to the annoyance of the Directors, but to the complacency of the expectant speculators. The price of one pond of cloves rose to 7.40–7.50 fl.[43] In 1668 as well only 150,000 ponds were sold, then the offer was increased to 200,000 ponds, but in 1670 again fell to the low level, viz. 150,000 ponds.[44] The last-mentioned quantity represented all the cloves at the Company's disposal in that year.[45] The stocktaking per 15 April 1670 showed that the whole stock had been sold.[46] During the following years the quantities increased, amongst other things because new plantations which orders had been given to lay out began to bear fruit. However, it was evident that the sales were no longer of an order of magnitude as before the rise in prices. The high prices of cloves had reduced the consumption. On several occasions the Heeren XVII touched on this problem in their letters to the East. Among other things people had begun using clove-bark (*nagelhout*) as a substitute for the expensive cloves.[47] The decrease in consumption also explains why the prices gradually declined in the course of the 1670's in spite of the fact that the Company for some years only offered 120,000–150,000 ponds for sale, indeed, it did not sell spices at all (apart from cinnamon) at the spring sale in 1672, which was connected with the outbreak of the war against France and England. For the same reason no cloves arrived in Nederland in 1673 and 1674. Finally, in 1677, the extension of the production had gone so far that it was possible to return to the old practice of fixed prices. The Heeren XVII kept to the price of 3.75 fl. per pond of cloves, and everybody then at any time could secure what he wanted. Cloves had been taken off the ration. Actually there was no abundance of cloves at the Company's disposal in Nederland in 1677. In the middle of April there were only 721,705 ponds,[48] or barely the quantity available when in 1659 it was decided to restrict the sales. The prospects of unhampered supplies from Batavia, which was now in a position to deliver was more decisive of the derationing than the stock in Nederland.

[41] Kol. Arch. No. 254, 4 March 1666.
[42] Kol. Arch. No. 255, 25 February 1667 (with a *stilstand* until the 1 March 1668).
[43] *Pieter van Dam* 1:II, p. 221; see also Appendix C.
[44] Kol. Arch. No. 255, 23 February 1668, 18 February 1669, and 10 February 1670.
[45] *Pieter van Dam* 1:II, p. 221.
[46] Kol. Arch. No. 10,235. The chambers of Delft and Rotterdam only had a stock of 42,008 ponds. This stock was sold, too, but had not been delivered at the date of statement.
[47] *Pieter van Dam* 1:II, p. 221.
[48] Kol. Arch. No. 10,236. The figure only applies to the stock of cloves. To this should be added some diminutive quantities of *capletten, poeier* and *bloem van nagelen.*

Pieter van Dam in his unique history of the Company made a calculation to illustrate the change that had occurred in the marketing of cloves during the period mentioned above. He calculated the sales before the rise in prices at 400,000 ponds a year. From the introduction of the fixed price system in 1677 down to and including the year 1700 he calculated the average annual sale to be 264,062 ponds on the basis of the Company's books. With an average price of 3 fl. per pond for the "old" sales as compared with the new fixed price of 3.75 fl. per pond, this meant that the Company's turnover of cloves fell from about 1.2 mill. fl. to about 0.98 mill. fl.[49]

As mentioned above, the trend of prices in the case of nutmeg during these years was very different. From the beginning of the 1660's to the end of the 1670's the prices of nutmeg on the whole were so low that to the Heeren XVII the problem was that of having them raised. Thus in September 1662 it was decided to reduce the offer from 300,000 ponds to 200,000 ponds of nutmeg and from 110,000 ponds to 72,000 ponds of mace. At the same time a minimum price of 50 st. per pond of nutmeg and 19 schellings per pond of mace was fixed, just as the period of *stilstand*, i.e. the period, normally one year, during which the Company bound itself to not selling any spices, was prolonged as far as 1 August 1664.[50] It was of little avail. The minimum prices were abolished at the following sale, but the market continued slack. The offer annually fluctuated between 200,000 and 375,000 ponds of nutmeg and between 60,000 and 135,000 ponds of mace. The outbreak of the war in the spring of 1672, as mentioned above, caused a suspension of the sale of spices. Under normal conditions it was to be expected that the prices then would rise, but this did not happen. On the contrary it was characteristic of spices as of several other commodities handled by the Company that the sales decreased and the prices proportionally did the same during wars, especially wars on land, which bordered on or touched Nederland. This reaction should presumably be explained by a reference to the increased risk, the unstable employment, and the fact that the consumers put aside their money and only bought the very necessaries of life. It may, e.g., be mentioned that the news of the French King's appearance with an army before Ghent in the spring of 1678 had the psychological effect on the simultaneous public sales in Nederland that the price of mace dropped to 15 schellings per pond. The Directors would not sell the mace at any cheaper price, so about 25,000 ponds remained unsold.[51] The sale of

[49] *Pieter van Dam* 2:III, p. 119. [50] *Pieter van Dam* 1:II, p. 218.

[51] *Ibid.* p. 239.

nutmeg during the last years of the war were comparatively great, viz. in 1676–78 an annual amount of 350,000 ponds, but only after the conclusion of the peace the prices rose in earnest. Another contributory factor was that the offer was reduced to 200,000 ponds by the Company. At the sales in the spring of 1679 the Heeren XVII fixed a minimum price of 60 st. per pond of nutmeg and 20 schellings per pond of the best mace. These prices were easily obtained. Varying quantities of *rompen* were added to the annual offer of 200,000 ponds of nutmeg, thus in 1682 no less than 90,000 ponds of two qualities. 80,000–90,000 ponds of mace were offered. In the spring of 1683 a reservation was made as regards the normal *stilstand* of one year, it being decided that if the price of nutmeg increased above 72 st. per pond during the year, the chambers should be allowed outside the public sales to offer nutmeg to intending purchasers at a price of 73 st. per pond.[52] However, this did not happen. The waves of purchases after the war had culminated and the prices had reached their summit. The sales in the season 1683/84 were extraordinarily slight. Only about 70,000 ponds out of the 200,000 ponds offered were disposed of.[53] Finally the Company in 1684 discontinued the auctions as to nutmeg. The price was fixed at 56 st. and in 1685 at 60 st. per pond.[54] Annually between some 200,000 and 300,000 ponds of nutmeg from all chambers were sold at this price. In the season of 1697/98 the sales rose to nearly 550,000 ponds of nutmeg, which meant receipts of about 1.7 mill. fl. Is it wrong to interpret this record as a manifestation of the great expectations after the peace of Rijswijk in the autumn of 1697? At that time, however, nature interfered and disturbed the balance so that the free-order system for some years had to be suspended and a rationing introduced in the form of public sales at non-fixed prices. The cause was a number of eruptions by the volcano Goenoeng Api on the island of that name in the Banda group in the years from 1690 to 1696. They did great damage to the cultures of nutmeg.[55] In July 1698 the Heeren XVII wrote that the Company in Nederland with the quantities just received by the returning fleet had supplies of nutmeg for half a year's consumption at their disposal.[56] In the spring of 1699 it was possible to offer 125,000 ponds of nutmeg at the public sales.[57] As appears from the statistics the price rose much as a consequence of the small offers. Nutmeg became a more expensive commodity than previously. When nutmeg in

[52] *Ibid.* p. 250.
[53] Accoding to Pieter van Dam's table of the sales in 1683–1700, Appendix V, *op. cit.* p. 298. At Kamer Amsterdam no nutmegs were sold at all in 1683/84, but 23,759 ponds of half pieces of *rompen*; see Kol. Arch. No. 10,237.
[54] *Pieter van Dam* 1:II, p. 251.
[55] *Ibid.* p. 279, Note 1. [56] *Ibid.* p. 283. [57] *Ibid.* p. 285.

the beginning of the new century could again be derationed and replaced by the free-order system, the price was fixed at the same level as cloves, viz. 75 st. per pond. This did not take place without any discussion; nor without any connexion with the Asiatic market, which we shall therefore consider in some more detail.

As mentioned above, the Asiatic market, to judge from the wording of the Heeren XVII's orders, held the priority at the distribution of the spices. "Soo veel te senden als buyten vercortinge van den inlandtschen handel sal connen werden gemist," was a set phrase in the orders for goods to be sent to Nederland.[58] Which, indeed, did not mean that the greater part of the spices were sold in Asia. Quantitatively it may probably during the whole period be considered that roughly two thirds were shipped to Nederland, while one third was sold by the Asiatic factories. It was first of all cloves which were of importance in the Eastern trade, especially the sales in Surat. Pieter van Dam quotes François Pelsart's famous publication from 1627, in which it was stated that old Indian merchants in Agra considered the sales of cloves in India to have been three times greater during the monopoly of the Portuguese than during the regime of the Dutch. The reason should be sought in the high prices that had been introduced by the Dutch. "Dat in die vorige tijden," writes van Dam with support in Pelsart, "niet een boer was, of de vrouwen en kinderen droegen daarvan braceletten om de armen en oock om de halsen."[59] We cannot say whether the Pelsartian opinion played any role for the Heeren XVII. As a matter of fact the Court of Directors repeatedly enjoined on the Government in Batavia the necessity of keeping moderate prices of the spices, especially the cloves in India. Thus in a letter dated at 21 April 1635, in which the Seventeen complained of the high prices in Persia, Surat, and on the Coromandel Coast. It only provoked the Asiatic merchant to try his hand in the trade in spices and break the Company's monopoly. It was also written in 1656, at a time when because of "extirpation" there was reason to expect a shortage of cloves that the prices in India should be kept at a not too high level, and when the price in Nederland in 1661 had risen to 97 st. per pond of cloves, the Heeren XVII stated that as long as the corresponding prices in India were 70–80 st. per pond, it was more profitable for the Company to prefer the Asiatic sales to the sales in Nederland.[60] The

[58] Cf. the comment of Pieter van Dam that the Company "'t vertier . . . in Indiën behoorde te prefereren voor dat van 't vaderlant", *Pieter van Dam* 2:III, p. 119 (in his "Aenmerckingen omtrent het werck van de speceryen, als nagelen, noten, foulie, mitsgaders caneel, en derselver prijsen in Oost-Indiën").
[59] *Ibid.* [60] *Ibid.* p. 118.

fact that, in the opinion of the Court of Directors, the spices on the other hand might be sold at too cheap a price, appears from the letter from 1653 quoted above (p. 97) in which the Heeren XVII found it necessary to fix minimum prices for the Asiatic market. But apart from this lower limit determined by the consideration for the European market the various factories had a fairly free hand in the price policy. The character of the sales at the most important factory, Surat, appears from Table F in the Appendix.[61]

As is seen, the increasing shortage ascertained above as regards the Dutch market also set in in Surat. About 1663/64 there was a turning-point at which the price of cloves rose to a higher level. In a calculation of the sales in Surat made in the beginning of the 18th century by Pieter de Witt[62] it was worked out that during a 22-year old period after 1664 in which the prices fluctuated between about 80 and about 101 st. per pond of cloves, a total of about 161,000 ponds more than in the corresponding period before 1664 were sold. This calculation was made by Pieter de Witt in order to prove that contrary to expectation the high prices had resulted in greater sales.[63] As a consequence of the rise in prices the Heeren XVII about the middle of the 1680's regulated the minimum prices. This was also done out of consideration for the Dutch market. The regulation came into force in 1687, the price of cloves being fixed there at 87 light st. per pond, while nutmeg, *rompen*, and mace were put at 60, 55, and 120 light st. per pond, respectively.[64] In these times one Surat rupee was counted equal to 30 light st.;[65] thus the minimum price stipulated corresponded to about 105 rupees per *man* at 36¼ ponds, which was no high price. As appears from the survey in the Appendix, the sales in the beginning of the 1680's were made at about 122 rupees per *man* and in 1685 at 109 rupees per *man*. From the same survey it also appears that annual sales fluctuated between about 50,000 and about 100,000 ponds of cloves. In 1692, however, the sales suddenly dropped to about 12,000 ponds. The fall gave rise to a violent discussion of the Asiatic price policy. The Fiscal in Surat, Pieter van Helsdingen, who together with Pieter van Ommen temporarily acted as Governor, was made responsible for the low sales. The cause of the unfortunate affair was that van Helsdingen had not wanted to sell the Company's cloves at a price below 117 rupees per *man*. Bids had been made of 109

[61] See p. 301. The table is based upon Kol. Arch. No. 1297, fos. 806 ff. ("Prijs Courant van alle de koopmanschappen die in 43 agter een volgende jaren sedert 1641 tot 1684 inkluijs door de Compagnie ten Comtoire Souratta verkogt sijn") and *Pieter van Dam* 2:III, p. 131.

[62] Collectie van Ghesel No. 198, "Concept-memorie van Pieter de Witt betreffende de noodzakelijkheid om in heel Indië uniforme specerijprijzen vast te stellen".

[63] Prices in light *stuivers*. [64] *Pieter van Dam* 2:III, p. 125. [65] *Ibid.* p. 120.

rupees, which corresponded to 90 light or 72 heavy st. per pond. It was maintained that at this price he would have been able to sell 96,500 ponds and that the Company by his intransigence had missed a profit of 420,000 fl. at a time when the office in Surat was already weighed down by large sums of interest to be paid on money borrowed. The Governor General and Council as well as the Heeren XVII agreed to denounce van Helsdingen's arrangements. The Fiscal therefore was dismissed from his office and the Commissioner Paulus de Roo was instructed to make an investigation. De Roo because of his death did not succeed in achieving his investigation – a later publication under his name was attributed to van Helsdingen – and was followed by the Commissioner Pieter Kettingh, who in 1696 took over the post as Governor in Surat.[66] The Government in Batavia thought that the price of 109 rupees or 72 heavy st. offered per pond of cloves was fully acceptable as no resale to Europe could take place on this basis considering the middleman's profit, which seemed reasonable if we keep in mind that the Dutch price of cloves since 1677 had been fixed at the level of 75 heavy st. Accordingly the Governor General and Council in 1694 ordered the staff at the Surat factory to sell cloves at 109 rupees per *man* or even less according to the opportunity of the time, and in the new set of minimum prices which came into force in 1696, and which included rises in the price of *rompen* and mace, the price of cloves remained unchanged: 87 light st. per pond.[67] It appears from the survey of the sales in Surat that sales were made at low prices in those years, the lowest being that of a sale in 1695 of a small quantity of cloves at 105½ rupees per *man*. The Heeren XVII made a point of increased sales of cloves at a time when supplies were again abundant, above all care should be taken that the prices were not put so high that "de gemeene luyden in de landen van den Mogol, de armen uytgesloten, daarvan souden moeten afsien."[68]

Pieter van Helsdingen, however, was ready with an answer to his attackers. In letters to Batavia and Nederland he sharply opposed the new instructions, maintaining that the Company's interests were not watched over by them. Amongst other things he accused his successor in Surat, Louis de Keiser, of being in collusion with the brokers of Surat and pocketing the profit obtained by the Company's low prices. Furthermore, he said that the commissioners' investigations had disclosed that some few months after a sale of cloves by the Company at 105½ and 107 rupees per *man*, it had been possible to buy the same cloves from the Indian brokers at 116 rupees per *man*. These statements

[66] *Ibid.* p. 120 *et seq.* [67] *Ibid.* p. 125. [68] *Ibid.* p. 121.

produced a deep impression in Nederland. De Keiser was dismissed. When in 1697 price regulations for the Asiatic trade in spices were issued it was actually van Helsdingen's policy that triumphed. The price of cloves was raised to 100 light st. per pond, which corresponded to about 121 rupees per *man*. The prices of nutmeg, *rompen*, and mace were raised correspondingly, viz. to 72, 68, and 160 light st. per pond, respectively.[69] As converted into heavy Dutch *stuivers*, this was 80 for cloves, 57.6 for nutmeg, 54.5 for *rompen*, and 128 for mace per pond. As to cloves this, again, means that the price was fixed at a level which, indeed, for several years in the last third of the 17th century had proved to be obtainable at the sales in Surat, but which nevertheless was 5 st. higher than the monopoly price in Nederland which had been fixed since 1677. The chance of cutting off the factory servants from their private trade by means of high and uniform prices undoubtedly was a decisive motive of this new policy. The investigations in connexion with the van Helsdingen affair had brought a good number of irregularities to light. Still, the actual problem was that of finding the point of monopoly, i.e. the price which with a view to the European level yielded the optimum sales. And in this respect the Government in Batavia thought that the Heeren XVII by the regulations of 1697 had overreached themselves. Therefore the Government granted exemptions from the regulations, a procedure in which they were supported by the merchants of the factories, including those of Surat. The following period showed decreasing sales, quantities of spices were returned to Batavia or were reshipped to Nederland. The Governor van Zwaardecroon in the spring of 1701 wrote from Surat that it had only been possible to sell 40,000 ponds of cloves at 114¼ rupees per *man*, and that the fixed prices endangered the whole market.[70] Still, the Heeren XVII maintained their new course, as appeared from the Court of Directors' letters to Batavia in the years 1700–1702. There was not, however, complete agreement in Nederland. In the winter of 1702/03 demands were made in Kamer Amsterdam for the appointment of a commission to inquire into the matter. Among its members was Pieter van Dam, who according to his own account of the price policy must be considered to have been among the opponents of the prices fixed in 1697. Van Dam especially stressed the problem of consumption, pointing out the tradition of moderate prices. A recurring theme in his 35th chapter about the Dutch public sales was just the slump in the sales in Nederland which was completed after the middle of the 17th century with the rise in prices. Spices were not necessities, their use in cooking in Europe was on the decline, something similar might

[69] *Ibid.* p. 122. [70] *Ibid.* p. 125.

happen in India. It was, writes van Dam, better business for the Company to sell e.g. 100,000 ponds of cloves at 108 rupees per *man* than 80,000 ponds at 116 rupees per *man*. Not only because it gave higher receipts, but first of all because it increased the requirements and consumption. Even in case the profit was the same, the great sales therefore were to be perferred.[71] Pieter de Witt, mentioned above, also sat on the commission, where he represented the opposite – official – point of view. The prices ought to stand, as they prevented frauds against the Company, hampered the interlopers' trade in spices, and excluded supplies to Europe behind the Company's back. On the basis of statistics regarding the turnover of cloves in Surat – though only down to 1684 – de Witt showed that the sales had increased by the rise in prices. He therefore was confident as to the future. With a little patience the Company would see that the new price policy would be a success. If a change of the prices would be started again, then "toonen wij niet oneijgen te sijn op een penningh het standtbeelt van de Comp: met een vrouw te verbeelden, als sijnde die sexe de ongeduldigheijd en wispelturigheijt meest eijgen."[72]

For a while it seemed that the commission had a majority in favour of reduction of prices. In the provisional order for returns worked out in September 1702 a reduction is mentioned. The Heeren XVII wrote that by the reduction of prices they counted on increased sales of spices in India, which was the more desirable as the Batavian Government because of the wars had orders only to send the very most necessary consignments by the homeward bound ships.[73] But in February 1703 the commission agreed to suspend the discussions until further information had been received from Batavia,[74] and in the beginning of March the Heeren XVII in their final order for returns wrote that they had now given full consideration to the matter and decided to cancel the promise of a reduction of prices. The Court of Directors would continue studying the arguments in favour of lower prices which the Batavian Government might advance, "bijvoegende dat niet altijt off indistinctelijck aan de hoge prijs waerop de specerijen allthans in Indien sijn gestelt de oorsaeck off reden van derselver verminderde sleet kan off magh toegeschreven werden, gelijck men het nochtans seer generalijck daerop in Indien schijnt geladen te hebben sonder veel aenschouw te maecken op veranderingen en constitutie van tijden en saacken, die noghtans daar omtrent veel ter eenre off andere sijde kunnen contribueren."[75]

[71] *Ibid.* p. 126 *et seq.*
[72] Collectie van Ghesel No. 198.
[73] Kol. Arch. No. 262, 13 September 1702.
[74] Collectie van Ghesel No. 198.
[75] Kol. Arch. No. 262, 2 March 1703.

This was definite. The prices were locked up at the high level, and the reports on the sales at the Asiatic factories show that the price regulations were actually carried into effect everywhere. Below, we shall give some random samples,[76] which show the prices of cloves up and down the East during the accounting years 1698/99–1699/1700, 1709/10–1710/11, and 1738/39–1739/40. The prices are in light *stuivers* per pond, and the quality is the best cloves, *garioffelnagelen* or *giroffelen*.

Table 20. *Prices of Cloves at Sales From the Company's Asiatic Factories. Light Stuivers per Pond.*

	1698/99	1699/1700	1709/10	1710/11	1738/39	1739/40
Batavia	60	60	—	100	100	100
Malacca	82.5	82.5	100	100	100	100
Negapatam	115	115	100	100	100	100
Porto Novo	114	115	100	100	100	100
Masulipatam	91.3	100	100	100	100	100
Hoogly	101.5	92.7	100	100	100	100
Cochin	100	100	100	100	100	100
Cananoor	99	100	100	100	100	100
Surat	92.3	91	106	105	102.8	104.4
Persia	100	—	100	100	100.4	101.1

It is seen that towards the end of the 1690's there was in a way a certain basis of enforcing the price of 100 light st. per pond, several offices on the Coromandel Coast selling cloves at higher prices than that. Similarly one can understand the Batavian Government's opposition to maintaining the 100 light st., considering that it appears from the survey that in Batavia itself cloves were sold at a price of only 60 light st. per pond. It is also remarkable that the factory in Surat during the following years was capable of selling cloves at a price above the minimum. It should be added that in 1728 a further rise in prices was carried through for the offices in Bengal, Coromandel, Malacca, Surat, and Persia. This was intended as an instrument in the fighting of the inter-Asiatic country traders. As the sales, however, suffered by this – especially on the Coromandel Coast – the prices in 1731 were returned to the old level.[77]

Thus it may be ascertained that the Company in the course of the last decades of the 17th century achieved a control of the trade in spices

[76] "Prijscourant der vercochte goederen" in Kol. Arch. No. 1521 (fo. 560), No. 1532 (fo. 315), No. 1694 (fo. 1916 *et seq.*), No. 1709 (fo. 2313), No. 2375 (fo. 2585), and No. 2406 (fo. 750).

[77] Kol. Arch. No. 732, Index: *specerijen.*

to such a degree that in Europe as well as in Asia it could fix the prices completely, first the prices of cloves, then the prices of nutmeg. The question then arises about conditions of production and sales. It is evident that it was constantly endeavoured to limit especially the cultivation of cloves on Amboyna. Through the 1690's the letters of the Heeren XVII to Batavia were full of complaints of the all too great results of the harvest on Amboyna. The Court of Directors in 1698 after being informed of the harvest of the preceding year, which because of its more than 1.4 mill. ponds was characterized as "overgroot" again gave orders for "extirpation".[78] The difficulties were not only due to the fact that the culture of spices for natural reasons was in the habit about every fourth year to yield a particularly great harvest, but it was also connected with the fact that the Company had to try establishing other cultures as a compensation to the population for the losses it suffered by the limitation of the production. During the first two decades of the 18th century the Heeren XVII recommended the transfer of the cultivation of indigo and coffee to Amboyna, which also took place, but results were long in coming. In 1710 it was learnt "with grief" in Nederland that the harvest of cloves on Amboyna in 1709 would amount to the extraordinarily large quantity of 1.85 mill. ponds.[79] Things did not turn out quite so bad. The harvest only was of 1.6 mill. ponds, but this was still too much.[80] What was aimed at during these years can be read out of the Heeren XVII's letter of August 1712, in which the harvest of 1711 was characterized as satisfactory. It was of about 500,000 ponds.[81] This did not, however, put an end to the "extirpation". Thus in 1716 it was stated that more than 150,000 young clove trees were exterminated. A stand of about 260,000 trees was still left.[82] How violently the production might vary from year to year appears from the fact that the harvest in 1714 yielded about 1.5 mill. ponds, while the harvest of 1715 – when the above-mentioned extermination had taken place to the undisguised satisfaction of the Heeren XVII – dropped to about 200,000 ponds.[83] The stores in Batavia had swollen up during the war as a consequence of the small consignments to Europe, and in the season of 1718/19 it was necessary to destroy large quantities of spices, thus more than 4.5 mill. ponds of cloves and nearly 1.5 mill.

[78] Kol. Arch. No. 461, 31 July 1698 (section on Amboyna). In the case of this and the following statements 1 *bhaer* or *bahar* of cloves is reckoned as equal to 550 ponds.
[79] Kol. Arch. No. 463, 29 September 1710 (section on Amboyna).
[80] *Ibid.* 23 July 1711 (section on Amboyna).
[81] *Ibid.* 1 August 1712 (section on Amboyna).
[82] *Ibid.* 24 June 1716 (section on Amboyna).
[83] *Ibid.* 28 September 1716 (section on Amboyna).

ponds of nutmeg.[84] In spite of fluctuations the "extirpation" at length yielded a favourable result, indeed, about the middle of the 1720's it even caused repercussions, nature starting her own campaign of extermination. Then the Heeren XVII pined for greater yields of the harvest. They still considered an annual yield of 500,000 ponds of cloves as the ideal,[85] but in 1724 the harvest was of about 450,000 ponds and in 1725 of only about 140,000 ponds.[86] The causes were stated to be old age and failure of crops. The Seventeen began fearing shortage. The Asiatic and European requirements could not be met. The harvest of 1726, it is true, yielded just under 600,000 ponds, but the harvest of 1727, yielding about 360,000 ponds, was poor.[87] Things went from bad to worse the following two years. The harvest of 1728 yielded nearly 770,000 ponds, but the harvest of 1729 failed completely, yielding only 52,250 ponds![88] There was a shortage of young fruit-bearing trees and new plantations had to be laid out in a hurry. In the autumn of 1733 the Heeren XVII wrote that they now hoped for better supplies of cloves. It had been learnt from Amboyna that the new plantations looked promising. The Court of Directors enjoined watchfulness; in future it should be tried with greater success to attune production and demand "zulx dat binnen wijnige jaaren zo wel het vaderland als de Indische comptoiren met een geproportioneerde quantiteijt, naar mate van den jaarlijkse vertier zouden konnen worden voorzien, het geen wij met verlangen zullen affwagten, en de Comp: van all verdere schade en winstderving die uyt dit gebrek onstaan is terwijl ondertusschen de lasten niet minder zijn geworden eenmaal weederom bevrijd te zien."[89] In view of the preceding account there is hardly anything surprising in the fact that this ideal programme of production could not be realized. There continued to be fluctuations. Furthermore, the production per tree seemed to be decreasing.[90]

As to the sales it is found as before that the greater part of the spices was sent to Nederland. During the great wars in the beginning of the 18th century the consignments were modest in agreement with the Company's usual policy. In Nederland they drained away the stores, while those in Batavia swelled correspondingly. After the war the demands

[84] Kol. Arch. No. 10,815, General Commerce Journal Batavia 1718/19, various accounts.
[85] Kol. Arch. No. 465, 21 September 1725 (section on Amboyna).
[86] *Ibid.* 28 August 1727 (section on Amboyna).
[87] *Ibid.* 17 August 1728 (section on Amboyna).
[88] *Ibid.* 15 September 1730 (section on Amboyna).
[89] Kol. Arch. No. 466, 8 September 1733 (section on Amboyna).
[90] See e.g. a letter from the Heeren XVII dated at 28 August 1742, in which the production per tree is stated to be $2^1/_3$ ponds as against previously 11 ponds. Kol. Arch. No. 468.

were highly raised and for some years were for 1.2–1.5 mill. ponds of cloves, 1 mill. ponds of nutmeg, and 5–600,000 ponds of mace. The conclusion of the peace brought about an increase in the sales. Thus the Company in 1714 sold about 435,000 ponds of cloves, about 284,000 ponds of nutmeg, and 80,000 ponds of mace.[91] On the whole it may be stated that the annual sales of cloves down to 1745 fluctuated between 300,000 and 400,000 ponds and thus bordered on the old figures of the sales from the first half of the 17th century, Pieter van Dam's frequently mentioned 400,000 ponds. On the long view the Company thus by the price of 75 st. per pond almost succeeded in recovering the trade, whereas the sales of nutmeg did not reach the same level although they also were increased after 1713 and normally varied between 225,000 and 275,000 ponds a year. It is, however, a fact that the Company at times felt hampered by its great stores of spices in Nederland, especially nutmeg and *rompen*, which were exposed to attacks from mites and similar pests. The stores of cloves, on the other hand, were small towards the end of the 1730's, which presumably was connected with the failure of crops mentioned above. Illustrative of the composition of the stores is a resolution of 17 August 1730, in which it was decided to burn nearly 400,000 ponds of nutmeg and 70,000 ponds of mace. The destruction took place during a period of four years. In 1730 they started by burning well over 100,000 ponds of nutmeg which all of it originated from the time down to 1711, i.e. nutmeg which was more than 20 years old.[92] In 1735 another clean-up of the warehouses was made. This time no less than 1.25 mill. ponds of *rompen* were destroyed; that gave food for thought. The Heeren XVII appointed a committee for the purpose of discussing what means might be used for increasing the sales of spices. The committee dealt with the most obvious problem, a reduction of prices, but when a report had been submitted in 1736, the Court of Directors decided that there should be no change.[93] In return there proved to be an increasing demand for mace, which by the annual figures of sales from 80,000 to 100,000 ponds reached the level from the 1660's, the 1670's, and the 1680's. In 1719 the Heeren XVII wrote that the European demand was constantly increasing; they gave orders for an extension of the production of mace on Banda, which the Court of Directors maintained was on the decrease.[94] The prices in Nederland, which were free, indeed, testify to great demands for this commodity.

[91] Collectie Radermacher No. 140.
[92] Kol. Arch. No. 201, 22 August 1730.
[93] Kol. Arch. No. 202, 8 November 1735 and 26 March 1736.
[94] Kol. Arch. No. 464, 27 September 1719 (section on Banda).

CHAPTER VI

Raw Silk

Admiral Jacob van Heemskerck's capture of the Portuguese carrack "S. Catharina" off Johore on the 25 February 1603 undoubtedly contributed to the fact that silks from the very first years of the Dutch East India Company's existence were placed among the most coveted returns on a line with pepper and the other spices. The "S. Catharina" had a cargo of, amongst other things, 1200 bales of Chinese raw silk to a value in Nederland of more than 2.25 mill. fl. The cargo was by the Admiralty in Amsterdam offered at a public sale in August 1604, and as at the same time there had been a failure of crops of silk in Italy, the run on the sale was overwhelming. From the whole of Europe intending buyers flocked to Amsterdam. The position of Amsterdam among the most important markets of silk may perhaps be dated from this sale.[1] It whetted the Company's appetite. In instructions from the Heeren XVII dated in April 1608 concerning the trade in Asia it was said that the trade to China should be increased by all means available, first of all in order in this way to provide silk "daerop goede profijtten sijn te doen ende oock seer groote quantiteijt can worden verhandelt, maecken oock seer groote neringhe ende welvaert onder het arbeijtsvolk."[2] If a direct trade to China could not be practised, the Company's factors were to buy the silk at the places to which the Chinese traded, e.g. at Patani. "Het is der Comp.[a] dienstelijcker veele penningen te besteden aen rouwe ongewrochte zijde als aen peper, alsoo de Portugesen den peper altoos in groote abundantie brengen en daermede cladden."[3] The consideration

[1] *Pieter van Dam* 2:I, p. 672; H. Terpstra, *De factorij der Oostindische Compagnie te Patani* (Verhandelingen van het Koninklijk Instituut voor de Taal-, Land- en Volkenkunde van Nederlandsch-Indië, deel 1, 's-Gravenhage, 1938), p. 118; H. E. van Gelder, "Gegevens omtrent den porceleinhandel der O.-I. Compagnie", *Economisch-Historisch Jaarboek*, vol. X ('s-Gravenhage, 1924), p. 165 *et seq.*

[2] Quoted from W. P. Groeneveldt, "De Nederlanders in China", *Bijdragen tot de Taal-, Land- en Volkenkunde van Nederlandsch-Indië*, 6th ser., vol. IV ('s-Gravenhage, 1898), p. 48.

[3] *Ibid.*

to the silk trade was just decisive of the activities of the Dutch during these years at Patani and in the smaller factories in Siam and Sengora. It is true that the Court of Directors were aware that there was also silk to be had in Persia. In the same instructions the Company's admirals in India were just recommended to enter into an alliance with the King of Ormuz against the Portuguese in order in this way to smooth the path for Dutch purchases of silk in Persia. As long as the Dutch factory at Patani existed, however, the Company did not gain a footing in Persia.

Although, as regards the greater part of the 17th century, we are poorly informed about the Dutch auction prices of silk, we have from the first decades a little information suitable to illustrate how the Chinese silk was placed on the European market and what profits it yielded. In the autumn of 1606 the Heeren XVII fixed the selling prices of a number of commodities, among them Chinese silk. The raw, white silk, i.e. unspun, white silk, was to be sold at 12.00 fl. per pond, while floss-silk (in Dutch: *floszijde*,[4] from which *florette garens* were spun) was to cost 16.20 fl. per pond, and spun silk was fixed at 15.60 fl. per pond. Raw silk was to be paid within 9 months.[5] The example shows the not insignificant distance between the prices determined by the quality or the working up, a fact which highly complicates the drawing up of exact statistics of prices. At that time – just as now – there were silk and silk. This becomes still more evident if we pass on to the section in the Amsterdam price lists dealing with silks, which is dominated by the multitude of products from the Italian industry. Thus the price list dated at 27 February 1624[6] shows that the cheapest silk was *Milano doppel* at 5.40 fl. per pond. This was followed by another kind of waste silk, boiled floss-silk, at 6.60 fl. per pond. Higher on the scale we find the Persian silks, *ardasse* and *legie*, at 9.60 fl. per pond. Raw silk from Messina at the date mentioned was quoted at 10.65 fl. per pond, and raw silk from Vicenza at 14.10 fl. per pond. Chinese raw silk also appears in the Amsterdam price list, where it is quoted at 16.20 fl. per pond. Most expensive were the Italian *organzini*, i.e. double-spun silks which were used for warp. In 1624 *organzini di Bologna* cost 20.70 fl. per pond, and the very finest organzine from Naples was quoted at a price from 21.60 fl. to 22.20 fl. per pond. This survey shows that Chinese raw silk was valued highest among the raw silks quoted, thus considerably higher than the Persian raw silks. As to the Company's profits we may mention a sale at the end of July 1621,

[4] From French "filoselle", cf. Dr. Stapel's glossary in *Pieter van Dam* 1:II.
[5] *Pieter van Dam* 1:II, p. 145.
[6] H. W. Aeckerle, "Amsterdamer Börsenpreislisten 1624–1626", *Economisch-Historisch Jaarboek*, vol. XIII ('s-Gravenhage, 1927), p. 105.

when Hubrecht and Samuel Saultijn bought a parcel of white Chinese raw silk of 1556 catti, i.e. 1868 ponds. The parcel originated from the Company's factory in Sengora. It had in January 1621 been shipped from Jacatra by the "'t Wapen van Hoorn" and the invoice price amounted to 7,116 fl., i.e. 3.81 fl. per pond. Messrs. Saultijn paid 15.90 fl. per pond, 15 months *in banco*.[7] Thus the Company's gross profit amounted to about 320 per cent. Another example from about the same time: Robert Baerle in March 1622 bought 1,009 catti Chinese white raw silk at a price of 16.88 fl. per pond, 15 months *in banco*.[8] This parcel had been sent home in April 1621 by the "Leyden".[9] Its invoice value was 4,833 fl. The silk had been bought on Formosa at a price of 200 Spanish rials per picul, i.e. 4 fl. per pond. The gross profit was about 325 per cent.

Thus it was a profitable and marketable commodity the Company had got hold of. In a survey of the various possibilities of sales in Nederland, dispatched in February 1617, the Heeren XVII modestly counted on an annual sale of about 72,000 ponds of Chinese raw silk.[10] Later on the figure rose, but the supplies – which were very irregular – as far as can be estimated, in the beginning of the 1620's were below 72,000 ponds a year. This is also connected with the fact that Chinese silk was a primary commodity in the trade to Japan which the Company was developing at the time. Where the Dutch demand collided with demand from the Company's factory in Japan, Japan was first of all taken into consideration.

The Persian King's capitulations to the Company in 1623 opened up possibilities of an extension of the Company's trade in silk. The Dutch secured "a share in the mighty international silk trade being carried on under the royal monopoly" (van Leur).[11] The basis of this was the collaboration which in 1619 was established between the English and the Dutch companies, conditioned by the struggle against the common enemies, the Portuguese, and by the Persian King's war against the latter.[12] In the years 1619–20, on an English initiative, a proposal was made for a division of the trade in Persian silk between the two Northwest European companies. The English company estimated the annual exports of silk from Persia to Europe at 6,000 bales. The exports exclu-

[7] Kol. Arch. No. 984, fo. 396 c; Kol. Arch. No. 249, 29 July 1621.
[8] Kol. Arch. No. 249, 24 March 1622.
[9] Kol. Arch. No. 985, fo. 15 *et seq.*
[10] Kol. Arch. No. 450, "Aenwijsinge ende particuliere memorie, etc.", dispatched February 1617.
[11] van Leur, *op. cit.* p. 187.
[12] Cf. Dunlop, *op. cit.* pp. XXV ff.

sively passed by way of Aleppo and Syria via the Levant and was distributed by 3,000 bales to Marseilles, 1,500 to Venice, 400 bales to the other Italian towns, Genoa, Lucca, Florence, Messina, etc., 600 bales to England, and 500 bales to Nederland. The Spaniards and the Portuguese had never gone in for conveying Persian silk to Europe. The English proposal was aimed at nothing less than a monopolization and waterborne redirection of the Persian export. The two companies were aware that such a project at the moment surpassed their combined economic strength, for which reason they also formed a minor plan for the purpose of ousting the Portuguese from Ormuz and from this strategic point on the Gulf supervising the imports of spices, sugar, textiles, and other Asiatic and European products to Persia (parts of the imports flowing further into Arabia and Turkey). In their main estimate the English calculated on a cost-price in Djask (southeast of Gamron) of 8 shillings per English lb. silk, which yielded a total investment of £ 540,000 for the above-mentioned exports of 6,000 bales.[13] A division of the booty – which in the English originators' opinion could be sold at 30–32 shillings per English lb. in Europe – would mean that the Dutch Company would have the disposal of 2.7–2.8 mill. fl. for the purchase of Persian silk.[14] Rumours of the plan made the English merchants in Aleppo trading to the Levant buy as much as 1400 bales of Persian silk in 1620, as it was reported that the Shah intended to direct his exports to the Persian Gulf.[15] However, the project failed. Neither the English nor the Dutch Company had sufficient funds for such an annual investment. By way of comparison it may be mentioned that the Heeren XVII in the spring of 1622 drew up an extraordinarily heavy programme for purchases of returns amounting to a total of 3 mill. fl. Of this amount it was recommended to invest 1.2 mill. fl. "aen rouwe sijde en waren."[16] But the English soon discovered that it was a Trojan horse they had led inside the walls of the Persian realm when allying themselves with the Dutch in the fight against the Portuguese. Economically the Dutch Company was the stronger, and after the conclusion of the capitulations in 1623 it behaved very energetically on the Persian market. As late as 1629 the two nations' co-operation was necessary because of the Portuguese danger. However, it was less tones of co-operation than complaints

[13] I.e. that the bale was counted as equal to 225 English lbs. The Dutch later in their invoices indicate 200 ponds per bale of Chinese as well as Persian silk. See also Kol. Arch. No. 250, 9 September 1638 ["... 800 á 1000 ballen Persiaensche sijde legie tot 200 ponden de bael"].

[14] Dunlop, *op. cit.* p. 10 *et seq.*

[15] *Ibid.*

[16] Kol. Arch. No. 4409, "Extract uyt missive van de mayores in data 14de April Ao. 1622 pr. "Erasmus" ges:, etc."

of competition on the part of the Dutch that were heard from the English merchants in Persia during these years.[17] It is also evident that even if the East India Companies did not succeed in redirecting the whole of the Persian export from the Levant to the Persian Gulf and the sea route round the Cape of Good Hope, their activities meant a serious inroad into Levantine trade. The Dutch minister in Constantinople, Haga, in 1626 wrote to the States General that the directors of the Dutch trade to the Levant had stated "dat de principale capitalen, die in Aleppo vertiert werden, bestaen in den incoop van de syde en dat deselvige nu door de Oostindische schepen uyt Persiae ende over Moscovia in de landen gebracht wordt."[18]

The new trade to Persia also meant that the Heeren XVII to a wide extent desisted from ordering Chinese silk for Europe, leaving this sort to the trade to Japan. In an order drawn up in November 1631, which only included returns to an amount of 1.3 mill. fl., the Heeren XVII thus asked for 400 bales or 80,000 ponds of Persian silk at a cost-price of 4 fl. per pond and only 10,000 ponds of Chinese silk at a cost-price of 3.50 fl. per pond.[19] As said above, this was a limited order. Towards the end of the 1620's the Heeren XVII had demanded up to 1200 bales of silk in Persia per season, i.e. 240,000 ponds,[20] and in the course of the 1630's they again approached to this level. In 1633 they fixed the order for Persian silk at 160,000 ponds and cut down the order for Chinese silk to 7,200 ponds.[21] The following year – in 1634 – they ordered still more, viz. 200,000 ponds of Persian silk, while the order for Chinese silk continually was very moderate, viz. 9,600 ponds.[22] This seems to have been the provisional culmination of the Dutch demand for silk from Persia. In 1636 the trend was declining, the order being for 160–200,000 ponds (800–1,000 bales).[23] The high figures mentioned are probably connected with Nicolaes Jacobsz: Overschie's endeavours to attempt a monopolization again, this time directed against the English East India Company. The Heeren XVII for some time supported Overschie in his attempt and in 1635 wrote that the Company's director of trade in Persia need not feel bound by the demands of Nederland. If his funds were sufficient,

[17] Dunlop, *op. cit.* p. XXXII; William Foster (ed.), *The English Factories in India, 1630–1633* (Oxford, 1910), p. XXXVII *et seq.*

[18] Dunlop, *op. cit.* p. LXV; K. Heeringa, *Bronnen tot de geschiedenis van den Levantschen handel*, deel 2 (Rijks Geschiedkundige Publicatiën, No. 34, 's-Gravenhage, 1917), p. 528.

[19] Kol. Arch. No. 250, "Lijste van retouren ter vergaderinge van de XVII in Nov. 1631 gearresteert, etc." We reckon 1 bale equal to 200 ponds, cf. above p. 113, Note 13.

[20] *Pieter van Dam* 2:III, p. 289, Note 5.

[21] Kol. Arch. No. 250, 17 September 1633.

[22] *Ibid.* August 1634.

[23] *Ibid.* September 1636.

he would be allowed to buy up additional quantities of silk, just as he should not be deterred by rising prices of silk in Persia as long as the English felt like buying.[24] The competitive factor in the purchases is evident. It is also evident that the Dutch had taken the lead. Soon after, however, they came to feel competition on the European market, which changed the Seventeen's view of the matter. The Persian silk, which about the middle of the 1620's in the Amsterdam price lists had been quoted at 34–36 *schellingen* per pond, i.e. 10.20–10.80 fl.,[25] had in 1634 dropped to 9.00 fl. per pond.[26] In December 1637 the Court of Directors wrote to Batavia that the silk received last had yielded but 25 per cent. It was therefore enjoined on the Government that only really good qualities should be shipped to Nederland. The others were of no interest. The Heeren XVII backed out. Overschie was taken to task for having made too great purchases at too high prices.[27] Measured by the standard of the 1620's a gross profit of 25 per cent. was, indeed, actually very low, and from a general knowledge of the Heeren XVII's view of profits it must be supposed that the figure was below the level which was considered lucrative.[28] If thus the interest in Persian silk cooled off, Chinese silk again gained ground in the Dutch orders for returns. In October 1637 an order was given for well over 50,000 ponds, but with the reservation that the trade to Japan should not be deprived of the silk by the fulfilment of wishes of Nederland.[29]

These features from the first third of the 17th century show marked fluctuations in offer and demand, which are typical of the conditions of trade in raw silk. Bounds had been set to the Dutch Company's activities in this field as in so many others. Actually the Company was very far from the monopoly they were raving about at intervals. On the European, i.e. the Amsterdam market, the supplies from Italy, France, and the Levant trade were first of all leading the fashion. The Company kept the pace in periods of shortage and boom and with great advantage put Asiatic silk on the market in Amsterdam, but it did not control the market and in periods of recession had to restrict its supplies of silk from the East.

[24] Dunlop, *op. cit.* p. 541. [25] Aeckerle, *op. cit. passim.*

[26] Dunlop, *op. cit.* p. LXVIII; *Economisch-Historisch Jaarboek,* vol. XII, p. XXXVIII. To judge from the orders the fall in prices was hardly, as supposed by Dunlop, due to great supplies of Chinese silk.

[27] Dunlop, *op. cit.* p. 541, Note 1.

[28] Thus we disagree with Dunlop in his estimate of this profit. Dunlop, *op. cit.* p. LXVIII *et seq.*

[29] Kol. Arch. No. 250, 3 October 1637; the order specifies as follows: 40–50,000 ponds of *witte rouwe Chin. syde,* 40–50 piculs of *witte Chin. getweernde syde,* 5–10 piculs of *couleurde ditto,* and 20 piculs of *pool syde.* On 9 September 1638 an order was given for only 360 piculs of *witte rouwe Chin. syde.*

Nor did it, in spite of ambitious schemes, control supplies in the East. Direct commercial intercourse with China could not be permanently established, and the barter in the Indonesian archipelago, along the neighbouring countries and islands of the Chinese empire, were characterized by competition with Asiatic, Portuguese, English, and other traders. In Persia the limits of the foreign trade actually were very narrow. The silk trade was a royal monopoly, and the Dutch only exceptionally succeeded in evading it. The silk had to be acquired from the Royal factor in Ispahan. The very fact that the Company was admitted to this market at all, was due to fortunate circumstances which actually were not brought about by the Dutch. It was connected with the Shah Abbas the Great's fight against Turkey. The attempt at redirecting the exports from the Levant to the Persian Gulf was conditioned by the Shah's wish for depriving Turkey of the receipts from the transit duty on silk and other Oriental goods. As mentioned in Chapter II, the Persian cultivation of silk was seated partly in an area comprising the provinces Shirwan, Segan, Shamakhi, Georgia, Berde, and Araxes, partly in the old realm or district Gilan. In the former area amongst others the *ardasse* silk was cultivated, in the latter the *legie* silk. The *legie* was most coveted by the Europeans, and the chief market for the purchase of *legie* was Resht, the capital of Gilan. There silk was on the market during the season from July to October. 14–15 miles from Resht was Laidsjan on the Caspian Sea, to which Russian ships from Astrakhan every year brought cloth and furs to be bartered for silk and other goods.[30] This northern trade route constituted the other possibility which presented itself to the Shah in his endeavours to direct the exports to Europe while getting round Turkey. The Russians were aware of this fact and pleaded their cause at an embassy to Persia in 1626.[31] Duke Frederick III.'s mission from Holstein to Persia through Russia in 1637 – well-known from Olearius' famous description – was also dictated by a wish for having a share in the Persian silk. With support from circles outside the duchy a plan had been drawn up to make Friedrichstadt on the Eider an entrepot and centre of the Northwest European trade in Persian silk.[32] The basis of this attempt at reviving the ancient route was the boom in Persian silk in the 1620's and 1630's and the commotion which on the Shah's initiative had been raised in connexion with the trade routes.

The falling prices of silk on the Dutch market cooled the eagerness of the Heeren XVII to secure Persian silk. Furthermore, the cost-price in

[30] *Pieter van Dam* 2:III, p. 282 *et seq.* [31] Dunlop, *op. cit.* p. 191. [32] *Ibid.* p. 627, Note 1.

Ispahan had risen. While the Company's buyers in the 1620's had obtained the silk at prices between 4.40 and 4.70 fl. per pond,[33] it cost more than 5 fl. per pond in 1637/38. The first trouble with the Shah amongst other things arose because the Company tried to buy the silk behind the back of the Royal factor.[34] In 1637 the Dutch were forced to pay 160,000 fl. export duties.[35] The Heeren XVII returned to their old acquaintance, Chinese silk. In 1636 the third great area of silk, Bengal, emerged in the orders for returns.[36] Through the 1640's the annual demand for Persian silk amounted to 4–500 bales, in 1648 it was 300 bales or 60,000 ponds. The order was for two thirds of *legie* and one third of *ardasse* at "reasonable" prices. The purchases were to be financed by the Company's supplies of spices, sugar, textiles, etc. No loans must be raised in Persia for the financing of the purchases of silk.[37] Conditions in Persia during the 1640's developed in such a way that the exportation of silk to Nederland for periods came to a standstill. The Company's servants were in open quarrel with the Shah. In 1643 the director of trade, Carel Constant, was imprisoned on his way from Gamron to Ispahan. The Government in Batavia were in favour of war, closing of the Company's office, and capture of Kishm, the largest of the islands at the entrance to the Persian Gulf. They were worried at the fact that Persian silk was again being exported to Europe in large quantities by way of Aleppo. The Company's profits decreased concurrently with this development.[38] The Heeren XVII had difficulties in making Governor General and Council be lenient – not least the "Moorish" trade to Gamron was a thorn in their flesh – but in 1652 they succeeded during Joan Cunaeus's embassy to Ispahan in having the commercial relations regulated. During many and long negotiations it appeared that the Persians especially fastened upon the surplus of the trade balance which was in favour of the Dutch. The Company had contracted for silk to a considerably smaller amount than they had realized in supplied goods. The silk and export of bullion and specie in connexion with duties were the chief items in the negotiations. As regards silk the result was that the Company engaged to take 300 camel lasts of silks, i.e. 120,000 ponds a year. The price was put at 50 *tomans* per last, which was 5.00 fl. per pond according to the usual rate of exchange, but only 4.37 fl. according to the new rate which

[33] Huybert Visnich's journal and ledger from Gamron 1623–24 show purchases of *legie* at 4.65 fl. per pond and *ardasse* at 4.37 fl. per pond. Dunlop, *op. cit.* pp. 118–9 and 114–5.

[34] *Pieter van Dam* 2:III, p. 294.

[35] *Ibid.* p. 296, Note 2.

[36] Kol. Arch. No. 250, September 1636: 20–30 piculs of *Bengaalse syde*.

[37] E.g. Kol. Arch. No. 251, November 1647.

[38] *Pieter van Dam* 2:III, p. 294 *et seq.*

at the same time was introduced between Persian and Dutch currency.[39] Finally, the Company was allowed to rebuild its factory house at Gamron, which had been destroyed during an earthquake in 1645. The new agreements were marked by the fact that Cunaeus contracted for 300 camel lasts of silk. It was, however, evident that in a way it was not on account of the silk that the Dutch accepted these conditions. It was first of all the profits from the sale of the goods in Gamron which inspired the work, the consideration for the favourable trade balance, and during the following decades it was not least the surplus of cash – "Moorish" gold ducats and silver coins – which made the Persian factories valuable. The circumstance that the gold and silver had to be smuggled out, was of minor importance. The agreement to take 120,000 ponds of silk annually was definitely inconvenient, apart from the fact that the bales of silk were as if cut out for concealing the ducats in them. It cost the Company some money for bribes to make the authorities connive at the evasion of the export clause, but, as Pieter van Dam states, these costs were small in proportion to the expense to which the Company would have put itself if it was to have taken the whole quantity in a period when the market in Nederland was very slack.[40] During the six-year period of 1655–1660 the Company got off with exporting only an average of 43,200 ponds of silk a year.[41]

The Heeren XVII certainly did not press on, but from 1653 inclusive gave the general order to the Government in Batavia only to send what the Persian King forced the Company's factors to receive. The less the better. In the beginning of the 1670's they got the bright idea of sending the Persian silk to Japan, where, however, it did not catch on.[42] The Court of Directors in Nederland encouraged invention as regards marketing the silk in Asia, but left it to the Batavian Government to solve the problem. They only wanted to see the surplus among the returns to Nederland. In 1682 the Persian silk disappeared from the list of orders of the Court of Directors and it did not reappear till 1701, when the situation was completely changed. How the gross profits developed during these slack years can be illustrated by the below example from 1668–70. We give the cost-price as known from the invoices, and as to the selling price it should be noted that it has been calculated from the sales at Kamer Amsterdam of all silks put together. As far as is known, no Chinese silk was sold during these three years, whereas there was some Bengali silk, though not so great quantities as those of Persian silk. As

[39] *Ibid.* pp. 299 ff. [40] *Ibid.* p. 313. [41] *Ibid.*

[42] This had once been attempted with a similar result; cf. W. H. Moreland, *From Akbar to Aurangzeb*, A Study in Indian Economic History (London, 1923), p. 66.

the prices of Bengali silk from the very few examples of sales named by quality from these years is seen to be above the prices of Persian silk, the figures adduced, in other words, are at the upper edge of the receipts from Persian silk.

Table 21. *The Prices of Persian Silk, 1668–70; Purchase and Sale. Florins per Pond.*

	Purchase		Sale
1668....	4.24–5.17	1668/69....	5.19
1669....	5.17–5.25	1669/70....	6.16
1670....	5.18	1670/71....	6.06

During the 1680's the prices became still lower, as appears from the statistics of prices in Appendix C. The gross profits became gross losses. The low was reached in 1685/86, when the Persian silk at the sales in Amsterdam only fetched a price of 3.95 fl. per pond.

It is evident that it was first of all the Company's Persian silk which could not hold its own on the European market during these decades. Other silks as well were occasionally lowpriced, but hardly involved losses. It was, however, uncertain what was left for Nederland of Chinese silk from the Asiatic turnover, and furthermore, the market for this silk was no longer particularly great. Instead, Bengali silk gradually inherited the leading place in the category of silk in the returns. During the first years the Heeren XVII contented themselves with cautious orders for 15–20,000 ponds of Bengali silk. In 1642 they estimated the cost-price at 2.25 fl. per pond.[43] This cheap purchase just made the commodity profitable, and already at an early stage the East India Companies had become aware of this fact. Thus representatives of the English company about 1620 related that unlimited quantities of silk could be acquired in Murshidabad, the most important centre for the cultivation of silk in Bengal, at prices "at least 20 per cent cheaper than any other place in India and was of the choicest stuff, wound off into what condition you shall require it, as it comes from the worm; where are also innumerable silk winders, expert workmen, and labour cheaper by a third than elsewhere."[44] Even though in the course of time the price rose, Bengali silk through the greater part of the 17th century was the cheapest of the three Asiatic groups of silks. Thus the invoice price in the returns of 1649 was 2.82 fl. per pond and in 1669–70 4.11 and 4.09 fl. per pond, respectively. The question then is to what extent

[43] Kol. Arch. No. 250, 29 November 1642.

[44] Bhattacharya, *op. cit.* p. 153 (from *The English Factory Records*, 1618–21, ed. Foster, pp. xxiii and 230).

the Bengali silk could be used in Nederland. On this point, however, the new silk proved suitable. As regards selling prices it was placed above Persian, but below Chinese silk. In the beginning of the 1650's the Court of Directors increased their annual orders to 50,000 ponds, which became the introduction to the first boom in the Dutch demand for the new silk. In September 1651 the Heeren XVII wrote that the Bengali silk "tegenwoordigh hier te lande met merckelijcke advance kan gedebiteert worden."[45] This optimistic estimate of the marketing of Bengali silk was strengthened to such a degree that they in January 1654 ordered 200,000 ponds or as much as could be bought in Bengal up to an amount of 1 mill. fl.[46] We know the selling price at Kamer Amsterdam in the season of 1653/54, when Bengali silk was sold on an average of 8.92 fl. per pond (the Persian silk rendered but 7.59 fl.). If we assume that the cost-price was just under 3 fl. per pond, this means that the Company could count on a gross profit of about 200 per cent on the silk from Bengal.

It may be asked why the Dutch Company only in the 1650's in earnest came to take an interest in Bengal as a supplier of silk, considering that, as mentioned above, it was already at an earlier date aware of the possibilities of cheap purchases there. Several different circumstances may serve as answers to the question. In the first place, the Company's trade in an area was rarely determined by one commodity only, but by a plurality of products. Purchase and sale were weighed against one another, for which reason the Dutch demand was not the only determinative factor. Not least the surplus of the total turnover in the area was an important guide to the management in Nederland as well as in Batavia. Secondly, the Persian trade must be taken into consideration. Apart from the fact that the balance there generally was very favourable, the Company was more or less bound by its past in Persia. This may be termed a historical factor, if we choose to look at it that way. The agreement of 1652 during the following period proved to be a drag, a capricious quantity which could not be calculated. It was important to attune the quantities of silk of the return cargoes in such a way that in years with sudden large supplies from the Persian Shah e.g. the Bengali quotas were reduced. The task, occasionally hopeless, of co-ordinating the purchases rested with the Batavian Government. The task, for that matter, became further complicated, since Bengali silk, as against Persian silk, could successfully be sold on the Japanese market, for which reason the rule was introduced that the wishes of the Japan office should come before everything else at the distribution. The third factor to be

[45] Kol. Arch. No. 252, September 1651. [46] *Ibid.* January 1654.

pointed out as contributory to the fact that the trade in Bengali silk developed comparatively late, was the unsettled conditions in Bengal during the first half of the 17th century. Thus the Portuguese to the best of their ability barred the access by holding Hoogly until 1632, and right down to 1666 their activities had a hampering effect in Chittagong. Coen, who otherwise did not shun war, characteristically wrote in 1627 that Bengal was a country "vol oorloch ende troubel, soodat alles aldaer buyten ordre staet;"[47] but during the 1650's the Dutch pushed forward, and the resolution of the Batavian Government in 1655 to appoint an independent director of trade in Bengal, which previously had been directed from Fort Geldria on the Coromandel Coast, is symptomatic.

The Company's head office in Bengal was at Hoogly, but in respect of silk Kasimbazar was the most important station. The English also in this period found their way to Kasimbazar, where they established a factory in 1658.[48] Although the Dutch were the leading as regards initiative – as stated by Moreland, "in Bengal their predominance is indisputable from the outset"[49] – the English company followed up the success in connexion with the new silk. The competition soon was considerable and at length in the first third of the 18th century resulted in the English taking the lead definitively. The development in Bengal thus was different from that in Persia. Tavernier in 1676 described Kasimbazar as a village which annually exported more than 20,000 bales of silk, each bale being of 100 ponds.[50] The silk was "reaped" three times a year. The local name of a "harvest" was "band". The so-called November "band" was gathered during the months from October to February, while the March "band" ranged from March to June and the July "band" from July to September. The winter cocoon was the best and hence the most expensive. This was followed by the March "band", and the poorest quality was the July "band".[51] In 1698 the Heeren XVII wrote that the staff of the Company should endeavour to buy November "band", "dewelke hier vetter en beter van sijde wert bevonden als wel die van andere teelten, en waer op wij vinden dat d'Engelsche wel haar meeste toelegh maeckende, boven onse sijde komen te prevaleren."[52] When the cocoons were "ripe" and the silkworm was killed by heating, the raw silk was to be rid of lime and other impurities

[47] Quoted from H. Terpstra, *De Nederlanders in Voor-Indië* (Patria, Vaderlandsche cultuurgeschiedenis in monografieën, No. XXXIX, Amsterdam, 1947), p. 143.
[48] Bhattacharya, *op. cit.* p. 153.
[49] Quoted from Terpstra, *De Nederlanders in Voor-Indië*, p. 153.
[50] According to Bhattacharya, *op. cit.* p. 153.
[51] Bhattacharya, *op. cit.* p. 154.
[52] Kol. Arch. No. 261, 24 July 1698.

by a washing. Then the thread was reeled into leas and the product was ready for export. Perhaps the silk might first be bleached or coloured.[53] The Court of Directors attached great importance to having a single-threaded reel of a not too long thread, which was the most easily saleable commodity. A good number of instructions and patterns were sent to Bengal to obtain the product which was most suitable for the Dutch industry. Not rarely it was tried to rouse the staff to carefulness by referring to the English company's good results with regard to quality. The Dutch were especially worried by badly reeled silk, several threads running double, and the Batavian Government for a while considered punishing the suppliers in Kasimbazar who did not comply with the instructions. This view was opposed by the Heeren XVII for fear of the English competition. They dared not risk that the suppliers should leave the Dutch Company and go over to the English.[54] Normally the Company did not want the silk to be worked up or coloured. In 1688 the Heeren XVII wrote that if so it must be considered that "de sijderederijen alhier niet alleen t'eenemael souden werden geruineert, maer oock heeft men hier de handelingh vrij beter en is het goet deughtsamer, gelijck uyt de vercoop van de in Indien geverwde en gerede sijde klaerlijck comt te blijcken."[55] As in the case of Persian and Chinese silk there were also special qualities of Bengali silk. The Portuguese terms of quality *cabessa*, *barriga*, and *pee*, were used to denote 1st, 2nd, and 3rd quality. The English correspondingly used the terms "head", "belly", and "foot".[56] Later a superfine quality appeared which was called *tanni* or *tanny*. This was a short-threaded reel of the best part of the cocoons, the so-called *patteni* threads, and therefore the quality was also called *tanni-patany* or in English "puttany".[57] This silk may have been named after the locality Thanna near Hoogly.[58] The Dutch Company down to the 1670's exclusively asked for *cabessa*, *bariga*, and *pee*, especially the two first-mentioned qualities. In 1676 the first order for *tanni* silk emerged in the demands,[59] and in a very short time it surpassed the other sorts. Thus the order of the Heeren XVII in 1681 was for "de Tannij zijde te prefereren gelijck d'Engelsche becomen."[60] The *tanni* itself, however, was different things; there were local variations, and as an example of the great variety of raw silk we shall adduce the following order sent in 1684 for the returns of 1686.[61]

[53] On the preparation of silk, see *Pieter van Dam* 2:II, pp. 67 ff., "Over de zijde teelt".
[54] Kol. Arch. No. 261, 25 February 1701. [55] Kol. Arch. No. 259, 26 November 1688.
[56] Bal Krishna, *op. cit.* p. 143. [57] *Ibid.*
[58] Dr. Stapel's glossary in *Pieter van Dam* 2:II.
[59] Kol. Arch. No. 257, 20 October 1676: 10,000 ponds of *Bengalsche rouwe syde tanni.*
[60] Kol. Arch. No. 258, 20 November 1681.
[61] *Ibid.* 9 December 1684.

Table 22. *Order from Nederland for Bengali Silk for the Year 1686.*

Tanni		100,000 ponds
Of which:		
A or *Cora*	15,000 ponds	
B or *Dom*	35,000 ponds	
C or *Cem*	25,000 ponds	
D or *Siarium*	18,000 ponds	
E or *Pansium*	7,000 ponds	
Cabessa		12,000 ponds
Bariga		12,000 ponds
Pee		12,000 ponds
	In all	136,000 ponds

For the sake of completeness it should be added that for some short periods there were also orders for small quantities of sewing and knitting silk and for Ceerpour silk from Bengal.

To return to the great order of January 1654 for 200,000 ponds or silk for 1 mill. fl., it should be pointed out that this order of magnitude was not representative of the orders for the years immediately following. As early as 1655 the Court of Directors reduced their orders for silk from Bengal to 100,000 ponds because of falling prices. The year after there was a reduction to 80,000 ponds, and during the following years the demand fluctuated between 50,000 and 80,000 ponds.[62] We shall not follow the orders in details throughout the period, but only point out that on the whole they fluctuated concurrently with the prices and were attuned to the supplies of other silks received by the Company in Nederland. The tendency was that with the very low prices in the beginning of the 1670's and in the beginning of the 1680's they were as low as for 40,000–60,000 ponds, whereas during the period towards the end of the 1670's characterized by higher prices they amounted to 60,000–80,000 ponds. About the middle of the 1680's a rise in prices began which in a decade made the orders for Bengali silk pass the level of 1654. The demand was increased by small supplies of Persian silk of poor quality. As indicated above, this increasing order was especially for *tanni*, whereas *cabessa* and *bariga* were less in demand. In November 1687 the Heeren XVII wrote that they were oversupplied by *cabessa* and *bariga*. It had only been possible to sell 30,000 ponds at the public sales. In the following year it was stated that the Company's stores of *cabessa* were of more than 48,000 ponds, which could barely be disposed of in less than two years.[63] As the *tanni* in Nederland obtained a foothold at the expense of

[62] Kol. Arch. No. 253, October 1656. [63] Kol. Arch. No. 259, 26 November 1688.

cabessa, the Heeren XVII asked the Government in Batavia to hold back the latter. There was also a surplus of *bariga* – about 30,000 ponds – but this sort was used by the workshops instead of the Persian silk, for which reason they still wanted to be supplied with that, indeed, in 1689 they demanded as much as 60,000–70,000 ponds of *bariga* "alsoo deselve door manquement van Persiaense sijde seer groote consumptie heeft, en dit jaer boven de 18 schellingen [i.e. 5,40 fl.] het pond verkoft is."[64] Therefore it was especially *bariga* and Persian silk which might collide in the consignments, as e.g. happened in 1692. The Company unexpectedly received a fairly large consignment of Persian silk, with the result that *bariga* at the public sales fell from 6 fl. to 3.50 fl. per pond, so the order was reduced to a modest 10,000 ponds.[65] Towards the end of the 1690's a shortage of Persian silk arose in Nederland, and the Seventeen for the first time in a long period gave a seriously meant order for Persian silk among the returns. For want of this they must have *bariga* "om dat hier te lande seer groot gebreck is aan stoffe van stick en naeij sijde te maecken waerto de Persiaense sijde mede komt te dienen."[66] Altogether the years about the turn of the century were characterized by greater possibility of sale and by top prices. The war in which Italy was involved for some time eliminated the presumably greatest supplier of silk in Europe, just as the French war discontinued the Turkish trade. The Persian supplies, however, were uncertain. The Shah and the merchants were more interested in selling the silk by way of Astrakhan and the Levant themselves than in supplying it by contract to the Company. In 1698 the Heeren XVII wrote that Armenian merchants for two years running had exported more than 1,000 bales of silk by way of Muscovy and Narva.[67] In 1701 the Heeren XVII asked for a total of 285,000 ponds of silk, viz. 40,000 ponds of Chinese silk, 220,000 ponds of Bengali *tanni*, and 25,000 ponds of *bariga*. Furthermore they expressed a hope of having the contract renewed with the Persian Shah, in which case political difficulties asserted themselves. Did they succeed in utilizing the situation? Or, in other words, how much did they get hold of? And how much did the Company sell during these years at the top? It is not mere words of praise which we find in the court minutes. In July 1698 the Seventeen complained of the modest quantities of silk coming from Bengal, which had landed the Company in difficulties. It was unable to supply the workshops of the country. Hundreds of looms were idle for want of silk, the artisans were unemployed and had difficulty in making both ends meet. If the manufacturers had not secured silk from

[64] *Ibid.* 9 December 1689.
[65] Kol. Arch. No. 260, 6 December 1692.
[66] Kol. Arch. No. 261, 27 November 1697.
[67] *Ibid.* 6 March 1698 (section on Persia).

England there would have been tumults.[68] These were drastic words. No less drastic were the excuses or explanations from Batavia and Bengal. They were about war, high living costs, desertion by weavers and reelers in Bengal. The Court of Directors in Holland, however, referred to the English company's success in getting silk home. To judge from the text it might seem that the Company had been outdistanced by the English in the silk trade; but this was not so. They still held their own against them, as appears from the following survey, which shows the English and the Dutch imports, respectively, during the years 1698–1700 and the sales from Kamer Amsterdam during the accounting years 1698/99–1700/01.[69]

Table 23. *English and Dutch Imports of Silk 1698–1700. Sales at Kamer Amsterdam 1698/99–1700/01. Ponds.*

	1698 1698/99	1699 1699/1700	1700 1700/01
TOTAL ENGLISH IMPORTS	37,507	37,507	106,469
TOTAL DUTCH IMPORTS	150,180	144,845	169,732
Of which from			
Bengal	72,191	142,189	133,867
Persia	74,090	—	—
China	3,899	2,656	35,865
SALES FROM KAMER AMSTERDAM ...	68,161	77,306	119,711
Of which from			
Bengal	35,742	75,840	109,369
Persia	30,577	—	—
China	1,842	1,466	10,342

[68] *Ibid.* 24 July 1698 (section on Bengal).

[69] The English figures have been taken from Bal Krishna, *op. cit.* p. 146, and are based on "the actual quantities of raw silk imported from the East and recorded in the Custom House." They are means converted into Dutch ponds. Professor Krishna finds that the English imports during these years were negligible. "Except for the two years of 1700–01, the imports were not significant." The background of this estimate is the "out of all proportion ... large quantities demanded in the preceding period" (p. 144), viz. the first half of the 1680's, when according to Professor Krishna the East India Company in 1682 and 1683 asked for more than 10,000 bales of silk per year. He states the demand during the five-year period of 1681–85 to be on an average "574,000 lbs. of 24 ozs. each." If, however, we are to compare the imports about the turn of the century with the imports in the 1680's, it would seem most natural to resort to the East India Company's ledgers in order to trace there the amounts actually received by the company. Such an examination discloses that the East India Company only received between one fifth and one third of the amount demanded in the first half of the 1680's. For the years 1682–1690 the figures are as follows (C. R. O. London, East India Company, Ledgers):

1682	135,566 lbs.	1687	71,292 lbs.
1683	173,087 -	1688	87,637 -
1684	110,106 -	1689	10,477 -
1685	118,877 -	1690	23,186 -
1686	6,702 -		

Although there was a great interest in Bengali silk, the China silk had not dropped out. About the middle of the 1680's there was a short-lived boom for China silk in Nederland. In December 1684 the Heeren XVII wrote that prices had risen to 12.60 fl. per pond. The commodity was in great demand, and the Court of Directors with the usual reservation asked for 30,000 ponds a year. In 1686 it was stated that prices had risen further, but the following year the market had become low. The sales only yielded 8.10 fl. per pond, and the *bewindhebbers* at the conclusion of the sales still had a lot of 20,000 ponds on hand, which they had kept back in order not to depress the market further. In 1688 the price dropped further to 3.90–4.20 fl. per pond, and the Company ceased asking for Chinese silk. The Court of Directors in 1690 stated that the Company had a stock corresponding to two years' sale "en deselve maer omtrent het uytgeleijde gelt off weijnigh meer comt te renderen."[70] In 1696 the picture again changed. The Heeren XVII in a letter to Batavia dated at 15 November mentioned that the abundance of the preceding years, which amongst other things was due to import from England and which had reduced the gross profit to 35 per cent., only, had now been replaced by increasing demand. This was intensified by a shortage of Italian silk. The Company had sold a small quantity of 3,170 ponds at 10.50–10.80 fl. per pond. They were somewhat uncertain as to the future, but did not expect any large-scale fall in prices and therefore wanted a quantity of 20,000–25,000 ponds of Chinese silk among the returns for the year 1698.[71] It seems somewhat surprising, considering that the Company, indeed, from the beginning of the century had imported Chinese silk, in the Seventeen's letters from 1698 to read that people had begun getting accustomed to the use of the China silk in Nederland,[72] which would seem to indicate that this silk previously has been re-exported. The assertion was repeated in several of the following letters.[73] Evidently there was again a boom. In the spring of 1699 the price of 15.00 fl. per pond was stated.[74] The war reduced the Italian production, by which the Dutch Company profited. The orders increased, culminating in 1701 by 40,000 ponds.[75] In 1703 the climax had been passed. Demands had then fallen to 12,000–15,000 ponds and the prices had dropped correspondingly. At the sales in Amsterdam the Company did not get more than 7.20 fl. per pond of Chinese silk, which was a very

[70] Kol. Arch. No. 259, 14 December 1690.
[71] Kol. Arch. No. 261, 15 November 1696.
[72] *Ibid.* 24 July 1698.
[73] E.g. Kol. Arch. No. 262, 25 February and 14 November 1701.
[74] Kol. Arch. No. 261, 6 March 1699.
[75] Kol. Arch. No. 262, 14 November 1701.

unsatisfactory result considering that the silk sold had been purchased at 6.30 fl. per pond. Consequently the cost-price got into the limelight. The order drawn up in 1706 was for 15,000–20,000 ponds conditioned by a cost-price of 5.40–5.60 fl. per pond.[76] The quality of the Chinese silk was criticized, too. The Heeren XVII referred to the fact that the French had brought fine sorts home, some lots of which had reached Nederland.[77] Other complaints of the quality followed, thus the Directors in the following year complained of a parcel of unsaleable silk, which had been "heel vliegigh, hairigh, en snolligh."[78] They also reproached the Batavian Government for having sent more than 40,000 ponds of Chinese silk to Nederland against the Company's orders. Two thirds of this parcel had been bought at 5.40–5.70 fl. per pond from Chinese junks at Batavia, and the Heeren XVII did not think it possible to sell the silk with a profit.[79]

30 to 40 years later the situation was very different. Then the English company had taken the lead as regards the import to Europe of Bengali silk and silk from the East on the whole. While the English import in the decade 1731–40 on an average amounted to 146,887 English lbs. annually, 139,511 English lbs. of which were Bengali silk, the rest Chinese,[80] the Dutch figures for silk offered for sale at all chambers, which in this period fairly corresponds to the supplies as there was no stock in hand worth mentioning, were on an average about 72,500 ponds a year during the five-year period of 1731–35. The Dutch turnover exclusively comprised Bengali silk. Only in 1732 a diminutive quantity of Chinese silk was sold. This development was fatal to the Dutch Company by the fact that it was not only with regard to raw silk that it fell behind. It also applied to the textiles, silks and cottons, both the Bengali textiles, which in this period were the most important, and the others. The Court of Directors were aware of these conditions. So to say constantly the Heeren XVII in their letters to the East complained of expensive purchases, wrong quantities, i.e. quantities which did not correspond to the proportions and designs which they on the basis of the market conditions in Nederland had drawn up. Nor were the qualities of the goods received satisfactory. Time and again they referred to the successful arrangements made by the English. Very characteristically they said in the introduction to their orders for 1737 – drawn up in March 1736[81] – "dat alle de lijwaten, sijde en sijdestoffen tot welkers inkoop soo groote somme van contanten nae Indien worden gesonden goed en kwaat 't een door het ander geree-

[76] Kol. Arch. No. 263, 2 March 1706.
[77] *Ibid.* 27 February 1708.
[78] *Ibid.* 3 April 1709.
[79] *Ibid.*
[80] Bal Krishna, *op. cit.* p. 198.
[81] Kol. Arch. No. 202, 22 March 1736.

kent, ende schade der vermiste, bedurven en gestolen goederen daer op afgereeckent sijnde, maar worden verkogt, geld om geld, houdende de Compagnie d'onkosten van d'equipagie dan nogh aen haar been." It appears from the same letter how this general characterization applies to the individual commodities, *in casu* silk. The Heeren XVII compared one of their demands for *tanni* silk with what they had actually received. The comparison looked as followed:

	Demanded	Received
Tanni A	12,000 ponds	4,097 ponds
B	25,000 -	7,086 -
C	25,000 -	8,953 -
D	10,000 -	19,132 -
E	10,000 -	13,725 -
F	2,000 -	18,367 -
In all...	84,000 ponds	71,360 ponds

Of the first three sorts, which had been sold at a gross profit of 23–24 per cent., the Company had received about 42,000 ponds less than demanded, whereas it had got almost 30,000 ponds more than demanded of the qualities D–F, which had only yielded a gross profit of 1 ½ per cent. These profits were very small, also as compared with the English company's profits, which were maintained to be 50 per cent. on the silk, thus in spite of the fact that the English auction prices were lower than the Dutch. In more than one respect the wrong composition of the silks in the returns was detrimental to the Company. It caused difficulties for the Company in its relations to its greatest customers, the silk manufacturers in Nederland. Thus *tanni* F could only be used for embroidering silk, and the qualities D and E were of no great importance, either. The Heeren XVII therefore concluded their analysis by, as usual, urging cheap and expedient purchases on the lines indicated. The Company could not discontinue its trade in silk "nademael dit een coopmanschap is waer bij niet alleen de Compagnie maar veele duysende van menschen, die van de zijde fabricq dependeeren, in 't vaderlandt moeten bestaan, en die het seekerlijk heel quaad zoude hebben, zoo eens schielijk den aanbreng van zijde men weet niet door wat consternarijen quam agter te blijven."[82]

The Dutch demand during the period from the turn of the century down to about 1740 did not reach the previous levels. From 1701 to 1706 the orders for silk fell from the extraordinarily high level of 290,000 ponds of Bengali silk to 230,000 ponds, after which it was reduced further

[82] *Ibid.*

and in 1712 reached a preliminary low with a demand for 142,000 ponds. Then a series of years followed with increasing demands, culminating in 1719 with a demand for 258,000 ponds, then again a downward tendency followed, with a low about 1728–29, when the Directors only demanded 94,000 ponds a year. Finally the demand was increased in 1730 and in the 1730's kept rather constant at 112,000 ponds. Neither the Chinese nor the Persian silk played any role worth mentioning during these decades. The quantities of Chinese and Persian silk received were very small. After 1716/17 no Persian silk at all was sold at the public sales in Amsterdam, and the sales of Chinese silk were very sporadic. Apart from a sale in the season of 1731/32, no China silk, as mentioned above, was sold in the 1730's. However, there is reason to emphasize the fact that it was not until the end of the 1720's that the English import surpassed the Dutch. Thus the average of the sales at Kamer Amsterdam – i.e. about half of the total sales at all chambers – during the years 1716/17–1727/28 was about 98,000 ponds of Bengali silk a year, while the total English import of the same silk during the 20-year period 1711–1730 amounted to about 68,000 English lbs. a year, to which were added about 5,900 English lbs. of Chinese raw silk.[83]

In the preceding chapter we have dealt with the chief raw article within the group of textiles, – silk. Apart from the invoices 1648–50, when the interruption of the trade to Persia gave rise to an extraordinarily low percentage for silk, the development in broad outline was this: in the beginning of the 17th century silk, as regards invoices, includes about two thirds of the whole group of textiles, about 1670 well over one third, and at the end of the century well over one fourth. Parallelly there was a vigorous growth in the group of textiles as a whole with the result that about 1700 it swallowed up more than half of the total capital placed in the cargoes of the homeward bound East Indiamen, i.e. that essential aspects of the Company's trade in this group of commodities are not illustrated sufficiently by a reference to silk alone. We must therefore try to draw a sketch of the other commodities in the group of textiles, as the main stress, as seen from a European point of view, should be laid on the period after 1670. Be it said at once that the other raw material, cotton, may very well be left out of consideration. It is true that the Dutch Company regularly imported cotton, but it was not a commodity of decisive importance, especially not during the time after 1670. The category which first of all is urgent, includes the piece-goods, the so-called *catoene lijwaten*, next, secondarily, the silks.

[83] Bal Krishna, *op. cit.* p. 198.

CHAPTER VII

Piece-Goods

In 1612 Hendrik Brouwer, later Governor General, wrote about the Coromandel Coast: "De Custe van Coromandel is den slincken arm van de Molucos, gemerckt sonder doecken, van daer comende, de negotie doot is in de Molucos."[1] As emphasized by the Dutch historian, Dr. H. Terpstra, there is hardly any doubt that the establishment of factories in India by the Dutch was first of all due to the need for Indian textiles to be traded to "de Grote Oost." The Coast was the chief supplier of these fabrics. If provided with a good cargo of *kustkleden* one might always count on a commercial profit in the archipelago. Cash and clothes were the only marketable commodities in the exchange with the population of the spice islands, and they also played a great part in the pepper trade. Already in the information given to Steven van der Hagen in 1603 when he left Nederland with a fleet of 13 ships, we find a clear view of the economic advantages to be derived by the Company from the establishment of permanent factories on the Coromandel Coast. The offices established in the course of time were not only situated along the Coast, but inland as well. Their geographical placing was not least determined by the technical specialization of the various areas; thus we may distinguish between North Coromandel, where the best white fabrics, i.e. unpainted fabrics, were made, and South Coromandel, the specialty of which was "pintados" or batik prints. The first contact with the Coromandel Coast took place by way of Achin. It was with an introduction from the Sultan of Achin to the Great Mogul that the Dutch in 1602 sailed to the other great textile area in India, Cambay, in Gujarat,[2] where Surat later became an important station for purchase

[1] Quotation from H. Terpstra, *De Nederlanders in Voor-Indië*, p. 40. The following is mainly based on this work together with Dr. Terpstra's dissertation *De vestiging der Nederlanders aan de kust van Koromandel* (Groningen, 1911) and his *De opkomst der Westerkwartieren van de Oost-Indische Compagnie*, Suratte, Arabië, Perzië ('s-Gravenhage, 1918).

[2] *Indonesian Sociological Studies*, Selected Writings of B. Schrieke, Part I (Selected Studies on Indonesia by Dutch Scholars, vol. 2, The Hague-Bandung, 1955), p. 44.

of the textiles of Northern India. In both cases the Dutch followed the old route of the Indian fabrics to Indonesia, and in both cases the Dutch push took place in competition with the Asiatic trade and in war with the Portuguese as well as in competition with the English East India Company. The Portuguese were not decisively defeated until 1658, when the strategically important Negapatam on the Coromandel Coast was captured. The same year Jafnapatam in Ceylon fell. While Coromandel and Gujarat from the very first years of the Company's existence stood out as main stations in the Company's trade, the third important Indian "textile country", Bengal, did not become of current interest until the second half of the 17th century, Bengal to a certain extent inheriting the position of Coromandel after the Coast had been harried by the great civil wars and thus had passed through the development aptly characterized by Daniel Havart in 1698 in the title of his work *Op- en ondergang van Coromandel.*

The textiles did not all go towards the east. The Portuguese had already cleared the way westwards to Africa and America via Europe for textiles from India. Evidence of this is names like *Guineesche lijwaten* and *negroskleden.* Here, too, the Dutch followed the usual trade routes, but they also took up export to Nederland with a view to creating a market at home. This might seem detrimental to the home linen industry. It should, however, be considered that the export to Europe during the first decades, indeed, probably down to about 1670,[3] was modest and at all events secondary in proportion to the sales in Indonesia. The majority of the textiles imported in Nederland were coarse goods which were re-exported through the West India trade. What was left was not particularly intended for clothing, but was used for table-cloths, rugs, towels, upholstery material, etc. Furthermore, a number of the fabrics were plain and used as basis of calico printing to which should be added the raw material of cotton when discussing the impact of early Indian textiles on Dutch industries. Let us, by way of example, mention what textiles the Heeren XVII in 1617 considered to be saleable in Nederland, including re-exports.[4] They asked for 6,000 pieces of "lijwaten à 2 stuyvers d'elle van 50 ellen lanck," and for 1,000 pieces of "Bengaelsche gingans," which were coloured table-cloths with a check pattern, in all 7,000 pieces. To this must, however, be added the silk fabrics, which were acquired not only by the traffic to India, but also by the intercourse with the Chinese in the archipelago, on Formosa, and elsewhere. The Direc-

[3] Terpstra, *De Nederlanders in Voor-Indië*, p. 62.

[4] Kol. Arch. No. 450, "Aenwijsinge ende particuliere memorie, etc.", dispatched in February 1617.

tors wanted a total of 4,800 pieces, viz. 2,000 pieces of *armozijnen*, i.e. fabrics made of thin silk, named after the town Ormuz, a product typical of Surat, but here, as in the case of the other silk fabrics rather of Chinese make, – 1,600 pieces of satin, furthermore 1,000 pieces of damask, and 200 pieces of velvet. The coloured designs were predominant. Otherwise it is in a number of cases difficult to make any sharp distinction between cottons and silks, as there were intermediary forms. These estimates of the sales may be compared to the statements of the imported textiles in the extant invoice material from the years 1619–21. From this it appears that the concept of "lijwaten" was identical with *guinees*, for the fabrics *montassis*, *bethilles*, and *mouris*, which later in the century were also included in "lijwaten", were listed apart. *Montassis* was a cheap cotton material which was mainly bought in Gujarat, *bethilles* were fine muslin table-cloths, and *mouris* were cheap blue fabrics. We find the following quantities of cottons and silks during these four years:[5]

Table 24. *Total Imports of Cottons and Silks, 1618–21, inclusive.*

Cottons	
Guinees	29,645 pieces
Montassis	6,750 -
Bethilles	100 -
Mouris	900 -
Silks	
Armozijnen	6,601 pieces
Damasten & Satijnen	4,379 -
Sundries	390 -

Guinees were sold in Nederland by the ell, but as the invoices do not indicate how many ells there were to a piece, we cannot make any definite statement as to the gross profit of it.[6] But the quantity of *montassis* listed in the survey was sold to Gerrit van Schoonhoven at a price of 50 st. per piece on 24 March 1622.[7] The cost-price was 3,448 fl. in all, which meant that the Company's gross profit was 484 per cent. The profit on the silks was more moderate. A quantity of 1,381 pieces of *armozijnen*, the cost-price of which had been 6,999 fl., was in September 1620 sold to Sr Jasper Wickevoort at a price of 9 fl. 5 st. per piece, which

[5] The number of *guinees* in 1619 has been estimated at about 11,000 pieces in 495 *packen*.

[6] A rough estimate looks like this: in 1617 one piece was stated to be of the standard measure of 50 *ellen*. Hence the selling price in Nederland in 1621 of one piece was 17.81 fl. and the gross profit about 250 per cent. Correspondingly the gross profit of another lot sold in the same year was about 235 per cent.

[7] Kol. Arch. No. 249, 24 March 1622.

yielded a gross profit of 82.5 per cent. The same merchant furthermore bought 956 pieces of *satijnen* at 24 fl. 5 st. per piece. The Company's cost-price in the East had been 11,670 fl. Consequently the gross profit was about 100 per cent.[8]

It is impossible to determine the origin of the fabrics from the invoices. However, it can hardly be a great mistake to assume that the majority of the silks during the first decades were of Chinese origin. In the extant orders from the 1630's the silks normally appear as Chinese. In an order drawn up in the autumn of 1633 the Heeren XVII asked for 50,000 fl. worth of silks, viz. "damasten en gefigureerde armozijnen meest coleurden en weijninge witte,"[9] and the following year they ordered to the same amount "aen Chineesche manifacturen, geen manifacturen die swart sijn."[10] In 1636 the amount was increased to 80–100,000 fl. to buy "alderhande goede Chineesche sijde manufacturen."[11] Similarly, in the case of the cottons it may be assumed that the majority of *guinees* originated from the Coromandel Coast, as on several occasions it was remarked that the *guinees* of the Coast should be preferred to those of Surat. During the 1630's and 1640's some new types were added to the above-mentioned kinds of fabrics, but *guinees* continued being the chief category. In 1631 the Heeren XVII ordered 400 "balen groff guinees lijwaet" to a total amount of 38,000 fl., besides "fijne lijwaten" to the amount of 25,000 fl. In 1633 the order was for 500 bales of *guinees*, one third of which was to be unbleached. The following year this order was repeated, but now with the postscript that one fourth should be "rouw". It may be estimated that 400–500 bales correspond to 8–10,000 pieces of *guinees*.[12] Below we shall render the order drawn up in November 1642, which is remarkable for its details as well as by the fact that the Heeren XVII have indicated the cost-prices which the Batavian Government ought to aim at.

[8] *Ibid.* 11 September 1620.
[9] Kol. Arch. No. 250, 17 September 1633.
[10] *Ibid.* August 1634.
[11] *Ibid.* September 1636.
[12] Moreland writes about a Dutch order from 1639 for 500 bales of *guinees* (longcloth) that "it would represent the equivalent of nearly 20,000 pieces of calico of the standard length," *op. cit.* p. 133. The standard length is given as 30–40 yards (*ibid.* p. 130). This conversion is correct, but can hardly apply to the Dutch pieces of *guinees*. In the invoices from the 1620's *guinees* are entered in packs or *corge*, which mainly were of 20–22 pieces. In Hindi *corge* denotes a number of 20, a figure which is often found in the conversions of the invoices. In our opinion the bales in the letters of the Heeren XVII therefore refer to *corges* or packs. This also agrees with the fact that the total purchase in the order of 1631 of 400 bales was calculated to cost 38,000 fl., which gives a cost price per piece of 4.75 fl., on the assumption that 1 bale = 1 corge. If we use Moreland's formula, the cost price becomes almost half of that of the 1620's. In the order of 1617 the piece of *lijwaten* was indicated to be 50 *ellen* long, and the cost price was booked at 2 *stuivers* per *el*, i.e. 5 fl. per piece. This length corresponds to about 34.50 m. and thus is in good agreement with Moreland's standard of 30–40 yards = 27.42–36.56 m.

Table 25.
Order Sent in 1642. Qualities and Estimated Purchase.

		COTTONS	
8–10,000	pieces	*Guinees*	60,000 fl.
6–8,000	-	*Bethilles*	31,500 -
6–8,000	-	*Mouris*	42,000 -
2–3,000	-	*Parcallen*	7,500 -
3,000	-	*Salempouris*	16,500 -
800–1,000	-	*Casse Bengale*	6,300 -
500	-	*Mallemollen*	3,500 -
500	-	*Semianen*	2,000 -
500	-	*Amberlijs*	2,000 -
2,000	-	*Chiauters-deriabadis*	4,000 -
2,000	-	*Adathaijs*	7,000 -
1,000	-	*Mamoedijs*	10,000 -
2,000	-	*Baftas, witte breede*	10,000 -
2,000	-	- *, swarte* -	12,000 -
500	-	- *, blauwe* -	3,000 -
2,000	-	- *, witte smalle*	6,000 -
500	-	*Lijwaten, geverfde*	1,500 -
500–1,000	-	*Gingans*	4,100 -
500	-	*Chalon gingans*	1,750 -
4,000	-	*Suratse kleeden*	10,000 -
2,000	-	*Negroskleeden, geschild:*	4,000 -
1,000	-	*Lijwaten, fijne*	2,600 -
		SILKS	
—	-	*"Zijde lakenen"*	150 à 200,000 -
50–100	-	*Japanse rokken*	2,800 -

This was an order for a total of 53,800–61,500 pieces of cottons to a cost-price of 246,250 fl., which, however, only corresponded to 7.7 per cent. of the 3.2 mill. which was the total of the order. Among the new qualities there may be reason to point out *salempouris*, a multicoloured fabric which in the course of time became a great article. Similarly *baftas*, which was a widespread name of fine cotton cloths with a great market in Asia. The best ones were considered to be the *baftas* from Broach (Gujarat).

The order mentioned above on the whole corresponded to the orders sent through the 1640's. If it is asked how they were executed, the answer may be found in the invoice material, from which we have borrowed the following figures for the years 1648–50. They cover all the homeward-bound ships.

	Cottons Received	Invoice Value
1648:	49,632 pieces............	228,618 fl.
1649:	40,155 -	182,839 -
1650:	55,128 -	256,702 -

Apart from a single parcel of Japanese kimonos Nederland in these years got no silks. The order for the years 1649 and 1650 was for 80,000 fl. in silks – though no black, grey, argentine, or sulphur-coloured – and the order was drawn up on the assumption that the fabrics could be dispensed with in the Japanese trade. As to the cottons received they corresponded to about 10.7 per cent. of the total value of the returns; the composition was in broad outline as desired. A calculation of the average price of the whole shows that it was from 4.6 to 5 fl. per piece of cotton fabric. At the public sales in the season of 1649/50 at Kamer Amsterdam a total of 22,946 pieces of various cottons was sold at an average price of 14.34 fl. per piece, and in the season of 1650/51 33,547 pieces were sold at an average price of 12.32 fl. per piece. Hence, we may very roughly estimate that there was a total gross profit of about 150–240 per cent. per season. While the Indian cost-price in 1620/21 was 4.7–5.1 fl. per piece of *guinees*, the Heeren XVII in the order drawn up in 1642 counted on about 6.7 fl. per piece. In the invoices of 1648/50 the cost-price of *guinees* was 5.6–6.0 fl. per piece.

Taking stock of the development down to the middle of the 17th century, we find an increase in the number of imported cotton fabrics from the order of 1617 for 7,000 pieces and an average import during the four-year period of 1619/21 of at least 9,350 pieces to the order of 1642 for 53,800–61,500 pieces and the average import during the three-year period of 1648/50 of 48,305 pieces. *Guinees* throughout the period constituted the chief single group. The cross section of 1648/50 shows that the piece-goods were becoming a highly specialized category covering a range of widely different fabrics, from fine muslins to canvas, but with the main stress laid on the coarse fabrics which were re-exported, and household textiles.[13] It is also evident that the textiles during this period from the Company's point of view were pronouncedly Asiatic goods. What was shipped to Nederland had not so great a share as

[13] Moreland has described the corresponding English trade in the following way: "The period with which we are dealing [i.e. from Akbar to Aurangzeb] does not cover the remarkable change in European fashions which occurred in the second half of the century. Up to the year 1660 there was practically no demand for muslin or prints as apparel; such dress-goods as were carried westwards were destined almost entirely for Africa or America, where the trade had been established by the Portuguese, and we are concerned in this section mainly with the adoption of Indian calico to meet European household needs – tablecloths, bed-linen, napkins, or towels – and to a very small extent with the use of Indian coloured for fancy goods as hangings or for decorative purposes", *op. cit.* p. 123.

regards invoices and sales. As stated by Moreland it was the English company which opened the West European market to cotton fabrics. The Dutch Company was more unobtrusive, perhaps in order not to compete with the staple commodity of the home country, linen, perhaps because Batavia offered a greater selection of returns, whereas the English traders to India often found it difficult to find return cargoes and therefore resorted to the textiles for want of something better.[14] The English import down to about 1646 obtained the majority of its textiles from Gujarat, Agra, and Sind, while the supplies from Coromandel only later became predominant. It is, however, impossible to draw a comparison between the two companies because the English import down to about 1646 laid the main stress on *baftas*, *semianen*, and other textiles from Surat, while the Dutch Company, as shown above, concentrated on *guinees*. A comparison in number of pieces does not yield much as the sizes are widely different. Thus the English import in 1619 by the "Royal Anne"[15] was of about 14,000 pieces of textiles of the ordinary length of 12–15 yards, while the Dutch ship "De swarte Beer" in the same year brought home on a rough estimate 10,800 pieces of *guinees*, which had a length of 30–40 yards. If we take the cost-price as standard, the value of the fabrics imported by the "Royal Anne" was 80,561 *mamoedijs*, i.e. £ 4,028,[16] while the fabrics of "De swarte Beer" cost 56,957 fl. According to the rate of exchange at Amsterdam[17] the English cost-price corresponded to 42,294 fl. In this case the Dutch import as regards invoice value must be rated higher than the English import, although the relation is the opposite as seen from a purely quantitative point of view, which alone is based on the actually incommensurable numbers of pieces. Unfortunately we do not know the value of the English import of piece-goods through a prolonged period. The Court of Directors of the English East India Company in the 1620's ordered a huge quantity of textiles from the factory in Surat, and the idea of the leading position of the English company is not least based on this demand. Thus it may be mentioned that in 1625 more than 200,000 pieces were ordered.[18] The famine in Gujarat in 1630 checked the activities, and the orders of the English company dropped to 100–120,000 pieces "calicoes, together with small quantities of fancy goods."[19] The 1630's were characterized by difficulties as regards the supplies to Europe. The immense distance which might occur between the quantities ordered and those actually

[14] *Ibid.* [15] *Ibid.* p. 126.
[16] One *mamudi* equals one shilling, cf. Bal Krishna, *op. cit.* p. 59.
[17] 19 August 1619: London 35 *schellingen*, cf. Posthumus, *op. cit.*
[18] Moreland, *op. cit.* p. 126. [19] *Ibid.* p. 127.

delivered, appears from the English Court of Directors' complaints in 1636, when "the factors were severely reprimanded for having provided only £ 1269 worth of calico against orders for £ 32,500 given in the previous five years."[20] The result of the reprimand was "a large consignment sent home by way of Surat in January 1639." It was worth 412,400 *mamoedijs*, i.e. £ 20,620, and included 66,141 pieces of textiles, 18,225 of them originating from Coromandel and 38,883 from Gujarat.[21] Moreland supposes that the trade during the following decade "was not expanding beyond the standard of 1640." Still, a great private import probably took place during the years when the trade practically was open, "for when the Company's monopoly was restored the English market was found to be greatly overstocked."[22] The £ 20,620 mentioned in 1639 corresponded to 222,696 fl.[23] As shown above, the Dutch Company's order in 1642 was for 246,250 fl. worth of textiles, and its actual import during the three-year period of 1648/50 was on an average 222,720 fl. worth of textiles per year. It is thus difficult immediately to accept the idea of the English company's leading position. We shall restrict ourselves to stating that the English company's demands for piece-goods from Surat in the 1620's were overwhelming. On the assumption that these orders were executed, the English import during this period was much greater than the Dutch. But the two companies' import during the 1630's and 1640's presumably were of fairly the same order of magnitude. A contributory circumstance may have been the fact that the English because of the failing possibilities of supplies from Gujarat in the 1630's were forced to attempt purchasing the piece-goods on the Coromandel Coast, where the Dutch Company held a secure position.

The simplest way in which to acquire the textiles was to buy them all ready from the Indian traders. These might be individual merchants or guildsmen. Pieter van Dam tells about the cloth merchants in Masulipatam on the Coromandel Coast that they were organized in four companies, "ieder met een hooft en secunde vorsien, maeckende te samen uyt een getal van 69 persoonen."[24] From such trading companies, which with their often considerable capitals were capable of effecting greater transactions than the individual merchants, the Company with sufficient funds in hand or with the necessary credit might rapidly secure large quantities of cloth. Already in the first years of their stay in Coromandel, however, we see the servants of the Dutch Company go direct to the

[20] *Ibid.* p. 128. [21] *Ibid.* pp. 101 and 129. [22] *Ibid.* p. 131.
[23] The rate of exchange has been estimated at 36 *schellingen*, cf. Posthumus, *op. cit.*
[24] Quoted from Terpstra, *De Nederlanders in Voor-Indië*, p. 63.

producers and place orders with the weavers and printers, hand in patterns, order definite designs, qualities, etc. The Company engaged in business by contracts. The best time in which to come to agreements with the artisans was in August or September. The textiles then might be expected to be finished and brought to the warehouses on the Coast for shipping in February or March. Normally the producers received part of the price agreed on in advance ("op de hand"). This is known from the first agreement, made in 1606, between the Company and the King of Golkonda. The King here promised "dat alle wevers, schilders, smits en alderhande ambaghtluijden, voor de Comp^{e} werckende offte gelt in handen hebbende, van wegen den Koningh offte ijmandt anders niet en zullen gemoeijt worden, tot dat het werck voldaen zij."[25] The Company got still closer to the production where they succeeded in taking the lease of the artisans' settlements – identical with the workshops. In this way the Company not only could exclude middleman's business, but also prevent that the weavers, printers, washers, etc., worked for other European or Indian competitive buyers. The artisans at the same time were protected from the often oppressive or arbitrary taxes and duties. As an example of this type Dr. Terpstra mentions the area Daatzerom with the two villages Golepalem and Gondewaron, which in 1676 was rented from the King of Golconda, which agreement in 1689, when Golconda had been conquered by Aurangzeb, was confirmed by the Emperor. Finally, the Company had factories in which Indian artisans worked under the supervision of the Dutch. As early as 1609 we find a number of 30 printers attached direct to the Company's factory at Tierepopelier. In some cases the Company owned the installations for the manufacture of the textiles, thus in Tegenapatam it had a dyeing-works, and Pieter van Dam relates how the Dutch in a small village an hour's walk from Nagelwanze had "een bleeckery opgeregt, wassers en kloppers uyt verscheyde quartieren byeenversamelt, en 't werck soo aan de gangh gekregen."[26]

It is obvious that the Indian textiles belonged to those commodities which made the greatest demands for technical knowledge. The process of manufacture was complicated. If, e.g., it was a question of making a woven fabric suitable for printing or painting, the raw cloth was first steeped in a kind of tanning material, then beaten "tender" with wooden sticks on benches. The contours of the motifs were indicated with charcoal on the fabric by means of a paper stencil and the lines were inked in with an iron solution. With an extract of sapan wood to which alum

[25] *Ibid.* p. 64. [26] Quoted from *ibid.* p. 66.

was added, the outlines of the figures which were to stand out in red were drawn. Next the fabric was boiled in water and afterwards was worked up with a decoction of goat's dung. Then it was bleached in the sun and later boiled again a few times. All these processes were introductions to the painting itself, which was started with the blue indigo colour, a system being used which from the Coromandel Coast was transferred to the Javanese art of batik printing, aiming at covering the areas of the fabric with wax which should not be blue (or green), after which the fabric was boiled blue in indigo. Then the artisans got busy with the other colours, which were painted direct on the fabric. The phases of this complicated process were executed by specialists, weavers, washers, beaters, dyers, etc. It soon proved necessary to have an insight in the technique if the Company should take part in the old export of Indian fabrics to the Moluccas, Indonesia, and other areas. As to the varieties, their name is Legion, a fact which explains the Dutch Company's eagerness to direct the production. With the increasing European demand influenced by fashion supervision of the manufacture became still more essential, and the most decisive competition between the European companies actually took place in the small Indian villages. In the 17th century the competition was first of all between the English and the Dutch Company. It became more and more pronounced as the century was drawing to its close. To this was added the activities of *La Grande Compagnie des Indes Orientales* founded in 1664. The companies took artisans from one another, tried to move them from district to district. Thus the Heeren XVII in 1698 gave orders to attempt a transfer of weavers from Pondicherry, where the best *guinees* were made at that time, to Negapatam, as the Company according to the conclusion of the peace with France was obliged to surrender Pondicherry to the French.[27] Or another event from the same year. The English had provided a great many textiles from the Sadraspatam area south of St. Thomé, and the Dutch Company supposed that their competitors intended to lease the neighbouring Alamparwe, well-known for its good weavers and painters. The requisite authorization was rapidly obtained from the presidency of the Coast, and the Dutch succeeded in snatching the lease of Alamparwe under the very nose of the English.

As pointed out by Professor Khan the English East India Company during the years 1665—1680 changed its commercial policy. It turned from the raw materials and the coarse textiles to the worked up, finer commodities. "We resolve to drive our trade through ... especially in

[27] Kol. Arch. No. 261, 24 July 1698.

silks and calicoes," wrote the London directors in 1683 to their officials in India.[28] The import created a demand, and the demand was covered by a new import. The last decades of the century were characterized by "the Indian Craze", the forerunner and counterpart of the later Chinese fashion in the 18th century. It is not our task here to describe this fashion,[29] only to point it out as an active economic factor. As appears from the analyses in Chapter II, fashion did not only change the structure of the English, but also that of the Dutch East India trade. If we are to believe Cary's pamphlet of 1699, the craze set in in the 1680's: "It was scarce thought about twenty years since that we should ever see Calicoes, the ornaments of our greatest Gallants (for such they are whether we call them Muslins, Shades or anything else) when they were then rarely used ... but now few think themselves well dresst till they are made up in Calicoes, both men and women, Calico Shirts, Neckcloths, Cuffs, Pocket-handkerchiefs for the former, Head-Dresses, Nightroyls, Hoods, Sleeves, Aprons, Gowns, Petticoats and what not, for the latter, besides India-Stockings for both Sexes."[30] It was a race for procuring novelties. "Now this for a constant and generall Rule," wrote the English company's directors in 1681, "that in all flowered Silks you change ye fashion and flower as much as you can every year, for English Ladies and they say ye French and other Europeans will give twice as much for a new thing not seen in Europe before, though worse, then they will give for a better silk for (of) the same fashion worn ye former years."[31] The companies watchfully analysed their competitor's returns. The English East India Company sent samples procured from Holland[32] in orders for its servants in India, or, as in 1683, demanded a large number of chintzes with the addition "they being the ware of gentlewomen in Holland."[33] Corresponding examples might be adduced from the Dutch Company's records. The tendency was towards finer textiles. The Indian silks replaced the Chinese ones in the homeward-bound cargoes, and above all Bengal emerged as the country of unexpected possibilities.

Turning to the Dutch Company's activities during the years after 1650 we may on the basis of the sales at Kamer Amsterdam give the following figures for the turnover of cottons, partly in pieces, partly in fl., in five-year totals for the period 1649/50–1733/34.[34]

[28] Vilh. Slomann, *Bizarre Designs in Silks*, Trade and Traditions (Published for the Ny Carlsberg Foundation, Copenhagen, 1953), p. 107; S. A. Khan, *The East India Trade in the 17th Century* (Oxford, 1923), p. 256. [29] Cf. Slomann, *op. cit.*

[30] J. Cary, *A Discourse Concerning the East India Trade* (London, 1699), p. 4, quoted from Slomann, *op. cit.* p. 104 Note 1.

[31] Quoted from Slomann, *op. cit.* p. 114.

[32] *Ibid.* p. 113. [33] *Ibid.* p. 115. [34] Regarding the sources see Appendix B, pp. 272 ff.

Table 26. *Sales of Cottons at Kamer Amsterdam, 1649/50–1733/34. Five-year Totals.*

Five-years	Quantities	Value	Five-years	Quantities	Value
	1,000 pieces	1,000 fl.		1,000 pieces	1,000 fl.
1649/50–53/54 ...	208	2,862	1694/95–98/99 ...	846	7,931
1654/55–58/59 ...	241	2,930	1699/00–03/04 ...	930	8,758
1659/60–63/64 ...	225	2,824	1704/05–08/09 ...	819	10,475
1664/65–68/69 ...	214	2,585	1709/10–13/14 ...	980	10,715
1669/70–73/74 ...	357	3,678	1714/15–18/19 ...	1,068	11,494
1674/75–78/79 ...	329	2,886	1719/20–23/24 ...	1,257	11,259
1679/80–83/84 ...	619	4,855	1724/25–28/29 ...	1,192	11,791
1684/85–88/89 ...	1,119	8,392	1729/30–33/34 ...	625	6,640
1689/90–93/94 ...	542	5,919			

The figures agree with the impression of an increase in the interest in cottons after 1670 and a boom in the 1680's obtained by a study of the Heeren XVII's orders. The complexity of the orders as regards qualities, however, makes it convenient to prefer the quantities sold as a guide to supply and demand on the Dutch market. The more so, as the accountants made a collocation of the very comprehensive and, because of lack of acquaintance with a number of textiles, so undeterminable category of "catoene lijwaten". The impression is also corroborated if we compare the section analysis of 1668/70 of the return cargoes with the corresponding analysis of 1698/1700. These analyses, furthermore, show a general increase in the cost-prices. Of the familiar *guinees* the average price in 1668/70 was about 8 fl. per piece, which is an increase from the section of 1648/50 adduced above, even when considering the changes during the intervening period, when the distinction between "light" and "heavy" *stuivers* was introduced. The cost-prices here are expressed in "light" *stuivers* or fl. In 1698/1700 the average price had increased still more, being 10 fl. per piece of *guinees*. Next, the analysis of 1698/1700 shows what an immense importance the Bengali area had acquired during the intervening about 30 years as a supplier of textiles to Nederland. While the analysis of 1668/70 is not in its structure essentially different from the analysis of 1648/50, the picture is very different in 1698/1700. It is true that we cannot with certainty determine the origin of the textiles in the analyses down to 1668/70 inclusive on the basis of the invoices. We can make a rough estimate from the names of the commodities and otherwise judge about the figures from the information of the general missives and the information from the individual districts. In the invoices from the turn of the century, on the other hand, the commodities are specified according to areas, which allows the following survey as regards the textiles.

Table 27. *Geographical Analysis of Piece-Goods in Return Cargoes 1697.*

	Invoice Values
Bengal	1,297,161 fl.
Coromandel	626,879 -
Tongking, China, Japan	283,570 -
Tutucorin	101,117 -
Surat	44,078 -
In all	2,352,805 fl.

It is seen that more than half of the textiles came from Bengal. The Company's total import in the year in question was to the amount of 5.4 mill. fl. Goods to an amount of nearly 1.75 mill. fl. or just under one third of the total originated from Bengal. The share of Surat in the returns is remarkably low. As to this we should no doubt take into consideration the tense conditions in Gujarat, although the Coromandel Coast and Bengal as well were characterized by unrest. If at this stocktaking, as above, we attempt a comparison with the English Asiatic trade, there is, as before, the difficulty that the value of the English imports of textiles is unknown. On the other hand, the value of the total import in 1698 was stated to be 356,509 £ sterling.[35] On the assumption that half of the import consisted of textiles, the two English companies consequently invested about £ 180,000 in East India textiles, while the value of the Dutch import – 11 fl. being reckoned as equivalent to 1 £ sterling – corresponded to nearly £ 214,000. The Dutch Company still maintained its leading position, but it was a near thing. The competition was severe.

An important phase in this struggle between the two competitors was introduced about the middle of the 1690's at a time when the old East India Company was hard pressed in English home politics. The interlopers successfully organized an opposition against the company's monopoly, and Child's seizure of the interloping ship "Redbridge" added fuel to the flames of the opposition. In January 1694 Parliament declared that all English subjects had equal rights to trade to the Indies. The following year the Scottish Parliament by law founded a Scottish East India Company, which, however, the English East India Company at first succeeded in making the King abolish. More serious were the complaints lodged against the old company for bribery of members of Parliament, which led Child and several directors to a short stay in

[35] Bal Krishna, *op. cit.* p. 137 Note 1.

the Tower. The English producers and merchants of woollens, badly battered by the increasing import of calicoes and silks, were not slow to participate in the attacks, the workers demonstrated; in short, public opinion demanded the dissolution of the East India Company.[36] In December 1695 the Heeren XVII wrote to Batavia that the Dutch with all means should further the trade in the East now that "d' Engelsen soodaenigh in onmaght sijn."[37] The *bewindhebbers* therefore had decided to send 3.2 mill. fl. in cash to the East, to which should be added the payment of an amount of 600,000 fl. in bills of exchange, besides a consignment to a value of nearly 400,000 fl., which amounted to a total of 4.2 mill. fl. (or 5.25 mill. fl. in "light" money) for the trade. It was hoped that this provision of fresh capital would result in considerable return cargoes and put an end to the usual complaints from Batavia of shortage of Indian trade capital. The Court of Directors made it abundantly clear that the Bengal factories should first of all be provided with money. The order for fine Bengali piece-goods had been increased, as they yielded the greatest profits, whereas the number of *guinees* and coarse Surat fabrics had been reduced, as they did not yield anything worth mentioning and furthermore took up more space in the ships than the fine textiles. The following year the Heeren XVII laid down as a rule for the cases in which not all the Company's Asiatic offices could have their wishes for cash fulfilled, that they should have allocations in proportion to their sizes, though with the exception of Bengal. This district must not suffer any want.[38] An interesting feature was the Seventeen's proposal to hold back as regards the factories which had no great results to show, e.g. the factory in Japan, where for some years considerable sums had been idle.[39] In a situation in which the factory Nederland had great profits, especially on Bengali goods, the trade capital ought to be directed according to the consideration for this. The profits on the Coromandel textiles were not satisfactory. The Directors complained that the gathering of textiles on the Coast was too slow and took place at rising prices. The Dutch Court of Directors greatly reduced a number of assortments of fabrics from the Coast, while other qualities dropped out completely, as e.g. in the case of canvas. In 1697 the Heeren XVII complained that the Company still received textiles which had been discarded from the orders, with the result that at the sales they had to be repurchased by the Company, because they had not been able to fetch the cost-price.

[36] M. E. Wilbur, *The East India Company and the British Empire in the Far East* (New York, 1945), p. 138 *et seq.*

[37] Kol. Arch. No. 260, 5 December 1695.

[38] Kol. Arch. No. 261, 15 November 1696. [39] *Ibid.* 27 March 1697.

The Company also in 1696 from Surat had received 35,470 pieces of black *baftas* and 12,900 pieces of black *hannekins*. Thus in spite of the fact that the Directors as early as 1692 had stated that they did not want any of these Surat *baftas* and *hannekins* as they were not marketable. The supply of the *baftas* was due to the fact that in Batavia they had on hand large stores which could not be sold in Asia. In 1694 the stock was of more than 85,000 pieces, which was increased the same year by a consignment from Surat of more than 63,000 pieces of *baftas*.[40]

In the summer of 1698 the Heeren XVII had become aware that a large number of interlopers had left England for India, either direct or by way of Cadiz. To this should be added the shipments of the English and the Scottish companies and the increased activities of the French. It looked like a conspiracy, "maar om dat wij niet geern souden sien dat sij boven ons quamen te triumpheren,"[41] the Directors gave orders for forestalling, especially in pepper, piece-goods, raw silk, and saltpetre. The factors should be allowed to pay more than ordinary prices for the products mentioned and otherwise put obstacles in the way for the competitors. Purchases would be accepted of textiles which were not of the very best quality. The important thing was to deprive the new East Indiamen of any hope of profit by forcing up their cost-prices and dumping the selling prices in Europe. The fact that the Dutch Company did not control the market, however, appeared from a worried remark in the same letter, in which the Heeren XVII lamented over the fact that four ships of the English company and one interloper in the spring of 1698 had carried home just as many fine fabrics as the whole of the Dutch homeward-bound fleet. The Directors ironically asked whether there were no war, famine, and shortage where the English were trading. The supply of coarse fabrics had also been unsatisfactory. It was especially the gathering of *guinees* and *salempouris* on the Coromandel Coast that failed. The Directors suggested that it should be attempted to transfer the production of these goods to Bengal, or, if possible, to supplement the deficiency on the Coast. On this point, too, the English according to the Heeren XVII's statement had been more successful. Complaints of the same character during the following years almost became set phrases in the *bewindhebbers*' letters to the Governor General and Council. The Batavian Government and the servants pleaded in their defence that they had too little money to fulfil the greedy wishes of Nederland. They referred to the fact that the English paid in cash and so got the best commodities. Or they only stated as the reason "het woelen der Engel-

[40] *Ibid.* [41] *Ibid.* 24 July 1698.

schen."[42] The Heeren XVII in reply attacked the practice of the factories of paying money in advance to the Indian merchants and artisans so that the Company was precluded from rejecting poor supplies.

Exports of bullion and specie were immense in these years, thus in 1700 greater than ever. The Heeren XVII's order in this connexion were for buying up everything and storing what could not be included in the return cargoes.[43] An attempt at moving the production of *guinees* from Coromandel to Surat was not successful. In February 1701 the Directors stated that the new Surat *guinees* were of too heavy material. They had yielded a small profit at the sales. The suggestion was repeated of attempting a production in Bengal. At the sales in October they had to hold back the Chinese silks because they could not yield the cost-price; they were struck off the orders with a remark that as long as the English asserted themselves so powerfully in the China trade, there would hardly be any change in this fact. The piece-goods from Bengal were not up to mark, either; neither as regards quality nor designs. Not least the fact that the cost-price of the textiles received in 1701 was about 20 per cent. higher than that of the supply of the preceding year contributed to the reduction of the profits. On the other hand, the consignments from Coromandel were highly praised. An abundant consignment of fabrics gladdened the hearts of the Heeren XVII. They stated their hopes that the improvement would continue "om als wackere coopluijden sigh door onse competiteuren niet te laten versnellen."[44] Aurangzeb's death in 1707 made the Directors hope for another flourishing period for the Coast.[45] A short interval in the general complaints of expensive and poor return cargoes occurred in 1704. The Bengali piece-goods were praised, thus also in 1705, when the textiles from Coromandel were characterized as better and cheaper than before. Especially the collection from Porto Novo was praised. On the other hand, the fine Bengali fabrics received in 1708 were unsatisfactory. The Heeren XVII ascribed this to the fact that the Government had agreed to liberalize the trade in Bengal, i.e. that the Company's servants had been allowed to trade on their own account.[46] In 1710 we find again the old note in the Heeren XVII's missives. The quality of the fine Bengali cottons was again the stumbling-block. The Directors referred to the English company's better qualities, obtained in spite of the fact that the English "aldaer geen vrijer negotie als wij sijn hebbende."[47] They accused the Company's factories of putting aside the most profitable assortments for their own benefit. Two years later the

[42] Kol. Arch. No. 262, 14 November 1701.
[43] *Ibid.* 21 September 1700.
[44] *Ibid.* 14 November 1701.
[45] Kol. Arch. No. 263, 3 April 1709.
[46] *Ibid.*
[47] Kol. Arch. No. 264, 4 March 1710.

Directors thought that the cause of the unsatisfactory supplies was that the merchants in Bengal were too late with their contractual supplies of textiles so that there was no time to reject the inferior qualities and secure substitutes. The factories were ordered to make new contracts.[48] The unsettled conditions in Bengal, however, had their share in the responsibility for the dear purchases, as, indeed, the Heeren XVII realized. Still, there were limits to acceptable prices, and in 1713 the Directors for the first time ventilated the idea of restricting the demands from Bengal because of the poor profits in Nederland.[49] The consignments from Coromandel, on the other hand, on the whole were good during those years. The qualities and cost-prices were praised; only in 1712 the Directors complained of having received too large quantities of piece-goods from the Coast, considerably more than desired, for which reason the prices had fallen at the sales.[50]

In a missive of 9 March 1716 the Heeren XVII wrote that it was a unanimous complaint among the Dutch merchants who for many years had been dealing in East India fabrics that the Company's auction goods from year to year had become poorer in quality and more expensive to buy. This condition had developed to such a degree that there were now qualities of manufactured goods which the Company bought in India at prices that were higher or almost as high as the prices at which the English sold the same commodity in Europe.[51] It was not least Bengal that was in the limelight. In the same missive the Heeren XVII appealed to the Bengali factories to make a special contribution, "dat de Nederlandsche Comp: door de meerder industrie der Engelsse en andere natien niet verder gepostponeert werdt."[52] Apparently these tickings off were of no great avail. The initiative had slipped out of the hands of the Dutch. Two years later, in 1718, the Heeren XVII complained that "de Bengaalse goederen dit jaar wederom wel 20 pCent hoger zijn ingekoft dan het jaar te voren."[53] The dissatisfaction amongst other things concerned muslin, which had been spoilt during the transport, because the white fabric interwoven with gold threads had been packed too close to the spices, the smell of which spoilt the gold threads. Later it was said that the muslin had been faked, having been interwoven with red copper instead of gold.[54]

To these, one might almost say, ordinary complaints then were added the complaints of the Ostend company's disturbing competition. On the

[48] *Ibid.* 10 March 1712.
[49] *Ibid.* 8 March 1713.
[50] *Ibid.* 10 March 1712.
[51] Kol. Arch. No. 198, 9 March 1716.
[52] *Ibid.*
[53] *Ibid.* 3 March 1718.
[54] Kol. Arch. No. 199, 3 March 1722.

English pattern the Ostenders concentrated on the import of Chinese fabrics. As mentioned above, Chinese silks for periods in the 17th century constituted an important group among the textiles, but the Dutch Company dropped them in the 1690's, when the Bengali silks became the fashionable goods *par excellence*. The English company had continued importing China silks and on the whole laid the greatest stress on the trade to China. In this respect the English were more far-sighted than the Dutch. The trade to China in the course of the first decades of the 18th century came to play a very great part in the Northwest European traffic to the East. About the turn of century the increasing English trade to China was the subject of a discussion between the Heeren XVII and the Governor General and Council in Batavia. The result of the discussion was that it was decided to do nothing about it apart from maintaining the old connexion with the Chinese junks in Batavia. The Heeren XVII characterized the English trade as speculative without any appreciable, or at any rate only a transient profit. The grapes were sour. Actually the Directors of the Dutch Company did not feel capable of preventing the English trade to China. It was consequently questionable "of het all met de ware koopmans maximes is overeenkomende, dat men sigh selfs evidentelijck schade toebrenght om een ander in de wegh off naedeligh to sijn."[55] The Company had to readjust this evaluation when in the beginning of the 1720's it was evident that the Ostenders advantageously imported considerable quantities of Chinese silks. In February 1723 the Heeren XVII's missive to Batavia had enclosed in it a list of the Ostend company's chief designs with a request to order the fabrics with the Chinese junks in Batavia. The purpose was the double one of getting a share in the profit and at the same time to make purchases difficult for the Belgian company.[56] A number of similar lists followed. It appears from the Seventeen's discussions that the Ostenders also disturbed them in the traffic in Bengali textiles. In February 1725 the Heeren XVII stated that an Ostend ship had just arrived with a full cargo of well sorted Bengali textiles of the same good quality as the English returns.[57] The silks received by the Dutch Company from China by way of Batavia proved a disappointment. The sales in the winter of 1726 and 1727 were characterized by greatly declining prices – cf. statistics – and some of the Chinese silks, e.g. *damasten*, had to be held back in 1727,[58] for which reason they dropped out of the orders for some time. The qualities of the cottons were not commendable, either. A number of them were

[55] Kol. Arch. No. 262, 14 November 1701.
[56] Kol. Arch. No. 200, 24 February 1723.
[57] *Ibid.* 26 February 1725.
[58] Kol. Arch. No. 201, 8 March 1728.

discoloured, which by the Directors was attributed to moistness at the packing. The English profitably imported *atlassen*, but the Dutch Company did not receive any *atlassen* in spite of their positive order for them. On this point the complaint bore fruit. *Atlassen* were received from Surat, though only to cause another reprimand from the apparently never satisfied Court of Directors: "de Suratse atlassen sijn seer slegt bevonden."[59] In the beginning of the 1730's some years followed about which it should in fairness be stated that the Heeren XVII on the whole were satisfied with the textiles received and with the results of the sales. Apart from some trouble about the length of *guinees*, the qualities were as ordered. The sales in the spring of 1733 "heeft ons veel genoegen gegeeven, waar van de Comp: en koopluyden bijde seer voldaan sijn,"[60] and as to the corresponding sales in 1734 it "is ... in 't geheel nog al reedelijk geweest."[61] About the middle of the 1730's everything was back in the old groove with references to the English and now also the French imports of piece-goods. The Dutch merchants to an increasing extent went abroad for purchases of piece-goods because the Company's own imports were not up-to-date.[62] In the general stocktaking made by the Heeren XVII in their missive of 22 March 1736 of the supplies with returns – summarized above in the chapter on raw silk[63] – the chief count of the indictment as regards the textiles was the very fact that the cargoes included too many rejects. Out of 81 different kinds of piece-goods from Bengal the Heeren XVII had had to strike off 31 items and for the rest had cut down their order. As an example of the poor service offered to the Company by its factories the Heeren XVII adduced a consignment of 19,500 pieces of *gerrassen* in 1733. The order had been for 60,000 pieces, while the French company in the same year imported 40,000 pieces. Significant also was a consignment of 27,500 pieces of black *baftas* from Surat in the return cargoes of 1733. These textiles had not been ordered since the end of the 17th century and therefore in the Directors' opinion must have been stored for very long in the Indian warehouses. They yielded a gross loss of 30 per cent. at the sale in Nederland.

The fundamental cause of the Heeren XVII's complaints, the variations of which have been mentioned for the years down to the end of the 1730's, was the English, to a less degree the French competition, and in the 1720's the competition from the Ostend company. In spite of the conscious and vigorous effort in the 1690's and the very first years of the 18th century, the Dutch Company did not succeed in tiring out the competitors. On

[59] Kol. Arch. No. 202, 21 March 1731. [60] *Ibid.* 5 March 1733.
[61] *Ibid.* 5 March 1734. [62] *Ibid.* 7 March 1735. [63] See p. 129 *et seq.*

the contrary, the Dutch got the worst of it. This development was completed in spite of the fact that the English wool and silk weavers by their protests in 1700 succeeded in having passed an Act which prohibited the import into England of "all wrought silks, Bengals and stuffs mixed with silk or herba, of the manufacture of Persia, China, or the East Indies and all calicoes painted, dyed or printed or stained there."[64] The Act caused an increase in the import of plain cottons and muslins. These semi-manufactures were finished in the rapidly emerging calico printing works, and in 1720 another Act had to be passed according to which the use of any calicoes was prohibited in England. The English East India Company, however, continually had a growing trade in textiles, re-export being splendid business. In an official report written in 1712 Davenant maintains that Holland during the four years 1702–1705 annually imported nearly £ 95,000 worth of silk and piece-goods from England.[65]

[64] Bhattacharya, *op. cit.* p. 158. [65] *Ibid.* p. 159.

CHAPTER VIII

Sugar

Sugar was a typical ballast commodity. As such it ranked with saltpetre, copper, and other heavy goods. Its example reveals the changeable character of the East India trade, just as it demonstrates the interplay between the European and the Asiatic market, the latter perhaps even more distinct than in the case of the other commodities, for while e.g. the export of Japan copper might at times be stimulated by the European demand, there had, partly because of the restrictive character of the trade to Japan, partly because of the necessary placing of copper in the Asiatic factories as a substitute for gold and silver, been set limits to the question how profoundly changes in the Dutch orders might interfere with the Company's arrangements in Japan. The case of sugar was different. The European demand in the 17th century started a cultivation of sugar in Java which soon gave rise to planters' interests which in several cases collided with the Heeren XVII's commercial points of view. Once established this cultivation was a factor to be considered, especially by the Batavian Government, which was engaged on the cultivation of sugar. When the Java sugar during the long period with low prices in the second half of the 17th century could no longer compete with the West Indian and Brazil sugar on the market in Amsterdam, difficulties arose for the cultivation of sugar in Java, which, however, were surmounted by the fact that the Company started a great export to Surat and Persia. This, again, became the introduction to no less than a commercial revolution in the Inter-Asiatic trade, as the sugar of the Dutch Company ousted the Bengali sugar which had hitherto had a market in Northwestern India. It should be added that this revolution was not only a result of the new trade in Java sugar; it was also promoted by the supplies by the Dutch to Bombay and Surat of other goods, thus Chinese silk. It should also be emphasized that like so many other "revolutions" this one lasted several decades.[1]

[1] Holden Furber, *John Company at Work*, A Study of European Expansion in India in the Late Eighteenth Century (Harvard Historical Studies, vol. LV, Cambridge Mass., 1948), p. 162 *et seq.*

Until 1637 the Dutch Company practically exclusively dealt in sugar originating from other areas than its own territories, i.e. sugar from China, Taiwan, Siam, and Bengal.[2] As early as 1616 the Heeren XVII had mentioned sugar in a missive in which they recommended sending old and superfluous ships to Nederland with sugar or other available goods.[3] We also know that in 1622 a quantity of about 220,000 ponds of Chinese sugar arrived in Nederland,[4] but otherwise sugar did not figure in the Heeren XVII's orders during these years, which may be explained by a reference to the relatively low prices in Amsterdam. The above-mentioned quantity from 1622 was sold at 0.27 fl. per pond. Towards the end of the 1620's and in the beginning of the 1630's there was a rather steep rise in the Amsterdam prices of sugar, thus the so-called *moscovades* – West Indian raw sugar – rose to a price of 0.59 fl. per pond after being only at 0.32 fl. per pond in 1624. The other kinds rose correspondingly.[5] The rise sharpened the Heeren XVII's interest in East India sugar. In an order drawn up in November 1631 to Batavia they asked for 400,000 ponds of sugar,[6] in 1633 the annual quantity wanted was increased to 600,000 ponds, in 1636 it was extended to 1 mill. ponds, and the following year the Directors asked for an unlimited quantity, which meant 3.75 mill. ponds or more. They first of all ordered Chinese *poeder* (powdered), *brood* (loaf), and *kandij* (candy) sugar, whereas the sugar from Bengal and Bantam could be dispensed with as long as China was capable of supplying the quantities needed as the qualities were inferior to those of Chinese sugar. Above all the Batavian Government must not send brown sugar from Siam.[7] It is not possible to make a complete survey of the quantities arriving in Nederland during this first period, but it is known that in 1631 just under 34,000 ponds of Bengali sugar were sent, in 1634 just under 430,000 ponds Chinese and Siamese sugar, and in 1637 more than 1.1 mill. ponds of white Chinese powdered sugar.[8]

The way in which the East India sugar was received on the market in Amsterdam appears from a comparison of its prices with the prices of some of the current qualities. Such a comparison has been made for the years 1631–1637:[9]

[2] J. J. Reesse, *De Suikerhandel van Amsterdam* (Haarlem, 1908), p. 160.
[3] *Ibid.* [4] Kol. Arch. No. 987, fo. 176 *et seq.*
[5] See Posthumus, *op. cit.* Table 57.
[6] Kol. Arch. No. 250, November 1631.
[7] Reesse, *op. cit.* p. 161. [8] *Ibid.* p. CXIII.
[9] The current qualities taken from the Amsterdam price lists ed. Posthumus, *op. cit.* Tables 57 ff. The prices of the East Indian sugar from Kol. Arch. No. 250.

Table 28. *Amsterdam Sugar Prices, 1631–1637. Fl. per Pond.*

	White candy	Refined sugar	Loaf-sugar	Brazilian white sugar	Mosco-vados	East India *kandij*	East India *poeder*
1631.......	1.17	0.82	0.78	0.67	0.59	—	0.54
1632.......	1.14	0.80	0.74	0.70	0.54	0.71	0.54
1633.......	1.12	0.80	0.75	0.67	0.54	0.49	0.46
1634.......	1.11	0.77	0.73	0.66	0.50	0.49	0.49
1635.......	1.11	0.76	0.73	0.66	0.51	0.55	0.49
1636.......	1.10	0.79	0.75	0.60	0.52	0.58	0.45–0.49
1637.......	1.36	1.06	1.02	0.85	0.67	0.83	0.68–0.72

We shall make the following comment on the table. The East India candy in the years 1632–34 was expressly stated to be Chinese. The powdered sugar in 1632–34 and 1637 was also Chinese, whereas the powdered sugar of 1631 was Bengali, while *kandij* and *poeder* for the other years was not specified. In the years 1635–37 Siam sugar was also sold. It was obviously so brown that at the sale in 1635 it was termed "Chiamse swarte suijkeren". The prices of this sugar were very low, viz. 0.26, 0.31, and 0.33 fl. per pond, respectively. The sorts of sugar in the Amsterdam price lists partly covered the origin of the sugar, partly the degree of preparation.[10] As mentioned above, moscovados was West India raw sugar, and it appears from the table that the East India *poeder* approached nearest to the prices of this sugar, but generally its price was a little lower. It should be added that the quantities imported as a rule were sold together, so that the buyer paid the stated price per pond plus a larger or smaller amount for the whole lot. Thus the Company in September 1633 sold the Chinese *brood* and *poeder* sugar to Paulus Timmermann and Arnout Pelt at 18$^3/_8$ *groot* per pond plus 1,001 fl. "op de parthye".[11] The average price consequently was a little higher, for which reason we hardly make any mistake in stating that the East India *poeder* sugar, which in the 1630's mainly was of Chinese origin, at the appearance in larger quantities on the market in Amsterdam was on a level with West India moscovados sugar. The fact that it was accepted as applicable in the refineries in Amsterdam appears from a passage in the Heeren XVII's order concerning goods from Formosa and Japan dating from 1637, in which it says that white Chinese *kandij*, *brood*, and *poeder* sugar

[10] As to the degree of preparation, see Reesse, *op. cit.* pp. 150 ff.
[11] Kol. Arch. No. 250, September 1633.

of the best qualities were applicable in Nederland "also nu hier de practijcken hebben uytgevonden omme die te wercke."[12]

The interest taken by the Heeren XVII in the trade during these years also appears from a calculation made of costs and profit at the dispatch of a flute of 170–180 lasts for the sole purpose of fetching sugar from East India.[13] The calculation, which dates from 1636, testifies to the fact that sugar in this case had not been considered a ballast commodity, but as an independent article of commerce which it might be profitable to import into Nederland by cargoes. The voyage there and back was estimated at 20 months. The flute was to be loaded in the East with 450,000 ponds of sugar placed in handy casks, and the cost-price was to be 3 *groot* per pond (or 7½ fl. per 100 ponds). The Company reckoned with a leakage of 15 per cent. of the weight of the sugar and an average auction price of 14 *groot* per pond (or 35 fl. per 100 ponds), which according to the above survey of the prices was made low. Hence the receipts would be 133,875 fl. and when the purchase of the flute and the costs were deducted there would be a profit left of 70,125 fl. or about 1¾ of the capital of 40,000 fl. which was necessary to have the flute sent off. After 20 months the 40,000 fl. had increased to 70,125 fl., i.e. that they had yielded a profit of a total of 75 per cent. or 52 per cent. per annum. So the Heeren XVII reasoned.[14] The calculation affords grounds for emphasizing that the usual calculations of profit in the records of the Company normally are of the gross profit. With a cost-price of 3 *groot* and a selling price of 14 *groot* per pond the gross profit in this case would have been 300 per cent. after deduction of 15 per cent. leakage. This should be compared with the Company's own calculation of the net profit of 75 per cent. This ratio between net and gross profit cannot, of course, be generalized. The example is only suitable to damp the ardour of the reader who is dazed by the idea of the enormous profits of the East India trade, as they have mostly been rendered in literature, – the gross profits. Information of the gross profit is not valueless, on the contrary, but it should not be identified with the net profit.

What about the cost-prices of sugar during this period? The amount of 7.50 fl. per pond mentioned in the calculation undoubtedly was a sober price. The white Chinese powdered sugar, which about the middle of the 1620's had cost 3.78 fl. per 100 ponds, in 1637 had increased to a price of 6.86 fl. per 100 ponds.[15] In the same year the Company bought sugar in Bantam at 6 rials per picul, i.e. 11.50 fl. per 100 ponds if

[12] *Ibid.* October 1637. [13] *Ibid.* November 1636. [14] See above p. 48. Note 122.
[15] Reesse, *op. cit.* p. LXXXVI.

the Spanish rial is rated at 48 st. The Heeren XVII, however, during these years deprecated getting any sugar from Bantam and only wanted Chinese sugar, so that the price of the estimate must be said to have been realistic in 1636. The European demand during the following period sent the prices up further in the East. As early as 1637 the Company raised the cost-price in Bantam from 6 to 9 rials per picul of sugar. This was a move against the English, who together with the Danes had tried to contrive that the Sultan of Bantam issued an embargo on transport of sugar from Bantam to Batavia.[16] In the same year the first step was taken towards cultivation of sugar within the Company's own area. They began laying out plantations, and in the year 1638 the Government could place 22 piculs of Batavia sugar as a trial consignment in the homeward-bound ships. However, a fairly long time still passed before the Batavia sugar appeared in large quantities. Before the middle of the century it was not mentioned apart in the invoices. In January 1649 245,000 ponds of the 1648 harvest were sent home, which is no impressive quantity.[17] The explanation is partly beginner's difficulties, partly the fact that the Company among other things through its trade to Taiwan could buy sufficient quantities of sugar, first of all Chinese sugar. Furthermore, there was in the beginning of the 1640's a perceptible decrease in the Heeren XVII's demands. In 1642 the Seventeen wrote that in Nederland there had been a considerable fall in prices as a consequence of great supplies from Brazil. It was therefore necessary in general to reduce the order for sugar. The order was for 600,000 ponds of *poeder* and 400,000 ponds of *kandij*, which in relation to previous conditions meant a reduction of the powdered sugar, but a relatively greater interest in the *kandij*. The Government and Council in Batavia accordingly were ordered to take a special interest in the purchase of *kandij* sugar. The following year there were reductions again, the Heeren XVII asking for 400,000 ponds of Chinese powdered sugar and 200,000 ponds of candy-sugar. In 1644 they halved the quantity of candy-sugar adding that they had plans for completely striking sugar off the list of orders, as the price in Nederland could no longer bear the expenses of purchase and freight.[18] The prices of sugar on the Amsterdam market during these years appear from the following table, which illustrates the Heeren XVII's characterization.[19]

[16] *Ibid.* p. 162.
[17] *Ibid.*
[18] *Ibid.* p. 163 *et seq.*
[19] Posthumus, *op. cit.* Tables 57 and 58. Regarding the prices of East Indian sugar cf. Note 20.

Table 29. *Amsterdam Prices of Sugar, 1638–1654. Fl. per Pond.*

	Brazilian white sugar	Moscovados	East India *kandij*	East India *poeder*
1638	0.68	0.54	—	0.50
1639	—	—	0.49	0.33
1640	0.55	0.49	0.64	0.47
1641	0.51	0.38	—	0.35
1642	0.46	0.34		
1643	0.44	0.31		
1645	0.46	0.39		
1646	0.65	0.57		
1648	0.60	0.43		
1649	0.66	0.52		
1650	0.67	0.49		
1651	0.73	0.53		
1652	0.69	0.50		
1653	0.66	0.51		
1654	0.69	0.51		

The Company's own prices are known from the contracts down to 1642, when it was decided to sell the sugar by public sale to the highest bidders. The *poeder* sugar sold in 1638 was Chinese, but the other sales were of aggregate quantities of Chinese, Bengali, and Javanese sugar, only the poor Siam sugar being sold apart.[20] It appears from the survey that the fall in prices stopped about 1645. So the Heeren XVII at once changed their minds. Instead of striking off the sugar from East India, as intended, they doubled their orders for powdered sugar as well as candy-sugar. Another and hectic demand from Nederland followed. The cause of the rise in prices was the fight of the Portuguese in Brazil against the Dutch West India Company. This fight reduced the supplies to Amsterdam, and a decade passed before the Brazil sugar was replaced by supplies from the sugar cultures transferred to other West Indian areas. During this decade great quantities again figure in the Heeren XVII's orders. In 1649 they ordered 2.5–3 mill. ponds of *poeder*. They did not want any candy-sugar, but in the following years they asked for 100,000 ponds of *kandij* besides the quantities of *poeder* mentioned. Sugar from China and Taiwan was still the sugar most in demand, but Batavia and Bengal are also mentioned. This second sugar boom of the Company

[20] Kol. Arch. No. 250, various dates. The sale of powdered sugar in September 1640 does not agree with Reesse, *op. cit.* p. 163, Note 1. From 1649 averages can be calculated from the accounts of Kamer Amsterdam, but the kinds of sugar are there entered together. Sugar is, however, so differentiated a commodity that we cannot build on it in this case.

lasted until 1655. Then a fall in prices set in.[21] In November 1655 the Heeren XVII only wanted to have the necessary quantity of *poeder* sent by the homeward-bound ships, besides 50,000 ponds of candy-sugar.

In spite of the interest of the factory Nederland in the East India sugar during the period 1645–1655, it appears that the Court of Directors in contrast to its previous orders added that the execution of the orders must be conditioned by the fact that the Company's domestic, i.e. Asiatic, trade did not suffer. This undoubtedly indicates that the various Asiatic factories to a greater extent had begun trading in sugar. Correspondingly we find in a missive from the Governor General and Council in December 1644 a mention of export to Persia.[22] The Batavian Government estimated that it could sell 1.8 mill. ponds of sugar a year from its Persian factories, but had preliminarily shipped 600,000 ponds of powdered sugar and 100,000 ponds of candy-sugar in order not to overstock the market, hoping that the prices would rise, as Taiwan in the preceding year had not sent any sugar to Persia. Another feature in the letters was the worry about the high cost-prices. As was the case during the brisk European demand in the 1630's, the prices of sugar rose. For the encouragement of the Batavian production of sugar the Government in 1647 increased the price per picul to 6½ rials. The increase bore fruit. The crops in 1652 were estimated at just under 1.5 mill. ponds. The Government on that occasion gave utterance to great optimism and in the missive to Nederland dated at 31 January 1653 concluded: "In somma, God lof, wij beleven in Batavia een florrissante eeuw."[23]

The flourishing was so so. At any rate the Batavia sugar was not to be triumphant in Nederland. Actually we must proceed to the very last years of the 17th century before finding a third brisk European demand. Prices on the market in Amsterdam after 1655 were low, the industry of refining in Amsterdam perhaps was on the decrease, too, and the Heeren XVII's wishes were restricted to an annual order to sell only the most necessary quantities, i.e. the surplus from the Asiatic trade, placed as ballast in the ships. Strict injunctions were given to watch the cost-price and the quality. Accordingly there was a reduction of the shipments from Batavia. During the boom in 1645–1655 the consignments had been of just below 1 to about 3.5 mill. ponds a year; now there was a gradual restriction. Thus the consignments in the years 1660–1668 were of 150,000

[21] It is true that the price material of Kamer Amsterdam from these years cannot be used as indicator of the prices of the various sorts – since, as mentioned above, all sorts have been merged – but the fall in prices can in fact be registered. While the average prices for all sugar during the years 1649–54 fluctuated between 34.66 fl. and 47.84 fl., they dropped in 1655 to 26.05 fl. per 100 ponds and during the following years kept at this level and at a still lower one.

[22] Reesse, *op. cit.* p. 165 *et seq.* [23] *Ibid.* p. 166.

to just below 800,000 ponds. Four years followed with shipments of 1–1.6 mill. ponds, then the quantities again were reduced, and in 1678 the Heeren XVII simply declined having any sugar. At the auctions in Amsterdam sugar was still sold in 1679/80, then there was an interval down to 1693.[24]

Conditions were better in the East. The loss of Taiwan meant a strengthening of the position of Javanese sugar. Chinese sugar disappeared from the consignments to Europe, and on the Asiatic market the Java sugar was able to compete. The competition, however, was keen. Above we have mentioned the incipient export from Batavia to Persia. It should be pointed out that there were no regular sales. The market was fluctuating. In 1675 the Batavian Government complained that Persia provided itself with so much Bengali sugar, a traffic in which the Company, for that matter, participated. Thus in the years 1680–1688 it sold a total of 5 mill. ponds of Bengali powdered sugar from its Persian factories.[25] In the 1670's the Company started its attempts at placing sugar, including Java sugar, in Japan. While the Java sugar in Persia and Northwest India especially had to wrestle with Bengali sugar, the competitor in Japan was Chinese sugar. In a missive of December 1671 the Governor General and Council gave information about a consignment of 7,900 piculs of sugar that had been sold in spite of the fact that Chinese merchants had placed 70,000 piculs of sugar in Japan.[26] Pieter van Dam in his work mentions that the Company in 1674 shipped 900,000 ponds of sugar to Japan.[27] But in this area the sales were not yet regular, either. They were not so until the middle of the 1680's. About the same time the Batavia sugar began to be a success in Persia. Another decade passed before the Company succeeded in creating a more constant market in Surat. Towards the end of the 17th century the Company also in Mocha found a market for its sugar. For a judgment of this important period in the history of the Java sugar we possess an interesting statistical material in the surveys prepared about 1710 in connexion with the report on the production of sugar which in 1711 was presented by C. van Swoll and H. van Zwaardecroon.[28] On this basis we shall first give a table which shows the relations as regards prices between Bengali and Indonesian powdered sugar on the Persian market during the years of transition, and the Company's gross profit on the two sorts.

[24] The annual consignments from Reesse, *op. cit.* p. CXIII *et seq.* and from the invoices.
[25] Kol. Arch. No. 8492.
[26] Reesse, *op. cit.* p. 169, Note 1.
[27] *Pieter van Dam* 2:I, p. 449.
[28] Copied in Kol. Arch. No. 8492.

Table 30. *Prices of Sugar at the Persian Factories, 1680–89. Fl. per 100 Ponds.*

	Bengali *poeder*			Batavia *poeder*		
	Cost	Sale	Gross profit	Cost	Sale	Gross profit
	fl.	fl.	%	fl.	fl.	%
1680....	9.29	23.02	147.8	12.65	28.33	124.0
1681....	9.14	24.79	171.2	13.61	30.10	121.2
1682....	8.84	23.02	160.4	13.51	32.76	142.5
1683....	9.83	17.71	80.2	—	—	—
1684....	8.90	24.79	178.5	13.45	31.87	137.0
1685....	8.03	23.76	195.9	—	—	—
1686....	—	—	—	—	—	—
1687....	11.63	18.20	56.5	—	—	—
1688....	10.32	27.01	161.7	14.19	34.53	144.0
1689....	—	—	—	10.71	28.33	164.5

It is seen how the selling price of the Batavia sugar constantly was higher than that of Bengali sugar. Indeed, the same applies to the cost-price, but the last years suggest that the cost-prices of the two areas approached to one another, those of Bengal rising and those of Batavia falling. At a judgment of the price policy of the Batavian Government towards the sugar planters – the verdict has always been severe – it is also worth mentioning the competitive qualities of the sugar, not least on the Asiatic market. The Batavia sugar had greater difficulties in holding its own on the markets nearer to the Bengali area, thus in Surat, which was abundantly supplied with Bengali sugar by Indian merchants.[29] In the accounting year 1686/87 the Company sold Bengali as well as Javanese sugar from its factory in Surat. The Bengali powdered sugar was sold at 15.31 fl. per 100 ponds, while the Javanese powdered sugar was sold at only 12.34 fl. per 100 ponds. That year, for that matter, was the only one in the period from 1680 to 1709 in which the Company sold Bengali sugar in Surat, but in the years 1695–1704 it sold some Batavia sugar, though not very large quantities. Closer to Bengal, on the Malabar Coast, on the Coromandel Coast, and in Ceylon, the quantities that could be sold were still more modest. It was in the outer areas of the Company's Asiatic trade that the Javanese sugar first was recognized, perhaps not least by virtue of the initial advantage of the

[29] In the Company's archives a great material dealing with this trade is found in the papers from Bengal, where the Dutch annually drew up statistics, not only of the extent of their own trade, but also of the imports and exports of Indian and other Asiatic merchants. See e.g. Kol. Arch. No. 1169 (1670/71) and Kol. Arch. No. 1516 (1697/98).

Dutch over the Indian merchants in long-distance transport. It may also be of some value to cast a glance at the quantitative distribution of the sugar to the various places during these years. It appears from the survey below and shows that Persia and Japan were the greatest buyers by far.[30]

Table 31. *The Company's Sales of Sugar at the Asiatic Factories, 1680–1709. Ponds.*

	Batavia		Bengali	
	poeder	*kandij*	*poeder*	*kandij*
Japan	20,603,675	2,608,501	—	—
Persia	24,139,183	4,542,722	5,407,558	34,755
Surat with Mocha	6,282,486	837,065	146,117	8,405
Malabar	217,403	27,583	25,407*	—
Coromandel	483,823	56,476	85,206	—
Total	51,726,570	8,072,347	5,664,288*	43,160

* Furthermore, 756 sacks and 14 1/8 chests.

If from the total of the quantities of Java sugar shipped from Batavia during the same period we deduct the exports to Europe, the figures show that the export to Europe of *poeder* was only 1/5 (about 13.7 mill. ponds) of the total export, while the export of *kandij* to Europe was 0.22 mill. ponds. To our knowledge no Bengali sugar was shipped to Europe during the years mentioned. The share of Europe, i.e. the factory Nederland, in the Java sugar thus was modest. It dates from the last years of the 17th century on. In July 1698 Java powdered sugar again appears in the Heeren XVII's orders for returns after being absent for a prolonged period. The Directors recommended sugar as ballast for want of saltpetre and copper and called attention to the fact that the prices in Amsterdam had risen. The Heeren XVII were not particularly optimistic about the future, as the conclusion of the peace was expected to promote supplies from Brazil, Barbados, Martinique, and Surinam. Furthermore, the *bewindhebbers* fastened upon the great leakage with consequent loss to which the sugar was subjected. During the following period they enjoined upon the Batavian Government that the sugar ought to be packed in chests and protected by pepper "dewijle deselve geen schade daar aan komt te doen, wordende hier meest gebruyckt om weder geraffineert te werden."[31] The cost-prices as usual were under observation. In February 1700 the Heeren XVII declared that 3¾ *groot* per pond was too much; they pointed out Japara as a cheap sugar-producing area.[32]

[30] Kol. Arch. No. 8492. [31] Kol. Arch. No. 261, 6 March 1699. [32] *Ibid.* 17 February 1700.

The Batavian Government, however, was not inclined to prefer Japara at its purchases, partly because the leakage was maintained to be greater at the transport, partly – and a rather more decisive factor – because of the consideration for the sugar producers around Batavia. The Seventeen in so far recognized the latter argument, but confronted it with the commercial point of view, writing that there "moet daer omtrent volgens coopmansmaximes behoorlijk acht gegeven werden op de inkoops-prijsen."[33] In September 1702 the Heeren XVII wrote that the Government could not send too much sugar to Nederland, which indicates that there was again a European boom. Supplies from Brazil, Barbados, and the Caribbees had, indeed, become great, as had been expected, and this informed the prizes, but no more than that the Court of Directors in the spring of 1705 characterized the East India sugar as a commodity which in many respects was very profitable to the Company, for which reason the sugar trade should be promoted in every way.[34] The Seventeen asked that the Batavia sugar appeared on the market in a condition which, as regards quality and quantity, approached to that of West India sugar. It was tried to make the sugar mills in Batavia produce or sort out two or three kinds of *poeder* in the manner of Barbados, where, after boiling and curing the sugar into sugar "loaves", these were divided into three pieces and the two upper "ends" were sold under the names of "blancos" and "moscovados" – which were the sorts most in demand in the Dutch refineries – while the third piece, the lowest one, called the "panel", was brownish and of an inferior quality.[35] The Heeren XVII even were willing to sanction a slightly higher cost-price for the better qualities.[36] During the following years an effort was made to improve the quality. The best qualities were sent in chests of 600–700 ponds, and it was considered to pack the sugar into still larger chests of 1000 ponds.[37] In this way the sugar was protected best and would stand being loaded beside pepper. The Directors referred the smaller chest to the Asiatic market.[38]

[33] Kol. Arch. No. 262, 14 November 1701. [34] Kol. Arch. No. 263, 2 March 1705.
[35] Kol. Arch. No. 262, 7 March 1704 [36] Kol. Arch. No. 263, 17 February 1707.
[37] Kol. Arch. No. 199, 14 October 1721.
[38] The troubles in connexion with the quality and the packing appear in part from the question of tare. In the 17th century the Company's sugar was packed in very different ways. As an example we may adduce the long list of tare published by the Heeren XVII in October 1642, when they decided to offer sugar at public sales (Kol. Arch. No. 250, 9 October 1642):

	Tare		Tare
1 Cleyne kist	45 pond	1 Pierre Semainspijp	120 pond
1 Groote kist	75 -	1 Seckboot	136 -
1 Toelast	145 -	1 Tousaens ooxhooft	120 -
1 Anjoupijp	140 -	1 Brandewijns ooxhoofft	130 -
1 Conjackpijp	120 -	1 Sack	—

In the 18th century it was attempted to obtain a greater uniformity. The models were the West India Company and the traders in Brazilian sugar. On a suggestion from the traders the

As during the previous booms powdered sugar was predominant. In the spring of 1709 *kandij* was omitted from the orders on the ground that the refineries in Holland would have nothing to do with that sort.[39]

The Dutch auction prices were particularly high at the sales in 1700–1703. Then the prices fell, but in spite of the lower prices the Heeren XVII, as mentioned above, considered the sugar trade to be profitable. About 1712 the prices began rising again, culminating in 1715–16. The quantities imported after 1700 varied between just under 1 and well over 2.5 mill. ponds. Especially during the second rise in prices the Heeren XVII found these quantities to be insufficient, fastening on the fact that occasionally large quantities of sugar were stored in Batavia. It is true that in 1701 they had declared that they would like to see a stock being built up in Java,[40] but now they wanted the sugar to be shipped to Europe. A contributory factor also was that the sales to private persons in the Indian trade in the Seventeen's opinion had assumed too large proportions. Furthermore, the supplies from the area near Tanjonkait rented from the Prince of Bantam were on the increase. Orders were given for a more rigorous supervision of the sugar mills and a concentration of all stocks in Batavia. At the same time the keels were laid down in Nederland of special sugar flutes which were to fetch Batavia sugar express to Holland. The first flutes were equipped about 1715, and in 1718 another number of flutes were put into service. They were specially built vessels of 130 feet which would carry 550,000–600,000 ponds of sugar.[41]

A result of these efforts was that consignments after 1716 increased considerably. Thus in the years 1719–27 they were between 3 and 6 mill. ponds a year. The European trend of prices, however, caused the Heeren XVII to begin beating a retreat about the middle of the 1720's. As early as 1721 the idea had been ventilated that the sugar flutes might be used

tare of the East India Company in 1714 was regulated in the way that tare of *kanassers* was increased from 26 to 30 ponds (Kol. Arch. No. 198, 9 October 1714). In 1721 the tare was further increased from 30 to 36 ponds per *kanasser* (Kol. Arch. No. 199, 14 October 1721). On 28 September 1728 the Heeren XVII dealt with a complaint from refiners and merchants in Amsterdam, Dordrecht, Rotterdam, Gouda, Middelburg, and Utrecht partly of the "frauduleuse afpakking der suijker canassers in Indie," with the occurrence of *kanassers* with two thirds of brownish sugar at the bottom and one third of ordinary sugar on top, partly of the tare, which was put too low. The Heeren XVII decided to increase the tare to 45 ponds for *kanassers* of up to 300 ponds and deduct 15 per cent. tare for *kanassers* of more than 300 ponds (Kol. Arch. No. 200, 28 September 1725). In February of the following year this decision was changed to the effect that 15 per cent. tare was to be deducted for all *kanassers*. In September the Company, however, returned to a fixed tare, which for all *kanassers* was put at 48 ponds, while the buyers had demanded 50 ponds (Kol. Arch. No. 200, 26 February and 19 September 1726). A similar development may be traced in the case of the chests.

[39] Kol. Arch. No. 263, 3 April 1709. [40] Kol. Arch. No. 262, 14 November 1701.

[41] Kol. Arch. No. 198, 14 July 1718 and Kol. Arch. No. 464, 15 July 1718 (section on Batavia).

for something else than sugar.[42] In September 1724 the Directors wrote to Batavia that they only wanted the sugar necessary for ballast "en voor al niet meer, om geen scheepsruijmte te verliesen voor andere kostelijker wharen."[43] This order, however, did not result in any clear reduction of the shipments from Batavia. Thus in 1732, to the regrets of the Heeren XVII, no less than 5.3 mill. ponds arrived, and the following year 4.6 mill. ponds.[44] The Seventeen were forced to fix their wishes for ballast at 2 mill. ponds of sugar a year. The sugar received in 1733 on an average yielded 5 ¼ *groot* per pond at the sales, and the cost-price had been 3 ½ *groot* per pond. It was no longer good business trading sugar. In spite of this fact supplies down to and including 1740 were considerably greater than the orders.[45]

The reason must be sought in the increase of the production of sugar in Java. In van Swoll & van Zwaardecroon's report of 1710/11 on the cultivation of sugar in the area surrounding Batavia the authors mentioned 131 mills with a possible capacity of approximately 13 mill. ponds of sugar annually and an actual production at the time of the survey of more than 8 mill. ponds,[46] which was a great increase as compared with previous statements in the 17th century.[47] The Company's purchases during the period after 1710 were about 8 mill. ponds annually. Even though the production might be decreasing, partly because of the price policy, partly because the plantations yielded less, there was a certain pressure of supplies. This was what caused that the factory Nederland in the years after 1724 received considerably more sugar than wanted, with the result that the profit was decreasing. An examination of the sugar accounts in the general commerce ledgers of Batavia after 1710 shows that the consignments to Europe constitute a greater part of the export than in the period of 1680–1709. The share of Europe in the consignments was lowest in 1715/16, when in the case of powdered sugar it was 27.8 per cent., and highest in 1724/25, when it was 69.6 per cent. The normal down to the middle of the 1730's was that one third to half of the sugar of Batavia was shipped to the factory Nederland. The distribution to the various areas appears from the following Table 32.

The survey shows a few important displacements on the Asiatic market. First of all there is the highly decreasing importance of the Persian

[42] Kol. Arch. No. 199, 9 October 1721. [43] Kol. Arch. No. 250, 29 September 1724.
[44] Kol. Arch. No. 202, 5 March 1733 and 5 March 1734. [45] Reesse, *op. cit.* p. 176.
[46] J. K. J. de Jonge, *De opkomst van het Nederlandsch gezag in Oost-Indië*, vol. VIII ('s Gravenhage-Amsterdam, 1875), p. 164.
[47] Thus 1.5 mill. ponds in 1652, cf. De Jonge, *op. cit.*, vol. VI (1872), p. 27.

Table 32. *Distribution of the Export of Powdered Sugar from Batavia, 1713/14–1734/35. In 1000 Ponds.*

Season	Nederland	Japan	Persia	Surat and Mocha	Ceylon	Coromandel	Various	Stock at expiry of the season
1713/14 ...	2,245	807	800	698	525	—	36	520
1715/16 ...	1,686	898	1,276	1,440	564	—	196	2,326
1718/19 ...	4,412	1,408	1,364	913	469	244	46	658
1721/22 ...	3,817	853	366	1,634	808	246	231	961
1723/24 ...	4,507	839	—	804	726	279	128	1,787
1724/25 ...	4,843	792	—	243	747	171	165	1,371
1726/27 ...	5,345	675	—	1,530	574	—	158	609
1727/28 ...	2,204	615	71	901	773	—	168	729
1730/31 ...	1,923	512	111	1,122	1,640	—	185	1,654
1732/33 ...	3,874	800	559	1,702	841	36	556	1,088
1733/34 ...	2,062	782	92	267	946	100	582	3,250
1734/35 ...	2,602	902	613	2,308	978	30	1,325	1,407

market. This was connected with the change of government in Persia about 1722, when the Sofi dynasty was dethroned, which caused a momentary interruption of the trade. Later the fights with the Afghans brought about so changeable conditions for the trade that the Company could not maintain its former position. The depressed market influenced conditions in Indonesia, the Batavian Government putting a check on the cultivation of sugar in the Prince of Bantam's areas, which previously had been promoted, when the European demand was at its height.[48] The figures from the Japanese market were also on the decrease, although not to a degree corresponding to that on the Persian market. On the other hand, the sales in Surat had increased as compared with those in the period of 1680–1709. Ceylon had made its appearance as a new market. The same applies to the Malabar Coast, which during these years on the whole became of greater importance for the Company. The great increase in the column of "Various" in 1732/33 and later is just due to exports to Malabar. The group of "Various" furthermore includes partly a constant small sale in the Indonesian archipelago (including sales in Batavia), partly varying shipments of sugar to Siam and in 1734/35 a quantity of 433,758 ponds to China. Thus we find that Europe during the years immediately after the change of government in Persia had to take a large amount of the Java powdered sugar – to a certain

[48] De Jonge, *op. cit.*, vol. IX (1877), p. XVI.

degree reluctantly – but that the Batavian Government also succeeded in selling sugar in new areas in Asia. The most important bright spot undoubtedly was that the Batavia sugar at length had found a good market in Surat.

It is well-known what a serious blow in 1740 was directed against the cultivation of sugar in Java by the fatal order for the banishment of a large number of Chinese from the area of Batavia. The order or the rumour about it provoked a revolt; at the terrible massacre on 9 October the number of Chinese victims was over 10,000. From the very first time of the cultivation of sugar, plantations and mills had mainly been run by Chinese people. The production afterwards decreased so much that in 1741 only 767,000 ponds were sent to Nederland, and the shipments during the years 1742–48 were practically at a standstill.[49] Only about 1750 the damage to the production was fairly repaired. The expectations from the Asiatic market during the new state of things appear from Governor General Mossel's reflections on the cultivation of sugar and the trade dated at 31 December 1750. Mossel sketched the following annual export figures for *poeder*:[50]

Japan	1.8 mill. ponds
Surat	3.6 - -
Persia	1.6 - -
Malabar	1.0 - -

Mossel was too optimistic. The decade 1751–60 according to his estimates should have brought an Asiatic export of 80 mill. ponds, but it was only of 64.5 mill. ponds.[51] During the same period there was normally an export of 0.5–1 mill. ponds a year to Nederland, and in spite of a boom in the period of 1758–62, in which the European supplies rose to more than 2 mill. ponds, sugar during the rest of the Company's lifetime remained a commodity the main sales of which took place in Asia.

[49] Reesse, *op. cit.* p. 178. [50] *Ibid.*

[51] During the nine years 1751/59 26.3 mill. ponds were sent to Surat, which according to the plan was 6 mill. ponds too little. Reesse, *op. cit.* p. 178.

CHAPTER IX

Japanese Copper

Japanese copper, too, offers a number of examples of the interplay between the Dutch and the Asiatic market, but in this case it is a commodity which in spite of periods with a considerable export to Europe predominantly belongs in the Company's Asiatic trade. In the course of the 17th century copper came to play an increasingly great part and at the end of our period was characterized by Governor General van Imhoff as altogether one of the Company's most important commercial products. The history of Japanese copper thus reflects an important course in the Dutch Company's trade in the 17th and 18th centuries.

Like so many other Asiatic commodities the copper from Japan circulated in Asiatic trade before the Dutch appeared on the stage. Through the activities of the Chinese merchants the copper was conveyed to Malacca, and Bantam, and from there was carried further to India, Persia, and Arabia. The Portuguese provided themselves with Japanese copper through their trade to China, i.e. by way of Macao, and much evidence shows that during the very years of war towards the end of the 16th century and the beginning of the 17th century, Japanese copper was a war material (guns) which was much in demand.[1] Japan, for that matter, was not the only copper-producing country in Asia. Copper also occurred in China, India, and Persia, but while the production of copper was decreasing in Northern India,[2] and China consumed her full output and more, the Japanese production for export was on the increase throughout the 17th century. The Persian winning of copper did not start in earnest until later in the 18th century and did not become of any importance in international trade during the period considered here. The use of copper was manifold. We have mentioned war material, but

[1] *Boletim da Filmoteca Ultramarina Portuguesa*, No. 2 (Lisboa, 1955), No. 49: Carta Regia Para O Vice-Reida India Matias de Albuquerque, Lisbon 8 February 1591. *Documentos Remittidos da India*, vol. I (Lisboa, 1853), p. 95 (18 January 1607) and p. 335 (17 February 1610).

[2] Moreland, *op. cit.* p. 183 *et seq.*

its function as coinage metal must be considered of primary importance. The small change in Japan, India, on the spice islands, and elsewhere was copper coins. The metal was also used in the building trade, for roofing, for decoration of temples, and for statues of Buddha. Numerous domestic utensils were of copper, jugs, vats for the distilling of arrack, for the refining of saltpetre, etc. The well-known gongs were also of copper. Finally the metal was used as material for shipbuilding, for sheathing, wires, compasses, etc. The Dutch Company regularly sent copper from Europe to its workshops in Batavia and elsewhere, e.g. graded plates of red copper for sheathing and yellow copper or brass for mountings.[3] To judge from the trade in the East, as its contours appear about 1620, it was not, however, a question of large quantities.[4] The copper in which the Company traded in Asia, was above all Japanese. On the whole its qualities were not inferior to those of European copper; consequently – apart from a few special sorts – there was no reason to take unnecessary trouble. In 1608 the Dutch got permission from the Emperor to trade in Firando in Japan, where the first factory was founded. The English also founded a factory, but for various reasons had to leave Japan in 1623. The Dutch, on the other hand, held their ground. Indeed, they had to leave Firando, but in return were referred to the island of Deshima off Nagasaki. There they had their permanent factory for the following two centuries and thus as compared with their European competitors enjoyed a monopoly of direct trade to Japan. Until Koxinga's conquest of Taiwan in the beginning of the 1660's the trade to Japan was placed under the Company's Governor in Taiwan, who was responsible for the supply of Batavia and the Indian factories with Japanese and Chinese products. In the case of the trade to Japan these were: silver, gold, copper, camphor, and a few other commodities.

The Dutch Company soon learnt to poach on the preserves of the Chinese merchants and the Portuguese by transporting copper to the Indies. The Coromandel Coast is mentioned at an early stage in the correspondence between Batavia and Firando as an important consumer of Japanese copper. In December 1614 the Resident at Firando, Jacques Specx, wrote to Jan Pietersz: Coen that he had increased the consign-

[3] In the 18th century the following sorts of copper figured in the printed schedules of the Company's equipment goods: (i) *koper, als latoen,* (ii) *Hamburger, rood blad dito,* (iii) *geelplat dito, dik en dunne,* (iv) *roodplaat dito,* (v) *roode kopere vullens,* (vi) *geele kopere dito,* and (vii) *roode kopere ketels.* Cf. Collectie Radermacher No. 121, "Rooster van de prijsen der goederen by de Kamer Zeeland ingekogt".

[4] In the extant invoices of ships equipped from Kamer Amsterdam in 1616–1620 copper thus is found only once in the cargoes, viz. in the ship "Den swarten Beer" leaving in the autumn of 1617 with 259 ponds red and yellow copper at a total value of 168 fl.

ment of copper wanted to 250 piculs as it "op de custe wel getrocken is,"[5] and in June 1617 Hans de Haze reported from Masulipatam that the coarse red copper from Japan had been sold at 90 Spanish rials per candy and the fine quality at 108 Spanish rials.[6] In 1620 we first find the idea ventilated of sending Japanese copper to Europe by the homeward-bound fleet. In February 1620 Coen wrote to Firando, asking for "een weinig koper als monster naar Nederland te senden,"[7] and literally at the same time Specx asked whether an attempt should not be made at sending coarse and fine copper as ballast to Nederland, which in his opinion would be profitable.[8] The small quantity of copper ordered by Coen was shipped to Nederland in April 1621 by the "Leyden".[9] The Heeren XVII had the Japan copper tested by a coppersmith in Amsterdam. The result did not come up to expectations. The leakage of the trial consignment was too great and the quality was not so good that the Directors thought that an import would pay, for which reason they wrote to Batavia in April 1622 in order to cancel Japanese copper as a return commodity until further orders were given.[10] At Firando, however, they were still optimists. In the same year as the Heeren XVII's order not to ship copper to Europe was dispatched to the Batavian Government, Lenaert Camps sent from Firando 1000 piculs of "schoon cooper, dat in't vaderlant naer onse gissinghe ongevaerlijck 1 ½ cent per cento avance geeven sal."[11] Camps was of opinion that a profit of 150 per cent. on a ballast commodity was good business, which it might well be worth while securing by making the ships of the homeward-bound fleet wait in Batavia until the Japan cargo arrived. The cost-price of the lot in Japan had been about 32,000 fl. and in Camps' opinion could fetch about 80,000 fl. The Batavian Government had a minor part of the lot shipped to Europe by the "Alkmaar" and the "Delftshaven" in February 1623, viz. 259 piculs of "fijn coper in ronde stucken" and 100 piculs of "fijnder coper in staefkens", to a total invoice value of 11,850 fl.[12] The cost-price was 10 taels and 10.8 taels per picul, respectively, to which was added expenses incurred in Japan for duties, etc., which were calculated at 4 per cent. of the cost-price. This lot of Japanese copper was sold in Nederland at 36 fl. for the round pieces (or copper

[5] (H. T. Colenbrander &) W. Ph. Coolhaas, *Jan Pietersz. Coen*, Bescheiden omtrent zijn bedrijf in Indië, deel 7:I ('s-Gravenhage, 1953), p. 19.

[6] *Ibid.* p. 238. [7] *Ibid.* p. 654.

[8] *Ibid.* p. 503. Letter from Specx dated at Firando, 24 February and 1 March 1620.

[9] See above, p. 19.

[10] Kol. Arch. No. 249, April 1622; *Pieter van Dam* 1:II, p. 163.

[11] (Colenbrander &) Coolhaas, *op. cit.*, 7:II, p. 1039. Camps' letter dated at Firando, 30 November 1622. [12] Kol. Arch. No. 989, fos. 286 ff.

"in brooden", as it was also named) and 49½ fl. for the copper bars, both sales being by the 100 ponds, which yielded a gross profit of about 44 per cent. and about 83 per cent., respectively. The Heeren XVII did not consider this any great profit, and again, in their missive of December 1623, asked the Batavian Government not to ship copper to Nederland, but recommended that they sent Japanese copper to Persia, where it had already given a good profit and where it would thus save cash.[13] At that time the Batavian Government was nevertheless shipping a fresh lot of Japanese copper to Nederland. The ships "Leyden" and "'t Wapen van Delft" left Batavia in January 1624 with a total of about 372 piculs of copper consisting of 645 "brooden".[14] At length a satisfactory profit was obtained, the lot mentioned being sold in Nederland at 56 fl. per 100 ponds, so the Heeren XVII gave orders to buy fairly large quantities of fine and refined Japanese copper for Europe.[15] The gross profit may be calculated at about 119 per cent. On another occasion the Heeren XVII specified the quantity of copper wanted at 2–300,000 ponds (i.e. 1600–2400 piculs). They assumed a cost-price of at most 31–32 fl. per 100 ponds and a good quality. Especially the latter factor seemed to have been of importance, for the Heeren XVII sent out a plate of copper as a model besides a direction how to assay the copper.[16] How these orders were effected cannot be decided with full accuracy, as the invoices are not extant from all the returning ships, but it appears from the extant material that in February 1626 about 123,000 ponds of copper were shipped to Nederland, and in November 1627 and January 1628 more than 300,000 ponds.[17]

What was the state of things in Nederland and Europe during those years when the East India Company, mainly thanks to its servants at Firando and Batavia, tried to place Japanese copper on the European market? The country with the greatest production of copper undoubtedly

[13] Kol. Arch. No. 4409, copy of missives from the Heeren XVII, "Japans cooper". The calculation of the profit is based on the invoice material (which gives the cost price), the selling price (stated in the missive mentioned), and the rate of conversion (from the invoices), 1 tael = 3 fl., besides the weight, 1 picul = 125 ponds (which does not appear from the invoices).

[14] Kol. Arch. No. 992, fos. 429 and 435.

[15] Kol. Arch. No. 184, September–October 1624, contract with Hans Loors, Amsterdam, dated at 7 October. Kol. Arch. No. 4409, 1 November 1624.

[16] Kol. Arch. No. 4409, 24 December 1624 ["om te proberen off het coper goet is, sal men een hoeck van de plate gloeijende maecken ende tselve dan uijt gereckt sijnde, soo't sonder scheuren ofte bersten blijft is een teijken van oprecht ende onvervalst coper, ende soodaniger plate als die plate was kan in Nederlant willich gelden 60 à 70 fl. 't cento"]. Dunlop, *op. cit.* p. 125.

[17] Kol. Arch. Nos. 998 (invoice of the "'t Wapen van Rotterdam", dated at Batavia, 3 February 1626), 999 (the "Amsterdam", dispatched on 2 February 1626), 1003 (the "'t Wapen van Delft", dispatched on 6 November 1627, and the "Vianen", invoice dated at Batavia, 13 January 1628).

was Sweden, but in Hungary, Transylvania, Thuringia, and Norway copper was also mined. The chief market of the copper trade was in Amsterdam. Even though Amsterdam was not the obvious market for Swedish copper, it was still under normal conditions the chief one. Next to Amsterdam Hamburg must be mentioned. Swedish copper was found on the market there, and large quantities of the Hungarian and Central European production reached the North German Hanseatic town. An important factor as regards the demand on the European copper market from about the turn of the century to 1626 was the copper coinage in Spain, the most powerful kingdom of Europe. Having had a silver coin which by continued debasements with copper had become more and more copper-like, the Spanish Government in 1599 went the whole length and introduced a pure copper standard of coinage. An occasionally tremendous minting took place and changed Spain to the greatest buyer of copper in Europe. We may distinguish between three periods of minting: 1599–1606, 1617–1619, and 1621–1626.[18] This Spanish demand in connexion with other factors such as the demand from the new-founded overseas companies of copper for ship-building materials and war materials[19] brought about a rising trend in prices, which lasted down to 1626. Then a fall in prices set in in 1626–27.[20]

Table 33. *Dutch Copper Prices 1624-1629. Fl. per 100 Ponds.*

	Swedish garcopper in the price-lists of Amsterdam	Japanese copper bars sold by the Company
1624......	64.55	56.00
1625......	67.27	—
1626......	56.82	43.85
1627......	—	44.10
1628......	55.78	—
1629......	48.00	40.75

The fall in prices may have been connected with the cease of the Spanish mintings, but in an interesting letter of 1633 written by the Swedish statesman Louis de Geer it says that the first fall in prices in Amsterdam was due to the East and West India Companies, which attracted by the high price had begun importing overseas copper. Especially the import of the East India Company was decisive.[21] De

[18] Eli F. Heckscher, "Den europæiske kopparmarknaden under 1600–talet", *Scandia*, XI:2 (Stockholm-København-Oslo, 1938), *passim* and p. 265.

[19] Albert Olsen, "Kobberpolitik i den svenske stormagtstid", *Scandia*, X:1 (1937), p. 57, and Astrid Friis, "Forbindelsen mellem det europæiske og asiatiske kobbermarked", *Scandia*, XII:1 (1939), p. 174.

[20] Posthumus, *op. cit.* Table 173. Kol. Arch. No. 184, September–October 1624, contracts dated at 29 October 1626, 23 July 1627 and 17 March 1629.

[21] Heckscher, *op. cit.* p. 268.

Geer stated that the copper from the East Indies in 1626 went to Aix in France.[22] One of the agents of the Swedish Crown in Amsterdam, Conrad van Falkenberch, estimated the Dutch import in 1628 at 136 tons,[23] which was somewhat less than the about 300,000 ponds mentioned above which the East India Company received that year. In 1629 Louis de Geer wrote that Japanese copper, although it was not so good as Swedish copper, had begun to find a ready market in Amsterdam, and this was one of the causes of the lower prices.[24] It is difficult to decide how much the Dutch imports of Japanese copper meant quantitatively as compared with Swedish copper on the market in Amsterdam. The calculated Swedish export during these years constituted 737 tons annually,[25] but only part of it went to Amsterdam. It is, however, certain that the presence of Japanese copper on the Amsterdam market in the years in question influenced the Swedish commercial policy. In the letter from 1633 quoted above, Louis de Geer points out how necessary it was for Sweden to have large quantities of copper stored, with which she might threaten the Dutch to beat down the price and in this way keep them from importing too much. The essential thing was to "ne reveiller le chien qui dort."[26]

The dog slumbered sweetly during the following years, not least because of the difficulties that had arisen for the Dutch in Japan during the years 1628–33 and the Japanese embargo laid on copper in 1638. The embargo was motivated by the fact that copper was war material,[27] and it lasted until 1645. At first it thus only came to a short guest-performance on the European stage, but the role opened up new vistas for the following time. The example showed that what moved the Heeren XVII when they finally decided to ask for larger quantities of Japanese copper, was selling prices which yielded a gross profit of more than 100 per cent.; only then the trade in this ballast commodity would be profitable. Louis de Geer therefore hit the mark when he sketched a Swedish policy of storing as the means of keeping the Company from a greater import of copper from the East. The element of competition is evident. As was the case of so many other imported goods of the Company, it also applied to the Japan copper that it was exposed to keen

[22] It is worth noting that the buyer of Japanese copper in 1626 was Elias Trip, Louis de Geer's brother-in-law. See above p. 34. Trip bought the Company's Japanese copper in 1627, too. Kol. Arch. No. 184, 29 October 1626 and 23 July 1627.

[23] Heckscher, *op. cit.* p. 269.

[24] Albert Olsen, "Kobberpolitik og Kritik", *Scandia*, X:2 (1937), p. 300.

[25] Heckscher in *Scandia*, XI:2 (1938), p. 236.

[26] Quoted from Albert Olsen in *Scandia*, X:1 (1937), p. 61.

[27] *A True Description of the Mighty Kingdoms of Japan & Siam by François Caron & Joost Schouten*, ed. by C. R. Boxer (London, 1935), p. LIV.

competition as regards qualities and prices on the European market, first of all from the European sorts of copper, to a less degree from the West India copper, i.e. copper from South and Central America.[28] Furthermore, it appears from the Heeren XVII's letters to Batavia that the Court of Directors placed copper as a commodity of importance for the Company's Asiatic trade. This is not fully known as regards these years, but it has been indicated that the Coromandel Coast and Persia were important consumers. The quantities mentioned now and then are mostly larger than the exports to Europe. Thus in 1627, 996 piculs were sent to Surat; in 1628 it was stated that Gamron bought 400 piculs a year, and in 1629 1477 pieces of coarse and 1252 pieces of fine copper were delivered to a factory in Persia.[29] Finally it is evident that the Company tried its hand at several different qualities, until it proved that only the quality called "fijn koper in staefkens" was most suitable for the European as well as the Asiatic market. This so-called bar copper became quite predominant when the export from Japan was started again after 1645.

During the Japanese embargo in 1638–45 copper was ordered from Nederland for India in quantities which were considerably greater than the imports to Nederland mentioned above. Thus in 1641–42 the Batavian Government asked for 100,000 ponds of copper in plates and in 1642–43 about no less than 600,000 ponds of Swedish or Hungarian copper plates. But by the re-opening of the export from Japan the copper bars poured out, and on 31 December 1646 the Batavian Government wrote to the Court of Directors in Nederland that they had no longer any use for European copper "sijnde de uytvoer van Japans coper tot 8 ende 9 tail 't picol toegestaen."[30] The first cargoes of copper bars were sent to Europe in 1649, the next lot in 1651. Then there was an interval of four years. Towards the end of 1655 the Heeren XVII for the first time entered Japanese copper in their list of the most important return commodities. On that occasion they stated that the price of copper in Nederland had risen from 36 to 56 fl. per 100 ponds, and asked the Batavian Government to ship as much copper as could be done without in the Asiatic trade.[31] In accordance with this order the Batavian Government in 1657 sent just under 40,000 ponds of copper to Nederland and

[28] In the first half of the 17th century American copper was sent to Seville, where i.a. it was used for the founding of guns. The proportion in which in 1629 it was mixed with Hungarian copper is known; cf. *The Spanish Rule of Trade to the West Indies* (London, 1702), p. 346, quoted from Albert Olsen, *Scandia*, X:2 (1937), p. 300 *et seq.*

[29] Cf. Albert Olsen in *Scandia*, X:2 (1937), p. 299.

[30] Kol. Arch. No. 10,061.

[31] Kol. Arch. No. 252, 1 November 1655.

in 1658 a quantity of even more than 1 mill. ponds. This was the introduction to a period of more than 20 years with constant and large supplies to Nederland. During this period it must be considered that Asiatic copper was a considerable factor in the offers on the European market. The supplies during the years when they were greatest, i.e. 1672–75, were equal to one third or half of the calculated Swedish exports.[32] This is in accordance with the fact that Japanese copper in 1669 was entered in the printed Amsterdam price-lists – together with Norwegian copper – where it figured until 1688.[33]

The impulse to this import period was the rising prices of copper in Europe. These prices appear from the following brief survey of the Company's sales of Japanese copper bars and the quotations on the Amsterdam exchange of Swedish garcopper during the years 1649–1655.[34]

Table 34. *Amsterdam Prices of Copper, 1649–55. Annual Average in Fl. per 100 Ponds.*

	Swedish garcopper in the price-lists of Amsterdam	Japanese copper bars at the public sales in Amsterdam
1649......	48.5	42.5
1650......	47.2	—
1651......	41.8	37.0
1652......	38.5	36.4
1653......	41.8	—
1654......	52.0	—
1655......	59.1	—

The Heeren XVII's interest in Japanese copper, however, may also to some degree have been aroused by the fact that there was a heavy fall in prices of East India sugar, which, as previously mentioned, was an important ballast commodity. Sugar, which in the beginning of the 1650's at the sales in Amsterdam had been sold at a price of 45–50 fl. per. 100 ponds, in 1654 dropped to a price of 35 fl. and in 1655 further to 26 fl. per 100 ponds. While the Directors in the autumn of 1655 asked for copper in homeward-bound ships, they ordered the Batavian Government not to send more sugar than necessary, i.e. only to send what could not be sold on the Asiatic market.[35] There is much to indicate that part of the Company's ballast capacity was switched from sugar to copper. In 1658 the Heeren XVII fixed their wishes for copper, ordering

[32] Regarding the Swedish exports, cf. Heckscher in *Scandia,* XI:2 (1938), p. 242.
[33] *Ibid.* p. 255.
[34] The Swedish garcopper prices from Posthumus, *op. cit.* Table 173.
[35] Kol. Arch. No. 252, November 1655.

600,000 ponds annually. The demand in 1659 was increased to 800,000 ponds, in 1663 to 900,000 ponds, and finally in 1668 reached the excessive quantity of 2 mill. ponds. In a postscript it was laid down that it was not possible at all to send too much Japanese copper to Europe. In 1674 the order of the Directors dropped to 1.2 mill. ponds, and in November 1679 they wrote that no copper ought to be shipped to Nederland except such quantities as were necessary for the ballast of the ships, or what the Asiatic market could not absorb.[36] These orders are far from expressive of what was actually shipped. Thus the consignments to Nederland during the period 1670–1675 on an average amounted to well over one fourth of the 2 mill. ponds ordered. The value of the orders is mainly that they give a certain clue to the intensity of the demand. In their fluctuations they correspond to the trend of prices at the public sales in Nederland. What was received by Nederland appears from the following table, in which also the total exports from Japan are listed, besides the quantities of copper bars sold at one of the Company's large factories in India, Surat.[37]

Table 35. *Export from Japan, Import to Nederland, Sales in Surat, 1646–1680. Five-Year Averages in Ponds.*

	Japan Export	Nederland Import	Surat Sales
1646–50	469,784*	28,648	39,974
1651–55	445,925	14,488	151,253
1656–60	1,368,315	378,816	272,168
1661–65	2,060,925	336,000	408,493
1666–70	1,447,713	383,450	326,930
1671–75	2,040,800	618,753	545,534
1676–80	2,554,600	257,922	660,267

* The export in 1648 is not known, therefore this figure is a four-year average.

The European demand undoubtedly gave a stimulus to the export from Japan, even though the boom of the export in the season of 1656 was rather more dictated by the Company's wish, by means of great purchases to reduce the Chinese supplies of Japan copper to Indonesia and Malacca, which was of vital importance to the activities of the interlopers.[38] However, it appears from the table above that in spite of the occasionally great supplies to Nederland, it was a main rule that the

[36] Kol. Arch. No. 255, 21 August 1668; Kol. Arch. No. 257, 14 November 1679.

[37] Based upon Kristof Glamann, "The Dutch East India Company's Trade in Japanese Copper, 1645–1736", *The Scandinavian Economic History Review*, vol. I (København, 1953), p. 52 *et seq.* and p. 64 *et seq.*

[38] *Pieter van Dam* 2:I, pp. 403 ff.

greater part of the Company's export remained in Asia. Indeed, the Heeren XVII seem to have realized this state of things, as, even in the years when they ordered most, they added that the shipments to Europe must not take place at the expense of the Asiatic sales. The export for that matter was somewhat hampered towards the end of the 1660's by a great minting in Japan of copper coins. In 1668 a temporary embargo was laid on copper, which was followed by trade restrictions. It was, however, of still greater importance that the Japanese at the same time laid an embargo on silver, an embargo which became permanent.[39] Furthermore, the price of Japanese gold coins was raised in the 1670's with the result that the share of gold in the Company's export decreased. Both factors gave a stimulus to the export of copper, which in 1670 again was set completely free. These phases can be traced in the export figures rendered above. The fact that silver disappeared and that the stream of gold flowed more sparsely from Japan meant that the Company tried its hand at the third coinage metal, copper, in the areas in which Japanese silver and gold had previously been sold, i.e. on the Coromandel Coast, in Bengal, Surat, Ceylon, Persia, and elsewhere. Especially the three areas first mentioned were important. The sales were promoted by the fact that the prices of copper in these places were higher than in Nederland. Thus the prices of Japanese copper in Surat were increasing from the beginning of the 1650's down to the beginning of the 1670's,[40] and the level at its culmination was about 30 per cent. higher than the corresponding Dutch level calculated from the official rates of conversion.[41] In Surat it is furthermore seen that only cloves yielded a greater profit to the Company than copper from out of a selection of commodities including 40 different items. At the same time it is evident that whereas Japanese copper at the Company's sales in Nederland meant gross receipts of at most 6–8 per cent. of the total receipts from the sales, it contributed to a much higher degree to providing cash for the Company at the Indian factories.[42] During the following decades the position of copper was further consolidated on the Asiatic market.

In 1681 the centre of disturbance in India shifted from the north to the south when the Great Mogul Aurangzeb attacked the kingdoms of Bijapur and Golkonda and tried to subjugate the independent Mara-

[39] *Pieter van Dam* 2:I, pp. 435 ff. Oskar Nachod, *Die Beziehungen der Niederländischen Ostindischen Kompagnie zu Japan im siebzehnten Jahrhundert* (Leipzig, 1897), p. 357.

[40] Glamann, "The Dutch East India Company's Trade in Japanese Copper", p. 64 *et seq.*

[41] This difference is settled when the distinction between "light" and "heavy" money is cancelled. In return the difference in the transport costs must be taken into consideration; so there is continually an actual difference.

[42] Glamann, "The Dutch East India Company's Trade in Japanese Copper", pp. 63 ff.

thas.[43] This is the background to the unique sales which the Company met with on the Coromandel Coast, thus in 1683/84 almost 2.3 mill. ponds of copper bars were sold, and more than 60 per cent. of the total gross profit in the accounting year on the Coast originated from the copper.[44] In Golkonda there was a veritable copper adventure, which, however, came to an abrupt end at the capture of the town in 1687. A native merchant of Golkonda, Zierum Chodenda, in 1684 contracted with the Company for the purchase of 12,000 chests of Japanese copper bars equal to 1.5 mill. ponds annually, mainly for the coinage of *nevels*. Large parts of the deliveries were made on credit. When Golkonda was captured Chodenda went bankrupt and the Company sustained a loss of more than 0.9 mill. fl. This caused that the directors of the factory were dismissed and an accusation brought against them.[45]

It is understandable that no copper was shipped to Europe during these years. Prices in Amsterdam even were low during the first half of the 1680's. Japanese copper did not reappear in Nederland until 1689. From this decade a project is known which throws an interesting light on the role of the European market in the Company's copper trade. Nederland here functions as a surplus market. The project i.a. appears from the Heeren XVII's missive to Batavia in 1684, in which the idea was ventilated that the Company ought to try to secure an actual monopoly of Japanese copper. The Chinese should be outmanouevred at purchases in Japan and elsewhere; the considerable surplus which in this way would arise might be shipped to Europe by the Batavian Government, which should be authorized to cancel saltpetre as a ballast commodity.[46] It was not the first time the Company tried to direct a blow against Chinese competition. In 1657 the Batavian Government thus had ordered the factory at Nagasaki to engross the copper, as the Dutch in the preceding year had felt much annoyed by the fact that Chinese junks had placed 17–18,000 piculs of copper in Batavia, where it was sold to private traders at 20–21 rials per picul, some of it being transshipped to the Coromandel Coast, Surat, and Persia by the Company's own ships.[47] In spite of the monopoly of the Dutch among the European nations in the Japan trade, their traffic in Asia with copper bars in other word was characterized by competition just as their copper trade in Europe. The Chinese trade to Japan – first of all based on silk –

[43] W. H. Moreland & Atul Chandra Chatterjee, *A Short History of India* (London, 1936), p. 251.
[44] Kol. Arch. No. 1287, fo. 387 *et seq.*
[45] Kol. Arch. Nos. 459 (8 October 1685), 460 (25 October 1686), 461 (8 July 1693). Daniel Havart, *Op- en ondergang van Cormandel*, deel 2 (Amsterdam, 1693), pp. 160 ff.
[46] Kol. Arch. No. 459, 11 December 1684. [47] *Pieter van Dam* 2:I, p. 403 *et seq.*

among other things resulted in large amounts of copper entering the market behind the Company's back. Thus it was also possible for the English, the Portuguese, and others to secure copper by trading with the Chinese on Macao, in Tongking, Siam, Malacca, Java, etc. So the dilemma was this: either to "engross" the market in Japan or to buy "free" copper at high prices in Malacca, Siam, Batavia, and elsewhere. The project formed by the Heeren XVII in 1684 estimated the total export of copper from Japan at a quantity between 50,000 and 60,000 piculs a year. According to the plan they offered the Japanese to take this huge quantity at a price of 11.9 taels per picul. Payment was to be made in the way that the Company undertook to provide Japan with the foreign goods which the country needed. The terms of trade were to be regulated according to the cost-prices of the imports, and the contract should the first time be binding for a period of three or four years.[48] The Japanese, however, refused to accept the plan. They maintained that the copper should be paid in cash, and furthermore they did not think that they would be able to supply the quantity estimated. The result therefore only was an order for the factory to buy as much copper as possible on the usual terms, and for the Batavian Government in various ways to put obstacles in the way of the trade to Japan of the resident Chinese.[49] At the same time the Japanese introduced a maximum limit to the whole of the foreign trade with the effect that the Dutch Company's trade to Japan was put at 300,000 taels annually. The corresponding Chinese quota was twice as high, while private traders had assigned to them a quota of 40,000 taels, against which the Company protested, but in vain.[50]

No opportunity arose to send any large surplus to Nederland for the simple reason that the plan for securing the whole export of copper from Japan could not be implemented. The Chinese trade continually meant a very considerable competition, and the share of the Chinese in the trade to Japan during the following years, if anything, became greater than the proportion assigned to them in 1685. About 1700 Pieter van Dam remarked that the Chinese junks at Nagasaki sold three times as much as the Dutch Company.[51] On the other hand, the rise in the price of copper in Amsterdam towards the end of the 1680's caused the Heeren XVII again to enter Japanese copper bars in their list of returns wanted. In 1688 they started with a modest 150,000–200,000 ponds, and in 1692

[48] Kol. Arch. No. 459, 8 October 1685; *Pieter van Dam* 2:I, p. 480.
[49] Kol. Arch. No. 460, 25 October 1686.
[50] *Pieter van Dam* 2:I, p. 487; Kol. Arch. No. 461, 14 September 1695.
[51] *Pieter van Dam* 2:I, pp. 534 and 543.

– with reference to an auction price of 61 fl. – they increased this quantity to 300,000 ponds. In 1694 the Batavian Government sent more than twice this quantity pleading that there was a shortage of saltpetre for ballast, for which reason it had been necessary to use copper. This caused the Directors to reduce their following order to 200,000 ponds.[52] But towards the end of the 1690's it was again raised concurrently with the rise in prices, and in 1699 the order was for 5–600,000 ponds, which level was maintained until the spring of 1705. Then a period followed with reduced orders, and in the spring of 1710 the Heeren XVII called attention to the fact that copper was being quoted at so low a price in Nederland that the sales of it yielded a very small profit.[53] About 1712 the market changed. The prices of copper rose again in Amsterdam, and in the beginning of 1715 the Directors increased their order to 5–600,000 ponds, which was motivated by the state of war in Sweden.[54] Already the following year, however, the demand was reduced to 3–400,000 ponds, at which level it was kept to the end of the 1730's.

The export from Japan and the import to or sale in Nederland during this period were as follows:

Table 36. *Export from Japan, Import to Nederland, 1681–1734. Five-Year Averages in Ponds.*

	Japan Export	Nederland Import
1681–85	2,720,000	—
1686–90	2,118,125	93,625
1691–95	1,800,000	293,190
1696–00	2,592,756	381,297
1701–05	2,019,096	210,899
1706–10	1,638,528	547,230
1711–15	1,207,584	87,145
1716–20	1,248,000	140,041
1721–25	1,248,048	210,320
1726–30	1,116,000	—
1731–34*	979,560	217,735

* Only four-year average.

Again it is clearly seen that the greater part of the copper remained in the Asiatic trade. This is so in spite of the fact that the sales on the Coromandel Coast were on the decrease from the end of the 1680's. Starvation and failure of crops followed in the wake of the war, by which trade suffered. At the factory at Nagasaki they pleaded that the rela-

[52] Kol. Arch. No. 260, 8 November 1694. [53] Kol. Arch. No. 264, 4 March 1710.
[54] Kol. Arch. No. 198, 4 March 1715.

tively low export figures in the beginning of the 1690's were due to the failing sales on the Indian market and inversely attributed the rise in the export towards the end of the 1690's to the increasing European demand. The fall in the Asiatic consumption can also be traced in the prices.[55] This depression continued down to about 1710, only interrupted by a short-lived rise about the turn of the century. The years 1703–06 were particularly poor, as the sales of copper completely failed in Bengal in 1703–1705 and in Surat in 1705–1706, while the market was low on the Coromandel Coast.[56] From about 1710 we may, however, note rising prices and increased sales in Asia. In spite of the very high European prices of copper bars during the years 1714–1717 – the highest in the 17th and 18th centuries – it was very small quantities that were sent from Batavia to Nederland, which partly was due to the fact that the Asiatic prices were just rising, partly to the fact that the export from Japan because of the restrictions of the Japanese authorities was at a considerably lower level than in the 17th century. During these conditions there was not much copper to ship to Europe. In the beginning of the year 1717 the Heeren XVII suggested that the cargoes to Europe might be supplemented by copper from Tongking.[57] The public sales in Nederland increased considerably from 1719 to 1723 as compared with those of the preceding period, which may have been due to supplies of Tongking copper, but while Asiatic copper had previously fetched prices which were very close to those of Swedish and Norwegian refined copper, they were now at a lower level. This may have been due to the poorer quality of Tongking copper. From 1724 to 1734 there were practically no public sales of Asiatic copper in Nederland. On the other hand, the rise in prices of copper continued at the Asiatic factories and was reinforced towards the end of the 1720's to such a degree that the level – allowance being made for the difference between "light" and "heavy" money – came to be considerably higher than that of Europe. When related to the quantities sold at the factories this rise must be characterized as due to shortage. Thus the basis was created of the export to the East of European copper which was introduced by the English in 1731 and which the Dutch on a number of occasions intended to start.[58] Another fundamental change which took place during these first decades of the 18th century was that Bengal

[55] Glamann, "The Dutch East India Company's Trade in Japanese Copper", p. 68 f.
[56] *Ibid.* p. 54.
[57] Kol. Arch. No. 198, 22 February 1717.
[58] H. Hamilton, *The English Brass & Copper Industries to 1800* (London, 1926), p. 280; Feenstra Kuiper, *op. cit.* p. 152.

became the chief area also in the copper trade. 27 per cent. of the Company's sales of copper bars during the first 25 years of the century took place in Bengal, while the Coromandel Coast, which previously had been the main customer only received 26 per cent. Surat got 24 per cent., Ceylon 12 per cent., and the Malabar Coast 8 per cent.[59] Simultaneously the English had succeeded in establishing regular direct commercial relations with China from Europe as well as from India. From 1716 they had a council in Canton. It is true that it was especially the trade in tea which benefited by these new trade routes, but at first the Dutch Company found its important Asiatic copper trade to be threatened. It was feared that the English company would advance closer to the Japanese market. Not least the fear of the English was decisive of the rejection of the idea of closing down the Japan factory which at intervals had been ventilated, as the profitableness during the 18th century became poorer and poorer. In 1724 a great inquiry into conditions of the Japan factory was started. Material was collected from the first 25 years of the 18th century and it was learnt that the copper by the sales in India had yielded a gross surplus of just under 8 mill. fl. The corresponding profit at the sales in Europe had been just under 2.5 mill. fl. The profit from the sale in Japan of the Company's imported products was just under 0.5 mill. fl. This result was not alarming, but during the following years the gross profit from the sales of commodities at Nagasaki decreased, and when in 1730 the accounting practice was introduced of deducting the constant losses on Japanese *koubangs* at their sale on the Coromandel Coast, the profit decreased from 64 per cent. in 1729 to 9 per cent., only, in 1730. As early as 1734 this method of accounting was given up again. During these years two points of view fought against one another. One was the point of view of sales, which laid the main stress on the profit at Nagasaki by the sale of the imported commodities, the other was the point of view of purchase, which was interested in Japanese export goods and their resale in India and Europe. The Japanese on several occasions had demanded higher prices for their copper, thus in 1729, when they maintained that they actually delivered the copper to the Dutch below the market price.[60] The point of view of purchases about 1740 was eagerly maintained by G. W. van Imhoff in connexion with his proposal for a complete revision of the Company's rates of exchange. In van Imhoff's opinion the Japanese tael ought to be reduced from 70 to 40 st. in the Company's accounts. It is true that in this way the Company could whistle for any profit at the office at

[59] Kol. Arch. No. 1931, fos. 2178–85. [60] Feenstra Kuiper, *op. cit.* p. 118.

Nagasaki, but on the other hand the advantage was involved that it would be possible to comply with the Japanese wish for a higher price of copper and thus secure a greater quantity than previously. Next to spices copper was the Company's most important article of commerce, and so the trade to Japan exclusively ought to be carried on from this point of view.[61]

[61] G. W. van Imhoff, "Consideratiën over den tegenwoordigen staat van de Nederlandsche Oost Indische Maatschappij", ed. J. E. Heeres in *Bijdragen tot de Taal-, Land- en Volkenkunde van Nederlandsche-Indië*, deel 66 ('s-Gravenhage, 1912), p. 494 *et seq.*; van Imhoff, "Consideratiën over den Jappanschen handel", *Tijdschrift v. Nederl.-Indië* 1853.

CHAPTER X

Coffee

The analysis of the Company's European auctions showed that coffee in the beginning of the 18th century became a commodity of a fair size from the point of view of sales. Like tea, coffee contributed to changing the character of the East India trade; so it is necessary to give a more detailed account of the Company's trade in these products.

The first coffee made its appearance at the Dutch Company's public sales in Amsterdam during the accounting period of 1661/62. 21,481 ponds of "cauwa de Mocha" were sold there.[1] During the following accounting year no coffee was sold, but from 1663/64 to 1666/67 varying amounts were disposed of, though in no case so large a quantity as at the first sale. Then there was a prolonged interval. During the accounting years of 1685/86 and 1686/87, respectively 1,792 ponds and 2,586 ponds of coffee were sold from Kamer Amsterdam, but apart from these small quantities the sales did not become regular until the 1690's, and not until then did the quantities exceed the original level. While coffee thus during the greater part of the 17th century played an insignificant role at the factory Nederland and, if anything, was in the nature of being a drug which tentatively was placed on the European market, conditions were somewhat different in Asia. There the Dutch had rather early become acquainted with coffee. This happened at Mocha, where Pieter van den Broecke in 1616 learnt about "een spetie van swarte boontjens . . . gelijck boontjens-holwortel, daer swart water van maken en warm indrincken."[2] At that time coffee was universally known in all Mohammedan countries and was found among the multitude of commodities which circulated in the Indian-Persian-Arabian maritime trade, in which Mocha

[1] In other words, it is possible to trace coffee five years before the time indicated by P. A. Leupe, "Invoering der koffijkultur op Java, 1700-1750", *Bijdragen tot de Taal-, Land- en Volkenkunde van Nederlandsch-Indië* (Amsterdam, 1859), pp. 53–71, viz. in a printed note on the spring sales at Kamer Amsterdam on 16 March 1666. Cf. Klerk de Reus, *op. cit.* p. 226.

[2] F. de Haan, *Priangan*, De Preanger-regentschappen onder het Nederl. bestuur tot 1811, vol. III (Batavia, 1910-12), § 804.

was an important station. The Dutch Company was involved in this trade and also dealt in coffee, e.g. in Persia and Surat, in Ceylon and elsewhere. The trade to Arabia, Persia, and Northwest India belonged under the head office in Surat. The places where the Company bought the coffee depended on opportunities and money. Towards the end of the 1640's and in the beginning of the 1650's the place was Mocha, and the quantities bought annually ranged from 120,000 ponds to just under 200,000 ponds.[3] Although these figures are high as compared with the above-mentioned European ones, it must be said that coffee was not a constant article in the Company's Asiatic trade in the 17th century, either. The Company had no possibility of nor any appreciable interest in participating in the trade through the Red Sea, where the greater part of the coffee was distributed to the Turkish sultanates, while the smaller portion, which was shipped eastwards to Persia and Gujarat, rather followed the old caravan routes than the sea routes. Furthermore, there were the insecurity which at intervals characterized the trade in Arabian waters and the high-handedness which might manifest itself in Mocha on the part of the Arabian authorities.

The basis of the Company's great coffee trade in the 18th century is to be sought in the European demand. The Europeans' increasing taste for coffee not only gave the East India Companies a main commodity to trade in, but also caused the cultivation of coffee, which had so far taken place only in Yemen and Abyssinia, in a comparatively short time to spread to Java, Isle de Bourbon, the West Indies, Surinam, and Brazil. Next to the introduction of Indian cottons to the European market, the import of coffee and tea was the most important contribution of goods from the East in modern times. As in the case of spices, pepper, and silk, the first coffee came to Europe by way of the Levantine trade. About the same time as Pieter van den Broecke tasted coffee in Mocha, the first bales were unloaded at Venice, and after that time we find the drink mentioned in the South and West European towns round about. In 1652 the first coffee-house was opened in London, in 1671 and 1672 coffee-houses were established in Marseilles and Paris. Tradition will have it that coffee in the latter place was introduced with pomp and circumstance, as an embassy sent by Sultan Mohammed IV – which stayed in the city from July 1669 to May 1670 – brought along coffee and introduced the drink to the notabilities of the Court as well as of

[3] *Dagh-Register gehouden int Casteel Batavia, Anno 1664*, ed. I. A. van der Chijs (Batavia-'s Hage, XXXX), p. 311.

the city.[4] Coffee, however, was still by many people considered a medicine, and opinions differed as to its qualities. It was mainly beer that was drunk in the first coffee-houses, where tobacco smoke drifted nauseatingly in the room. The patrons of the houses were not held in great esteem. The Parisian coffee-house of 1672, which belonged to an Armenian, was maintained to be patronized only by Knights of Malta and foreigners, while the *bourgeoisie* stayed away. In these years a new figure made his appearance in the varied Parisian street-life. A small limping man named Candiot walked about crying coffee. He wore a white apron and carried, fastened to his belt, a bright metal box with coffee, sugar, cups, and other implements. In one hand he had a brazier with a *cafetière* mounted on it, in the other a kind of water tank.[5] It was a far cry from Candiot's quickly served coffee – price: 2 *sols* including sugar – to the elegant *cafés* which about 30 years later were found around la Foire Saint Germain: shops decorated with mirrors and crystal candelabra and with marble-topped tables, where writers, philosophers, and other beaux-esprits met "en prenant de café en bonne compagnie."[6] At that time there were about 300 *cafés* and coffee-houses in the metropolis. Coffee was getting victorious, and about 20 years later Jac. Savary in his well-known manual tells about the splendid Parisian *cafés*, in front of which even "les Dames de la première qualité" often had their carriages stopped and had a cup of coffee served at the carriage door on a silver tray.[7] France and England soon acquired a reputation for having a particular taste for coffee.

If François Valentijn is to be believed, it was the English who taught the Dutch to drink coffee. In 1726 Valentijn wrote that 40 years back coffee was a practically unknown drink in Nederland, but later "zoo algemeijn in ons land doorgebroken dat de meijden en naeisters nu smorgens hare coffi moeten hebben, of de draad wil door het oog van de naald niet."[8] To the literary evidence of the triumph of the drink should be added the fiscal one as the reverse of the medal. Savary gives an account of the French system of duties and the French retail distribution, a perfectible system which was to prevent all illegal traffic. In Amsterdam the Revenue Contractor Pieter de Veth in March 1692 sent out his spies on a raid among the coffee-houses of the town and spoilt the idyll, i.a. at Daniel Admirael's coffee-house behind the Exchange which

[4] La Roque, *Voyage de l'Arabie Heureuse* (Amsterdam, 1716), pp. 308 ff.
[5] *Ibid.* [6] *Ibid.*
[7] *Dictionnaire Universel de Commerce*, vol. I (Amsterdam, 1726), article on *café*.
[8] François Valentijn, *Oud en Nieuw Oost-Indiën*, deel 5: I (Dordrecht-Amsterdam, 1726), p. 190.

bore the concise name of "The Two Coffee-Bales", where a large number of people sat smoking and drinking coffee at 2 st. a cup.[9] Everywhere the authorities sharpened the control. It was not only the companies and the traders to the Levant who had got a great commodity to deal in; the smugglers, too, got busy.

Concordant with the marked French and English demands for coffee was the considerable trade to the Levant from these two countries, which was on a larger scale than the Dutch trade.[10] As seen from the point of view of the Company, however, there is nothing to indicate that the Dutch Company started the trade in coffee later than the English and French companies, whereas it is evident that at any rate the English company traded more regularly in coffee in the 17th century, which was conditioned by the greater sales in England. We have a basis for a judgment of the Dutch demand in the Company's orders to India for returns. From the year 1686 inclusive, coffee appears permanently in the orders for returns. In December 1689 the Directors for the first time mentioned the increasing sales, calling attention to the fact that coffee came into use more and more, for which reason they asked for 75–80,000 ponds. The Heeren XVII emphasized that the coffee should be fresh and good. When the following year they received a quantity of old and inferior coffee, the order was reduced to 40–50,000 ponds, while at the same time it was stated that the English had secured a much better and cheaper quality. The note struck here – the complaints of the quality and the high cost-prices – as will be seen below, was to be something of a leitmotif in the Directors' estimate of the Company's purchase of coffee. In 1695 they increased the order violently from 50,000 ponds to 3–400,000 ponds, which, amongst other things, was connected with very low supplies. This level was held until falling prices in 1699 made the Court of Directors reduce the order by half. In 1703 the annual order for coffee was increased to 200–250,000 ponds, the following year to 400,000 ponds, in 1707 to 500,000 ponds, and in 1711 to 600–700,000 ponds. Let us provisionally make a halt here and see how the orders were effected and at what prices the imported coffee was sold.

The factory in Mocha was closed down in 1684. The orders for coffee during the 1680's were directed to the Company's factories in Persia,

[9] Gemeente-Archief, Amsterdam, Not. Arch. No. 4435 (Not. Michiel Bockt), 21 March 1692. There 24 Amsterdam coffee-houses are enumerated, which had been inspected. According to kind information by Dr. Simon Hart, Amsterdam.

[10] The material of the Amsterdam Notarial Archives from about 1700 to about 1706 (Gemeente-Archief, indexes) shows practically exclusively Levant coffee in the various *insinuaties*. The coffee was imported from Leghorn or Genoa, from Marseilles, or by inland route by way of Geneva.

and the Heeren XVII gave orders for the Batavian Government to buy coffee in Persia and Surat as well as on the Malabar Coast or in other places where the "Moorish" merchants traded. They did not, however, succeed in getting hold of any large quantities, and what was bought was second-rate commodities. The Court of Directors complained that the contact between the various factories was not as it should be. In some cases they had omitted buying coffee because they assumed that other factories had made the purchases, and inversely. At the sales at Kamer Amsterdam the prices of coffee rose highly at the autumn sales in 1693, 1694, and 1695. The figures in 1695 show a trebling of the 1693 level and explain the violent increase of the order for coffee contained in the missive to the Governor General and Council sent in December 1695. The Heeren XVII in this letter gave orders to make use of all mercantile means at the purchase of coffee. This intense request was of no avail, on the contrary. During the following years no coffee at all came to Nederland by the returning ships. In the meantime the prices in Amsterdam rose to undreamt-of heights. In March 1697 the Heeren XVII maintained that coffee had been sold at 4 fl. or 80 st. per pond. Great supplies were on their way from the Levant, which had made the price fall to 46–47 st., but in spite of the possibility of a further fall in prices, the Directors thought that the coffee trade was still profitable. The supplies, however, continued being modest as compared with the orders. In July 1698 complaints of this were made in severe terms: because of failing purchases in Surat and on the Malabar Coast the Company had missed the great profits from the unique boom in Europe, where much money had been earned by trade in coffee. Now the prices had fallen to 24 st. per pond and "wij sullen achter het net konnen vissen," as it said in the letter. After this despondent message had been sent off, 129,931 ponds of coffee arrived by the returning fleet. The invoice price was about 0.54 fl. per pond and at the following auctions in the autumn of 1698, where the greater part of the coffee was sold at Kamer Amsterdam, an average price of about 1.08 fl. per pond was obtained, i.e. a gross profit of exactly 100 per cent. The Heeren termed this a "redelijcke winst", and reduced their orders for the following period. As so often in the Company's history it proved difficult to regulate and harmonize supplies in step with the fluctuations in the European demand. The time factor interfered. While the order of the Heeren XVII had been reduced to 150–200,000 ponds of coffee, 246,856 ponds were on the way home. Some of it was lost by shipwreck; but the following year 316,343 ponds of coffee were shipped from Ceylon, where the

Arabian, Persian, and parts of the Indian returns were gathered. The average cost-price of this lot was about 0.51 fl. per pond, and at the auctions in Amsterdam in the autumn of 1700 273,928 ponds of coffee were sold at 0.78 fl. per pond. The profit was decreasing which made the Directors cautious. They again enjoined the importance of having a close contact between the factories, and this time made Ceylon responsible for the large quantities which against orders had been shipped home. The cost-prices came under observation. It was important to make cheap purchases.

This was much easier to write than to execute in practice. In the East the Company, as it proved impossible to secure sufficient quantities of coffee by purchases from the Moorish merchants in Surat and elsewhere, had resumed the earlier traffic to Mocha. In 1696 Nicolaas Welters was appointed "hoofd te Mocha"[11] with Adriaen van den Heuvel as "secunde", and this was the introduction to the probably intensest phase of the Dutch Company's commercial intercourse with the Arabian world. During the following 30 years the Company had practically regular communications with Mocha and from 1707 a permanent residence in the town.[12] Mocha belonged under the Bassa of Yemen – the ancient Arabia Felix – who again was in vassalage to the Turkish Sultan. Towards the end of the 17th and in the beginning of the 18th centuries the town was of the same order of magnitude as the Dutch town of Dordrecht, its population being estimated at 10–12,000 inhabitants.[13] Its composition reflected the brisk trade that flourished in the town. The majority of the population consisted of Arabs, but also Persians, Turks, Abyssinians, and a few Jews lived in Mocha. Furthermore, there were the Indian traders, the banians, who had a limited religious liberty. The Bassa governed the town through a Governor, whose power was great, and who, amongst other things, regulated all conditions connected with duties and excises. The town was fortified towards the Red Sea by two forts, which controlled admission from the sea. On the other hand, there was no landward protection worth mentioning, as an old stone wall had fallen into disrepair. The climate seemed insufferable to the Europeans. Apart from a sea breeze which every day freshened a little in the morning, the heat was stifling. The drinking water was bad, and people were pestered by insects. It might happen that loading and unloading of ships in Mocha

[11] W. Wijnaendts van Resandt, *De gezaghebbers der Oost-Indische Compagnie op hare buitencomptoiren in Azië* (Amsterdam, 1944), p. 232.

[12] J. A. van der Chijs, *Realia*, Register op de generale resolutien van het Kasteel Batavia, 1632/1805 ('s Hage-Batavia, 1882–1885), 3 October 1707.

[13] Valentijn, *op. cit.* p. 189.

had to be interrupted for days as the crew were ill because of the heat.[14] A passage characteristic of the Dutch merchants' attitude towards life in Mocha is that which slipped in when the residents Abraham Pantzer and Gabriel Scholten in February 1719 learnt that they would be relieved: "Waar voor den Almagtigen zij gelooft en gedanckt, die ons nog de hoope heeft overgelaten, om ons eerlang uyt deese ongesonden landen en quaadaerdige caste te zijn gered."[15]

As in so many other places in the Asiatic trade it was the monsoons that indicate the rhythm in the trade of Mocha. In the spring months of March and April the ships arrived, either in order to trade or to go on with pilgrims to Jidda, the port of Mecca. They came from Persia, from Surat, from Diu, Goa, Calicut, Cananoor and Dabhol, from Masulipatam, and from as far away as Achin. Furthermore, from Mozambique and Abyssinia. Almost at the same time the caravans came from Cairo, Alexandria, and Aleppo, generally a number of 1500–1600 camels. The stream of commodities also passed by sea through the Red Sea. There the commodities of the Levant trade and Asia Minor met with commodities from Arabia, Africa, Persia, India, and Indonesia and with the products of the Far East. J. C. van Leur on the basis of the material published by Dr. Terpstra has drawn a vivid picture of this trade in the beginning of the 17th century – the trade of travelling pedlars – and has compared life in Mocha at the time with the scene in Macalla, as it might be experienced in 1931.[16] The large amounts of precious metals which were realized in Mocha at an early stage made a profound impression on the Dutch merchants. Thus Pieter van den Broecke in 1616 saw the arrival of two caravans which brought about 200,000 rials of eight and 100,000 Hungarian, Venetian, and Turkish gold ducats.[17] Not least the prospect of obtaining part of this stream of specie had made the Dutch East India Company send its ships to Mocha, but in the 17th century the Company nevertheless preferred Persia to Arabia, partly because of the unsafeness, partly because an export to the Red Sea of e.g. pepper was not expedient, considering the near connexion with the Levant.[18]

When the Dutch trade to Mocha was resumed, the factory in Surat because of the piracy rampant in the waters around Socotra and the Cambay Gulf by the Prince of Gujarat and the Great Mogul was forced

[14] Kol. Arch. No. 1810, "Daghregister Mocha", 26 March 1719.
[15] *Ibid.* 14 February 1719. [16] van Leur, *op. cit.* pp. 75 ff.
[17] Valentijn, *op. cit.* p. 189 *et seq. Pieter van Dam* 2:III, pp. 262 ff., "Beschryvinge van Mocha" (about 1623).
[18] M. A. P. Roelofsz, *op. cit.* p. 92.

to establish a convoy service from Surat to Mocha together with the English and the French companies. This meant that some of the Indian trade to Arabia took the form of freightage by the company ships. The tense relations in Gujarat between the Europeans and the Prince – which later necessitated the embassies to the Great Mogul – could not but have a hampering effect, especially during the years from 1702 to 1706. At first the trade yielded a good result from a traditional point of view. The Residents informed the Company that during the period from November 1697 to November 1699 a net profit – i.e. all costs in the place being deducted – of 219,334 fl. had been won.[19] As compared with the previous expeditions to Mocha, it was even a great profit.[20] The balance had mainly been derived from the sale of pepper, cloves, sugar, Japan copper, Siam tin, and lead, to which should be added the freightage from the convoy ships. From the balance 10,747 rials of eight were shipped to Surat, while 12,694 pieces of different "Moorish" ducats were sent to the Malabar Coast to be used there in settlement of bills of exchange drawn on Surat. The latter procedure took place for reasons of currency, as the ducats mentioned were at a low rate of exchange in Surat. Trade in Mocha, for that matter, had shown that not everything could be sold at a profit. They had to return 77,795 pieces of China porcelain – which were forwarded to Europe – and some silk fabrics. The sales of pepper had not been satisfactory either, which by the Residents was ascribed to great supplies of Malabar pepper by Indian ships to Aden and Mocha. They had also suffered disappointments as regards Ceylon cinnamon. The Arabs had no taste for genuine cinnamon, they used wild cinnamon imported from the Malabar Coast, and purchases by the Turkish merchants failed.[21]

The re-established trade to Mocha should not, however, be viewed traditionally. Peddling and specie were no longer primary factors.[22] The Company wanted coffee, coffee for Europe. In order to have their wishes fulfilled it soon proved necessary to leave Mocha and go north, to the very coffee districts at the foothills of Yemen, where Arabian peasants in the dampest and shadiest places had their terraced gardens with the coffee bushes placed in long, dense rows, some of them protected by trees. Often the gardens were provided with canals and small ditches

[19] Kol. Arch. No. 1504, General Letter dated at Batavia, 20 January 1700.

[20] Kol. Arch. No. 1297, fos. 823–32, "Memorie van de winsten op verscheyde voyagies na Mocha" (1641–1684).

[21] Kol. Arch. No. 1491, letter dated at Mocha, 23 August 1698.

[22] Cf. Milburn, who in *Oriental Commerce* about 1800 wrote that the trade to Mocha constantly yielded a surplus of bullion and money when viewed from Bombay, but that the total picture was in disfavour of Europe when the purchases of coffee were taken into consideration.

for irrigation. There the town of Beit-el-Faki was situated, the centre of the coffee trade, where merchants from Hejaz, Egypt, Syria, Constantinople, Fez, Morocco, Habbesh, Persia, and India met. It was the centre of a trade of a world-embracing character which had hitherto been closed to European activities. Now the companies' servants so to say walked in at the backdoor. Beit-el-Faki was only a day's journey from the outermost districts of the coffee hills and a day's journey and a half from the port Hodeida. By land to Mocha the journey took four days by camel and six days into the hills to the ancient town of Sana.[23] Another important market was farther north about Zilba with the port Lohaya. From Beit-el-Faki to Lohaya by land the distance was four days' journeys and a half. The coffee, which began to ripen in January-February, and which in a few districts might be harvested twice a year, which was not the normal, was named after the various districts. The name also was a description. The coffee from Wosab and Suffal had a reputation for being the best, but it was difficult to secure at Beit-el-Faki. This was followed by the sorts of coffee from Harras, Rimma, Himma, and Doran, which became the sorts the Europeans provided themselves with, whereas the coffee from Zilba and Sinan was not unconditionally to their taste. In Mocha it was also possible to buy Abyssinian coffee, but its quality was poor. It was bought by the native population and some of it was exported to Surat, but on the whole in very small quantities.[24]

The backdoor could be opened, but not without resistance. To the Turkish merchants the question was by what channels the European demand was to be met, and there the Levant – as indicated above – so far had the upper hand. In August 1698 the Dutch merchants wrote from Mocha that a large number of Turkish merchants from Jidda had arrived at Beit-el-Faki and had purchased coffee for the Levant. The native merchants at Mocha had held their coffee off the market, hoping for a further profit by the rise in prices. This caused the average price of the total Dutch purchases in 1698 to be well over 10 *penningen* above the price of 1697 in Surat.[25] It was evident that the Dutch Company's purchases were not of such a volume as to have any appreciable influence on prices in Arabia. The demand from the north was decisive. Two facts, however, during the following period came to be in favour of the maritime trade to Mocha. One was that the Egyptian Bassa, inspired by the

[23] Carsten Niebuhr, *Reisebeschreibung nach Arabien und andere umliegenden Ländern*, vol. I (København, 1774), p. 318 *et seq.*

[24] C. R. O. London, Egypt & Red Sea, vol. I, 1644–1726, Mocha General Letters, No. 29, 20 July 1721 and No. 182, 6 August 1725.

[25] Kol. Arch. No. 1491, General Letter dated at Batavia, 10 February 1699.

large transits of coffee in 1699 – in conflict with existing "capitulations" – got the idea of raising the transit duty by 12 ½ per cent.[26] The increase meant a temporary interruption of the coffee-trade in the Levant, as it occurred at a time when the European market provisionally was saturated and the European merchants therefore could refuse taking the dearer coffee. During the following years the Governor at Mecca and Jidda showed a similar high-handedness in his attitude towards trade.[27] The other fact simply was that the Turkish Sultan's effective authority in Yemen did not prove sufficient for him to restrict, still less prohibit the increasing European trade in coffee at Mocha and Beit-el-Faki. Thus in 1719 the Sultan sent several envoys to Yemen in order to obtain a prohibition of export by the Europeans. However, they received the answer that if the Sultan wanted to acquire all coffee from his countries, such a monopoly must be secured by the Turkish merchants if they guaranteed the Arabs an annual amount in cash which at least corresponded to that introduced into Yemen by the Europeans. The envoys did not like that answer, but there was nothing to be done about it.[28]

The low prices in Nederland during the first years of the 18th century about 1704 were followed by a rise. Again the problem arose of having demand and supply co-ordinated. In March 1705 the Heeren XVII complained that they had not received any coffee from the East. In their letter they mentioned a Dutch price of 28 st. per pond of coffee and increased their order for the year 1706 to 400,000 ponds. The Directors were aware of the difficulties against which the Company's servants had to fight in Surat, but thought that the coffee might be bought on the Malabar Coast. The trade to Mocha during those years came to a complete standstill. From 1702 to 1706 inclusive, no coffee came to Europe by the ships from Ceylon. But coffee – probably from the Malabar Coast – arrived from Batavia. The quality gave occasion for complaints. In February 1707 the price in Holland rose to 38 st. per pond. This price was maintained at the auction in the autumn when 276,381 ponds of coffee were sold in Amsterdam. At the autumn sale in Amsterdam in 1708 the average price rose to 54 ½ st. per pond. Only 48,409 ponds were sold, and part of the coffee was Mocha coffee of good quality, which to some degree explains the high price. At the same sale 40.13 st. was quoted at Kamer Zeeland, and the total average was stated to be 49.13 st.[29] The improvement in quality was not only due to the fact that the Company had again started buying coffee in Arabia, but also that greater

[26] Heeringa, *op. cit.* p. 280. [27] *Ibid.* p. 474.
[28] Kol. Arch. No. 1810, "Daghregister Mocha", 7 and 10 July 1719.
[29] Kol. Arch. No. 10,228; cf. Appendix B.

care had been taken as to the transport of coffee. The practice was introduced as far as possible to place the coffee in ships where no pepper was loaded. When the trade was resumed, it appeared that the cost-prices had not fallen since the Dutch last traded to Mocha. The coffee of the season of 1707 was bought at an average price of about 12 ½ st. per pond or 0.63 fl. per pond. During the following years the prices fluctuated between 0.55 fl. and 0.58 fl. per pond. Even though the auction prices in Holland left the excessively high level of 1708 and during the two following years were respectively about 31 st. and about 37 st. (in Amsterdam), the profit was considered satisfactory. Failing purchases at Mocha during the season of 1710 caused the Governor General and Council in Batavia to try having the coffee dispatched more quickly and effectively. Hitherto the coffee had been sent from Mocha to Surat and from there to Ceylon, where it was finally transshipped to the homeward-bound vessels. In other words, they had followed the traditional route along the coast to and from Mocha. By the growing European demand the ships were increasingly provided with cash for the purchases, whereas the Indian commodities receded into the background. Hence the idea arose of making special "coffee ships" sail direct from Batavia or Ceylon across the ocean to the northernmost point of Madagascar and from there farther to Mocha, and return by the same route to Ceylon or direct to Europe. This was a bold attempt at reducing the time factor. The first attempt, however, was no success, resulting in the Company's purchases of coffee in 1712 being very small.[30] By following the Dutch Company's supplies with coffee during these years the impression forces itself upon us that it was behindhand as compared with its competitors. As early as 1708 the French East India Company at St. Malo to the indignation of the Marseilles merchants had sent two ships direct to Mocha for coffee and in 1712 the experiment was repeated.[31] The English company started a similar traffic. In the season of 1711 the two nations together imported 2 mill. ponds of coffee from Mocha. The Dutch, whose purchases, as mentioned above, had failed in 1710, and who in 1712 bought a negligible quantity, in 1711 secured a quantity corresponding to somewhere between $^1/_4$ and $^1/_3$ of the total English-French purchases.

It is evident that the trade in coffee about 1712 was changing character. The European companies during the following period sent large amounts of cash to Mocha, often by the direct route; the export quantities became of an order of magnitude which rendered a revaluation of the profit percentages necessary; simultaneously the Levant trade lost ground in the race for carrying the coffee-beans to the Europe thirsting for coffee.

[30] Kol. Arch. No. 264, 10 March 1712. [31] La Roque, *op. cit.* p. 107 *et seq.*

A piece of evidence of this new situation is the Heeren XVII's letter to Batavia dated at 10 March 1712.

In the letter, which contains the order concerning the homeward-bound fleet of 1713, they asked for 1 mill. ponds of coffee from Mocha, Surat, and other places, or as much as can be held in two "coffee ships". No means or efforts should be spared, it says, to secure for the Company this costly commodity, which with the greatly increasing sales in Nederland gave the Company great profits. The Heeren XVII did not hesitate to characterize coffee as one of the most profitable commodities in the commerce. Only spices and a few other products were more profitable. It was recommended that Bengali raw silk and silk fabrics should be kept back in order to obtain sufficient cash for the purchase of coffee.[32] How did this optimistic evaluation agree with fact? At the auctions later in the year 476,982 ponds of coffee were sold at Kamer Amsterdam at an average price of 1.40 fl. or 28 st. per pond. This was the greater part of the Dutch purchases in Arabia during the season of 1711, of which the lion's share had been bought by contract in the month of May at 70 ½ rials per bahar or about 11 ½ st. per pond, in other words, a gross profit which roughly – the factory expenses incurred are unknown[33] – amounted to about 141 per cent. As mentioned above, the Company's servants at Mocha did not succeed in effecting the large order for the season of 1712, but in the following season they were successful. The invoices of the ships from Ceylon show that a total of 1,117,538 ponds of coffee bought in 1713 at an average price of about 11.6 st. was sent home. At that time, however, the prices in Europe were falling. In a letter to the Governor General and Council in Batavia dated at 1 March 1714 – thus sent before the large quantities bought in the season of 1713 had reached Nederland – the Court of Directors advised caution as the price of coffee had fallen considerably as a consequence of the huge quantities of coffee-beans which the English and the French had sent to Europe for two successive years. The Heeren XVII therefore only asked for one cargo of coffee by the returning fleet in 1715, or about 500,000 ponds. The fall in prices continued at the Company's autumn sales. At Kamer Amsterdam 733,370 ponds of coffee were sold at an average price of 1.18 fl. per pond. The gross profit was about 104 per cent. Still, the increasing sale meant that the Company actually earned more by this sale than by the sale of 1712, the gross profit in money in 1712, when the price was 1.40 fl. per pond, amounting to 391,125 fl. as against a profit of 440,022 fl.

[32] Kol. Arch. No. 264, 10 March 1712.

[33] As far as can be seen the material of invoices from Ceylon is not complete for that year.

at the autumn sale in 1714, when the price was 1.18 fl. per pond. As long as the cost-prices at Mocha did not rise, there was thus no problem. They did not do so during the following three seasons, 1714, 1715, and 1716. Therefore it was no calamity that the Company in 1715 received 1,100,926 ponds of Mocha coffee instead of the 500,000 ponds ordered. The gross profit from the sales in Amsterdam in the autumn of 1715 was 464,246 fl.[34] It seemed that the Dutch market could absorb the large quantities, and a rise in prices in the spring of 1716 made the Heeren XVII order 1.2–1.3 mill. ponds of coffee or two cargoes from Mocha. The Government in Batavia was ordered to supply the factory at Mocha amply with cash, and it was decided to make the ships from Mocha return direct to Europe instead of going by way of Ceylon. The route along the African coast, however, was dangerous to the ships, for which reason the direct homeward voyage was abandoned. In 1718 the Heeren XVII decided that the ships from Mocha should again go to Ceylon, where refreshments should be taken in. They should not, however, await the rest of the homeward-bound fleet, but go to the Cape of Good Hope and wait for the rest of the fleet there. The order was repeated in 1721, a sailing plan being recommended according to which the coffee ships in the month of August should be sent from Mocha and arrive at Gale on the southern point of Ceylon in September. From there they were to follow the ordinary route of the Ceylon fleet until they were off the Sunda Strait, and then continue in the wake of the Batavia fleet to the Cape. After a short stay in Cape Town the coffee ships were to finish the voyage home alone round the north of Scotland. In this way the coffee ships would sail after the Batavia fleet, but before the Ceylon fleet, which according to plan left Gale in November. The background to these rearrangements of the routes was the dissatisfaction with the quality of the coffee brought home. The damp and hot climate at Mocha and in Ceylon spoilt the coffee, which easily became mouldy and musty.[35]

In the spring of 1718 the Heeren XVII increased the order for Mocha coffee to 1.4–1.5 mill. ponds. Four years later it was further raised to 2 mill. ponds or three cargoes. Proportionally to this rise in the demand there was an increase in the dissatisfaction with the quality and the cost-prices of the coffee sent home. Throughout the 1720's the complaints

[34] 725,384 ponds of coffee were sold at an average of 1.18 fl. According to the invoices from Ceylon the cost-price at Mocha was about 10.8 st. per pond.

[35] Kol. Arch. No. 198, 9 March 1716 and 3 March 1718. Furthermore, Kol. Arch. No. 464, 15 October 1721. In 1722 we find for the first time special invoices for the two coffee ships dated at Gale in October, while the invoices of the Ceylon ships were dated at Gale 25 November 1722, Kol. Arch. No. 1866, fo. 152, and Kol. Arch. No. 1868, fo. 1600 *et seq*. Cf. the fact that the coffee imported was sold by auction on 2 August 1723, i.e. about three months prior to the normal autumn auction.

were permanent and amongst other things resulted in the Dutch First Resident at Mocha, Joan van Leeuwen, being arrested and held responsible for his arrangements in connexion with the purchases in the season of 1720, but in spite of this there was no material improvement in the Heeren XVII's opinion. The rise in prices was due to the supply and demand at Mocha. The central point of the Directors' criticism of the purchases in Yemen, however, was the assertion that the Dutch merchants bought too poor and too expensive coffee as compared with their English, French, and Belgian competitors. As this criticism touches on something absolutely essential in connexion with the Company's commercial activities, we shall, in what follows, in some detail consider conditions of purchase during the years in which the Dutch Company's trade to Mocha was at its height.

While the cost-prices at Mocha during the years from 1708 to 1716 inclusive had been at quite a stable level, ranging from just below 11 to well over 11 ½ st. per pond, the price in the season of 1717 rose to about 13.6 st. and in the season of 1718 to about 17 st. per pond. The Company's servants at Mocha explained to the Directors that the coffee had become so expensive because the Europeans had started buying to an extent as never before. They substantiated their explanation by statistics which showed that while the Company during the years 1707–15 inclusive had bought a total of 4,143,252 ponds of coffee for 8 ships, they had in the three following years, 1716–18, sent off 5 ships from Mocha with a total quantity of 3,768,494 ponds of coffee. The English and French purchases had increased in the same proportion, and furthermore, the sales to the Turkish, Persian, and Indian areas had increased. The production in Yemen simply could not keep pace with this demand; especially in the season of 1718 the shortage was pronounced,[36] as the crops failed that year and the country was ravaged by famine. Comprehensive new plantations had been made, which promised a larger supply. Furthermore the Company's servants explained that while during the quiet years they had comparatively easily and in good time been able to enter into contracts with the native brokers or coffee merchants at Mocha – they employed banians – these had understandably been very reserved during the rise in prices. Conditions of purchases were characterized by engrossing, and often the coffee at Beit-el-Faki only appeared in small lots, i.e. 20–100 camel loads a day during the harvest time. The arrival of European or other ships at Mocha – or only rumours of ships to be expected – made

[36] Cf. also C. R. O. London, Egypt & Red Sea, vol. I, 1664–1726, No. 29, letter dated at 20 July 1721.

the prices rise. There were cases on record of the price per bahar rising in a week by 25–30 rials at Beit-el-Faki.[37] In short, during such unsettled conditions accidental factors supervened. The actual cause of the rise in prices in 1718 was an abnormally great demand and an also abnormally small supply.

After the high rise in prices in 1718 it was awaited in great suspense what the following years had in store. On the basis of the extant journal we may – as an illustration – follow the season of 1719 at close range, as it developed for the Company's merchants Abraham Pantzer and Gabriel Scholten.[38] The journal is introduced by a statement on 5 December 1718 that various Turkish merchants from Jidda had arrived at Beit-el-Faki in order to buy up old coffee. It says that at Jidda there were only small stocks of coffee and that the price there was 36 rials per 100 ponds. The Turks' appearance at Beit-el-Faki made coffee rise to 160 rials per bahar so that an Arabian merchant named Mahmet Macboel – according to the Dutch merchants' statement the greatest merchant in the place – earned 25–30,000 rials. One month later the Dutch noted that the price of old coffee had dropped again at Jidda (to 30–28 rials per 100 ponds) as well as at Beit-el-Faki (to 150–148 rials per bahar). At the same time the new crop was ripening. It was of excellent promise. The first berries had among the Arabs been traded at a price of 125–130 rials at Beit-el-Faki, but they were still too green to be good. For that matter conditions were characterized by quiet, not only commercial, but political conditions as well. On the 14th of January the Company's broker, F. Wiera, sent a first sample of the new crop to the Residents at Mocha. Having weighed and dried the coffee-berries the Dutch established that there was a loss in weight of 10–15 per cent., for which reason they made up their minds not to enter into any contract. The prices at Beit-el-Faki then were respectively 140–145 rials for coffee of the old harvest and 120–130 rials for the new crop. On 24 January the Company's servants received a second sample of the new crop from the broker. Pantzer and Scholten, who by the Government in Batavia had been ordered to make their purchases in good time, found two sorts suitable, being of dry, good coffee, which was offered them at a price of 125–130 rials (per Beit-el-Faki bahar). The broker declared himself willing to contract for 2–300 bahars (Mocha weight), but the Residents wanted to contract for 1,000 bahars. Wiera replied that he dared not contract for so large a quantity, reminding the Dutchmen of

[37] Kol. Arch. No. 1810, letter dated at Mocha, 19 August 1719, and "Daghregister Mocha".
[38] Kol. Arch. No. 1810. Regarding the following prices see Appendix G.

the violent rises in prices which in the last two years had set in on the arrival of the European coffee ships. He stuck to the 2–300 bahars; but the Dutch merchants pointed out that there was much coffee on the market at Beit-el-Faki, but few buyers, that prices would fall rather than rise owing to the supplies which every day arrived more abundantly, as the crop to all appearance would be great, that the coffee prices at Grand Cairo, i.e. Medina, and Jidda were falling, and that the arrival of the European ships was uncertain. Furthermore, they thought that the demand from Turkish as well as European quarters would hardly reach the heights of the preceding years. The broker shrewdly replied that the Dutch merchants themselves might send a man to Beit-el-Faki to buy coffee on his own account. If so, he offered to assist him at a reasonable brokerage. The Residents excused themselves. As Pantzer had been ill and was still weak, he could not spare a man for this purpose. The result was a compromise: a contract for 500 bahars of coffee at 82 ½ rials (per Mocha bahar) free of carriage on the Dutch scales. In the merchants' opinion this was a profitable contract.

On 14 February 1719 the Company's ships the "Vrieswijck" and the "Amsterdam" arrived at Mocha. Onboard the ships were the merchants Joan van Leeuwen, Pieter Zeegers, and Jan van Alderweereld, who were to replace Pantzer and Scholten as Residents. On 16 February they were introduced to the Commandant, who welcomed them "met alle vriendelijckheid en blijdschap" and offered the Arabian national drink, *kitscha*, consisting of coffee extract and rose water. The appearance of the Company ships made the prices at Beit-el-Faki rise from 125–130 to 135–140 rials per bahar. On 1 March the Dutch entered into a second contract with the broker for 1000 bahars of coffee. Unfortunately the particular terms are unknown.[39] Some days later the Residents received a message that Wiera's men at Beit-el-Faki had difficulties in getting camels for the transport to Mocha of the coffee contracted for. The Company complained to the Governor. The lack of camels was due to great export of coffee to Jidda, Babylonia, and Persia. The camels took the coffee to the port of Hodeida, and as long as this transport lasted, it was difficult to find a sufficient number, as the camel-drivers preferred the shorter road, which was more lucrative, to the longer road to Mocha. On the 22nd of March van Leeuwen was sent off to Beit-el-Faki in order to inquire into the matter. He reported that the sales of coffee to Persia and Babylonia were great, and that the prices for some time had been as high as 145–148 rials, but now again were at a level of 135–140 rials per bahar. In the beginning of the month of May it was rumoured that

[39] The journal refers to the Minutes of the Residents, which it has not been possible to find.

30 plums of rials had arrived at Hodeida from Jidda for the purchase of coffee. The price at Beit-el-Faki leapt by 10–15 rials to 155–160 rials per bahar. The rumour, however, proved to be greatly exaggerated. Only three plums had arrived, and the price dropped to 140–145 rials.

On the 12th and 13th of May no less than seven ships arrived at Mocha, viz. three ships from Surat, two ships from the Malabar Coast, and two ships bound for Europe, viz. the French "Le Paix" from St. Malo and the Ostend ship "The Empress Elisabeth". The Dutch merchants noted that the captain and supercargo of the latter were English, and that both vessels almost exclusively carried cash for the purchase of coffee. On the 16th of May a fourth ship arrived from Surat. The coffee then was quoted at 100 rials per bahar. While the French merchants already on the 19th of May went to Beit-el-Faki with a banian in order to make purchases, the men of the Ostend ship hesitated. It was reported that the Imperial merchants tried to get their coffee from the English consul at Mocha, Mr. Hill, who according to the Dutch Residents had on hand 400 "camels", i.e. bahars, and who offered to have the remaining quantity bought by his sub-merchant, Mr. Seijs. On the 28th of May Mr. Seijs left for Beit-el-Faki with two Ostenders. The Dutch merchants about that time mentioned a price of 155–160 rials at Beit-el-Faki. On the 7th of June it says in the journal that letters from the coffee centre reported greedy purchases made by the French and the Imperial company merchants. The latter had paid 161 rials per bahar for their coffee. On the 10th of June the Dutch Residents entered into their third contract, which was for 1000 bahars (Mocha weight), this time with the broker Amier Zient. The contents of this contract are not known, either. By the middle of June it was stated that the coffee at Jidda cost 24–25 rials per 100 ponds, which was a little more than the price at Mocha and Beit-el-Faki. The Turkish merchants at Jidda said that the large quantities exported by the Europeans were the cause of the high prices. On the 27th of June the Company's ship "Vrieswijck" was full-laden. This time the Dutch had finished very early, also as compared with their European competitors. On the 6th of July they entered into the fifth and last contract for a quantity of 500–600 bahars of coffee for the "Amsterdam". The price was 100½ rials (per Mocha bahar). In the middle of July the journal was concluded with a specification of the ships found on the roads of Mocha for commercial purposes in the monsoon or season of 1719, a total of 22. Furthermore, there were the vessels from the local trade (provisions, ivory, gold, slaves, etc.), i.e. ships from Musquette, Jidda, Hodeida, and other places.

At the loading of the last coffee into the "Amsterdam" the Company was exposed to one of the not infrequent interferences on the part of the local Commandant. The road down to the ships was barred and the Commandant prohibited his Arabs to unload and load the ships, whether Dutch, English, French, or Imperial. Futhermore, all banians in European service were told that the Commandant would refuse to give his permission to the shipping of a single bale of coffee if they did not buy the coffee on hand at Mocha. The English consul protested on behalf of himself and the Imperial merchants with reference to the fact that he had previously in the season unsuccessfully tried to buy coffee at Mocha. The French merchants lodged a similar protest, but added that they were willing to buy the coffee mentioned – which of course belonged to the Commandant – if they could get credit for a year. Perhaps this proposal was accepted, at any rate the prohibition was soon repealed. For that matter the high-handedness experienced by the Europeans at Mocha was nothing as compared with what the Asiatic merchants had to put up with on the part of the Commandant. Altogether the European nations during these years enjoyed greater commercial privileges at Mocha than the Asiatics. While the latter paid an export duty of 9 per cent., that of the Europeans was only 3 per cent., indeed, the French had succeeded in having their duty reduced to 2.75 per cent. The Dutch and the English furthermore had a quota of 600 bales of coffee free of duty. Besides, the clearance for the Europeans was very lenient as compared with that for the native merchants, who had their commodities closely inspected. The last feature was by the English considered an important factor as it might contribute to the trade to Surat passing to a higher degree from Indian to English hands. Often a complaint to the Governor was effective, not least when accompanied by a present in the shape of rials, "which is the strongest argument you can urge."[40]

It is also characteristic that the Imperial merchants could make their purchases without being annoyed by their European competitors. It applied at Mocha as at Canton that if the Ostend ships had reached port, they were under the protection of the foreign jurisdiction. As is well-known, the Courts of Directors of the Dutch, English, and French companies wanted to fight the Ostend company by all means. When the decision of the British Parliament to arrest British subjects outside the service of the East India Company reached the factory at Mocha, the company's servants at the factory replied that "attempting such a thing here, would bring us into a dispute with the government, who we believe

[40] C. R. O. London, Egypt & Red Sea, vol. I, 1644–1726, No. 84, 16 July 1722.

would interfere to protect the people of any ship that came to the port as they show an equal respect without distinction to Europeans."[41]

The Dutch purchases in the season of 1719 were 1,626,748 ponds of coffee at an average invoice price of about 15.3 st. per pond. The rise in prices thus had stopped, although the prices had not dropped to the old level. The lower prices, however, only lasted for three years. In 1722 the curve rose again, culminating in the season of 1725 with an average cost-price of no less than 22 st. per pond. The table below shows the annual average prices at Mocha during 1713–27, as they appear from the material of invoices.

Table 37. *Dutch Purchases of Coffee at Mocha, 1713–1727.*

Season	Amount	Average	Season	Amount	Average
	1,000 ponds	st. per pond		1,000 ponds	st. per pond
1713......	1,118	11.6	1721......	1,699	14.4
1714......	1,101	10.8	1722......	1,685	15.8
1715......	568	11.3	1723......	864	17.7
1716......	711	11.1	1724......	808	19.2
1717......	1,471	13.6	1725......	462	22.0
1718......	1,585	17.0	1726......	561*	14.6
1719......	1,627	15.3	1727......	534	10.4
1720......	1,772	14.9			

* Estimated at 2,150 bales of 261 ponds (cf. Appendix G).

One might suppose that the Heeren XVII would be pleased with the falling prices during the years immediately after 1718. They were not satisfied, however, but continually maintained that the cost-prices were too high. Especially severe was the criticism of the purchases in the season of 1720, for which the above-mentioned Resident van Leeuwen was held responsible. The total amount bought was 1,771,742 ponds of coffee shipped by the "Rotterdam" and the "Lugtenberg". According to the invoices the price of these cargoes amounted to a total of 1,317,055 fl., which gave the average price of about 14.9 st. per pond, as indicated in the table above. But besides, there were various expenses which in the Directors' opinion should be included, the total expenditure thus being 1,362,507 fl., the average price consequently being well over 15 st. per pond. Inquiries were made into the prices of coffee at Surat, at the Persian factories, and at Basra; it was learnt that towards the end of 1720 and in the beginning of 1721 coffee had been sold in these places at respectively 9.6–11 st., 17–18.4 st., and well over 7 st. per pond.[42]

[41] *Ibid.* No. 29, 20 July 1721.
[42] Kol. Arch. No. 1843, fo. 1222, survey dated at Batavia, 14 September 1721.

By a decision of 16 September 1721 van Leeuwen was dismissed as First Resident at Mocha and summoned to Batavia under arrest with his salary written off, as the Government considered his purchases to be fraudulent. The best basis of comparison, however, must have been the purchases of the competing companies for Europe. In this respect the Heeren XVII maintained that the English company always bought better and cheaper coffee in Arabia than the Dutch, but apart from the fact that it appears from their records that the Directors sent samples of English company coffee to the factory at Mocha in proof of their assertion,[43] it has not been possible to find any satisfactory documentation concerning this serious count of the indictment. We must consult the material of the English company, partly the letters from Mocha, partly the accounts, for a possible answer to the question.

The English merchants as well had difficulties about the prices at Mocha in the second decade of the 18th century. They thought that the famine in 1718 was the immediate cause of the violent rise in prices during this season. The reason why the level was still high was that the Europeans had adopted the practice of permanently settling at Mocha which promoted engrossing. From one season to another they started the purchase of coffee earlier and earlier. Another factor which influenced the price was the time of arrival of the ships with cash. On all those points their explanations did not differ materially from those of their Dutch colleagues. But a new feature appears in the English letters from Mocha in 1721.

The English merchants in the early spring of 1721, for money which had been left over from the previous season, had made cheap purchases for the "Sutherland". However, they only succeeded in obtaining part of the cargo of the "Sutherland" on the cheap, as the French merchants at Beit-el-Faki tried to capture the market and in this way forced up the prices. Then one of the ships of the Ostend company arrived, and prices at Beit-el-Faki leapt from 115 to 125 rials (per bahar). The arrival of two English ships produced a further rise in the price of coffee to 130 rials, the result being that the following English purchases were made at considerably higher prices. At the race for coffee in that year the French gained the victory, first of all because their ships arrived first. The English merchants estimated the French cost-prices at an average of 120 rials, and that of the Ostend merchants at about 130 rials. "But there's no knowing what the Dutch's stand them in, their method of providing being different from other Europeans, what they purchase is by contract with the banians for certain quantities, which is kept very secret, and

[43] Kol. Arch. No. 464, 7 October 1720.

sometimes they make three or four contracts in a season," it says in the English general letter of 1721. The English traders further relate how the Dutch in 1721 put off making a contract for coffee, hoping that no English or French ships would arrive from Europe. Disappointed in their expectations they had under compulsion to contract for coffee "at a very high rate." Their late purchases drove up the prices of camels to the detriment of the English, who were also rather late. "It is the general opinion," concludes the report from Mocha, "[that] the Dutch buy their coffee dearer than other Europeans, and have it not so well garbled, their export this year will be about 7,000 bales."[44]

The English merchants in the season of 1722 mention prices rising from 114 to 164 rials,[45] but then the purchases were very great. The English purchases alone were of 7,343 bales of coffee by two ships to London and one to Bombay, so far the greatest English purchases of coffee at Mocha. They were concluded in the month of July. In the letter about it, dated at 11 August 1722, it says: "The Dutch and Ostenders have now done buying and when Mr. Geekie came down which was the ultimo July, it was then worth from 135 to 145, we are informed that the Turks now begin to buy."[46] In May 1723 the English merchants at Mocha wrote that the Dutch already on 13 December 1722 had started their purchases at Beit-el-Faki with a view to the season of 1723 and secured 600 bales at 144 rials, whereas the English traders did not start until the end of February and had to pay 169 rials for their coffee.[47] In spite of a cheap first round the total Dutch purchases were made at very high prices in the season of 1723. In the month of August the English factory wrote as follows: "The fall in the latter season has proved somewhat beneficial to us, and the Dutch coffee so much exceeding the rest is occasioned by their purchasing, mostly at an advance price for ten or more days forbearance for want of ready money."[48] Plenty of rain promised better prices for the following season, but the hope was disappointed, as grasshoppers spoilt many bushes and trees, and already in January 1724 the servants of the English factory wrote that coffee appeared on the market in small quantities only and at a price of 177–180 rials. Internal unrest also contributed to forcing up the prices, "so that should your Honours send out the same tonnage this season as you have the three

[44] C. R. O. London, Egypt and Red Sea, vol. I, 1644–1726, No. 29, 20 July 1721.
[45] *Ibid.* No. 84, 16 July 1722. [46] *Ibid.* No. 96, 11 August 1722.
[47] *Ibid.* No. 114, 31 May 1723.
[48] *Ibid.* No. 1, 21 August 1723. It appears from a survey in No. 123 that the Dutch cost-price was 180, that of the Ostenders 178–79, and that of the French 174; Persian and Turkish merchants bought coffee at 145, 159, 165, and 170 Spanish rials per bahar.

preceding we apprehend great difficulty in fitting them."[49] The shortage led to an attempt at making an agreement between the Europeans not to offer more than 150 rials. According to the English merchants the Dutch chief at Mocha was the originator of the idea. However, the attempt failed, as his "seconde" at Beit-el-Faki did not sanction it, but in February made purchases at 166–173 rials.[50] When the ships from Europe arrived at Mocha, the prices even rose to 180–200 rials.[51] Later it says in the report from the English factory, "The price of coffee at Beit-el-Faki . . . [has] fallen from 200 to 170 dollars per Bahar upon the Dutch's having compleated their investment and our gentlemen there agreeing with the French not to bid upon each other but buy in conjunction and to divide equally what was so purchased, but in a very few days the want of coffee in the country, which from the beginning was apprehended, appeared to be real and the price soon started to 195 Spanish dollars per Bahar which gave us no small concern least we should not be able to give the "London" a loading."[52] The English factory servants had gradually realized that they must adapt themselves to the high prices of coffee at Mocha, as there were no signs that the European demand should decrease. In the very summer of 1724 they learnt from their French colleagues that the French company had made a contract with the Government to provide the kingdom of France with coffee at a maximum price of 100 *sols* per French pound, for which reason the French had to send at least one ship to Mocha every year. They also reckoned with a constant demand on the part of the Dutch and the Ostend company.[53] These misgivings for the season of 1725 came true, even though the Dutch contrary to expectation sent only one ship to Mocha for coffee. At the arrival of the ships the prices rose from 180 to 200–202 rials. Furthermore, food became more expensive because of a drought, and a disease among the camels made the transport cost rise. The packers at Beit-el-Faki had to have higher wages as a consequence of the high cost of living.[54] After the ships had left, prices as usual fell at Beit-el-Faki. At length it seemed that the peak had been passed. The English mentioned a price of 125 Spanish dollars in the cheap season. The arrival at Hodeida of some native boats from Jidda and the Dutch factory servants' purchases in December at the same time as the French made purchases with a view to the season of 1726, made the price rise to 157 rials. The English put off their purchases. In March one of their ships arrived and they bought coffee at a price of 135 rials. An unexpected Dutch ship from Batavia

[49] *Ibid.* No. 129, 26 January 1724.
[50] *Ibid.* No. 132, 15 March 1724.
[51] *Ibid.* No. 137, 29 June 1724.
[52] *Ibid.*
[53] *Ibid.* No. 151, 11 August 1724.
[54] *Ibid.* No. 175, 12 July 1725.

and a French "country" ship from Pondicherry made the price of coffee rise to 142 rials, but on the whole the prices for the season of 1726 were considerably lower than those of the previous seasons.[55]

The English letters from Mocha in the 1720's corroborate the Heeren XVII's criticism of Dutch purchases at too high prices. Furthermore the English records offer the interesting piece of information that at any rate in the case of some of the seasons there was a difference between the Dutch way of buying coffee – viz. by contracts at Mocha – and the practice of the other European nations, where the merchants themselves, assisted by Arabian brokers, went to Beit-el-Faki and secured the coffee from day to day, as it came down from the hills. This fact perhaps explains the difference in prices. At other times also the Dutch merchants stayed at Beit-el-Faki, where they bought coffee on the spot. The purchase by contract, therefore, is not the only decisive factor, any more than it should necessarily be identical with unprofitable purchase. The merchants' cash in hand was another important factor, but to this should be added the judgment of the varying crops, the uncertainty as regards the European as well as the Turkish demand, besides local conditions, as sketched above. The extent to which the Dutch and the English cost-prices differed appears from the following table.[56]

Table 38. *Dutch and English Average Cost-Prices of Coffee at Mocha, 1713–1727.*

Season	Dutch	English	Season	Dutch	English
	Rials per bahar at 735 ponds			Rials per bahar at 735 ponds	
1713........	129	128	1721........	161	151
1714........	120	missing	1722........	176	167
1715........	126	129	1723........	198	195
1716........	124	123	1724........	213	211
1717........	152	missing	1725........	245	189
1718........	189	175	1726........	163	152
1719........	170	171	1727........	115	missing
1720........	165	145			

It is not possible to state the part of the coffee trade which the Europeans during these years succeeded in securing by way of Mocha. It is true that we occasionally find some estimates in the English and Dutch letters from Mocha, but they can only in part be verified as regards the figures for Europe, and we are without any means to check the figures

[55] *Ibid.* No. 197, 12 June 1726. [56] As to sources and calculations, cf. Appendix G.

for Asia. Thus the English wrote in 1721 that the Turkish and Persian traders' annual export from Yemen could be estimated at about 40,000 bales of coffee, 10,000 of which went by the trade routes to Basra and Babylon, while about 500 bales went to Surat. In 1723 the Turkish-Persian export was said to have been only 5,200 bales, while English and Dutch sources agree in estimating the total European export at just under 16,000 bales, nearly half of which was the share of the English, while the Dutch exported 3,300 bales, and the Ostenders, the Brandenburgers, and the French the rest. It is not evident whether the Turkish-Persian export figures originate from Mocha alone or from a larger area. In 1724 the English factory at Mocha stated that the Persian and Turkish merchants exported just under 11,000 bales of coffee from the ports of Mocha, Hodeida, and Lohaya, while the Europeans bought just under 13,000 bales.[57] Finally it may be mentioned that the Dutch in 1727 estimated the Asiatic export to Persia from Mocha at 5,000 bales.

The rising cost-prices at Mocha in connexion with the falling selling prices came to influence the Company's gross profit on coffee. A comparison of the cost-prices with the selling prices at the various chambers shows that the profit from having been 0.61 fl. per pond on the coffee bought in the season of 1718 fell to being 0.05 fl. per pond for the quantities bought in 1724. The profit on the lots of 1725, bought very dear, was 0.10 fl. per pond. As compared with the quantities imported, this meant that the gross profit calculated on a season's Mocha coffee fell from about 1 mill. fl. to about 40,000 fl. This alarming fall, which in fact was tantamount to the Mocha coffee involving a loss, however, was fully counterbalanced by the fact that this was the years of the great break-through of Java coffee. While 90 per cent. of the quantities of coffee imported in the season of 1721 came from Mocha and only 10 per cent. were Java coffee, the ratio five years later was the exact opposite. Furthermore, the Company imported quantities of Java coffee which by far exceeded the standard of previous years. In the season of 1718 the Company received just under 30,000 ponds, in the season of 1721 just under 200,000 ponds, in the season of 1724 well over 2.5 mill. ponds, and in the season of 1726 well over 4.2 mill. ponds. These figures give an idea of the rate of the increase. In 1725 the Court of Directors enforced a great reduction of the cost-price in Java, i.e. the price paid to the coffee planters. From having paid 0.50 fl. per pond of Java coffee, they reduced the price to

[57] C. R. O. London, Egypt & Red Sea, vol. I, 1644–1726, No. 151, letter dated at Mocha, 11 August 1724.

0.13 fl. per pond. The result was that the gross profit increased from about 1 mill. fl. at the sales in 1725 to more than 3 mill. fl. at the sales in 1727. In this way the Company's coffee trade entered a new phase. The new level of the sales was maintained for several decades. With a certain justification this level may be denoted as the final phase of the expansion of the coffee trade. Therefore we shall see how this development was completed, and the problem which it produced for the Court of Directors. In brief, it was a question of a transition from trade to cultivation.

While the Company's trade in Mocha coffee has not previously been studied, the history of the cultivation of coffee in Java is well-known, i. a. from de Haan's work about Priangan. We shall therefore content ourselves with very briefly reminding of the chief data. As early as 1696 the first coffee bushes are said to have been sent to Batavia for purposes of cultivation, but they were spoilt in 1699 by earthquakes and inundations. Greater success was achieved with some young plants which Governor General van Zwaardecron had brought to Java from the Malabar Coast. In 1707 the Heeren XVII gave orders for the planting of coffee bushes to be encouraged by all means.[58] Governor General van Hoorn showed the very greatest interest in the cultivation. He had coffee bushes distributed to the princes in the Preanger countries, to the chiefs in the Jacatra and Cheribon highlands, and at the suggestion of Major Knol in 1709 had coffee bushes for planting distributed to princes and chiefs in the districts of Samarang and Kartasura. In 1711 the Batavian Government could write home that it had reaped 894 ponds of coffee. The coffee was immediately shipped to Nederland and sold at the auctions in Amsterdam and Middelburg in 1712 at prices of 27.88 st. and 19.50 st. per pond, respectively, i. e. at prices somewhat lower than the price of Mocha coffee, which at the same sales maintained an average of 28.10 st. per pond. It is true that the cultivation failed in Central Java, but in the Preanger countries, in the highlands near Batavia and at Cheribon it developed at a brisk rate. The rate at which the Java coffee flowed into the Company's warehouses at Batavia appears from the following survey:[59]

[58] Klerk de Reus, *op. cit.* p. 227; De Jonge, *op. cit.*, vol. 8, p. 139 *et seq.*

[59] The survey has been made on the basis of the General Commerce Ledgers of Batavia, which books include a complete survey of the turnover of the year, whereas the figures communicated by De Haan only cover the countries belonging under Batavia, *op. cit.* p. 920 *et seq.*, and the figures adduced by De Jonge, *op. cit.*, vol. 9, pp. 158–61, indeed include other areas, but follow the season of harvest or gathering, which is the greater part, but actually covers only half to two thirds of the twelve months of the year.

Table 39. *Coffee Purchased and Delivered at Batavia in the Accounting Years 1713/14–1732/33; In Ponds.*

	Rest carried over at the beginning of the year	Purchased and delivered during the year
1713/14	1,868	1,774
1715/16	2,894	9,084
1718/19	27,817	36,267
1721/22	191,453	618,765
1723/24	56,778	1,804,797
1724/25	464,219	2,603,628
1726/27	255,335	5,310,084
1727/28	1,292,884	3,462,770
1730/31	1,314,045	3,686,695
1732/33	2,408,265	5,857,399

While the greater part of the quantities down to about 1726/27 originated from the highlands near Batavia, the share of Cheribon increased very much after that time and became almost as great as the quotas from the highlands. In the last account selected, that of 1732/33, the coffee from Cheribon was placed "Aan de westzijde", while the Java coffee was placed "in 't Casteel" at Batavia. The coffee received in the season of 1721/22 included 18 ponds from Amboyna, where the Company also tried to start a cultivation of coffee, viz. from the ulterior motive of restricting the cultivation of cloves and the illicit trade connected with it. The coffee from Amboyna, however, did not come to play any role, which was due to the violent reduction of the price of production made by Governor General de Haan on Amboyna in 1726, where at that time there were 161,066 young and 17,126 fruit-bearing coffee bushes. The cultivation actually was crushed at birth. In Ceylon, too, the Company during these years encouraged the laying-out of coffee plantations. Ceylon appeared for the first time in the material of invoices in October 1722.[60]

In 1724 the Heeren XVII realized that Java was in a position to deliver coffee to such an extent that it was sufficient to send only one ship annually to Mocha. They gave orders for the disestablishment of the residency at Mocha, as the trade in future should be directed from the ships.[61] They assumed that the decreasing Dutch demand would lead to lower cost-prices at Mocha and decided that Mocha coffee might at most be bought at a price of 10 st. per pond,[62] the same price at which they wanted the Javanese to deliver their coffee.[63] The reason why the Dutch trade to

[60] Kol. Arch. No. 1866, fo. 152.
[61] Kol. Arch. No. 464, 23 June 1724 (section on Mocha).
[62] Kol. Arch. No. 200, 26 February 1725.
[63] Kol. Arch. No. 465, 21 July 1725 (section on Batavia).

Mocha was not discontinued was that it yielded a profit and meant sales of some Company goods. Furthermore the Company was not interested in being undercut on the European market with cheap Mocha coffee. By annually sending a ship to Mocha for coffee it would, in the Heeren XVII's opinion, be possible to keep the cost-price at such a level that it would benefit the Java coffee,[64] – an interesting piece of economic reasoning, which amongst other things was based on the Company's experiences at Mocha in the beginning of the 1720's, when the arrival of a single ship would raise the price considerably. The Heeren XVII's orders at the same time reached a peak of 4 mill. ponds of coffee a year from Java, to which should be added the coffee that might be fetched at Mocha with one ship.[65]

So far the prices at Mocha were at a level a good deal higher than the maximum price fixed, and the complaints of the high cost-prices continued for some years. Now and then the Heeren XVII threatened to close down the Mocha factory completely, without, however, carrying out their threat. They welcomed a proposal for shipping 10,000 ponds of Java coffee for sale on the Coromandel Coast in order in this way to relieve the Moorish demand at Mocha, where the Moors raised the bidding to "so een excessive prijs".[66] In 1727, however, the fall in prices had set in at Mocha. Having paid between 19 and 22 st. per pond of Mocha coffee the Company in 1727 bought coffee at 10.4 st. per pond. The joy at the fall in prices was mingled with anxiety that it should draw the price of Java coffee with it. The European market began to show signs of being glutted with coffee. At the auctions in 1728 the price of Java coffee beans dropped to 14–15 st. per pond, and the Heeren XVII therefore concentrated on the possibility of greater sales in the East and on the prime costs there. The Ceylon factory was ordered to increase its sales by reducing the selling price from 12 to 10 "heavy" st. in order in this way to hamper the Arabian sales.[67] At Surat the Heeren XVII hoped that the Company could sell the Java coffee at a price of 12 "heavy" or 15 "light" st. per pond, referring to the fact that the factory servants at Mocha had previously with great force maintained that an important cause of the high cost-prices there was the great export of coffee from Mocha to Surat, where it had been sold at a price of 23–30 rupees per *man* (at 36.25 Dutch ponds), i.e. about 19–25 st. per pond. Otherwise they left it to the Batavian Government to consider the special circumstances of each single

[64] *Ibid.* 28 August 1727 (section on Mocha).
[65] Kol. Arch. No. 200, 21 September 1725.
[66] Kol. Arch. No. 465, 17 August 1728 (section on Mocha).
[67] *Ibid.* 18 August 1729 (section on Ceylon).

factory as regards the price policy, only that the Government should always pursue the one goal of making the Java coffee hold its own against the Mocha coffee on the Indian market.[68] Finally it gave rise to no little anxiety that the Java coffee had emerged among the goods imported by the competing companies, thus in France, just as supplies of coffee from the West Indies to Europe were annoying.[69] As to the emerging of the Java coffee at the auctions of the competing companies, this in a way was no unpleasant fact, as it proved that Java coffee was a success as regards taste. What in the Heeren XVII's opinion was unpleasant was the fact that the coffee had reached the competitors by other routes than the official ones.[70]

West India or Surinam coffee found favour on the European market and caused a further fall in prices in the 1730's.[71] The Heeren XVII realized that coffee was a commodity which without detriment to the quality could be transported all over the world and that the new areas of production meant keener competition. Above all the original illusions of acquiring a monopoly were lost. There was no longer any prospect of the competitors flocking to Batavia in order to secure the coffee beans there.[72] The Dutch Company was in a situation in which it was of vital importance to have accurate knowledge of the costs of production and transport. While the prices of coffee fell in Europe, the production increased in the East. In 1737 the Heeren XVII increased their order for coffee from 4 to 6 mill. ponds.[73] Amongst other things this was done on account of the large stocks that had accumulated at Batavia. It was recommended on the same occasion to limit the cultivation of coffee by "extirpation", and rice and pepper were pointed out as the commodities which in the immediate situation were suitable to replace coffee. The large stocks at Batavia, however, not only were expressive of overproduction, but was also inspired by an attempt at improving the quality of the Java coffee by storing it for a year in order to give the coffee a sufficient dryness in this way. The Heeren XVII in 1731 had sanctioned an increase in the price of production from 5–6 to 6–7 rixdollars per 125 ponds of coffee. The Directors had also suggested that a surplus corresponding to a whole year's "Europe crop", i.e. 4 mill. ponds, was accumulated at Batavia in three or four years.[74] Gradually it became

[68] *Ibid.* (section on Surat).
[69] *Ibid.* (section on Mocha).
[70] Kol. Arch. No. 466, 14 September 1731 (section on Ceylon).
[71] Kol. Arch. No. 467, 17 September 1737 (section on Ceylon).
[72] *Ibid.* 25 August 1740 (section on Persia).
[73] *Ibid.* 17 September 1737 (section on Batavia).
[74] Kol. Arch. No. 466, 14 September 1731 (section on Batavia).

evident how difficult it was to obtain increased sales of Java coffee in India. For good reasons the Heeren XVII were sceptical as to an assertion that it would be possible to make the natives in the Banda district drink coffee or tea. Both products were too dear for the poor Bandanese.[75] On the other hand they fastened on the chances of the Java coffee in the old "coffee-drinking" areas in Asia, Surat and Persia. The Company's servants stated that the taste for Mocha coffee was too deep-seated for the Java coffee to compete with it. Therefore it fetched so low prices. This assertion gave occasion for the high Directors to have a taste, which made them return the following angry verdict: "Wij zouden gelooven dat 'er een mensch ter wereld zo fijn van tong is die onderschijt kan proeven tussen goede en welgedroogde Javaense en Mochase boonen; wat ons aengaet als wij die proeff eens en andermal genoemen hebben, heeft niemant dat onderschijt konnen gewaer worden, hoe is dan te geloven dat een parthij lompe Turken en Persianen zo veel fijner van tong zouden weesen als wij en andere menschen."[76] It was, however, a fact that the prices of Java coffee sold in these quarters were lower than the prices at which English, French, and Indian merchants sold Mocha coffee. In some cases the lower price was intentional – the Company would in this way create a taste for Java coffee – but even at the cheap price the coffee could not always be sold. Thus the Heeren XVII in their letter of 1739 remarked that the French in Persia had sold coffee at 13.60 st. per pond, while the Dutch Company had not succeeded in selling its Java coffee, which had been offered at 11 st. per pond.[77] The Mocha coffee could not be cut out in the Asiatic area, and the fear that its cost-price at Mocha should fall disproportionately, proved quite unfounded. Indeed, the Dutch in 1730 bought coffee at Beit-el-Faki at a price of 9 st. and at Mocha at 9.25–11.50 st. per pond, so that they secured a total of 186,998 ponds at an average of 10.19 st.[78] But it was far from a full cargo, and in spite of the fact that the maximum price was raised to 11 "light" st.,[79] the Mocha ship often had to return with very small quantities onboard, although there was cash available at Mocha.[80]

[75] *Ibid.* 3 September 1735 (section on Banda).
[76] Kol. Arch. No. 467, 10 September 1738 (section on Persia).
[77] *Ibid.* 4 September 1739 (section on Persia).
[78] Kol. Arch. No. 466, 30 August 1732 (sections on Surat and Mocha).
[79] *Ibid.* 14 September 1731 (section on Mocha).
[80] E.g. Kol. Arch. No. 466, 3 September 1735 (section on Mocha).

CHAPTER XI

Tea

"People who study hard and use their brain diligently, should take good care not to drink tea, as they are enfeebled by the work of their brain in advance and therefore should not strive after further exhaustion, quite apart from the fact that tea will disturb their night's sleep, which is bad, as people who think much need a rest. But tea is a good drink for fat people and those who have a hot and yellow gall or who suffer from hot vapours or of too much sleepiness." More poetic lines have been written about tea, but as a matter of fact François Valentijn never quite reconciled himself to this novelty, which he first became acquainted with in 1681, when an Indian preacher offered him a cup of tea "die niet beter dan hooy-water smaakte." Later on, things went smoothly. It was better when tea became cheaper. The ratio between investment and enjoyment became more reasonable. As late as the 1720's Valentijn amazedly remembered the gentleman at Rotterdam who in 1684 had poured out tea for him which had cost 80 fl. per pond.[1] Actually there was good reason to muse upon the course of things, for the 40 years had changed tea from an expensive – and much debated – drug on the chemist's shelf to a popular drink steaming deliciously in pots and cups, the twin sister of coffee, but of a gentler temper. In the large towns tea-houses and -shops attracted custom.

"Ga niet voorbij
Indien dat gij
Soekt goeje Thee
Sie, ruijk en smaak
Tot U vermaak
En neemt wat mee."[2]

[1] Valentijn, *op. cit.* p. 190.

[2] Signboard from shop in Oude Liliestraat in Amsterdam. Gemeente-Archief Amsterdam, Aantekeningen de Roever, thee.

The analyses of the Company's Dutch auctions showed that tea in the course of the first third of the 18th century became a commodity of great importance from the point of view of sales. This feature is not unique for the Dutch Company. Other European companies as well flung themselves into the tea trade. The European market apparently was insatiable in its demand. The competition was conspicuous, and often it was questions concerning the trade in tea which were discussed when "onze competiteurs" were mentioned in the Heeren XVII's discussions. Actually these thirty years marked a decisive transition in the Asiatic trade. The direct trade to China furthered interloping, as it had the great advantage from the point of view of interlopers that it was not burdened with disbursements for expensive building of forts, etc. The final Chinese standpoint that all European nations should have free admission to trading at Canton, to a certain degree made the great companies' monopoly of the trade east of the Cape of Good Hope illusory. The old dream of regular trade relations with the Celestial Empire finally was realized. During the last part of the 17th century a regular trade had been established – also in tea – by land along the caravan routes through Manchuria and Mongolia, between Russia and China, after the conclusion of the Nerchinsk Treaty in 1689, with Kiakhta as emporium.[3] Now the sea route was established as the contact decisive to Northwest Europe, a contact which as regards transport as well as economy gave rise to new conditions for the East India trade.

There are many different kinds of tea. In his description of East India Valentijn distinguishes between three main sorts, viz. (i) Bing or Imperial tea, (ii) Singlo or green tea, and (iii) the brown Bohea tea. This division agrees with the Dutch Company's names in accounts, surveys, etc., from the first decades of the 18th century, the green tea, however, in the reports on the purchases of tea from the Chinese junks at Batavia being called *witte the*. In our day it is a custom to distinguish between green and black (or brown) tea, a third category, however, being separated out, viz. flower tea, which may be both green (Imperial tea) and black (Pekoe), flower tea meaning the pickings of the young, downy, silky, white or orange, not yet quite unfolded leaves, while the terms of "green" and "black" refer to the preparation of the leaves. Green tea is heated for a few minutes soon after being picked, through which process the leaves are withered and give off a considerable amount of moisture. Then they are rolled between the hands and dried. Black tea is after the

[3] On the caravan routes in the 17th century see John F. Baddeley, *Russia, Mongolia, China*, vol. II (London, 1919), p. 223 *et seq*. The author is indebted to Professor Owen Lattimore for his reference to this unique, but little known work.

rolling left for some time on bamboo mats exposed to the action of the air, through which a slight fermentation takes place that changes the colour and taste of the tea. After the fermentation the tea is dried under constant stirring, sometimes after being rolled once more. At that time as now there were a long series of grades. First of all this applied to black tea, of which there were the sorts of Pekoe, Souchong, Congho,[4] Rosemary, ordinary Bohea, etc., while besides the green tea termed Singlo also Hyson and others were bought. The way in which tea cargoes in the 18th century might be composed appears from the following analysis of the English and the Dutch Companies' purchases during the triennium of 1720–22 and the triennium of 1730–32.[5]

Table 40. *Analysis of the Composition of English and Dutch Cargoes of Tea 1720–22 and 1730–32.*

	English		Dutch	
	1720–22	1730–32	1720–22	1730–32
	%	%	%	%
GREEN TEA				
ord. Singlo or *Witte the* ...	37.5	44.0	57.5	11.1
Bing or Imperial	3.1	2.7	2.9	2.9
Hyson	0.6	3.8	—	1.6
BLACK TEA				
ord. Bohea	46.3	42.3	39.6	78.4
Congho	10.5	6.5	—	3.6
Pekoe..................	2.0	0.6	—	0.7
VARIOUS.................	—	0.1	—	1.7
In all %	100.0	100.0	100.0	100.0
Mill. lbs.	3.37	4.21		
Mill. ponds			0.95	4.27

The analysis indicates that in spite of the large number of qualities, there were especially two sorts in which the companies were interested, viz. ordinary green tea and the ordinary black called Bohea. The latter was named after the Bohea (Wu-i)-mountain in the province of Fukien,[6] where a great part of the tea bought by the Europeans was cultivated. The peasants had their tea bushes growing in small gardens. There the

[4] Perhaps identical with Kanhoe; cf. Kol. Arch. No. 1793, fo. 867, Batavia, 29 September 1718, purchases from Chinese junks of 13,839 ponds of tea Bohea = 507 ponds of Pekoe + 13,332 ponds of Kanhoe.

[5] For the years 1720–22 the Dutch material only gives information about the main qualities, the figures being entered under Singlo (*Witte*) and ordinary Bohea, respectively.

[6] Hollingworth, "List of the principal tea districts in China, etc.", *Journal of the North China Branch of the Royal Asiatic Society*, New Series, No. X, Appendix p. 10.

leaves were picked in the height of summer and sold to buyers who transported it to the merchants at Canton, where the further packing took place in the warehouses. The new tea came to Canton in the months of September to December.

The Dutch had early in the 17th century become acquainted with tea in Asia, both Chinese and Japanese tea, and they also at intervals shipped it to Europe.[7] In the Chinese settlement in Batavia the Company's servants had, as it were, every day an opportunity to see what tea was used for. The supplies of tea from China, however, were an affair which the Chinese themselves attended to. The commercial intercourse between China and Batavia has been mentioned several times as one of the important inter-Asiatic trades the existence of which can be traced far back in time. The traffic between China and Batavia was attended to by Chinese junks manned by Chinese crews and with Chinese merchants as owners. The junks came from Canton, Amoy, Ningpo, and other places. As a rule they put to sea in the month of December by the north monsoon and arrived at Batavia in the beginning of the new year where their presence for that matter gave a vivid colouring to the town. When their cargoes had arrived great busyness arose in the Chinese shops, where everything was displayed in the most alluring way, a scenery which in many ways reminded the Dutch of the kermisses and annual fairs in their home country.[8] Besides by way of the direct Chinese maritime trade, Chinese commodities reached Batavia indirectly by way of Macao, Manila, Malacca, etc. In the General Letters which the Governor General and Council at Batavia every year in November or December sent to the Heeren XVII in Europe, the turnover with the Chinese junks and the traders from Macao and Manila was summarized together. This turnover during the first decades of the 18th century as a rule displayed a surplus in favour of the Dutch, ranging from 100,000 to 500,000 fl.

The Chinese commodities comprised a jumble of tea, gold in bullion, Mexican rials, Japanese and Tongking bar copper, white alum, raw silk, silk fabrics, tutenag, which was an alloy of zinc, furthermore white wax, radix China, i.e. the root of a plant which in China and India was used as a medicament, and chinaware. Among the commodities which the Dutch sold to the Chinese, pepper undoubtedly was the most important, but also cinnamon could be sold together with Dutch manufactures,

[7] Cf. G. Schlegel, "First introduction of tea into Holland", *T'oung pao*, Series II, vol. 1 (Leiden, 1900), pp. 468 ff.

[8] The following is mainly based on Dr. I. de Hullu's thorough study "Over den Chinaschen handel der Oost-Indische Compagnie en de eerste dertig jaar van de 18e eeuw", *Bijdragen tot de Taal-, Land- en Volkenkunde van Nederlandsch-Indië*, deel 73 ('s-Gravenhage, 1917), pp. 32–151.

amber, lead, and occasionally larger or smaller quantities of sandalwood, benzoin, caliatour wood, red coral, and bird's nests. Towards the end of the 17th and in the beginning of the 18th century the main stress in the China-Batavia trade as seen from the point of view of the Company was on the sales to the junks and the traders from Macao and Manila, first of all of pepper, which in China was used not only in the European way, but in the northern provinces and by poor people "tot verwarming van de maag met water of andere vochten gedronken werd."[9] In the General Letter of 6 February 1694 the Governor General and Council thus pointed out the profit to the Company of having the pepper trade with the Chinese concentrated in Batavia and in this way to avoid smuggling. Later, in December 1700, it was said that the contracts for pepper with the princes of Bantam and Palembang had resulted in a surplus which it had not been possible to sell in India, for which reason the Batavian Government had sold large quantities of pepper to the Chinese at low prices, i.e. without loss, but also without any appreciable profit. This arrangement was criticized by the Heeren XVII, amongst other things because they feared that the low selling prices of pepper should give the English and other European nations occasion for providing cheap return cargoes in China and thus inflict a competition on the Company on the European market. The Heeren XVII indeed wanted a successful trade to China, but it must not be obtained at the expense of the profit – "de oogwit en de ziel der negotie" – and therefore they ordered the Government in Batavia to fix a minimum price of 7.50 rixdollars per picul (at 125 ponds) of pepper and slowly to raise the price to 8 or 8.50 rixdollars. In the letter of 9 July 1715 the Heeren XVII gave orders for the pepper price to be raised to 10 rixdollars, referring to the fact that pepper at the last public sale at Batavia had been sold at 9.50 rixdollars per picul.

By the increasing European demand for tea, the centre of gravity, however, in the Batavian turnover was shifted from sales to purchases, and the purchase of tea just became the cause of a dramatic interruption of the old trade in the year 1718, an interruption which lasted until 1722. On 2 March 1717 the Governor General and Council decided to regulate the cost-prices of tea so that Singlo tea (ordinary green tea) was put at 40 rixdollars per picul (at 125 ponds), Bing or Imperial tea at 60 rixdollars per picul, Bohea tea of the first grade (Kanhoe) at 80 rixdollars per picul. This custom of fixing the prices was not new and was used in many places, e.g. in Japan. The decisive fact, however, was that the Chinese

[9] Letter dated at the Dutch factory in Canton, 25 December 1764, quoted from De Hullu, "Over den Chinaschen handel", p. 38.

were not prepared for these prices, which, as compared with those of the preceding years, were characterized as very low. The Chinese maintained that amongst other things because of the high bottomry they could not sell their green tea at less than 60 rixdollars per picul. The Batavian Government, however, maintained the prices mentioned and recommended the junks to return to China with the tea if they found the prices unreasonable. The 14 junks chose to sell, but in return promised that they would never more go to Batavia. The annual statement for the buying season of 1717 at Batavia showed that the Company got the Bohea tea at the above-mentioned price of 80 rixdollars per picul for the best grade and the inferior grades at 75, 70, 65, and 60 rixdollars per picul. The Chinese Emperor answered by prohibiting his subjects to trade to Batavia.[10]

The Governor General and Council were not pleased at the new situation and amongst other things discussed the possibility of sending a ship to China, but dared not implement the plan for fear of Chinese reprisals. The free citizens of Batavia were willing to run the risk and privately applied for permission to trade to China, but were refused as the Government dared not give such a permission out of consideration for the Chinese settlement in the town. In this emergency they were obliged to buy what the Portuguese traders in Macao brought to Batavia. So far the quantities were not large – in 1718 only about half of the quantity ordered by the Court of Directors – and the prices were clearly influenced by the extraordinary circumstances. The quantities purchased in 1718 cost 115–125 rixdollars per picul of Bohea tea or on an average just under 75 per cent. more than in the preceding year. The Directors in Holland were worried. They encouraged the Batavian Government to lure the Chinese to Batavia again – though not in the way that pepper and spices were sold at prices below the minimum prices fixed –, and thought that if the attempts were not successful, the Company ought to send one or two ships to China from Batavia, amongst other things in order to hamper the Ostend company in its purchases at Canton. The Batavian Government, however, remained passive. Even though the Dutch had learnt that the Portuguese in Macao had tried from the Emperor to obtain a permanent prohibition against Chinese trade to Batavia, the Government trusted that the local governors in the coastal districts suffered so great losses that they would soon be sorry for the relation broken off. Presumably the Chinese losses first of all were losses of freightage; for in Dutch

[10] General Letter dated at Batavia, 20 March 1718, and resolution of the Governor General and Council dated at 3 May 1718; cf. De Hullu, "Over den Chinaschen handel", p. 42.

sources it is repeatedly stated that the traders from Macao to Batavia mainly attended to carriage on Chinese account. The Dutch East India Company had to pay much for the tea for a couple of years. The supplies, indeed, were abundant in the seasons of 1720 and 1721, in which they rose to a quantity between 200,000 and 350,000 ponds, but still the Company in 1721 on an average paid almost 80 per cent. more for the Bohea tea than in 1717, the year of the junk affair. Furthermore, this trade as a whole resulted in a deficit, about 30,000 rixdollars in 1720 and about 160,000 rixdollars in 1721.

In 1722 the prospect was getting brighter. On the 31st of March the Batavian Government could inform Holland that Chinese junks had again made their appearance at Batavia, two from Shanghai and three from Tongking. Another two or three junks were expected. The credit for the solution of the crisis is ascribed to Governor General van Zwaardecron and the Chinese settlement in Batavia. Probably the Emperor Kang-hi's death in December 1722 was contributory as well. Economically the resumption of the traffic meant a violent fall in the prices of tea. In 1721 Bohea tea had cost the Company an average of about 59 "light" st. per pond when bought from the Macao traders. In 1722 the Company bought it at a price of 22 "light" st. per pond and in 1723 at 19 "light" st.

The fluctuations during the years 1717–1723 are mainly explained by the special commercial conditions mentioned, but should not be judged without consideration to the trend of prices in China. A comparison between the Dutch cost-prices at Batavia and the English prices at Canton gives the following result:[11]

Table 41. *Dutch and English Cost-Prices of Bohea Tea at Batavia and Canton. Taels per Picul at 122.5 Ponds.*

Season	Batavia	Canton
1717/16	56.9	39.1
1718/17	97.5	31.3
1719/18	70.3	32.7
1720/19	70.0	39.2
1721/20	100.5	43.6
1722/21	37.4	34.1
1723/22	32.4	27.8

Owing to Valentijn's description the compulsory prices in 1717 have been considered as expressive only of the Batavian Government's cupidity. The knowledge of the prices on the market in Canton, however, may also be supposed to have supervened. The difference between the prices of

[11] See Appendix H.

the buying season of 1717 and the prices in Canton in the autumn of 1716 is marked especially if compared with those from the years immediately after the resumption of the trade. A difference in prices between the two places is to be expected considering the freightage, but it is impossible to determine this difference as the freightage is unknown. Another uncertainty concerns the quality of the tea. It may be thought that the tea conveyed to Batavia by the Chinese was what was left after the Europeans in Canton had secured the best qualities and that parts of the freightage cost thus in fact were eliminated by the difference in quality. Furthermore, the European market should be considered. If there was not in 1717, owing to the European selling prices, any direct reason for forcing down the cost-price – apart from cupidity – the question in return, as we shall see below, came up with a vengeance two or three years later, when about 1720 a great fall in prices set in in Europe. At that time, however, conditions had come to a deadlock at Batavia and the purchases were made at so high prices that the Company for almost three years in succession must have sustained losses on its tea. This also appears from the comments of the Court of Directors.[12] To the commercial deficit in Batavia we should therefore add the loss in Europe when we are to compute the cost to the Company of trying to force the prices in Batavia down towards the level of the Canton prices.

While during the years before the interruption of the commercial intercourse with China 12–16 junks a year came to Batavia, no less than 21 junks appeared in 1723, and in 1724 18 junks. The Company's purchases reflect the increased traffic. The prices did not long remain at the low level of the season of 1723 (i.e. 19 st. per pond). In 1724 there was very little Bohea tea to be had, and the average therefore was no less than 35 st. per pond. The lowest annual average price during the following seasons from 1725 to 1730 inclusive was just under 24 st. per pond (in 1725), and the highest price was just under 28 st. (in 1728). The quantities bought increased from season to season, starting with 130,000 ponds in 1725 and ending with 1.2 mill. ponds in 1730. The Company's European selling prices in these years showed a stabilizing trend down to 1728 inclusive, when Bohea tea was sold at an average price of 71–73 st. per pond. Then the turn of the tide came. At the auctions in 1729 tea was sold at 48 st., in 1730 at 33 st., and in 1731 it only fetched 24 st. per pond (see below). The profits must be compared with the turnover, but in spite of a high increase of the quantities bought and sold, it is evident that the Company was again in a serious situation, in

[12] E.g. Kol. Arch. No. 200, 24 February 1723.

which the Batavia tea in the case of certain lots involved a loss. This development could only confirm the Heeren XVII in their decision in 1728 of opening a direct route from Nederland to Canton.

The basis of this decision was increasing dissatisfaction with the Batavian Government's ability to provide Holland with tea. As seen in proportion to the quantities which the English company and the Ostend company shipped to Europe the supplies from Batavia seemed insufficient to the Heeren XVII. They had several times requested the Governor General and Council to send ships direct from Batavia to China for tea and other commodities, but the Government had excused itself with reference to lack of expert knowledge and insufficient stocks of silver; thus the Government said in May 1724 that a trade to China based only on the sale of merchandise carried there was impossible. Silver was a necessity, and the Government had not even silver enough for obtaining the ordinary returns from the Indian factories, which was particularly serious in Bengal. The decision of following the example of the competing companies and go direct to China did not involve that the purchases in Batavia of Chinese goods from the junks should be stopped. In March 1728 the Governor General and Council were ordered continually to buy unlimited quantities "tot een redelijken prijs en inzonderheid in betaling voor specerijen."[13] The motto was the greatest possible purchases to the detriment of the Ostend company, and remembering the success of the Java coffee the Heeren XVII also gave orders for trying a cultivation of tea in Java, Ceylon, Cape Colony, and in other places where the Company possessed suitable territories. As to the intended cultivation of tea the Heeren XVII stuck to their usual principle that no cultivation should be made by the Company itself, but everything should be left to the planters.They recommended an awarding of prizes for the new cultivation, but the memory of the discontinuation of the awarding of prizes for the cultivation of coffee in 1726 was so fresh that the Governor General and Council do not seem to have considered offering new prizes.[14]

The increase in the Dutch demand appears from the Heeren XVII's orders for returns. In 1715 they asked for a modest 60–70,000 ponds, 6–7,000 ponds of which should be Bing tea, 12–14,000 ponds of Bohea tea, and the rest green tea. The following year the order was raised to 100,000 ponds, viz. 10,000 ponds of Bing tea, 10,000 ponds of Bohea tea, and the rest green tea.[15] In 1719 the order was more than doubled. It

[13] De Hullu, "Over den Chinaschen handel", p. 65.
[14] De Haan, *op. cit.*, vol. II, p. 864.
[15] Kol. Arch. No. 265, 4 March 1715 and 9 March 1716.

was fixed at 200–250,000 ponds with a distribution of the sorts corresponding to that sketched above. The Heeren XVII added that they could not offer any precise information to the Governor General and Council in Batavia how much tea it would be desirable to import, the trade seemingly being too unsettled. The reason why they raised the order so much was the consideration to "onze Europeese competiteuren," who carried large quantities home.[16] The initiative was clearly influenced by the other companies' activities. In the following years the precise statements of quantity are left out in favour of orders for "een ongelimiteerde quantitijt", with an addition that all the sorts sent home should be of the best quality, this addition being provoked by complaints of the bad properties of the tea sold. The complaints of the quality continued, and in 1724 the Heeren XVII with reference to the tea that had arrived by the "Baanman" wrote that indeed the tea was well graded, but still the prices had not been so high as they ought to be for the reason that the tea had been packed in the usual way in "canassers en bladen van bamboes." During the voyage it had lost much in freshness and flavour. Therefore it was recommended to follow the example of the English and the Ostend company by packing the tea in large chests covered inside by lead, which packing would also make stowage easier.[17] This, again, was a proof that the Company lagged behind its competitors. In 1728 600,000 ponds were ordered for the Netherlands, an order which in a later letter in the same year was raised to 1 mill. ponds.[18] All imaginable means should be used for buying up tea and putting obstacles in the way of the competitors.

In a way the many different sorts of tea make it difficult to judge the trend of prices during the eventful years after the end of the War of the Spanish Succession, as it is absolutely necessary to have prices determined by quality as the basis. Otherwise chance will come into play too much, as will appear from the following example selected from among many instances showing how great differences in prices there were between the various sorts.[19] The table shows the predominant prices at the English East India Company's sale in London in October 1719.[20]

[16] Kol. Arch. No. 265, 3 March 1719.

[17] Kol. Arch. No. 464, 29 February 1724 (section on Batavia).

[18] Kol. Arch. No. 465, 15 March 1728 (section on Batavia).

[19] The differences in prices have also been stated by Henri Hauser in his *Recherches et Documents sur l'Histoire des Prix en France de 1500 à 1800* (Paris, 1936), p. 487, the French material, however, being very incomplete.

[20] Gemeente-Archief Amsterdam, Archief Brants No. 401, Brieven aan David Leeuw, vol. I, letter from Peter Crellius dated at London, 27 October 1719.

Table 42. *English Prices of Tea in October 1719. Shillings: Pence per English Lb.*

Green tea	high grade	19 s. 2 d.	
	medium grade	10 s. 4 d.	to 10 s. 6 d.
	ordinary grade	9 s. 2 d.	- 9 s. 4 d.
Imperial tea ...	high grade	15 s.	- 16 s.
	medium grade	12 s. 6 d.	- 13 s.
Bohea tea	high grade	19 s.	- 20 s.
	medium grade	15 s.	- 16 s.
	ordinary grade	13 s. 6 d.	- 15 s.
Pekoe tea	high grade	19 s.	- 20 s.
	medium grade	16 s.	- 17 s.
	ordinary grade	13 s.	- 15 s. 2 d.

The fullest material is the Dutch, while the rest of the Northwest European material is more fragmentary. Reference is made to Appendix B for a detailed description of the Dutch sources. In what follows the outlines of prices will be given on the basis of the two largest imports, green tea and Bohea tea, both of them of the ordinary grade. Two turning-points in the price movement may be observed, one about 1720, the other about 1730. While the total average for all chambers of the Dutch Company during the years 1714–19 fluctuated between 3.25 and 5 fl. per pond of green tea and between 4.60 and 8.44 fl. per pond of Bohea tea, the prices during the years 1720–29 ranged between 1.21 and 4.11 fl. per pond of green tea and between 2.09 and 3.78 fl. per pond of Bohea tea. The change is marked. Green tea and Bohea tea were sold at the autumn auctions in 1719 at the prices of 3.25 fl. and 4.67 fl. per pond. In the autumn of 1720 the corresponding figures were 2.20 fl. and 2.29 fl., respectively. As an external sign of this fall it may be mentioned that the auction prices from 1720 came to be quoted by *stuivers* instead of fl. as previously. Unfortunately it has not been possible to find any English prices from 1720, but if we compare the auction prices of the East India Company from 1718 and 1719 with its prices in 1721, the fall is also reflected there. Before 1720 green tea was sold at 9 s. 2 d.–10 s. 8 d., after 1720 at 6 s. 6 d.–7 s. per English lb.; Bohea tea was in 1719 sold at 13 s. 6 d.–15 s. and in 1721 at 6 s. 2 d.–6 s. 8 d. per English lb. It seems natural to connect the fall in prices with the great crisis. It is evident that the crisis influenced the Dutch Company's sales as a whole. When the Heeren XVII in April 1721 drew up a balance sheet of the latest auctions, they explained the poor result by a reference to the South Sea Bubble in England, the troubles of the West India Company in Holland, and the Mississippi Bubble in France. The Dutch correspondents had received no orders from abroad. The whole trade was tight.[21] But the Heeren XVII did not think that the consequences of the crisis would be serious to the Company. The very fact that the fall in 1720 brought the prices of tea down to a permanent, lower level indicates that the crisis was not of any appreciable importance. The fall in prices should rather be linked with the fight against the Ostend company, the offers from Ostend, and the large number of projects for new companies propounded at that time.[22]

The interloping which during the second decade of the 18th century developed from the Austrian Netherlands, on several occasions had occupied the English as well as the Dutch East India Company. It even led to a kind of collaboration. In September 1718 thus one of the Directors of the English company, Mr. Decquer, arrived in person at the assembly of the Heeren XVII. He wanted amongst other things to discuss the means which might be used by the two companies in common in order to prevent the trade from Ostend.[23] Among the methods applied by each of the two companies also was the economic. In the sphere of the trade in tea the measures of the English East India Company were decisive, as this company was the leading importer. In the beginning of July 1719 the "Prins Eugen" arrived at Ostend from China carrying a cargo of about 170,000 ponds of tea. Already towards the end of July it was rumoured in London that the East India Company would suspend its usual minimum prices at the auctions in September and sell a large quantity freely "om de Oostendenaars van die vaart op Oost-Indien te verhinderen."[24] This did not happen, however. The cargo of the "Prins Eugen" was sold in the Austrian Netherlands in the middle of August at about 4 fl. per pond of Bohea tea and about 2.75 fl. per pond of green tea Singlo.[25] The East India Company as usual fixed its auction prices and had good sales, to which various special terms of payment also contributed. The dumping of which rumours had been abroad did not come

[21] Kol. Arch. No. 199, 4 April 1721.

[22] Thus about 1720 it was rumoured that in Denmark it was intended to found a combined insurance and East and West India trading company (the Ostenders also in the beginning traded to the West Indies) with equipments from the Elbe; Archives Nationales, Paris, Archives de la Marine, B 1, No. 48, p. 458 *et seq.*, 28 September 1720. The buccaneer Morgan from Madagascar suggested to Karl XII of Sweden that the King should found a similar company with Gothenburg as European port, and also tried to get John Law to take an interest in such a scheme; Eskil Olán, *Ostindiska Compagniets Saga* (Göteborg, 1923), pp. 12–14; C. R. O. London, E. I. C., Miscellaneous Letters Received, vol. 13, 1722, No. 148 (undated letter in code from Mr. Forman, Paris, about Morgan's project). On Prussian projects from these years see Viktor Ring, *Asiatische Handlungscompagnien Friederichs des Grossen* (Berlin, 1890), *passim.*

[23] Kol. Arch. No. 198, 15 July, 10 September, 19 September, 26 September 1718.

[24] Gemeente-Archief Amsterdam, Archief Brants No. 401, Brieven aan Dav. Leeuw, vol. I, letter from Peter Crellius dated at London, 21 July 1719.

[25] C. R. O. London, E. I. C., Miscel. Letters Received, vol. 10, Nos. 141 and 144.

until the spring of 1721, but then it was violent. The fall in prices, as mentioned above, had already started at that time. Now the East India Company announced that at its autumn sales it would offer green tea at 5 s. per English lb. and Bohea tea at 6 s. per English lb.[26] The prices did not fall quite so low, the actual selling price of e.g. Bohea tea corresponding to an export price of 1.44 fl. per English lb.[27] This step gave rise to protests from the East India Company's customers, viz. the merchants who had procured supplies at the sales in 1719 and 1720 with a view to the English market as well as those who were engaged on the re-export to Holland and other countries. The tea merchants pointed out "that, to their great loss, they have for some months past, been obliged to sell tea from 4 to 6 s. per pond less than they gave at the candle for it. The vast quantity of tea clandestinely imported from Ostend etc. having for generality supplied city and country."[28] The exporters maintained that they had lost half of their money on the old tea which they had declared after the company's announcement "as your declaration was intended, and had the desired effect of falling the foreign markets."[29] The protests resulted in the company at the declaration releasing the buyers from some of the payment for the old tea.[30] At the beginning of the 1720's the French tea prices also seemed to have been brought down to the low level.[31]

In order to throw a light on the development of the tea market down to the next turning-point about 1730 we shall first render the quantities of tea sold in Holland and England.[32]

[26] C. R. O. London, E. I. C., Court Books, vol. 49, 23 June 1721 (p. 391).

[27] Calculation based on a rate of exchange of 35 s. and a drawback of 3 s. 11 d. per lb. of Bohea tea. The Dutch auction-sale price was 2.18 fl. per pond of Bohea tea.

[28] C. R. O. London, E. I. C., Miscel. Letters Received, vol. 12, No. 210 undated ("Case of the buyers of tea read in Court 6th September 1721"); cf. Court Books, vol. 49, 6 September 1721 (p. 451 *et seq.*).

[29] C. R. O. London, E. I. C., Miscel. Letters Received, vol. 12, No. 211 undated ("Paper sign'd by Mr. Stretfield & several Tea Buyers – read in Court 13th September 1721 vide Minutes").

[30] 1 s. per lb. of tea bought at 9–13 s. 11 d., 2 s. per lb. of tea bought at 14–19 s. 11 d., and 3 s. per lb. of tea bought at 20 s. and more. C. R. O. London, E. I. C. Court Books, vol. 49, 28 September 1721 (p. 474 *et seq.*).

[31] Archives Municipales Nantes, Compagnie des Indes, HH 222, auctions 22 September 1722 and 12 October 1722: green tea Singlo was sold at a predominant price of 72 *sols* per *livre* and Bohea tea at about 103 *sols* per *livre*. With the Amsterdam rate of exchange of November 1722 (Posthumus, *op. cit.* p. 597) – which, however, was very low – these prices correspond to 1.22 fl. and 1.73 fl. per *livre*, respectively. From before 1720 we have found only one price at Nantes to be stated, viz. from 1712, when green tea was sold at about 230 *sols* per *livre*; Compagnie des Indes, HH 200.

[32] DUTCH FIGURES: Kol. Arch. Nos. 10,242 and 10,242A (cf. Appendix B). ENGLISH FIGURES: C. R. O. London, E. I. C., Correspondance/Memoranda, vol. 10, 23 February 1733 ("An account of the quantity of teas sold by the East India Company from Christmas 1716 to Christmas 1732, in which is distinguished the quantity at each sale, drawn out by order of the directors of the said Company"). The statistics are drawn up per accounting year, i.e. 1720/21 comprises the auction sales during the autumn of 1720 and the spring of 1721, etc.

Table 43. *Sales of Tea in Holland and England by the Auctions of the East India Companies 1720/21–1730/31.*

	Holland	England
	ponds	lbs.
1720/21	94,917	316,182
1721/22	238,611	1,056,263
1722/23	295,142	1,569,224
1723/24	186,007	110,459
1724/25	249,074	489,423
1725/26	192,247	334,242
1726/27	200,912	581,712
1727/28	204,062	633,182
1728/29	157,003	1,353,866
1729/30	529,789	1,490,355
1730/31	1,005,845	1,049,593

It is not possible to set up similar series of sales for the Ostend company and the French company. It may, however, be stated that the Ostend company's supplies down to 1729 was of an order of magnitude corresponding to the English rather than to the Dutch supplies.[33] In 1726 the Heeren XVII declared that the Ostenders glutted Europe with Asiatic goods,[34] an assertion repudiated by the directors of the Ostend company, although with the reservation decisive in this connexion that they acknowledged importing large quantities of tea.[35] The French sales during the years 1723–34 exclusively took place at Nantes. They were less regular than the Dutch and English sales. In 1722 nearly 220,000 *livres* of tea were sold by auction, the following year well over 100,000 *livres*. Then there was an interval down to 1726. In the years 1726, 1727, and 1728 about 60–75,000 *livres* of tea were sold annually. In 1729 the sales increased to more than 300,000 *livres*, and in the beginning of the 1730's they amounted to about ¾ mill. *livres*.[36]

[33] Stadsarchief Antwerpen, G. I. C., No. 5729 (1725), No. 5733 (1726), No. 5730 (1728), No. 5724 (1729), No. 5732 (1730), No. 5734 (1731).

[34] Kol. Arch. No. 200, 13 September 1726.

[35] Stadsarchief Antwerpen, Insolvente Boedelskamer LXII (de Pret), No. 1320, letter to Mr. Pattijn, Soissons, dated at 2 July 1728.

[36] The *Nouvelle Compagnie Royale de la Chine* founded in 1712 was in 1719 united with the old company, the united company being called the *Compagnie Royale des Indes et de la Chine*. Before 1723 the return commodities were sold at Nantes as well as elsewhere, e.g. Saint-Malo. After 1734 they were sold from Lorient. Especially after 1715 Nantes developed highly and a considerable re-export can be followed from the end of the 1720's on. The auction figures originate from the Archives Municipales, Nantes, Compagnie des Indes, HH Nos. 222–226. See further: Leon Vignols & Henri Sée, "Les ventes de la Compagnie des Indes à Nantes, 1723–1733", *Revue d'Histoire des Colonies Françaises*, vol. XIII (1925), pp. 492 ff., Gaston Martin, *Nantes et la Compagnie des Indes*, 1664–1769 (Paris, 1926), p. 65, and H. du Halgouet, "Pages coloniales – Relations maritimes de la Bretagne et de la Chine au XVIIIe siècle," *Mémoires de la Société d'Histoire et d'Archèologie de Bretagne*, tome XV: 2 (1934), p. 434 *et seq.*

If we consider the prices there are two things that ought to be mentioned. One is the fact that green tea during the 1720's became comparatively more expensive and about 1730 in Holland as well as England cost more than Bohea tea. In 1728 it was said in a report on the market in the Netherlands: "het schijnt dat sedert eenigen tijdt den groenen thee wat meer in de mode begint te comen t'gene den bohée wat druckt."[37] The letter-writer thought that this change in taste was in favour of the English company, which seems reasonable, considering that the English in the 1720's laid the main stress on green tea, while the Dutch concentrated on Bohea (see the analysis above of the return cargoes of the two companies). The other feature is the stabilization of prices. This is a common feature, too. We may point to the moderate sales after the dumping years were over. The tariff reform of Walpole in 1723/24 contributed to stabilizing the English and hence also the Northwest European market.[38] The immediate effect was a more effective check on smuggling, which affected the Ostend company, furthermore, a rise in the English prices of tea and a reduction of the re-export, which amongst others affected the Dutch buyers and through them the smugglers, too, as good portion of the English re-exports by way of Holland was smuggled back into England. A comment on Walpole's new system by a London merchant in April 1724 is instructive. The merchant tells his Dutch correspondent about the rise in prices, which in a couple of months brought green tea from 6 s. 6 d. to 7 s. 6 d. and Bohea tea from 8 s. 9 d. to 11 s. 6 d.–12 s. per English lb. and exclaims, "Kon se [i.e. the tea] van Holland wederom gebraght worden sou men die prijs hier haast sien daalen."[39] While to our knowledge the price of Bohea tea kept rather constantly at about 12 s. per English lb. during the years after 1724, the price of green tea rose further and in October 1727 reached a level of 14 s. 6 d.–16 s. 10 d. per English lb.[40] A factor contributory to the rise presumably was the psychological effect of the Emperor Charles VI.'s decision under compulsion to suspend the Ostend company in May 1727. The prices at the Ostend company's auctions also rose about 1727/28. The predominant prices of the Bohea tea at the sales at Ostend in 1725 and 1726 were 54 st. and 51¾ st. per pond, respectively. At an auction in April 1728 Bohea was sold at 79½ st.

[37] Stadsarchief Antwerpen, Insolvente Boedelskamer LXII (de Pret), No. 1321, letter to Mr. Charles Pike, Amsterdam, dated at 8 November 1728.

[38] On the tariff reform see Stephen Dowell, *A History of Taxation and Taxes in England*, vol. IV (London, 1888), pp. 220 ff.

[39] Gemeente-Archief Amsterdam, Archief Brants No. 401, Brieven aan Dav. Leeuw, letter from Gilb. de Flines, London, dated at 17 April 1724.

[40] *Ibid.* letter from Gilb. de Flines, London, dated at 3 October 1727.

per pond as the predominant price.[41] These high prices surprisingly evoked a certain anxiety in the directors of the Ostend company. The anxiety especially related to the English market. The high prices caused a stop to the smuggling from Ostend to England while at the same time the English company's price policy in connexion with Walpole's system hampered the re-export with the result that "daer door het vertier van den Engelschen thée merckelijck vermeerdert."[42] The prospects were that the East India Company would be appropriating the English market.

It was the Dutch rather than the Ostenders who put an end to the stabilization period. In September an English correspondent to the Ostend company commented on the Dutch decision to start a direct trade to China as follows, "I see the Dutch are in earnest to send ships to China, this is a fine turn on our Company here but they have always been our good allies, I am sure if they go on, they will do more harm to this trade than ever the Ostenders did, or ever would have done."[43] The suspension of the Ostend company also gave rise to some disturbance. The company which was finally dissolved by the second Treaty of Vienna on 16 March 1731, in spite of this continued its commercial activities, trying to conceal them under foreign colours. Plans were teeming for moving the company to Hamburg, to Copenhagen, to Gothenburg, or to a Prussian port. Single expeditions were sent out, e.g. the famous ship "Apollo", which in 1730 was sent to China in the name of the merchant Jean Adam Pruner and provided with the passport and under the colours of the Prussian King. In spite of its being chased energetically in Asiatic as well as European waters neither the English, the Dutch, nor the French succeeded in seizing the ship, which achieved its voyage and in the autumn of 1731 arrived in the Elbe, where its cargo was sold in Hamburg.[44] Danish plans for founding a branch of the East India Company of Copenhagen at Altona on the Elbe in 1728/29 was pointed out to be the doing of the Ostenders. This was not so; on the other hand, several of the captains and supercargoes of the Ostend company went north and obtained appointments in Denmark and Sweden. In the autumn of 1730 the first ship to trade direct to China was sent from Copenhagen with the former Ostend supercargo Pieter

[41] Stadsarchief Antwerpen, G. I. C., Nos. 5729, 5733, and 5730.

[42] Stadsarchief Antwerpen, Insolvente Boedelskamer LXII (de Pret), No. 1321, letter to Louis Bernaerts, Ostende, dated at 1 October 1728.

[43] *Ibid.* letter to Mr. Nennij, Brussels, dated at 6 October 1728.

[44] C. R. O. London, E. I. C. Home Miscellaneous, No. 74 (3), abstract of letter from Brussels to the company's directors dated at 31 August 1731 containing an account of the "Appolo's" voyage. Stadsarchief Antwerpen, G. I. C., No. 5676, 20 November 1734, § 2, on a remuneration to Mr. Pruner. Alg. Rijksarchief, 's-Gravenhage, Kol. Arch. No. 202, 7 April 1731. J. de Hullu, "Over den Chinaschen Handel", pp. 132–135.

van Hurck as commercial chief. The first ships of the Swedish Henrik König Company left for China in February 1732.[45]

This was the background to increased supplies of tea to the Northwest European market. The Dutch imports surpassed the English. The supplies became greater than the consumption, which for that matter was increasing, could absorb. The prices fell. As early as the autumn of 1728 the East India Company reduced its fixed price of Bohea tea by 2 s. per English lb., in 1729 by another 1 s.[46] The fall in prices can be traced in Holland as well as Ostend and Nantes, see the opposite survey (Table 44).[47]

The fall in prices again promoted smuggling to England. In spite of Walpole's system the control was far from sufficient. In Sir John Cope's report of 1733 we may read the smuggler Gabriel Tomkins' description of the shady traffic. He used to hire ships for Zeeland, where the tea was bought. It was then landed on the coasts of Kent and Sussex. Armed groups of 10–12 men conveyed the tea to the neighbourhood of London, where it was stored in rented houses some five or six miles from the town. The further transport took place on horseback with portions of 100–200 English lbs., which were distributed to wholesale dealers or druggists, direct or through middlemen, such as "one Caleb Leigh, who used to receive goods from him at The Saracens Head in Carter Lane."[48] The beginning of the 1730's was furthermore characterized by large stocks, not least in the English East India Company. With reference to this the company in 1733 prolonged the period within which it was possible to obtain drawbacks, from three to six years. The dumping was at the same time intended and involuntary. The old companies watched each other and together kept an eye on the new companies' growth in the rough economic climate. In an English report on the autumn auctions in Copenhagen 1737 the meagre Danish profit was pointed out. What was not consumed in Denmark – and the Danish consumption was trifling – was "taken off at very low rates by certain Dutch mer-

[45] Kristof Glamann, "Hollandske Indberetninger om Altona-projektet 1728–29", *Danske Magazin*, 7:V (København, 1953), pp. 263–302. The same, "En ostindisk Rejse eller Thomas Thomsen på Galejen", *Sjöhistorisk Årsbok 1953–54* (Stockholm, 1954), pp. 15–43.

[46] C. R. O. London, E. I. C., Court Books, vol. 53, 24 April 1728 and 29 August 1729. Stadsarchief Antwerpen, Insolvente Boedelskamer LXII (de Pret), No. 1321, letter to Louis Bernaerts, Ostende, dated at 1 October 1728.

[47] DUTCH PRICES: Kol. Arch. No. 10,228, cf. Appendix B. OSTEND PRICES: Stadsarchief Antwerpen, G. I. C., Nos. 5730, 5724, 5732, 5734, 5735, 5736, 5712, 5722, and 5738 (auction-sale books and catalogues). NANTES PRICES: Archives Départementales de Loire-Inférieure, Nantes, Série C, Chambre de Commerce de Nantes, No. 706, statistics of export. – While the Dutch and the Ostend prices are auction-sale prices, the French prices are export declarations of value (*ad valorem* prices) and thus only intended as a guide.

[48] *Reports from Committees of the House of Commons*, vol. I (London, 1803), p. 610.

Table 44. *European Prices of Bohea Tea, 1728–1734.*

	Nederland Batavia tea	Nederland China tea	Ostend	Nantes
	Average fl. per pond	Average fl. per pond	Predominant st. per pond	*Ad valorem* *sols* per *livre*
1728				140
April			79.50	
Aug.–Sept.	3.69			
Dec.	3.58			
1729				missing
May			71.50	
Nov.–Dec.	2.40			
1730				72
April	2.28			
June			43.00	
Oct.–Nov.	1.69	2.13	41.00	
1731				50
April			36.00	
May–June	1.64			
Oct.			32.00	
Oct.–Nov.	1.18			
Dec.	1.36–1.44	1.40		
1732				50
April			28.00	
Nov.-Dec.	1.24	1.50		
1733				64
April–May	1.53			
May			29.50	
Oct.			33.25	
Nov.–Dec.	1.43	1.63		
1734				50
May			35.14	
Nov.–Dec.	1.63	1.66		

chants, who seem to be the only foreign purchasers at present." The reporter prophesied a short life for the Danish as well as the Swedish company, a prophecy which to some degree was predetermined by the view that both companies "have been prejudicial to ours, and must continue so to be, as long as they subsist." He concluded by making this statement: "Could the more wealthy and better established companies contrive for a while to overpurchase and undersell the others they might possibly by that means hasten their dissolution."[49] Things did not take

[49] C. R. O. London, E. I. C., Home Miscellaneous, No. 57, copy of Mr. Walter Titley's letter to my Lord Harrington, dated at Copenhagen, 5 October 1737.

quite so bad a course. On the other hand, the dumping was not without results; it contributed to weakening the old opponent, the Dutch Company, which in the 1730's gave up its recently established direct trade to Canton.

The initiative with respect to the direct trade came from the chamber in Amsterdam. Ironically enough, the Dutch Company, which zealously took care that its expert captains and traders did not go into foreign service, in the case of the direct trade to China was in a sphere where its own personnel was not sufficient, for which reason it had to take into its service people who had previously served the Ostend company. One of the three supercargoes who were hired for the first direct ship, the "Coxhorn", a native of Amsterdam named Jan de Jongh, had been twice to Canton by the ships of the Ostend company. Altogether it is evident that the pattern of the direct equipments deviated materially from those of the Company's ordinary voyages. The pay of the crew was higher, the "privilege tonnage" was ampler, the pattern was foreign.[50] The Directors at Kamer Amsterdam had decided to send two ships to China, but due to various unfortunate occurrences only the "Coxhorn" started. The ship put to sea on 5 December 1728 with a cargo of just under 300,000 fl. in silver coins, the majority being *dukatons*, the rest Mexican rials and pillar dollars. On 2 August 1729 she anchored at Macao.

The "Coxhorn" without any obstacles sailed up the river to Canton and began trading within the framework set up for the Europeans by the Chinese authorities. A century old project had thus been realized. Was it symptomatic that when the gate to the great Chinese empire was set ajar, the Dutch Company was among the last to arrive? It had displayed much energy throughout the 17th century and made a number of attempts at making its way to a direct commercial contract with China, by or without force. The rule of the Portuguese at Macao was an essential obstacle, and at Coen's time the Company therefore formed the grandiose plan – among many other grandiose plans whirling about in the head of that bellicose gentleman – of chasing the Portuguese away, striking a blow at the Spanish silver fleet at Manila and in this way monopolizing the trade to China and Japan. China should be provided with all foreign goods by the Dutch. It all came to nothing. Macao

[50] See Collectie Radermacher No. 495, "Stukken concernerende de directe vaart in China" i.a. containing information on the Ostend company's purchases in Canton in 1726; Kol. Arch. No. 8471, Papieren Hope, "Consideratiën over de vaart naar China door Nic. Hartman aangeboden aan Prins Willem V, 17. august 1751"; De Hullu, "Over den Chinaschen handel", p. 70.

held out. The Dutch gained a footing on the Pescadores, but had to leave the islands under a threat of attack by the Chinese governor of Amoy. The Company moved its forces to Taiwan and held that island until Koxinga captured it in 1661. Time and again the Company succeeded in making single expeditions, more or less clandestinely, to Amoy and other ports in Fukien, but in each case it had to buy a permission to trade there from the local governor. In the 1680's the Company made another push and i.a. sent off the embassies under the leadership of Vincent Paets and Louis de Keiser, but this was in vain, too. Canton was never reached. The Dutch Company's successful arrangement in Japan with a permanent factory could not be repeated in China. Here the English company got better off. Although it also had great difficulties to fight, it established a fairly regular traffic towards the end of the 17th century, mainly to Amoy. At the turn of the century the "Macclesfield" safely returned from an exciting stay at Canton with a large and valuable cargo. The ship belonged to the English Company Trading to the East Indies founded in 1698, which was a competitor of the old East India Company. It is in the English company records that we first learn about conditions of trade in China, in Amoy, Chusan, and Canton.[51]

In the southernmost Chinese areas, in Tongking, where the population was Indo-Chinese, and where there was nominally a state of vassalage to China proper, the Europeans were exposed to the same high-handedness and fortuitousness as those which they had met with time and again in the Arabian commercial area. All purchases and sales took place through the King, the Prince, or their representatives; they fixed the prices and rates of conversion, through them the goods wanted were delivered. Any trace of native merchants was gone. In Amoy, too, the private merchants kept in the background. In Canton, however, they met a more freely developed system. It is true that the influence of the Imperial Customs Officer, the Hoppo, was great, but the decisive new feature which the supercargoes of the "Macclesfield" experienced, was "the Great Mandarins Merchants", among whom especially the Viceroy's merchants represented an attitude towards trade with the foreigners which heralded a new era. As pointed out by H. B. Morse they were the forerunners of the later on so well-known Hong merchants, whose "wonderful combination of business shrewdness and commercial honour has been praised by so many foreign observers."[52] It was generally agreed by the English supercargoes that of all the Chinese ports known,

[51] H. B. Morse, *The Chronicles of the East India Company Trading to China*, 1635–1834, vol. I, (Oxford, 1926), pp. 99 ff. [52] *Ibid.* p. 101.

Canton was the most pleasant place in which to trade. The reason why they arrived at this place last was partly the resistance of the Portuguese and their own unwisdom, partly (in Morse's words) "because the Manchu hold on that wealthy and important mart was for some years precarious, and the military authorities did not venture to give free scope to the commercial abilities of the Cantonese, barely subdued, always inclined to rebellion, and then and now, the most self-assertive of all the Chinese."[53] From the first years of the 18th century it may be assumed that the English trade to Canton was permanent, and by the increasing activities of the Ostenders during the second decade the European element in the commercial life of Canton became characteristic. When the English company's servants reached Canton in 1720, they learnt from the Chinese merchants that the Ostenders had tried to engross the tea market. The preceding year they had contracted for 1,500 piculs of tea more than they could carry off by their ships. The tea merchants had had to bear the loss due to the breach of contract. This experience may have given rise to the establishment of the famous Co-Hong. This new "combination for the control of the foreign trade"[54] saw the light of day on 25 December 1720. The Co-Hong was a guild consisting of the greatest Chinese merchants who traded with the foreigners. They made a charter with 13 articles. The purpose was that of preventing abuse, fostering foreign trade, and protecting the foreigners from the unworthy among the merchants of Canton. The foreign and the Chinese merchants, it was said, were members of one family, and owed all they had to the service of the Emperor. The profit ought not to be the result of individual profit, but ought to appear as the benefit of an agreement made for the common good. The foreign and Chinese merchants should be on an equal footing. If the Europeans succeeded in selling dear and buying cheap, the Chinese would only suffer losses and thus be tempted to sell false goods for true. Therefore the members of the guild would meet the foreign merchants and agree upon prices. If a Chinese merchant tried to trade behind the back of the guild or to deliver poor goods, he would be punished. Chinese traders from other places who came to Canton in order to bargain with the Europeans, must act through the Co-Hong. A foreign ship might do half of its trade through a single merchant, while the rest of it should be divided among the guild members. At the making of contracts the Europeans must pay their money in advance. All deliveries of goods to foreign ships should be recorded. The declaration of green tea should be net weight. A number

[53] *Ibid.* p. 147. [54] *Ibid.* p. 163.

of minor, special commodities, e.g. chinaware, which required technical knowledge, were free and might be bought outside the Co-Hong. Still, the dealers in chinaware should pay 30 per cent. to the guild without regard to profit or loss. The articles finally decided the share which the members of the guild should have in the foreign trade. The members were divided into three classes, the first class consisting of five Hong merchants, the second class of another five Hongs, and the third class of six Hongs, i.e. 16 members in all. New merchants might be admitted on paying 1,000 taels, for which amount they should be enrolled in the third class.

These platonic and pleasantly sounding articles were not at all to the taste of the English company. The London Court of Directors in so many words declared that the intention of the Chinese was "to set their own prices on the goods to be sold Europeans, and to have their proportions of the real profits on said goods whoever appeared to be the seller."[55] The English reacted by making their supercargoes form a council at Canton, which appealed to the Hoppo.[56] In the immediately following seasons after 1720 they succeeded in avoiding the Chinese selling cartel, a contributory factor being disagreement between the Canton merchants. In return they had trouble with the Hoppo, who amongst other things in 1728 tried to impose a 10 per cent. extra duty on the goods, against which the Europeans as well as the Chinese merchants lodged a protest. It was customary to pay a duty of 6 per cent., besides various presents and the like for the permission to trade. The European supercargoes refused to pay the new duty of 10 per cent., after which the Hoppo made the Canton merchants responsible for the duty. The controversy with the fiscal authorities is difficult to unravel, but undoubtedly it strengthened the position of the greatest Hong-merchants, whose connexion with the Hoppo was most effective. In 1728 the English supercargoes wrote that actually there were four merchants who aimed at securing a monopoly of trade with the Europeans. They were Suqua, Ton Hunqua, Tinqua, and Coiqua, "whom the English and other Europeans have always transacted their affairs with, these are now combined together and supported by the Hoppo and other mandarins."[57] This was the first step towards the so-called "security merchant" system, which was clearly developed about 1740.[58]

[55] Instructions to the supercargoes of the "Townsend" dated at 24 December 1725; quoted from Morse, *op. cit.* p. 169 *et seq.*

[56] This did not mean that there was any resident factor at Canton. Only the French used this practice during the years from 1698 to 1724. Later in the 18th century "staying over" was common.

[57] Morse, *op. cit.* p. 195.

[58] Earl H. Pritchard, *The Crucial Years of Early Anglo-Chinese Relations, 1750–1800* (Research Studies of the State College of Washington, vol. IV., No. 3–4, Washington, 1936), p. 116.

When the "Coxhorn" arrived at Canton, the Dutch especially entered into connexion with one of these Hong-merchants, – or rather two, viz. Ton Hunqua and his colleague Tinqua. On 9 August 1729 the first contract for tea was made, with a term of delivery of 100 days, the commodity being delivered on board at the Company's risk and all expenses for packing, etc., and duties being included in the price. During the following months the whole return cargo was secured, and on the 27th of December the commercial transactions were concluded. The "Coxhorn" had to pay about 3,100 taels for tonnage and anchorage, fees for passports, etc. The homeward voyage began immediately after the new year, and on 13 July 1730 the ship anchored at Texel. It carried a cargo consisting of nearly 270,000 ponds of tea, 570 pieces of silk fabrics, and chinaware. The cost-price corresponded to an amount between 270,000–280,000 fl., and after the auction the Court of Directors made up that the expedition had yielded a net profit of about $3^1/_4$ plums of gold, i.e. 325,000 fl.[59] The Heeren XVII were satisfied. The result seemed to them to encourage continuing the direct trade to Canton; so during the years 1731–35 11 ships in all were sent, 8 of which were equipped by the chamber of Amsterdam.

The appearance of the Dutch on the tea market of Canton caused anxiety to the English East India Company. The Chief of the English Council at Canton in 1729 was informed that the "Coxhorn" was coming and ordered to put obstacles in the way of the Dutch ship in every manner, to spoil the market for its supercargoes, and to try to make it miss the monsoon on its homeward voyage.[60] These pious instructions reminded very much of those concerning the ships of the Ostend company, which the companies fought against together. They could not, however, be put into practice. As at Mocha the conflicting parties were protected by the local jurisdiction. Indeed, the Dutch supercargoes when leaving Canton were accompanied onboard by a party consisting of Portuguese, Chinese, Armenian, and – English merchants. A more serious matter was the assertion which was later made from English quarters, that the Dutch supercargoes had been fraudulent in their purchases of tea in the season of 1729. It was rumoured in London that the tea in the invoices was put at 20 per cent. higher than the actual prices, viz. at 24–26 taels instead of 19–20 taels.[61] For that occasion the Heeren XVII decided to authorize the Company's "advocate" to correspond with the Company's connexion in London, Gerard Bolwerk, about the matter, but nothing

[59] Kol. Arch. No. 10,419, the account "Voyagie naer China".
[60] Morse, *op. cit.* p. 193. [61] De Hullu, "Over den Chinaschen handel", p. 101.

was heard about it later. The Dutch cost-prices, for that matter, were on the whole lower than the English prices, as appears from the survey of the buying seasons of 1729–33.

Table 45. *English and Dutch Cost-Prices of Bohea Tea at Canton, 1729–1733; Taels per Picul.*

Season	English	Dutch
1729	27.3	24.6
1730	21.4	18.8
1731	17.4	17.3
1732	16.8	14.5
1733	13.2	14.9

The discussion of the cost-prices in 1729 was rather expressive of the fact that the English company's own servants had come under suspicion. The English factory records quote more than 24 taels for green tea and more than 26 taels for black tea, i.e. amongst others Bohea tea (from the table it appears that the average for Bohea was 27.3 taels) as against a predominant price of 19 and 20 taels in the preceding season.[62] The English had contracted with the Hong merchant Suqua, but two of his rivals, Ton Hunqua and Tinqua, from whom the Dutch Company had made purchases, sent the English Court of Directors a letter in which they accused the Chief of the English Council at Canton, Mr. Fazakerley, of having entered the purchases at too high prices. An inquiry into the matter made in the season of 1731 did not lead to any actual result apart from the fact that the East India Company decided to leave Suqua as a supplier and instead chose Ton Hunqua and Tinqua.[63]

When the English Canton fleet – consisting of four ships and one sloop – in the summer of 1730 was on its way to China, it made a stop at Batavia. The Chief of the Council of Supercargoes, Mr. James Naish, noticed that in that season 20 junks had arrived at Batavia from Chusan, Amoy, and Canton, besides six ships from Macao, with a total of 25,000 piculs of tea.[64] Mr. Naish thought that 5,500 piculs would cover the local demand, while the rest was intended for Europe. If this estimate might be exaggerated,[65] it is at any rate a fact that large quantities of tea were sold at Batavia in that year, actually the largest amounts that had been seen there so far. The price of Bohea tea was considerably above the

[62] Morse, *op. cit.* p. 194. [63] *Ibid.* p. 202 *et seq.* [64] *Ibid.* p. 197.

[65] The buying statistics show total purchases in 1730 of about 1,345,000 ponds, about 1.2 mill. ponds of which were Bohea tea, i.e. roughly 11,000 piculs of tea were bought by the Company. To this should be added the purchases of the interlopers, which were unknown, but which undoubtedly were great, too. Kol. Arch. No. 2036, fo. 3337 *et seq.*

price that had been paid at Canton in 1729, viz. 42 taels per picul. The following year, however, there was a heavy fall in prices with the result that the prices at Batavia came to be below the prices at Canton. It cannot be precluded that supplies from Amoy and Chusan contributed to bringing about the fall in prices, as it is known that these towns had several times tried to regain their lost position and actually invited the English company's servants to make their purchases there. It should be added that there was a general downward tendency on the market in the beginning of the 1730's. The Ostend company had dropped out as a purchaser – the last ship to go to Canton was the above-mentioned "Apollo", which made purchases in 1730 – the European market showed signs of being temporarily saturated, and the production in China had probably been extended by new plantations, which now yielded tea. Furthermore, the Dutch at Batavia in 1732 – under the influence of the Heeren XVII's reduction of their orders to Batavia from 1 mill. to 100,000 ponds – almost sifted their purchases of Bohea tea with the result that the Canton merchant Suqua lost 30,000 taels on his cargoes. This reacted on the market at Canton in the autumn and brought about a fall in prices.[66] In the Batavia seasons of 1731, 1732, and 1733 the average cost-prices of Bohea tea were 19.9, 12.9, and 13.2 taels per picul, respectively. The very level to which the prices of tea gradually dropped, was intended by the Batavian Government. The Heeren XVII, who a few years before had complained of too high prices at Batavia and reduced their orders accordingly, suddenly got afraid that the "ongemeene laage prijsen" should put an end to the junk traffic, as they could not pay the freight and other expenses for the Chinese.[67] It was considered to stop the direct trade from Nederland to China and on this basis they were anxious of a repetition of the affair of 1717. Having the direct trade stopped was just what the Governor General and Council were working at. It had always been a thorn in their flesh; they felt it as a disavowal and limitation of their power. The Government by its price policy now tried to create an impression that it was cheaper to buy the tea at Batavia than at Canton.

In August 1732 the Kamer Amsterdam set up a commission to consider possibilities of economies in the direct trade to China. The costs seemed too great to the *bewindhebbers*. They especially wanted to reduce the crews and their pay as well as the "privilege tonnage", which was more abundant than the normal. As pointed out in the chapter on the factory

[66] H. B. Morse, *op. cit.* p. 212, and the Dutch statistics of purchases, which show a purchase of only 71,500 ponds of Bohea tea. Kol. Arch. No. 2103, fo. 3765.

[67] Kol. Arch. No. 202, 7 March 1735.

Nederland, the Dutch freight charges per ton really were not essentially different from the charges paid by the English company. They might be a little higher than the normal English charges, but to the Heeren XVII it was obviously more natural to compare the charges with those of the trade to Batavia and Ceylon and think of the consequences a higher pay might have to the rest of the Company's sailors.

The annoyance at the newly started Danish and Swedish trade to the East Indies and China in the same year led to a proposal of partly in Europe buying up Spanish rials under the nose of the Scandinavians, partly in the East engrossing the markets in concert with the English. The Heeren XVII suggested that a permanent factory should be founded at Canton in order in this way to extend the knowledge of trade in China and especially to investigate what Dutch and Indian commodities might be disposed of. By such an arrangement the Court of Directors thought that the Company could better secure prime qualities of tea and the choicest chinaware. Besides the factory at Canton, the Company might also establish a subfactory at Amoy. According to the plan it should be the task of the Batavian Government annually to send three or four ships from Batavia to Canton with spices, pepper, sapan wood, and other commodities which the Chinese used to import by their junks. The Chinese returns should only go to Batavia to the extent needed in the Company's inter-Asiatic trade, while the greater part of the tea and the chinaware should be shipped direct to Europe in two or three ships, through which arrangement time as well as money would be saved. As regards time, the Heeren XVII assumed that the tea could reach Nederland about two months earlier than usual, and in money the purchases would become cheaper when they were made out of the season. As regards quality the project furthermore involved the advantage that all the Company's tea would be packed in chests in the Chinese manner, in contrast to the Batavian junk tea, which in spite of repeated orders still mainly reached Europe in bamboo cases, which gave too much tare. The new organization of the Company's trade to China would involve a prohibition of the Chinese and Portuguese trade to Batavia. The Court of Directors did not think that a total ban could be carried into effect, but wanted that it should be tried to restrict the trade to only one cargo of tea annually, whereas other Chinese commodities might without hindrance be shipped to Indonesia. The private traders should be prohibited to deal in tea. The Heeren XVII maintained that the private traders annually sent 2.5 mill. ponds of tea to Europe, the ships thus being overloaded with a consequent risk to the navigation.[68] This surprisingly great clandestine import, the existence of which was not denied by the Governor General and Council, requires further comment.

It was mentioned in the Introduction that interloping must be considered a practically unknown phenomenon in Nederland in the period under consideration. On the other hand the Company's officers and crew were allowed to carry goods to Nederland in the form of "privilege tonnage". The "privilege tonnage" together with the Company's own goods was unloaded in the Zuider Zee and carried to the chambers, where the sailors made their appearance for a kind of customs examination, some commodities having been declared contraband. Furthermore, the volume of each man's "privilege tonnage" was checked, this volume being proportioned to his rating and the length of his stay in the East.[69] This private import was legal, being part of the pay of the men employed, but besides that, officers and crew smuggled private goods home by the ships. Neither the volume of the legal private import nor that of the smuggling by the ships is known. From the account of seized goods it can be seen how much was discovered. Occasionally it was a question of considerable amounts, thus at the Kamer Amsterdam seized goods to an amount of more than 171,000 fl. were sold in 1713/14, and in 1714/15 the amount was more than 175,000 fl.[70] Although smuggling is known from the whole of the Company's lifetime, there are various indications that it grew to be a serious problem and just did so in connexion with the trade in tea. The general increase in the Company's trade contributed to make effective control difficult. It was easier to supervise an annual returning fleet of 15 ships than inspecting the fleets of the 1720's and 1730's which were of some 30 ships. The activities of the Ostend company in this special field, too, produced a minor revolution. The Ostend company's foreign captains and supercargoes understood how to benefit by the great personal risk connected with the prohibited trade by demanding and getting a "privilege tonnage" which was considerably greater than usual. The example was infectious. When the Dutch opened the direct trade to China, they had, as mentioned above, to grant a great "privilege tonnage" to officers and crew. What the Company's other captains and officers had not legally accorded to them, they took for themselves. We are disinclined to attach so great importance to the corruption as has previously been done, at any rate as regards the period of 1620–1740, but it cannot be

[68] De Hullu, "Over den Chinaschen handel", pp. 129 ff.

[69] J. de Hullu, "De matrozen en soldaten op de schepen der Oost-Indische Compagnie", *Bijdragen voor de Taal-, Land- en Volkenkunde van Nederlandsch-Indië,* deel 69 ('s-Gravenhage, 1914), pp. 352 ff.

[70] Kol. Arch. No. 10,412.

completely disregarded. The evidence is too great for that. With a President like de Haze at the head of the Company it does not require much imagination to picture to oneself the way in which an illegal import by the Company's ships could be arranged, considering his outrageous affairs in connexion with Pieter Backer. Finally there were the activities of the private traders in Asiatic trade. The element of free burghers at Batavia gradually increased, and so the pressure through the hidden channels increased as well. In the beginning of the 1730's it seems as if every nerve was strained to carry tea home. The private traders bought up tea on a scale which corresponded to the Company's purchases at Batavia, and the legal "privilege tonnage" actually was great when it was practically exclusively used for a single commodity.[71] The size of this capacity appears from the answer given by the Governor General and Council to the Heeren XVII's demonstration of the private import to Nederland of about 2.5 mill. ponds of tea. The Batavian Government in so many words replied that half of this quantity ought to be considered as "privilege tonnage" – about 2,000 piculs for the sailors and about 8,000 piculs for the officers – while the second half was due to smuggling, which ought to be legalized in the way that the private traders at Batavia should be permitted to convey such a quantity to Nederland against payment of freight.

Besides, the Batavian Government in their answer to the Heeren XVII's proposal on the whole doubted its practicability. It would hardly be possible to prevent the Scandinavian countries from securing silver, amongst other things because they could buy it at Cadix, as the Swedish company did. Nor could an engrossing of the Indian markets be realized, and in the case of China it was evident that any nation could freely trade there and even could count on assistance from the Chinese authorities if it was tried to impede them. The Dutch Company might very well establish a permanent factory at Canton, but the Governor General and Council foresaw that the other nations would soon follow up this idea and then the Company was back again where it started. This would involve that there would be nothing left for the junk traffic, as the junks had hitherto supplied themselves with the surplus from each season at Canton. The Batavian Government stated its interest in the junk trade,

[71] As compared with the total official capacity, on the other hand, it was not impressive. We do not know the tonnage of the Company's ships (cf. above), but the annual transport of the chief pond goods in the 1720's and the beginning of the 30's was of at least 15–20 mill. ponds, i.e. that the privileged tonnage and smuggled goods together included 10–15 per cent. That mainly tea was smuggled is concluded from the fact that the goods seized in the 1730's were dominated by tea. See e.g. Kol. Arch. No. 8335, the "Versamelingh van de verkoopinghen" of Zeeland, 1724–1736.

which meant an income for the town, and pointed out that the Europeans as regards the freight rates would be unable to compete with the Chinese.[72] The annual supplies of tea by the junks were estimated at about 30,000 piculs.[73]

The final results of the deliberations were that the China trade in 1734 was reorganized in the way that the direct trade from Europe to Canton was discontinued, and the management was passed on to the Governor General and Council at Batavia. What was left of the Heeren XVII's plan was that the Batavian Government should every year send two ships to Canton, the largest of which should go direct to Nederland, while the other should return by way of Batavia, where its cargo should be regulated; besides, the junk tea should be placed in the units of the ordinary homeward-bound fleet. This arrangement was determinative of the development until 1756. The prohibition of the private trade in tea was not carried into effect. At G.W. van Imhoff's suggestion the Government in 1743 made the realistic decision of legalizing the activities of the private traders, so that the latter should be permitted within certain limits to use the Company's ships from China to Batavia against a payment of freight of 4 rixdollars per picul. Three years later the payment was reduced to one fourth, the price thus being brought down to the same level as the rates of the junks and the Portuguese.[74] Furthermore, also on the initiative of van Imhoff, it was effected that the country traders might freight tea to Europe, i.e. Nederland, by the Company's ships against a remuneration of 40 per cent.[75] The central element of the reorganization of 1734 was the fact that the Company by an export drive with Indonesian goods in China hoped to relieve the pressure on the Company's resources of silver. The Heeren XVII in 1735 stated that their chief purpose in discontinuing the direct trade to China had been the consideration for the shortage of money at Batavia "en allerweegen soo veel doenlijk te brengen tot die florisanten staat waar in het voor deesen is geweest."[76] They would try to buy tea for commodities instead of using cash. The English East India Company grappled with the same problem and – assisted by enterprising country traders – towards the end of the 18th century discovered that while the Chinese had little taste for European goods, they were eager to accept the articles of India, particularly raw cotton and opium, though China itself produced the one and prohibited the other.[77] Almost simul-

[72] *Ibid.*

[73] *Memorie boek van pakhuismeesteren van de thee te Amsterdam, 1818–1918, en de Nederlandsche theehandel in den loop der tijden* (Amsterdam, n.d.), p. 35.

[74] *Ibid.* p. 36 *et seq.* [75] See Kol. Arch. No. 8471. [76] Kol. Arch. No. 202, 7 March 1735.

[77] Michael Greenberg, *British Trade and the Opening of China*, 1800–42 (Cambridge, 1951), p. 9.

taneously with the Dutch project we find the first mention in the English factory records of the smuggling of opium to Canton by British ships from Fort St. George. The English supercargoes in 1733 warned their colleagues from India against conveying opium to Canton, pointing out the great risk to which they exposed the whole trade to Canton. The Emperor in 1729 had issued a prohibition of the smoking of opium.[78]

The regulation of 1734 was of good promise. The Zeeland *bewindhebber* Samuel Rademacher later wrote that the returns which arrived from China by way of Batavia during the first years yielded the Company a greater profit than the direct trade carried on by the Heeren XVII.[79] The quantities imported and sold annually ranged between just under 200,000 ponds (in 1741) and just under 1 mill. ponds (in 1732) in the period from 1732 to 1742 inclusive.[80] Still, about the middle of the century the Heeren XVII raised severe criticism of the Batavian Government's management of the trade in tea. The hotbed of the criticism was the *bewindhebbers*' assembly in Holland and its chief count was that the Company's auction prices of tea gradually had sunk to a level of 40–50 per cent. below those of its European competitors. A report made in 1754 by a committee of principal stockholders pointed out the danger of carrying on the trade to China solely from the point of view that at the sales of Indonesian and Indian commodities at Canton the Company ought to obtain the greatest profit possible. The report called attention to the fact that the Batavian Government since 1734 had gradually increased the rate of conversion of the Chinese tael from 71–72 st. to 88 st. which veiled the profit on the goods sold at Canton. The principal stockholders were of opinion that cash was the most marketable commodity of all in China, and purchases of tea against payment in silver would always give the best quality at the cheapest price. It must always be a principal rule for a merchant, it was said, to seek the market where he will get the greatest profit on his goods. The Governor General and Council had offended against this rule by sending commodities to China which ought to have been sold elsewhere. This, e.g., applied to a number of the fine spices, of which some, for that matter, had a very limited market in China, thus nutmegs and cloves, in the case of which a sale of more than 40 piculs of each commodity depressed the market. The principal shareholders acknowledged that the Batavian Government had succeeded in selling between 2.3 and 3 mill. ponds of pepper a year at Canton, but

[78] Morse, *op. cit.* p. 215.

[79] J. de Hullu, "De instelling van de commissie voor den handel der Oost-Indische Compagnie op China in 1756", *Bijdragen tot de Taal-, Land- en Volkenkunde van Nederlandsch-Indië*, deel 79 ('s-Gravenhage, 1923), p. 523. [80] Kol. Arch., Aanwinsten 1901, III, No. 5.

thought that the pepper in the case of several years could have been sold more profitably elsewhere. They also thought that the large quantities of pepper actually indicated that the Government had needed silver for the equipments. Finally they remarked critically on the export of Japanese copper and tin to China. It was poor economy to carry copper from Japan to Batavia and from there to Canton, not least considering that the Chinese carried on a considerable trade to Japan (the ratio between the Chinese and the Dutch trade in copper was put at 16:10). Tin, on the other hand, was a commodity which was much in demand in China. The criticism in this case referred to a sale of 1.4 mill. ponds at prices which actually were lower than the price in Europe, for which reason the tin ought to have been placed in the homeward-bound ships instead of unprofitable goods such as sugar, Persian red chalk, and the like.[81]

The Dutch Company started its trade in tea at a late stage. For a long period it bought tea from the Chinese junks at Batavia. The increasing English traffic to the Chinese ports, which already from the first years of the 18th century had been of a regular character, in connexion with the Ostenders' interloping brought the Batavia tea into the limelight, both because it was dear, and because qualitatively it was not on a level with tea bought by direct trade. Furthermore, the increasing demand of the competing companies manifested itself in decreased supplies by the junk route. The interruption of the commercial intercourse between the South Chinese ports and Batavia as a consequence of the attempt at enforcing lower prices in 1717 actually became an expensive affair to the Company, which for two or three years must have suffered losses on its trade in tea. A factor which contributed to starting a direct trade was the budding plans in Denmark–Norway and Sweden for trying their hand at the trade to China. In 1729 the Company finally ranged itself alongside the other European companies and sent its first expedition to Canton. The fact that the supplies from the junks were maintained is evidence partly of the private traders' increasing interest in trading in tea, partly of the great drive actually tried by the Company when finally it got started. A purely quantitative comparison shows that the Dutch Company during the following years occupied a leading place among the importers of tea to Europe. The great efforts taxed the Company's strength. The Batavian Government greatly disliked the direct trade from Nederland to China, as the ships passed the head office, which was always starving for men, materials, and commodities. The cargoes mainly consisted of cash and bar silver. The reorganization of the tea trade in

[81] De Hullu, "De instelling van de commissie voor den handel op China", pp. 523 ff.

1734 is evidence of the necessity of relieving the pressure on the Company as regards its shipment of silver to China. The direct trade was discontinued, though only in one direction. The Company continued buying on the market at Canton and the greater part of the goods purchased was sent to Nederland by the direct route while the rest was sent home by way of Batavia after the local demand had been covered. The decisive factor therefore was the attempt at buying tea with Indonesian and Indian goods instead of buying it with silver. The plan was in the nature of an export drive in China with the products of Batavia. Of necessity this would be detrimental to the old trade of the junks, i.e. the Chinese and Portuguese merchants, at Batavia, as the export drive would involve a limitation or perhaps prohibition of sales of e.g. pepper to the foreigners. The trade at Batavia did not, however, dwindle to nothing. It played a role to the private traders and in the 1740's it is seen how the Company actually drew the activities of the private traders into their endeavours to secure sufficient quantities of tea for Nederland. As a whole the Dutch Company during these years lost ground in the European race for the China tea. The English competing company had again become the greatest importer. The private traders were permitted to freight tea by the Company's ships from Canton to Batavia as well as from Batavia to Nederland. The Company only reserved to itself the ships on the direct route from Canton to Nederland. It is certain that the export drive in China produced results. Whereas the Company towards the end of the 1730's sold about ½ mill. ponds of pepper a year at Canton, it succeeded during the 1740's to have the sales raised to 1½–2 mill. ponds and in the 1750's in a few cases to about 3 mill. ponds. The sales of tin were also increased. These examples are interesting. The English also sought for suitable export commodities for China and for some time on the pattern of the Dutch went in for pepper. Still, it must be said that the marketing possibilities were limited, considering the size of the area. Bullion and specie were in our period the most marketable commodity in China and thus the most suitable means of payment for purchases of tea. Thus we see two tendencies clashing in Dutch commercial policy in China. One, represented by the Court of Directors in Nederland, lays the main stress on the cost-prices, the qualities, and the sales in Europe, while the Government at Batavia to a higher degree looks on the traffic to China from a producer's and seller's point of view and in its policy amongst other things uses a devaluation of Dutch currency in an attempt at showing trade to be as profitable as possible. Suggestions for the cultivation of tea in Java were made, but while coffee became an object of cultivation, tea so far remained a question of trade.

CHAPTER XII

Profit and Loss

What does the accounts of the Company tell about the period from 1620 to 1740? In order to have this question answered we must first briefly elucidate the character of the accounts, specify what they contain and what they do not contain. Actually the accounting of the Company was very heterogeneous. In a few cases we may in some of the factories find a bookkeeping which seems quite modern. In other places we find the elements of a capitalistic bookkeeping, without it, however, being clearly developed. The weakest feature from a present-day point of view was the general accounts and hence the balance-sheets. This is conditioned by the fact that the Company, in spite of several attempts, never attained to a central bookkeeping including the whole of the concern. Not least practical conditions put obstacles in the way. Owing to the long distances it took three or four years to collect all books. Accounts were kept of the Dutch activities, chamber by chamber, and the final result was set up in annual balance-sheets comprising all the six chambers. The general account of the Asiatic establishments was kept at Batavia. There, too, annual balance-sheets were set up, and the most obvious expression of the Company's total balance, therefore, was obtained by comparing the balance-sheets of the two areas. In the relation between the home country and Batavia the principle was followed that each of them should pay its own "house-keeping". Cargoes sent out and return cargoes were exchanged in the sense that each party entered the cost-price and the costs immediately connected with the acquirement of the cargoes.[1] It was an adapted form of factorage bookkeeping. Externally the Company's general accounts appear as double-entry bookkeeping – there are journals and ledgers and balances in the ledgers – but actually it is not what is understood by double-entry bookkeeping today. There is no capital account nor any effective profit-and-loss account. In the Dutch ledgers there is, indeed, an account for the total costs of equipment – the so-called *equipagie-generaal* – which is compared

[1] Mansvelt, *op. cit.* p. 95.

with an account for the total receipts of the sales of returns of the year – the so-called *retouren-generaal* – after which the difference is made out as profit or loss. But this "profit-and-loss account" is very primitive and is no auxiliary account to which losses and profits are consistently transferred from the various trading accounts. As a logical consequence of the practice outlined here we shall in the Company's Dutch balances under assets search in vain for the whole of the Indian enterprise, in some cases also buildings and plants in Nederland, furthermore the ships and the goods and cash being under transport. Under liabilities the share capital is missing.

The factorage accounting system was historically determined. Its defects were not so conspicuous to the time as on a later view. In a certain respect it may perhaps even be said that the Heeren XVII were interested in the defective balance-sheet. As pointed out by Dr. Mansvelt it was necessary for the Court of Directors to veil the surplus and deficit to the shareholders, who were speculating for a profit.[2] One of the decisive differences between the English and the Dutch Company which came to light in the first decades of the 17th century, was the very fact that the Dutch were able to invest capital in their Asiatic establishments in spite of the shareholders' protests and claims for having the general account closed when the profits were insufficient to them. The second English Joint Stock Company of 1617 had at its disposal a share capital of nearly 1.6 million £ sterling, which was roughly 2 ½ times as large an amount as that with which the Dutch started in 1602. Still the great English effort failed. When trade was going badly the shareholders demanded their money back and got it. In 1628 the Joint Stock Company was dissolved without there having been an investment in Asia to an extent similar to that of the Dutch. We may get a certain idea of the Dutch Company's situation in the 1620's by looking at the few balance-sheets extant. From October 1621 we have found a balance-sheet drawn up on the basis of "de generale boeken" at Batavia. It looks like this:[3]

DEBIT Table 46. *Balance Batavia, October 1621.* *CREDIT*

DEBIT		CREDIT	
Ongelden	7.3 mill. fl.	*Winsten*	3.8 mill. fl.
Arrears, etc.	0.2 - -	Goods captured	2.0 - -
Effects	5.2 - -	Various receipts	0.2 - -
		Balance: the Company	6.7 - -
	12.7 mill. fl.		12.7 mill. fl.

[2] *Ibid.* pp. 84 ff. [3] Kol. Arch. No. 986, fos. 228–231.

This balance is typical of the balances at Batavia. For its interpretation serves the fact that *ongelden* sums up all the costs which had been defrayed in the form of wages, pay, ships, fortifications, prizes, etc. *Winsten* similar sums up the Company's receipts by its commercial activities in the East, i.e. the goods it had acquired as surplus. As the expenses were defrayed out of the capital which the Directors in the course of time had sent from Nederland and the receipts on the whole represent that which Nederland had received in the form of returns, the difference indicates the costs of the establishment of the Dutch rule so far, though we must also consider the other receipts summed up (goods captured, duties, etc.).

A corresponding balance from the end of September 1627 shows the following picture:[4]

DEBIT Table 47. *Balance Batavia, End of September 1627.* *CREDIT*

Ongelden	16.2 mill. fl.	*Winsten*	12.3 mill. fl.
Arrears, etc.	0.4 - -	Goods captured	3.2 - -
Effects	6.4 - -	Various receipts	1.5 - -
		Balance: the Company	6.0 - -
	23.0 mill. fl.		23.0 mill. fl.

It is seen that the debts of Batavia to the Company or to Nederland had improved somewhat, though not much. As to the effects it is pointed out in a note added to the 1627 balance that these actually constituted 4.1 mill. fl., only, when the factory stocks of food, ammunition, etc., were deducted, besides the value of the returns sent home during the year, while the value of the cargoes going out during the same period were added. The note shows that the values of ships and goods at sea were not considered at the balancing time.

In Nederland the following balance from May 1625 may serve as an example:[5]

DEBIT Table 48. *Balance Nederland, May 1625.* *CREDIT*

Cash in hand	339,923 fl.	*Penningen à deposito*	6,702,301 fl.
Outstanding debts	2,225,324 -	Debts to the States General, etc.	129,479 -
Goods not sold	2,374,871 -	Debts of profit	73,807 -
Sundries	104,560 -	Sundries	29,634 -
Balance	1,890,543 -		
	6,935,221 fl.		6,935,221 fl.

[4] Klerk de Reus, *op. cit.* Beilage XI (a).

[5] On the basis of Kol. Arch. No. 10,233A, "Sommier staet van de respective cameren der O. I. C. 'tsedert d. 20 Junij Ao. 1624 tot 20 Mayo Ao. 1625".

The balance illustrates what was said above about the absence of the share capital among the liabilities and of buildings, ships, etc., among the assets. Just as in the working account it was the current receipts and payments that were recorded, so the balance is a survey of the cash in hand and the short-term – urgent – amounts and debts. In the beginning of the 1620's the short-term amounts were still greater.[6] The total picture is not particularly bright. If the general account had been closed in the 1620's the profit would undoubtedly have been just as poor as that of the English Joint Stock Company. The *bewindhebbers*, however, were staunch in their conflict with the shareholders and were supported by the States General. Although the concept of "reserve capital" as regards accounting was as unknown a quantity as the concept of "share capital", the Court of Directors continued to build up an invisible trading capital in the East and the results did not fail to appear.[7]

We get an impression of the changes that took place during the 17th century by considering the balances for Batavia and Nederland in 1689.[8]

DEBIT Table 49. *Balance Batavia, End of March 1689.* *CREDIT*

Ongelden	240.0 mill. fl.	*Winsten*	265.4 mill. fl.
Arrears, etc.	7.5 - -	Goods captured	5.7 - -
Effects	18.1 - -	Various receipts	23.7 - -
Balance: the Company	29.5 - -	Creditors	0.3 - -
	295.1 mill. fl.		295.1 mill. fl.

DEBIT Table 50. *Balance Nederland, Middle of May 1689.* *CREDIT*

Cash in hand	0.8 mill. fl.	Bonded debts	12.2 mill. fl.
Stock-in-trade	12.4 - -	Short-term debts	0.8 - -
Stock of materials	0.8 - -	Bill debts	0.1 - -
Arrears	0.3 - -	Arrears	0.5 - -
Buildings, etc.	0.6 - -	Balance	1.3 - -
	14.9 mill. fl.		14.9 mill. fl.

It is seen that in the balance-sheet of Nederland there is now an item of assets comprising buildings, warehouses, etc., – in 1717 the Heeren XVII decided to cut out the real estate as an asset again – but apart from this there is neither in one balance nor the other a fundamentally changed arrangement. It may be added that the bookkeeper Paulus de

[6] See above, p. 34.

[7] Mansvelt, *op. cit.* p. 87.

[8] Klerk de Reus, *op. cit.* Beilage XI (b) and Beilage II (a).

Roo, who prepared the Batavia Balance, suggested that the amount of the creditors should be deducted from that of goods and chattels in order to find the Company's actual capital in India. If it is wanted to insert the examples from 1689 in the financial development, it may be done by resorting partly to the Dutch balances rendered in van Dam and de Reus, partly to the calculations which B. van der Oudermeulen set up in his memorandum towards the end of the 1770's.[9]

Van der Oudermeulen drew up his memorandum on the basis of several years' studies of the Indian account books, and some of his results from the 17th century thus are very valuable, as this material has been lost. If, with van der Oudermeulen, we strike a balance in 1654, we find a total surplus of 25 mill. fl., since all the receipts calculated from 1613 down to 1654 had constituted 101 mill. fl., while the disbursements during the same forty years amounted to 76 mill. fl. About 15.3 mill. fl. of the total surplus were placed in effects or *restanten*, which is van der Oudermeulen's term for the values of what was left over in the Indies. The remaining 9.7 mill. fl. represented the surplus of the Indian returns as compared with what was sent from Nederland. Twenty years later the total profit, after 60 years of commercial activity, had risen to 44 mill. fl. of which 23 mill. fl. were placed in *restanten*, while Nederland had received a total of 21 mill. fl. more in the form of returns from India than cargoes sent out. This increase in the Indian surplus culminated in 1693 with a surplus of more than 48 mill. fl., 25 mill. fl. of which were placed in the Indies in the form of effects. Then there was a decline which van der Oudermeulen could establish as early as 1696, as the total surplus of this year could be stated at only 40 mill. fl. The decline, however, did not manifest itself in a decreased stock of effects, on the contrary. The *restanten* in 1696 had increased to a total of 26.5 mill. fl. The trend during the short period from 1693 to 1696 was symptomatic of the rest of the period. The surplus, i.e. the difference between the total receipts and the total disbursements, became smaller and smaller. In 1713 the surplus was 16 mill. fl. and in 1724 only 1 mill. fl. After 1725 it was negative. In 1730 it amounted to −7 mill. fl., and a statement in 1743 showed that during the 130 years' trading period a total of 41 mill. fl. had been lost.[10] During the same period the value of the effects increased from the above-mentioned 26.5 mill. fl. in 1696 to 40 mill. fl. in 1711, 55 mill. fl. in 1735, and then dropped to 51 mill. fl. in 1743. In other words, the *bewindhebbers* in Nederland during these

[9] Printed in Dirk van Hogendorp, *Stukken raakende den tegenwoordigen toestand der Bataafsche bezittingen in Oost-Indië* (Den Haag-Delft, 1801), pp. 43 ff.

[10] The statement of 1743 printed in Klerk de Reus, *op. cit.* Beilage XI (c).

years were not only able through the annual consignments to cover the increasing deficit, but also to enlarge the effects in the Indies with the result that the Government at Batavia in 1743 owed an amount of 92.4 mill. fl. to the home country. This happened simultaneously with the fact that the Company in Nederland improved its balance. After about 1700 the Heeren XVII reduced the bonded debt of the factory Nederland, and in 1718 it was possible to enter a surplus of 11.5 mill. fl. on the balance-sheet, the greatest in the history of the Company. As stated by Dr. Mansvelt, this development took place at a time which traditionally has been pointed out as marked by the Directors' improvident policy of dividends.[11] The four decades about 1700 were the period of great dividends in the Company's history, when during six successive years a dividend of 40 per cent. was declared (1715–1720). As compared with the reserves in Nederland and the Indies the dividends would not seem to have been unjustifiable, and therefore it is hardly probable that the explanation of the Company's later decline is to be found in the policy of dividends. It was not so in van der Oudermeulen's opinion, either. Instead he points out how things had taken an unfavourable turn in the Indies since 1696. This was the origin of the decline. It was the failing inter-Asiatic trade which produced the whole wretched business, not as supposed by van der Oudermeulen's contemporaries, the dividends and the violent competition in the beginning of the 18th century as symbolized by the deficit which after 1736 constantly figured on the Dutch balance-sheet. The substantial profits on the import to the home country delayed the process of ruin. Dr. Mansvelt lays the main stress on the factor of administration. He agrees with van der Oudermeulen in his demonstration of the insignificant importance of the dividends, but is of opinion that van der Oudermeulen overestimates the Company's profitable position in Nederland.[12] For the very reason that the Court of Directors looked on the whole commercial enterprise from a one-sided Dutch point of view "als een groote import-zaak van koloniale producten,"[13] the comprehensive view and control were lost. The *bewindhebbers* in Nederland preferred to pay the Indian deficit, i.e. some of the Indian working expenses, instead of keeping the Indian administration separate from Nederland and e.g. permitting the Batavian Government to calculate a profit of 20–30 per cent. on the goods shipped to Nederland. The great profits in Nederland in the beginning of the 18th century as

[11] Mansvelt, *op. cit.* p. 99.

[12] Mansvelt, *op. cit.* p. 105 ["Het komt ons voor, dat van der Oudermeulen eenvoudig de dupe is van Compagnie's comptabele voorstelling"].

[13] *Ibid.*

a consequence of the rise in prices in Europe actually veiled the picture. Only when the proceeds of the returns in the second half of the century decreased – from 1700 to about 1780 it may be established that the costs of equipment increased by 100 per cent., while the proceeds from the sales of the returns only increased by 50 per cent. – the shortcoming became obvious. The chief blame thus according to Dr. Mansvelt rested with the administrative insufficiency. The receipts and expenditure in Nederland were compared without it being considered that these figures bore relation to widely different questions. It was calculation of profit of the very most primitive kind, quite insufficient for a company of the dimensions of the Dutch Company. "Het handelsbedrijf van de Compagnie wordt gekenmerkt door de volslagen afwezigheid van kostprijsberekening."[14] The administration neglected to divide the expenses into capital expenses and costs. Furthermore it neglected to add specific costs to the prices of the various commodities, such as freight, interest, and insurance. This was done in spite of the fact that the Company paid interest on money borrowed and in spite of the fact that the time of circulation of the capitals sent out was extremely different at the various offices. The reason why the Company did not charge any freight was that, as mentioned above, it built and owned the ships itself, as against the English company, which mainly used hired ships, which not least instigated the company to shorten the time of the voyage. The fact that the Dutch company direct wrote off its ships was not due to reasons of solidity, but was a result of lack of ability in respect to administration and bookkeeping. The ship and freight expenses rested with the same weight on all commodities. The bookkeeping of the Company might be compared with two large pans of a balance, not a sensitively distributed weighing system with minutely weighing small pans. On the large pans the total result could be read, but it could not be seen where profit and loss occurred. Therefore the Company for years continued trading to places and in commodities which long had incurred losses, and inversely it neglected starting trade in new commodities and to new places. Even the greatest reserves could not in the long run remedy such defects.[15]

Although there are many correct features in Dr. Mansvelt's shrewd analysis and criticism of the Company's accounting, we cannot quite accept his conclusion, – for several reasons. In the first place, because the Directors were aware where the shoe pinched and knew how a better system of accounting was to be made in principle. Next – and more decisively – because beside the accounts proper surveys were regularly

[14] *Ibid.* p. 108. [15] *Ibid.* p. 110.

made which covered a number of the areas not included in the factorage accounting system. These surveys or calculations were no more than the accounts satisfactory in a modern sense, but apart from the unreasonable idea of measuring the Company by the standard of our day, they were calculations which were highly taken into consideration when the Company's trade was discussed and planned. This means that we ascribe somewhat greater skill in registering progress and decline to the Company than Dr. Mansvelt did on the basis of his studies of the Company's accounts.[16] The reason why the Company's traffic decreased was less a lack of knowledge than of the actual changes in the structure of the trade.

Let us begin the examples of the contemporary criticism of the accounts with a concrete account which in itself demonstrates that it was possible on a small scale to practise the principle of double-entry bookkeeping. From the Gamron office a journal and ledger from the season of 1623/24 have been brought to light and published by Dunlop in the edition of sources of the Company's activities in Persia.[17] In the ledger the capital account is identical with the account for the Head Office at Batavia, for this was the entrepreneur. As there was not at the factory in Persia any fixed trading capital, nor any permanent plants or the like (but indeed rent and other expenses in connexion with the office at Gamron), the entrepreneur's contribution to the business was identical with the capitals and commodities received by the ships. These amounts were credited to the Head Office at Batavia. Inversely, this account was debited with the values which the entrepreneur drew from the business, i.e. first of all the values of the returns which were shipped from Gamron, to which should be added wages for the servants of the factory and expenses in connexion with the handling of ship and cargo (provisions, etc.). The actual profit on the commercial activities at Gamron, the balance of the profit-and-loss account, about 163,000 fl., was credited to the account of the entrepreneur with a balance amount of about 12,000 fl. The profit-and-loss account was credited with the profits from the sales of various parcels of commodities and debited with various losses and expenses, amongst others loss on exchange. The special balance amount denotes debts. It is part of a remaining debt of about 30,000 fl., which the factory owed to the Shah Abbas's factor Molaim Beg on a

[16] Van Leur follows Mansvelt and Sombart, when he writes: "The history of the development of modern capitalism – something completely different from the history of the acquisition of wealth in general, and colonial wealth in particular – has very little directly to do with the history of the Company as an entrepreneurial form, unless it would be in the fields of financial and banking affairs of later Company times. As a commercial enterprise the Company represented an old-fashioned, extremely conservative type", *op. cit.* p. 233.

[17] Dunlop, *op. cit.* No. 57.

quantity of silk. The reason why the Head Office at Batavia was made responsible for under half of this amount was that the other about 18,000 fl. was supposed to be present in the form of cash in hand, equipment, outstanding debts, and other assets. The cash in hand was insignificant, 313 fl., and the same applied to the value of the equipment, etc. The most important item among outstanding debts was about 13,000 fl., which the Company had been forced to pay as duty, which it did not think that it was liable to pay. We shall not commit ourselves as to the question whether this duty was an outstanding debt that could be cashed, but establish (1) that in the journal at the end of September 1624 there is a balance of assets and liabilities at the office at Gamron, (2) that there is in the ledger a special account for the trading capital, a profit-and-loss account, and a balance account, and (3) that otherwise there is in the ledger a detailed division of the various constituents (cash-, merchandise-, debtors' and creditors', and other accounts). It may be added that the ledger furthermore includes a special statement of the gross profit on the commodities sold (presents, however, being deducted). This amounts to 232,740 fl. – 54,114 fl. = 178,626 fl., or about 33 per cent.; but as mentioned above, the entrepreneur was only credited with a net profit of about 163,000 fl. In other words, it is possible from the accounts to read practically all that one would expect to read out of a modern account.

The most searching criticism on the Company's accounting system is found to have been passed towards the end of the 17th century by Johannes Hudde. His ideas are so lucid that they might enter unabridged into a good modern description of the theory of balances. Therefore they deserve a closer presentation, the more so as among economic historians the view may be found that bookkeeping in the 17th and 18th centuries served limited purposes, and that the striking of balances exclusively were aimed at the merely technical transfer of the items from one book to another.[18] Indeed, this is how the picture appears in the textbooks of the time, but the following summary shows what the President of the greatest trading company of the world thought about the question. His considerations furthermore throw light on the practical difficulties connected with the preparation of a total balance with which the Company, as indicated above, had to struggle.

Johannes Hudde places the following groups among the assets: effects, outstanding debts, legal claims as a consequence of octrois and of con-

[18] B. S. Yamey, "Scientific Bookkeeping and the Rise of Capitalism", *Economic History Review*, Sec. Ser., vol. I (London, 1949), pp. 99 ff.

tracts with Eastern princes. Among liabilities we find debts in the form of loans with or without interest, trade debts, unpaid wages, unpaid amounts according to contracts, etc. Elsewhere it is seen that Hudde realized that the Company's share capital also ought to figure among the liabilities in the balance.[19] The effects ought to include all goods and chattels in the Indies, in Nederland, and at sea. They consisted of two groups: (1) merchandise (including cash) and (2) non-merchandise, i.e. ships and equipment of ships, forts and war material, buildings and real property, ammunition, food, etc. It also applied to the other groups that they should cover the Indies as well as Nederland. The balance should be a total balance. It should be drawn up in one and the same standard of value (the quantities consequently be made uniform in respect of units) and referred to one definite market at one definite time. He chose Dutch units, Amsterdam, and 15 May 1683 in his own rough outline of a new balance-sheet, unfortunately not complete in its extant form. Hudde honestly called attention to the work and great insight required for the drawing up of such a balance-sheet. It would be necessary to master the most heterogeneous Asiatic units of coin, measure, and weight, and their rate of conversion into Dutch units. It was still more difficult to transfer the values to Amsterdam, for the valuation of the commodities should be made with reference to the local marketing conditions and at the transfer of the amounts be charged with risk, freight, convoy duties, and other costs. As to the date of the balance, 15 May 1683, the principle should be adopted that an estimate was first made of the time at which the goods could be sold to the best advantage, after which this value should be referred to 15 May 1683 "tegens een raisonnabel interest gerabatteert."[20] Furthermore, the time factor should involve costs of warehouse rent, wages, duties, risk of fire and theft, etc. Special attention was given to the valuation of spices, which is connected with the fact that the Company's storage problem was first of all a question of storage of spices. It is interesting to notice Hudde's sense of finding an applicable basis through a statistical collection of information. 10-year statistics of production, consumption, and stock in Nederland and the Indies were necessary besides a statement of losses during the transport as a consequence of shipwreck, etc. If this analysis showed that the annual production plus the stocks available exceeded the annual sales considerably – and Hudde was under an

[19] F. W. Stapel, "Johannes Hudde over de balansen van de Oostindische Compagnie", *Economisch-Historisch Jaarboek*, deel XIII ('s-Gravenhage, 1927), p. 222 Note 1.

[20] *Ibid.* p. 219.

impression that this was so; cf. the chapter on spices[21] – two forms of regulation should be considered. One was drastic and was to the effect that the surplus in Nederland or the Indies should be destroyed. Destruction in Nederland was most expensive, as the spices there were charged with freight, convoy duties, and other costs. It was more economical to exterminate some bushes on the Spice Islands or to destroy the fruits at Batavia, where they were booked at so low a price.[22] The other form of regulation was more peaceful. It consisted in either merely passively holding off or in a more active price policy. The passive method counted on a regulation by nature through failure of crops, disease, famine, and the like, or losses as a consequence of war, shipwreck, etc. If, on the other hand, the price policy was chosen, the method would be through a reduction of prices to create greater sales and a consequent greater demand, which again might condition a later rise in prices when production and stock had been equalized. As an alternative Johannes Hudde, however, mentioned the possibility of creating greater sales without reduction of prices "door het introduceeren van een modegebruijk aan considerable hoven, als onder anderen Vrankrijk, door schenkagiën of anderzints."[23] In order further to make it clear how important this estimate of the stocks was, Hudde advanced some theoretical examples. The first ran as follows: "The merchant has a stock of 100 ponds of cloves. The annual sale is 50 ponds and the annual production 50 ponds. What is the value of the 100 ponds stored?" Answer: "Nothing, on the contrary they involve losses, as they cost warehouse rent and other expenses." In the second example conditions were as in the first case, but with the change that the production failed completely in the seventh year. What would the value be of the 100 ponds stored? Answer: "As much as the value of 50 ponds at seven years' discount plus the value of 50 ponds at fourteen years' discount less the costs of the two amounts for warehouse rent, fire-insurance, etc." The third example is only found as formulated, the answer has been lost. What is the value of the stock after a reduction of prices – three ponds are sold at the price of two ponds – with a consequent two thirds greater sale? It may seem that this is a very mechanical or quantitative way of treating the mechanism of prices, but what is of central importance in this connexion is the author's sense of marketing conditions and price policy besides a statistical empirical material at the valuation of the Company's stocks for use at drawing up the balance-sheet. He was completely inspired by

[21] See above p. 109.

[22] Nutmeg at 1¼ st., cinnamon at 6 st., foelie at 10 st., cloves at 7½ st. "light" money per pond. [23] Stapel, "Johannes Hudde", p. 220.

a wish for having the "right" valuation carried through. The Dutch market price could not simply be used as a basis of the valuation of the stocks of the chambers, as the market price was conditioned by the sales, just as the "outlet" of the stock was determined by production and supplies. Under special circumstances (Example I) even the invoice value of the spices would be too high a basis of valuation. The same problem was present in the case of the stocks at Batavia. There an increment should be added to the low cost price in the accounts, viz. the expected profit, as it is done in our day in the case of commodities bought in order to be realized at a profit. If anything, this was the case with the spices. The principle of increment should also be carried through in the cases in which the profits of the Asiatic factories should be referred to one and the same time, as it was a well-known fact that up to three or four years passed before the books of the remote factories reached the Head Office at Batavia. It was therefore necessary to calculate a probable profit, and Hudde suggested as a basis a numerical working up of the results of the preceding 25 years' accounts.

Unfortunately Hudde's own attempt at creating a new type of balance-sheet is not extant. But there are a few fragments of it, one of which, prepared on the basis of the balances in Nederland in the middle of May 1686 and at Batavia at the end of January 1685 will be given here:

Table 51. *Hudde's Draft of a Balance-Sheet 1685/86.*

CREDIT: THE DUTCH INDIES, end of January 1685		25,267,927 fl.
viz.		
Effects	21,350,234 fl.	
+ Bills of exchange	506,335 -	
	21,856,569 fl.	
— Dead effects	1,172,244 -	
	20,684,325 fl.	
— Cargoes shipped	2,824,565 -	
	17,859,760 fl.	
+ Cargoes not booked and being under transport	7,408,167 -	
	25,267,927 fl.	
DEBIT: NEDERLAND, middle of May 1686		2,319,888 fl.
viz.		
Credit balance	287,437 fl.	
+ Returns outside the balance of the Indies	2,032,451 -	
	2,319,888 fl.	
BALANCE		22,948,039 fl.

The item of "Returns outside the balance of the Indies" denotes cargoes from Bengal, the Coromandel Coast, and Ceylon, which because of the time factor were not debited to the balance of the Indies. This is in agreement with Hudde's rule of crediting the balance with cargoes which have been debited to the account of effects in the home country, but not yet credited to the account of effects in the Indies, and similarly crediting the balance of cargoes debited to the account of effects in the Indies, but not credited to the account of effects in the home country; inversely of debiting the balance with cargoes received in the home country and credited to the account of effects there, but not at the balancing time debited to the account of effects in the Indies. Hudde does not mention the fourth possibility – which was very theoretical – of debiting the balance with non-debited cargoes sent from the home country and credited in the Indies. The principle is that of double-entry bookkeeping, viz. that no transaction is imaginable in the assets without there being at least one account which is credited with value estimated and one or more accounts which are debited with the same value.

As stated above, we do not know the continuation. The manuscript breaks off at the most interesting stage, where the author is going to realize his fine thoughts of booking the other effects and debts, which do not figure in the ordinary books, of carefully valuing the stocks – the adduced credit balance in Nederland was based on the traditional valuations of stocks and stores – and of referring the values at a fixed time, and finally of equalizing the difference between "light" and "heavy" coins. We must content ourselves with Hudde's suggestion that "al des Compagnies effecten, praetensiën etc., gediminueert met alle deszelfs schulden, nog vrij hooger moeten werden geschat als de bovenstaande somme van fl. 22,948,039 fl."[24] Perhaps Hudde did not himself succeed in having a finale complete balance-sheet drawn up. It would be a tall order for a busy man, who besides the Presidency of the Heeren XVII discharged the duties of Burgomaster of Amsterdam. But before he withdrew from the Court of Directors he started others on the work, just as he took the initiative in the project for a general account of the history of the Company. The latter plan was realized in Pieter van Dam's impressive work *ad usum delphini*. The balance project was shipwrecked, although the originator of the idea, as shown above, had laid down so distinct outlines. The former general bookkeeper at Batavia, Daniël Braams, in 1690 was appointed general bookkeeper to the whole Company with the task of managing "het formeren en redresseeren van de

[24] Stapel, "Johannes Hudde", p. 230.

boecken, soo hier te lande als in Indiën, en daeruyt de generale boecken, met tgene wijders daaraan dependeert, te maken, om dan vervolgens daeruyt jaarlijcx te kunnen opstellen en voortbrengen een Generale Staat van winst en verlies en sulcx daeruyt klaar voor oogen te brengen, wat van den Generalen Staat van de Compagnie is en in wat effecten die, so hier als in Indiën, bestaat."[25] But as ill-luck would have it, Braams died after making the first drafts. In 1697 the Heeren XVII decided to appoint a general bookkeeper again. The decision, however, was never carried into effect. Things relapsed into the old groove.[26]

If we follow the Company's practice at the statement of the value of the Dutch stocks, it is evident that it was always kept below the market price.[27] In the case of spices cloves ("in soorten") in 1637 were estimated at 60 st. per pond, which estimated price in 1645 was reduced to 50 st. Five years later the price was raised to 54 st. and in 1666 to 60 st. At this value the Company annually took stock of the stores of cloves down to 1688, when the price was reduced to 54 st. As mentioned in the chapter on spices, the price of cloves at the sales, and hence the market price, from the end of the 1670's was kept at 75 st. per pond, which level was maintained to the end of the period. Still, the estimated price was reduced during the following decades, first to 45 st. in 1701, then, in 1718, to 30 st., and the following year to 20 st. per pond.[28] Perhaps this was done on the basis of considerations similar to those of Johannes Hudde's mentioned above. Assorted nutmegs kept more constant, viz. at 42 st. per pond from 1637 down to 1718/19, when the estimated price was reduced to 30 st. and 20 st. per pond.[29] The reductions were still greater in the case of *rompen* and *foelie*. *Rompen*, i.e. "in soort", in the 17th century were estimated at a price of 39–30 st. per pond. In 1719 whole *rompen* were reduced even to 6 st. and half *rompen* to 3 st. per pond. This was due to overstocking. Similarly, the estimated price of *foelie* in the 17th century had ranged between 120 and 90 st. per pond. In 1719 it was reduced to 36 st. per pond.[30] Pepper and saltpetre, too, were estimated at values between the invoice price and the market price. In the case of textiles, however, the practice was followed of entering them into the

[25] Pieter van Dam quoted from Stapel, "Johannes Hudde", p. 217.

[26] de Heer, *op. cit.* p. 55 *et seq.*, is of opinion that in the archives of the Company there is proof that the balances were worked up into a whole, referring to Kol. Arch. No. 8396. But this is a survey made later in the 18th century (the Collectie Hope) and therefore is no evidence of any aggregate bookkeeping.

[27] See the material in *Pieter van Dam* 1:I, pp. 344 ff., on which this characterization is based. Van Dam's prices of pepper in 1669, 1688, and 1671 (pp. 346–7) are not *schellingen* but *grooten*. Furthermore, Kol. Arch. No. 250, 3 December 1637.

[28] Kol. Arch. No. 198, 14 July 1718 and No. 199, 21 July 1719.

[29] *Ibid.* [30] *Ibid.*

balance-sheet at the invoice value, as elsewhere with due allowance being made for leakage, etc.

Next we come to the estimates made outside the accounts. They were the so-called *rendementen* drawn up after each auction at the suggestion of the Heeren XVII, i.e. lists showing invoice price and selling price for each commodity and the gross profit calculated on it. To judge from the Heeren XVII's missives these lists were considered the corner-stones in the Company's commercial policy. The orders for returns were drawn up on the basis of the *rendement* lists, and the lists accompanied the orders to Batavia, where they were to be a guide for the Batavian Government's composition of the returns. Unfortunately they are not found in the Dutch Record Office. Perhaps they were not copied. Perhaps they suffered the same fate as much everyday price material else, e.g. the price-lists, viz. that as rule it was not found to be worth while keeping it. The Government at Batavia similarly made calculations of gross profits on the cargoes received. A number of these surveys are found from year to year in *Overgekomen papieren.* A similar case was that of the Indian factories, an instance of this being found in the ledger of Gamron 1623/24. Moreover a general Indian price-list was drawn up every year at Batavia and sent to Europe. It is no exaggeration to say that calculations of the gross profit on each commodity was the Alpha and Omega of the Company's trade. To the weighing of receipts against disbursements demonstrated by Dr. Mansvelt we should therefore add the Company's annual calculations of the gross profits on the individual products in Nederland as well as in Asia.[31]

When going through the chief articles of commerce we several times indicated that there was a lower limit to the gross profit. If the profit dropped below that, the article was cancelled from the orders or the order was reduced with a remark about having the level of the cost-prices lowered. In a way the Company operated with a kind of net profit determined by the costs. The way in which the costs came into play in the Court of Directors' considerations may be illustrated by a couple of examples. In a letter of 22 March 1631 from the *bewindhebbers* in Amsterdam to the Governor General and Council at Batavia[32] the trade to Persia was mentioned. From the end of October 1628 to the end of October 1629 the Company had at Gamron on a capital of 400,000 fl. earned 332,000 fl., to which should be added the profit on the silk sent home, on which the Company counted on having a further gross profit

[31] Another estimate drawn up out of the accounts is Kol. Arch. No. 10,228 (cf. Appendix B); also a *rendement*, but of a different character.

[32] Dunlop, *op. cit.* No. 200.

of 50 per cent. in Nederland. In all the 400,000 fl. would yield a gross profit of 698,000 fl. or 174.25 per cent. The Amsterdam *bewindhebbers*, however, had their doubts that this profit was sufficient to cover the costs. The Company's debts in Nederland and the Indies were great because of the great equipments and warfare, the building of forts, etc. The prices of wood, iron, hemp, and provisions were high. Indeed, the trade to Persia was carried on from Surat, and if the Company wanted to maintain the Surat trade, it might as well maintain the trade to Persia, too. At that time the Company used six ships for the trade to Surat, which meant an annual disbursement of about 200,000 fl. for wages and 300,000 fl. for the maintenance of the ships, etc. If the Company counted on a year's outward voyage and a year's homeward voyage, the total expenditure for the six ships thus would be 1 mill. fl., but the trade to Persia, extended the trading period to three years, which together with interest on money borrowed meant an annual cost of 400,000 fl.[33] A considerable gross profit on the Asiatic and Dutch commodities would be required to pay such costs. The *bewindhebbers* therefore entertained the idea of discontinuing that trade, but shrank back on the ground that large amounts of money had been spent on the establishment of the trade and that a closing down would strengthen the position of the Portuguese. They contented themselves with proposing direct trade from Nederland to Surat/Persia, in which way it would be possible to save a whole year, while the country trade might be kept going by having a sloop trade from Batavia to Surat and Persia. It is seen that estimates of costs in connexion with calculation of gross profits were not alien to the *bewindhebbers*.

They would also consider the wear and tear on the ships, as appears from the above-mentioned example from 1636, in which the Heeren XVII made a calculation of the costs of equipment of a sugar flute of 170–180 lasts with a crew of 40.[34] The gross profit amounted to about 300 per cent., when 15 per cent. was deducted for leakage. The net profit, however, only amounted to 56 per cent. for a total trading period of 20 months, or 33.6 per cent. per annum. The calculation is a pure "equipagie-calculatie", with a specification of initial cost and wear and tear on the flute, pay of the crew, and provisions, but without considering the capital to be invested in the cargo; nor is there any amount of money for payment of interest on the equipment costs or the costs at the sales of the cargoes in Nederland.

[33] It is not evident how the figures are to be interpreted.

[34] See the chapters on the Factory Nederland and on the Company's trade in sugar, pp. 48, Note 122, and 155.

As to the booking of the direct trade to China in the accounts of Kamer Amsterdam we find an exception from the rule that receipts and disbursements are entered as more or less anonymous elements on the accounts of *equipagie-generaal* and *retouren-generaal*. Here everything is collected in a special "voyage" account, so that finally a clear balance could be struck. The first "voyage" accounts were debited with the value of the ship sent out, while after its return the ship was subjected to a fresh valuation, the result of which was credited to the account. In the case of the later "voyages" only the difference i.e. the wear and tear was entered as a disbursement. It amounted to one fourth to one fifth of the original value of the ship. Thus the "Coxhorn" before its first voyage to Canton was booked at 55,888 fl. Then it was new-built. After its arrival home it was valued at 45,450 fl. When it was sent out again after being repaired, it was booked at 54,141 fl., and after its second return was valued at 45,400 fl.[35]

Another example which illustrates possible causes for reflection in connexion with the calculations of the gross profit dates from 1735. It is a so-called "commercial account" concerning the Bengali returns.[36] It includes all the goods having arrived in Nederland by way of Batavia and Ceylon as well as direct from Bengal. According to the invoices the purchase was of 2.2 mill. fl., which at the sale in Nederland yielded 3.8 mill. fl. or about 71 per cent. gross profit. In the case of the textiles the gross profit was on an average about 71 per cent., for saltpetre about 165 per cent., and for Bengali silk about 33 per cent. The commercial element appears by the fact that a number of costs should be deducted from these gross profits. These costs were: costs in connexion with the arrival of the returns in Holland, expenses and wages in India calculated in relation to the annual deficit in the Indies, writing off on the ships for wear and tear on the homeward voyage, brokerage, and three years' interest at 4 per cent. of the cost-price. Hence, the net profit proper was about 4½ per cent. Finally, we shall from a collection of calculations concerning the Company's Asiatic sugar trade from the 1750's, select a draft for a balance from Surat 1757/58.[37] The usual *rendement* showed a gross profit of more than 52 per cent. on powdered sugar and 80.5 per cent. on white candy. The *rendementen* were exclusively based on the profit on the quantities sold. They did not indicate anything as to the quantities which were left unsold at the end of the year, nor the length of the time at which they had been stored in the warehouses. This was

[35] Kol. Arch. Nos. 10,419, 10,420, 10,421, and 10,422.
[36] Kol. Arch. No. 8476. [37] Kol. Arch. No. 8492.

considered in the balance of 1757/58, as the stock was charged with an annual interest of 4 ½ per cent. Furthermore the freight, risk, and costs in Surat were entered into the balance. The total result was a deficit of about 37,000 fl. or 9 ½ per cent. of the Batavian invoice value of the sugar placed in Surat.

It is true that the Dutch Company stuck to a form of accounting which already in the 17th century proved unsatisfactory and which in the 18th century was antiquated as compared with the exemplary accounts kept by e.g. its small Danish competitor.[38] On the other hand, calculations on more expedient principles were made on various occasions; furthermore, calculations of gross profits on which the investments were based, were made outside the accounts. The Directors were also aware of surplus and loss from season to season in each single place in Asia.[39] Therefore it is hardly unreasonable to assume that the Heeren XVII fairly soon registered progress and decline in the various fields. An examination of their orders for returns is evidence that they had a keen eye for the changes in trade. That they should voluntarily continue trading in non-saleable commodities is out of the question. Not least the flourishing period in the decades about 1700 give ample evidence of the Heeren XVII's watchfulness and incessant criticism of the returns, based on the own profit percentages, the profits of the competitors, the costs, and the state of the Asiatic factories. They were aware of the weak points. Nor was there any lack of proposals for reforms. The high fixed expenses for forts, military forces, patrol ships, etc., were felt to be hampering. They criticized the placement of the whole enterprise at Batavia, various factories were at intervals sentenced to being closed down, but few of them actually were so. The sailing time was the object of great interest, and commissions worked at proposals for its reduction. Then there was abuse of office in connexion with private trade. Once exposed, this abuse was particularly conspicuous, and corruption has later been the perhaps most frequently emphasized cause of the ruin of the Company, until Dr. Mansvelt through his inciting analysis added administrative flaws. The occurrence of corruption is incontestable. It was closely connected with the development of private trade in the years about 1700, not least the English country trade, which was one of the most important new features in the Asiatic trade.

[38] On the Danish accounts cf. Aage Rasch & P. P. Svejstrup, *Asiatisk Kompagni i den florissante periode*, 1772–1792 (København, 1948), pp. 53 ff.

[39] Cf. Klerk de Reus, *op. cit.* Beilage IX, "Liste der Gewinn- und Verlustziffern auf den verschiedene indischen Comptoiren van 1683–1757".

But in our opinion there are other commercial causes left which have not previously been realized, simply because the Dutch Company has not been studied as what it first of all was, viz. a trading company. In spite of its monopoly of spices developed during the 17th century, the Company cannot be characterized as an economically monopolized enterprise. It is true that it had a national monopoly of the Asiatic trade, but if the Northwest European market is regarded as a whole – and a Dutchman had good reasons to do so because of his country's free trade policy – there were several companies to determine the supplies. Comparative studies of prices show that there was a distinct connexion between the national markets for East Indian products, which is not surprising, considering the great role played by re-export. Historians have in too high a degree fastened on the provision in the octrois for trade east of the Cape of Good Hope and on the great profits on spices, but have overlooked that also on markets where there were few competitors price competition and other forms of competition might break out, just as it has been forgotten that spices did not dominate the export from Asia and that gross profits were one thing and net profits something else. A considerable part of the Dutch East India Company's import included goods which on the European market had to compete with related products from Europe or from other countries overseas. This applied, e.g., to silk and cotton, textiles, saltpetre, indigo, sugar, copper, and coffee. In a number of cases it was the prices of these related products which decided whether an import from Asia was profitable or not. The Northwest European market for Asiatic goods was far from being stable. The changes in the European demand is read best in the Heeren XVII's orders and in the analyses of sales. It is evident that not least the 40-year period about 1700 presented quite a small revolution. The East India textiles, besides coffee and tea, radically transformed the usual habits. New areas emerged and created changed conditions for the purchases. Furthermore, there was a pronounced competition from new or revived companies at Ostend, Gothenburg, and Copenhagen. "Onze competiteurs" became a set term in the Heeren XVII's letters to Batavia. If we turn to the Asiatic markets, we find that the competitive factor is still more evident. There the competition was not only with the European companies, but first of all with the Asiatic traders. There is a long way to go before we have arrived at a sufficient understanding of the character of the Asiatic trade and economy during this period. It is to be hoped that not least the Asiatic historians will continue the investigations which have already been started, and thus contribute to making the Asiatic background clear to us. From the point of view of the history of the Company not least an account of conditions in Bengal during the years after 1680 will be of invaluable importance. The Company's Asiatic trade was not only an enterprise within definite areas, but also a traffic from one country to another, an international affair, which in Asia extended over distances of almost the same order of magnitude as the sea route from the North Sea to Ceylon and Batavia. At the treatment of conditions of a single area the commercial contributions from other Asiatic countries will therefore in many cases be as decisive as the European ones. Among the particularly distinct changes in the Dutch Company's Asiatic trade, there may be reason to adduce the changing stream towards the west of the Chinese and especially the Japanese precious metals. The Chinese stream of gold to the Coromandel Coast flows until Koxinga's conquest of Taiwan. The Japanese stream of silver flows until 1668, when it was replaced by a stream of gold, which, however, already in 1672 decreased perceptibly and was changed into a stream of copper. The Company was also able to draw precious metals from Persia and this pull became stronger as the export of silk lost ground and the supplies of gold and silver from China and Japan were made more difficult. The Persian supplies could not, however, counterbalance the loss of the supplies from China and Japan, for which reason a great need for European shipments of silver and gold arose towards the end of the 17th century. This was the more decisive as the changes in the European demand fairly simultaneously stimulated the need for bullion and specie by asking for commodities from areas consuming gold and silver. Another conspicuous feature was the rise and fall of the Coromandel Coast – to quote Daniel Havart's words once more. With the ruin of the Coast through the Indian civil wars the Company lost hold of a large area, to which it had given its greatest attention from the beginning of the 17th century. The Company's "left arm" withered, and even though the Dutch took the initiative in starting a trade to Bengal, it did not there succeed in getting the start of its nearest European competitor, the English, in a similar way as on the Coromandel Coast. Furthermore, the Dutch indirectly through their initiative in other fields contributed to establishing new connexions within inter-Asiatic trade, first of all the direct trade between Bengal and China, which in time became the axis of the English commercial mechanism. The Dutch export drive in the Surat area and in Persia for the products of the new Javanese sugar plantations contributed to cutting the old connexion between Bengal and Surat based on Bengali sugar, raw silk, and Surat cotton. The supplies to Northwest India of Chinese silk and sugar had a similar effect. During the 18th century the Bengali trade was directed towards the East, towards China, and an indirect country trade developed between Bombay and China. The English country traders were the leaders in these developments. The background of the new trade routes was the increasing European demand for tea, which gave rise to a violent pressure on the European resources of silver and consequent endeavours to find in India an applicable substitute for silver to China. This substitute was found. It was called opium, and with it also considerable parts of the private trade carried on from the Coromandel Coast to Indonesia were transferred to the English possessions.[40] The trade to China, which about the same time was opened by direct route from Europe brought the Dutch Company into a dilemma. At first the Directors undoubtedly underestimated this trade. Later, when its success was evident to everybody, they vacillated between direct trade from Nederland and indirect contact by way of Batavia. The latter possibility saved cash, as the Chinese tea could be paid with pepper, spices, and other commodities. It represented a development of the old Asiatic route between Canton and Bantam, which had been so conspicuous to Dutch observers on their arrival in Indonesia about 1600, even before the Company had a great part of the Indonesian export of pepper redirected from China to Europe and before the Chinese trade to the Indian seas withdrew as a consequence of the fights of the dynasties in China. An advocate of this route was the Batavian Government, whose position was strengthened by the successful transfer of the cultivation of coffee to Java. It was a repetition of the success in sugar and meant that a new factor of planting emerged alongside of the commercial considerations. Nor was there any lack of projects for a transfer of the cultivation of tea to Java. On the other hand, the direct route was recommended by the Directors in Nederland. Their motivation was the competition, which necessitated purchase on the spot and fast transport to Europe. The English commercial drive in China paved the way for other European nations and made the Dutch control of the navigation around the Spice Islands more necessary. But this meant continued great costs for the maintenance of the monopoly of commodities which only yielded one fourth of the receipts at the most profitable factory, Nederland. A fear that the English (and others) would advance farther, led to a stubborn maintenance of the trade to Japan, although eventually it yielded but a modest profit. The Dutch succeeded in keeping the English out, but still the Japan copper, which played so

[40] Holden Furber, *op. cit.* p. 162 *et seq.*

great a part in the Company's Asiatic trade in the course of the 18th century, was threatened when the English began exporting English copper to India.

Competition and changeableness rather than monopoly and constancy was what characterized the Dutch Company as a trading company or "business enterprise". From a European point of view there is just in the commercial aspect many features which indicate that in the period of 1680 to about 1740 there was a number of displacements that depreciated the Company's position in Asia, which had hitherto been so advantageous. These decisive years changed the character of the European-Asiatic commercial intercourse. In the volume of trade there was a boom on the basis of the cottons and silks, which were in great demand. A couple of new articles, coffee and tea, developed into main commodities, the profitableness of which came to consist in a great turnover at moderate profits and in fast transport. The displacements in the requirements of the European market, its fashion and taste, changed Asiatic conditions, and an increasing number of competing companies strained the company system and undermined it. The Company has previously been considered a nearly historyless, evergreen pagoda-tree, whose golden fruits the Court of Directors had a monopoly of shaking into its turban at suitable intervals, from which it was only finally prevented by fraudulent, lazy, and incompetent officials. We are inclined, instead, to characterize the Dutch Company as a hard-working enterprise in occasionally keen competition with the other European companies and with the Asiatic merchants. Once engaged on the Asiatic trade it had to continue, expand, and find new markets for purchase and sales. It was never at rest. The Company's history includes many features: wars, subjugation, trade, mission, administration, working of plantations, science, etc. These are all aspects of the relations of the Dutch to the Asiatic peoples. In the case of the 17th and the 18th centuries not least the commercial conditions are decisive of our understanding of the European initiative.

APPENDICES

APPENDIX A

The Invoice Material

The analyses of the composition of the cargoes imported are based on the invoice material in the large collection of *Overgekomen papieren* in Kol. Arch. The invoices there are found singly or more or less summarized in connexion with the missives of the Governor General and the Council to the Heeren XVII. They may enter in the missive as a so-called *sommarium* of the cargoes of a homeward-bound fleet. Apart from the mostly complicated and laborious work of finding the invoices in the unwieldy folios – the *Overgekomen papieren* number more than 500 fat volumes from the 17th century – the material is without any greater problems. For a period in which, apart from a single exception, no accounting material from Batavia and Ceylon is extant, the invoices are the most reliable basis on which to estimate the supplies to Nederland, both the quantities and the values. The extent to which the triennia selected are covered by the invoices preserved, appears most clearly from a summing-up of the material adduced.

The first triennium includes the following ships:

The "De Witte Beer" and the "Tholen" (Kol. Arch. No. 979, fos. 114 and 176), the "Zierickzee", the "Mauritius", and the "Delft" (Kol. Arch. No. 980, fos. 212, 317, and 402-403), the "De Eenhoorn" and the "De Swarte Beer" (Kol. Arch. No. 981, fos. 398 and 462-80), the "De Goude Leeuw", the "Dordrecht", the "West-Vrieslandt", and the "De Orangieboom" (Kol. Arch. No. 982, fos. 45, 406-07, 408-09, and 410), the "De Witte Beer" and the "De Vreede" (Kol. Arch. No. 983, fos. 69-70 and 295), the "Mauritius" and the "'t Wapen van Hoorn" (Kol. Arch. No. 984, fos. 296 and 396 c), and the "Leyden" (Kol. Arch. No. 985, fos. 15-16).

The only ship, the invoice of which has not been found, is the "Walcheren", which left in October 1620, destined for Kamer Zeeland, its cargo being of an invoice value of 118,121 fl.; cf. Valentijn, *Oud en Nieuw Oost-Indiën*, vol. I, pp. 216 ff.

The next triennium includes

the "Walvisch", the "Tijger", the "De Vreede", the "Zutphen", the "Coningh van Polen", the "Orangie", the "Henrietta Louijsa", the "Noordmunster", the "Nieuw Delft", the "Rotterdam", the "West-Vrieslandt", and the "Enckhuijsen" (Kol. Arch. No. 1064, fos. 81-82), the "Malacca", the "Princesse Royale", the "Oliphant", the "Vogelstruijs", the "Drommedaris", the "'t Hoff van Zeelandt", the "De Provintie", the "Schiedam", and the "Zeelandia" (Kol. Arch. No. 1649, fos. 140-01), finally the "Den Diamant", the "Salmandar", the "Zutphen", the "Den Lastdrager", the "Orangie", the "Henrietta Louijsa", the "N: Rotterdam", the "Breda", and the "Leeuwaerden" (Kol. Arch. No. 1068, fos. 118-20).

The extant invoice material for this triennium is complete.

The analysis of the triennium 1668–1670 is based on the invoices from the following ships:

The "'t Wapen van Hoorn", the "Alphen", and the "Constantia" (Kol. Arch. No. 1152, fos. 101), the "Hollantse Thuyn", the "'t Wapen van Middelburgh", the "Dordrecht", the "Kattenburg", the "Outshoorn", the "Tijger", the "Vrijheyt", the "Jonge Prins", the "Amerongen", and the "De Spreeuw" (Kol. Arch. No. 1152, fos. 173, 193, and 198), the "Zuidpolsbroek", the "'t Wapen van Terveer", the "'t Huis te Velzen", the "'t Wapen van der Gouw", the "'t Wapen van Rotterdam", the "De Rijzende Zon", the "De Vrije Zee", the "Batavia", the "De Handelaar", the "Oostenburg", the "'t Stigt van Utrecht", the "Nieuw Middelburgh", the "Voorzichtigheid", the "Papenburg", the "Hazenberg", the "De Cogge", and the "'t Huys te Muizenburg" (Kol. Arch. No. 1156, fos. 209-10, 233, 283-4, 541, and 725), the "Hollantsen Thuyn", the "Amersfoort", the "Burch van Leyden", the "Ternaten", the "Damiaten", the "Tulpenburch", the "Wapen van Zierickzee", the "Wapen van ter Goes", the "Wapen van Middelburg", the "Wapen van Vlissingen", the "Eendracht", the "Delftshaven", the "Jonge Prins", the "Medenblick", the "Gekroonde Vreede", the "Osdorp", and the "Uitdam" (Kol. Arch. No. 1159, fos. 22 and 475).

All these ships came from Batavia with the exception of the "De Cogge" and the "Huys te Muizenburg", which came from Ceylon. While the information about the ships from Batavia is complete, the invoices for seven ships from Ceylon are missing. The total value of the cargoes of the missing ships is 881,610 fl. Their cargoes can in part be reconstructed from the cargo lists in the newsletter *Hollantse Mercurius* (1668, p. 126, 1669, p. 114, and 1670, p. 107 *et seq.*). However, it must be taken into account that the cargo lists are marred by some misprints, for which reason the uncertainty of a reconstruction is considered to be too great. For instance it may be mentioned that *Hollantse Mercurius* states the cargoes of *guinees* of the "Osdorp" and the "Uitdam" to be of 400 pieces – they were of 4,000 pieces – of cotton yarn to be of 32,567 ponds – they were of 42,567 ponds – of saltpetre to be of 226,400 ponds – they were of 326,400 ponds, etc. Finally it should be added that Valentijn in his list of returning ships makes the "De Cogge" belong to the ships from Batavia. As stated above, the "De Cogge" came from Ceylon.

As to the last triennium, the basis is the following ships:

The "s Lands Welvaaren", the "Grimmestein", the "Nigtevegt", the "Donkervliet", the "Domburg", the "Beyeren", the "Merestein", the "Overnes", the "Schoondyke", and the "Den Ijsel" (Kol. Arch. No. 1475, fos. 395 *et seq.*), the "De Gent", the "De Carthago", the "De Boor", and the "De Zandloper" (Kol. Arch. No. 1477, fos. 1229 and 1607), the "De Lek", the "De Berkel", the "Ijselmonde", the "De Beloys", and the "De Schellack" (Kol. Arch. No. 1479, fos. 1231 and 1239), the "Oosterstein", the "De Unie", the "Brandenburg", the "Vosmaar", the "Reygersdaal", the "'t Hof van Ilpendam", and the "Dregterland" (Kol. Arch. No. 1488, fos. 272 *et seq.*), the "'t Huis te Nieuburg" and "'t Huis te Dieren" (Kol. Arch. No. 1490, fos. 906), the "Berkestein" (Kol. Arch. No. 1491, fos. 1287), the "De Waalstroom", the "Bambeek", the "Spierdijk", the "Sir Jans Land", and the "Nieuwland" (Kol. Arch. No. 1495, fos. 1259 ff.), the "Kattendijk", the "s Lands Welvaaren", the "Nigtevegt", the "Merestein", the "De Concordia", the "De Gent", the "Voorschooten", the "Meydrecht", the "De Handboog", the "Overrijp", the "De Geelvink", the "De Vegt", the "De Voetboog", and the "Eykelenburg" (Kol. Arch. No. 1504, fos. 1025 ff.), the "De Spiegel", the "Berkenrode", the "Overnes", and the "Grimmestein" (Kol. Arch. No. 1508, fos. 1214 ff.).

The invoices from the "Huys ter Loo", the "Drijbergen", and the "Tamboer", all from Batavia, are missing. It appears from the Governor General's missive of 20 January 1699 that the "Tamboer" was bound for Cape Colony, where its cargo, which had a value of 66,168 fl., was to be transhipped to the ships returning from Ceylon. The two other ships had a total cargo at a value of 617,564 fl. (Kol. Arch. No. 1490, fo. 890 verso). For that matter, Valentijn's indications of value disagree with the figures in the missive.

Finally it should be added that the invoices for the triennia 1668–1670 and 1698–1700 contain a few items of costs. These are not included in the analyses as they cannot be distributed on the various groups of commodities.

APPENDIX B

The Material Concerning the Public Sales

In the extant Northwest European company material the Dutch part is exceptional as regards statistical particulars concerning the goods imported. This is connected with the peculiar way in which the main source of the sales statistics, the accounts, was kept. As mentioned in the chapter on Profit and Loss the receipts from the sales of the year were transferred to a special account, the *retouren-generaal*. It was the total gross receipts which figured on this account. Furthermore the books included special accounts for the various commodities: pepper, nutmegs, saltpetre, etc., where the sales were registered in more detail with statement of the various buyers and the quantities sold. The sum of the volume of the commodities sold was also transferred to the account of the *retouren-generaal*. Copies of the *retouren-generaal* circulated among the chambers together with the other parts of the Company's balance. The best records are a set of balances in the papers left by the chief bookkeeper in the "Departement van de thesaurie" of Kamer Zeeland.[1] On this basis it is possible to prepare statistics of quantities and prices from the sales at Kamer Amsterdam from 1649/50 on. In the case of the other chambers it is not possible to carry the statistics so far back. Considering the leading part played by Amsterdam we have not found it necessary for later decades, i.e. from the middle of the 1660's, to extend the statistics to the other chambers. In the case of a number of commodities we have made the Amsterdam quantities and prices be representative of the quantities sold and the prices of the Company. Roughly the Amsterdam turnover corresponded to approximately half of the total turnover. In the text we have as far as possible called attention to the cases in which this rule is not valid.

[1] Kol. Arch. Nos. 10,234–10,242 F: "Generale staten van verhandelde goederen, uitstaande schulden en onverkochte goederen van de verschillende kamers".

This continuous source not only enables us to estimate the conditions of sales in Nederland in a much more reliable way than in the case of the other Northwest European companies, but it also enables a critical inquiry into the other statistical sources. Actually a wealth of statistical surveys is extant in the archives of the Company and in the "*bewindhebber* papers". One of the most comprehensive surveys is Kol. Arch. No. 10,228 entitled "Bijeenbrenging van verkoopingen, register van de opbrengst der verkochte Oost-Indische goederen, 1693–1760".[2] What is its relations to the balance in the accounts of commodities sold?

The statistics among other things include the commodities of pepper (white and black), powdered sugar, saltpetre, cinnamon, Japanese copper, tin, tea (various sorts), Bengali silk, Chinese silk, *salempouris*, and *guinees*. They indicate the quantities sold at all chambers, the price, the total amounts of the sales of each commodity, and the total amounts of the public sales, all figures drawn up for each year of the long period. Thus apparently a source which may form the basis of a quantitative estimate of the total number of the Company's sales. If, however, we try by means of the accounts or the transcripts of the *retouren-generaal* to check the statements, certain peculiarities of the tabulations are revealed. First, there are the quantities stated. For instance, it is stated that the sales of tea at the chamber of Amsterdam in the autumn of 1714 amounted to a total of 36,766 ponds. The Amsterdam account books run from the 15th of May to the 15th of May, and in the accounting year of 1714/15 two public sales were held in Amsterdam, viz. the autumn sales on 22 October 1714 and the spring sales on 15 April 1715. At that time it was customary that tea was only offered at the autumn sales, and hence the Amsterdam accounts for the year 1714/15 state the quantity of tea actually sold. It amounted to a total of 31,452 ponds, i.e. 5,314 ponds less than stated in Kol. Arch. No. 10,228. What is the origin of this difference? If we go through the Court Minutes of the Heeren XVII with special reference to the autumn sales of 1714, we shall see that the Directors on 20 September 1714 decided to offer 6,775 ponds of Bohea tea, 22,368 ponds of green tea, and 7,623 ponds of Bing tea at the sales in Amsterdam, i.e. a total of 36,766 ponds of various sorts of tea or exactly the quantity stated by Kol. Arch. No. 10,228 to have been sold in the year 1714. This and similar examples indicate that the quantities stated are not the quantities sold at the auctions, but those offered by the Company's

[2] From Kamer Amsterdam. On the back of the volume the old designation No. 390 from *Inventaris De Munnick*, i.e. "Inventaris van het Oost Indische Archief berustende in het West Indisch Magazyn te Amsterdam opgemaakt ingevolge resolutie van den Minister voor de Marine & Kolonien van den 6. December 1828 La: G & H No. 46".

Directors. Having thus elucidated the statements of quantities in the statistics, the question arises of the character of the prices indicated. Here it applies that the statistics as rule in the case of each commodity indicate only one price, which according to the form of the tabulation must be supposed to be a kind of average price. For a few, particularly differentiated commodities, however, several such average prices are indicated in connexion with the quantities. Thus in the case of tea. This time we shall adduce the autumn sales of 1721. There we find as sold (i.e. offered) at Kamer Amsterdam 23,485 ponds of Bohea tea at 38 st. per pond (value 44,621 fl.) and 38,561 ponds of Bohea tea at $44^4/_5$ st. per pond (value: 86,376 fl. 13 st.). Furthermore, 46,922 ponds of green tea at $29\frac{1}{2}$ st. per pond (value: 69,209 fl. 19 st.) and 31,439 ponds of green tea at $32^2/_5$ st. per pond (value: 50,931 fl. 3 st.), besides the small quantity of 492 ponds of Bing tea at $48\frac{1}{2}$ st. per pond (value: 1,193 fl. 2 st.). This gives a total of 160,899 ponds of various sorts of tea at a value of 252,331 fl. 17 st. The actual sales at Kamer Amsterdam were only of 112,953 ponds of various sorts of tea. According to the accounts the receipts were 212,484 fl. 13 st. in all. Hence, the average price according to the accounts was 1.88 fl. per pond of tea, while the average for the 160,899 ponds of the table amounts to 1.57 fl. per pond. It would, however, be insufficient on the basis of a simple average in the case of such a differentiated commodity as tea to judge the reliability of the prices recorded in Kol. Arch. No. 10,228. Unfortunately the Amsterdam accounts and hence the transcripts of the *retouren-generaal* were kept in such a way that it is impossible to calculate the average for the various sorts of tea, all sorts as a rule having been lumped together. The actual sales minutes have been lost; but from the autumn sales held on 10 November 1721 and the following days a printed price-list from the chamber of Amsterdam is extant.[3] From this it appears that Bohea tea was sold at prices from 34 to 72 st. per pond and green tea at 25–38 st. per pond (Bing tea is not mentioned; cf. the insignificant quantity offered). In both cases the average prices of Kol. Arch. No. 10,228 are found within the respective ranges and in the case of green tea very close to the midmost price of the range ($31^1/_2$ st. $> <$ $29^1/_2$ and $32^2/_5$ st. per pond), whereas the averages for Bohea tea keeps under the midmost price of the range (53 st. $> <$ 38 and $44^4/_5$ st. per pond). As we have not, however, any detailed knowledge of the structure, we must try in a different way to provide some authentic average prices to be used as a standard of comparison. Here a transcript of *retouren-generaal* from Kamer Rotterdam comes to

[3] Gemeente-Archief Amsterdam, Bibl. 6, Verkopingen der O.I.C.

our assistance, as among the sales in the accounting year 1721/22 two quantities of green tea are mentioned, one of 5,913 ponds sold at a price of 8,703 fl. the other of 3,648 ponds at 5,844 fl., which gives averages of 29 ½ and 32 st. per pond, respectively, to be compared with the Rotterdam figures of Kol. Arch. No. 10,228, viz. 5,883 ponds at 30 st. per pond and 3,897 ponds at $31^1/_8$ st. per pond, actually a fair agreement as regards the prices. The average prices for Bohea tea show an equally close correspondence. The respective sales at Rotterdam were of 2,647 ponds at 5,048 fl. and 4,084 ponds at 9,588 fl., or averages of $38^1/_5$ and 47 st. per pond. Kol. Arch. No. 10,228 mentions 2,917 ponds at $37^1/_8$ st. per pond and 4,916 ponds at $47^1/_4$ st. per pond.

From this and similar comparisons it may be concluded that whereas in the collection of statistical tables entitled Kol. Arch. No. 10,228 the quantities recorded are not those actually sold, but those offered for sale by the Company's Directors, the average prices indicated in the same source correspond to the average prices at the sales. In the case of tea the comparison also shows the limited value of the printed price-lists, which give the range of prices, but are not suitable for an exact judgment of the average price. If, finally, we want to inquire into the character of the total average for all chambers, this may be illustrated by the following example comprising the autumn sales of Bohea tea in 1714. Kol. Arch. No. 10,228 has a tabulation as rendered in Table I.

Table I. *Autumn Sales of Bohea Tea in 1714.*

A	6,775 ponds	4 $^2/_5$ fl.	29,810 fl.	—:–
Z	3,262 -	4 $^3/_{10}$ -	14,026 -	12:–
D	1,205 -	5 $^3/_8$ -	6,476 -	17:8
R	1,195 -	5 -	5,975 -	—:–
H	1,195 -	4 $^3/_4$ -	5,676 -	5:–
E	1,168 -	4 $^3/_5$ -	5,372 -	16:–
	14,800 ponds	4 $^3/_5$ fl.	67,337 fl.	10:8

It is seen that the sales amount at each chamber has come out by multiplication of the quantity offered with the average price known. The total average price (i.e. for all chambers), however, is not a fraction of the fictitious quantities, 14,800 ponds and 67,337 fl. 10 st. 8 penn., for which reason the last line in the tabulation is not correct, as 14,800 ponds at $4^3/_5$ fl. per pond gives 68,080 fl., i.e. that the total average was not constructed any more than the average of the chambers, but was ascertained.

The information of the price lists is not in all cases made superfluous by Kol. Arch. No. 10,228. Let us as an example chose the silk fabrics, *armozijnen*. In Kol. Arch. No. 10,228 they are entered together, but the price lists distinguish between a number of different qualities. In Table II we shall render the information of the two sources concerning the autumn sales in 1737–39.[4]

Table II. *Amsterdam Auction Prices of "Armozijnen", 1737–39. Fl. per Piece.*

The Price Lists	1737	1738	1739
Armozijnen, effene dubbelde	12.63–13.13	12.38–13.00	13.13–13.38
— *, effene enkelde*	7.25–7.38	7.38	8.13–8.25
— *, gestreepte*	12.00–12.63	12.75–13.38	13.88–14.38
— *, geblomde*	13.88–14.25	14.88–15.50	—
— *, enkelde geruyte*	7.13–7.50	8.13–8.38	8.25–8.75
— *, dubbelde gekettingde*	14.38–14.63	16.25	—
Kol. Arch. No. 10,228			
Armozijnen	12.50	12.63	12.38

The two sources may be said to supplement one another, as the price lists throw light on the multitude of qualities, while Kol. Arch. No. 10,228 shows that weighing of the material which can no more be done, because the sales books and catalogues have been lost. This appears still more clearly in the case of one of the commonest cotton fabrics, *salempouris*, cf. Table III.

Table III. *Amsterdam Auction Prices of "Salempouris", 1737–39. Fl. per Piece.*

The Price Lists	1737	1738	1739
Salempouris, gemeene gebleekte van Bengalen	5.63–6.50	5.75–6.13	5.88–6.75
— *, gemeene gebleekte van de Kust*	5.50–8.25	5.75–7.50	5.75–7.38
— *, gemeene gebleekte van Matura*	4.38–4.75	4.38–4.88	4.63–4.88
— *, fijne dito van de Kust*	10.38–10.63	10.75	9.88–10.00
— *, fijne dito van Matura*	9.63–9.75	9.75	9.00
— *, rouwe dito van de Kust*	5.25–5.75	5.88–7.63	5.50–6.38
— *, rouwe dito van Matura*	4.25–4.38	4.38	4.50
— *, bruyn blaauwe dito van de Kust*	9.00–9.38	8.63–9.38	8.13–8.38
— *, roode dito van Jaffanapatnam*	7.50	7.00–7.50	8.00
— *, bruyn blaauwe dito van Matura*	—	5.00–5.63	—
— *, rouwe gebl. van Mallabaar*	—	—	5.63–5.75
— *, gemeene gebl. van Mallabaar*	—	—	6.50
Kol. Arch. No. 10,228			
Salempouris	5.88	5.94	6.38

For a number of commodities Kol. Arch. No. 10,228 presents more detailed information about prices than the extracts of *retouren-generaal* and the accounts. In cases where great qualitative differences are connected with some commodity we have therefore preferred Kol. Arch. No.

[4] The price lists are kept in Collectie Radermacher No. 121.

10,228 to the accounts. As to other commodities Kol. Arch. No. 10,228 summarizes the differences in quality in an estimated average, which is found in this source, only. Furthermore, Kol. Arch. No. 10,228 offers the advantage of having an average for all the chambers of the Company.

Finally it is natural to ask, Who prepared Kol. Arch. No. 10,228? What purpose did this "Bijeenbrenging van verkoopingen" serve? Linguistically *bijeenbrenging* only means collocation or counting, a statistical survey. As mentioned in Appendix E, Pepper, the Company every year prepared a "Bijeenbrenging van de specerijen", a summary of which was entered in the Court Minutes and indicated the shrinkage of the volume of the spices. The oldest register of the Company's archives[5] shows that both of these annual surveys figure among the volumes from the commercial department and the warehouses of the Kamer Amsterdam. There we also find the so-called "Rendementen der gehoudene verkoopingen van retouren", the acquittance-books for commodities sold and delivered, and the registers of commodities not sold. Thus there is no doubt that Kol. Arch. No. 10,228 is a contemporary document originating from the Company's administration. Why, then, were the results of the sales calculated on the basis of the quantities offered and not on the basis of those actually sold? Presumably because the Heeren XVII needed a quick survey of the probable volume of the sales, amongst other things with a view to liquidity. The fact that the Heeren XVII received such surveys – after the fashion of the surveys of the cargoes of the returning fleet – amongst other things appears from the entry in their Court Minutes dated at 17 May 1670 on the sales of pepper and saltpetre in the month of May.[6] With the credit granted at the sales it took some time before the final result could be drawn up. Possible buyers who did not fetch their goods produced a similar effect. If, therefore, an estimate of the expected total proceeds from the sales was wanted, there were only the gross quantities offered and the prices on which to base the survey. The quantities offered were published before the sales – as mentioned above, printed cargo lists were issued already on the arrival of the returning fleet – special sale catalogues were printed, advertisements were inserted in Dutch and foreign newspapers, the large firms sent lists of the sales to correspondents far and near.[7] Furthermore, price lists were made as soon as the sales were over, and these, too, were printed and sent far and wide. The progress of the sales, lot by lot, was registered in a sales

[5] *Inventaris De Munnick*, fo. 24 *et seq.:* "1ste Charterolle der Administratie hier te Lande".
[6] Kol. Arch. No. 255, 17 May 1670.
[7] Copies of the printed lists announcing the auction sales from the various chambers may be found in Collectie Radermacher No. 115 (sales 1720, 1731, 1732, etc.).

book – *venditieboek* – with statement of buyer and price. At the delivery of the commodities the lots and the names of the buyers were entered in a so-called *leverantieboek*. There the tare fixed was deducted from the quantities. These books have not been preserved; but in the archives of Kamer Zeeland there is a "Versamelingh van de verkoopinghen",[8] drawn up on the basis of the *venditieboek* and *leverantieboek*. They run from 1724 on. Nor are the above-mentioned *rendementen* extant.[9] As mentioned in the text, they were in a way the Alpha and Omega of the trade, and copies of them were sent to the East. The Heeren XVII's orders were drawn up in immediate connexion with the sales and were accompanied by *rendementen*, from which the gross profit appeared. The *rendementen* were prepared on the basis of the invoices, which in certain cases were followed very closely, viz. if the point was that of having qualitative differences defined, e.g. in the case of new commodities. As an example of such *rendementen* we may render the result of the autumn sale in 1701 of a quantity of Javanese indigo received by the ship "De Drie Kroonen",[10] see Table IV.

Table IV. "*Rendiment: Javaanse Indigo.*"

27	ponds in 1 *kasje*	fl.	1:2:8	't *catti*	56	st. per pond
115½	- - 1 -	-	1:2:8	-	56	- - -
37½	- - 1 -	-	1:10:-	-	75	- - -
148	- - 1 -	-	1:10:-	-	72½	- - -
125	- - 1 -	-	1:5:-	-	64¼	- - -
19	- - 1 -	-	1:6:-	-	64½	- - -

[8] Kol. Arch. No. 8335, Kamer Zeeland, Dept. van de koopmanschappen.
[9] Possibly they are kept in the former Provincial Archives at Jakarta.
[10] Kol. Arch. No. 262, 14 November 1701.

APPENDIX C

Public Sale Prices

Table V: Average Prices, Kamer Amsterdam, 1649/50-1737/38.
SOURCE: Kol. Arch. Nos. 10,234-10,242 F.

Table VI: Estimated Averages, All Chambers, 1698-1740.
SOURCE: Kol. Arch. No. 10,228.

Table V. *Average Prices, Kamer Amsterdam, 1649/50–1737/38.*

	Black Pepper	Cloves	Nutmegs	Mace	Cinnamon
	fl. per pond	fl. per pond	fl. per pond	fl. per pond	fl. per pond
1649/50	0.49	—	2.52	5.94	1.29
1650/51	0.46	3.27	2.52	5.94	1.28
1651/52	0.42	3.27	2.52	5.94	1.26
1652/53	0.38	—	2.52	5.94	1.23
1653/54	0.70	3.19	2.46	5.81	1.99
1654/55	0.59	3.21	2.45	5.80	1.46
1655/56	0.40	3.17	2.47	5.81	1.32
1656/57	0.36	3.20	2.49	5.76	—
1657/58	0.49	3.20	2.47	5.77	2.28
1658/59	0.41	3.20	2.48	5.99	2.67
1659/60	0.53	3.73	2.52	5.84	3.23
1660/61	0.48	3.95	2.71	5.67	3.96
1661/62	0.48	4.72	2.42	5.14	3.75
1662/63	0.54	4.56	2.10	4.27	3.71
1663/64	0.43	4.55	2.48	6.04	3.76
1664/65	0.58	6.08	2.39	5.23	3.44
1665/66	0.61	5.48	2.26	4.93	2.56
1666/67	1.10	6.38	2.25	5.51	2.71
1667/68	0.66	4.88	2.25	5.37	2.24
1668/69	0.64	5.57	2.23	5.49	2.61
1669/70	0.47	4.63	2.29	5.62	3.36
1670/71	0.43	5.35	2.26	5.98	3.04
1671/72	0.42	5.40	2.30	6.16	3.58
1672/73	0.40	—	—	—	2.71
1673/74	0.45	4.76	2.28	6.03	2.67
1674/75	0.41	4.28	2.28	5.66	3.08
1675/76	0.34	4.00	2.54	5.46	3.00
1676/77	0.28	3.75	2.22	5.09	3.14
1677/78	0.26	—	2.13	4.50	3.06
1678/79	0.32	3.68	3.00	5.91	2.61
1679/80	0.35	3.68	3.05	7.35	3.35
1680/81	0.33	3.68	3.38	7.83	3.18
1681/82	0.29	3.68	3.99	7.05	2.65
1682/83	0.26	3.69	3.40	5.90	2.50
1683/84	0.35	3.72	—	6.76	2.50
1684/85	0.38	3.72	2.83	5.69	2.69
1685/86	0.35	3.72	2.97	5.85	2.90
1686/87	0.37	3.72	2.97	5.79	2.68
1687/88	0.44	3.72	2.97	5.98	2.77
1688/89	0.56	3.72	2.97	6.06	2.47
1689/90	0.65	3.72	2.97	6.18	2.33
1690/91	0.63	3.72	2.97	6.46	2.45
1691/92	0.72	3.72	2.97	6.87	2.80
1692/93	0.54	3.72	2.97	7.80	2.50
1693/94	0.43	3.72	2.97	5.90	2.35

Table V (continued)

	Black Pepper	Cloves	Nutmegs	Mace	Cinnamon
	fl. per pond	fl. per pond	fl. per pond	fl. per pond	fl. per pond
1694/95	0.40	3.72	2.97	5.82	2.49
1695/96	0.40	3.72	2.97	7.50	2.84
1696/97	0.51*	3.72	2.97	9.61	2.73
1697/98	0.63*	3.72	3.11	11.68	3.07
1698/99	0.54*	3.72	4.62	12.03	2.92
1699/00	0.37	3.72	3.55	8.47	2.71
1700/01	0.55	3.72	4.21	10.53	2.57
1701/02	0.45	3.72	3.72	6.65	2.20
1702/03	0.42	3.72	3.72	6.76	2.44
1703/04	0.45	3.72	3.72	7.26	2.40
1704/05	0.39	3.72	3.72	6.48	2.86
1705/06	0.41	3.72	3.72	6.75	2.69
1706/07	0.44	3.72	3.72	6.52	2.90
1707/08	0.57	3.72	3.72	7.33	2.85
1708/09	0.45	3.72	3.72	6.63	2.76
1709/10	0.52	3.72	3.72	6.62	2.63
1710/11	0.49	3.72	3.72	6.27	2.18
1711/12	0.54	3.72	3.72	6.07	2.00
1712/13	0.64	3.72	3.72	6.23	2.55
1713/14	0.92	3.72	3.72	6.26	2.46
1714/15	0.59	3.72	3.72	5.93	2.62
1715/16	0.46	3.72	3.72	8.29	2.47
1716/17	0.56	3.72	3.72	6.36	2.70
1717/18	0.48	3.72	3.72	5.79	2.58
1718/19	0.47	3.72	3.72	5.80	2.48
1719/20	0.42	3.72	3.72	5.60	2.63
1720/21	0.34	3.72	3.72	5.80	2.49
1721/22	0.31	3.72	3.72	6.62	2.52
1722/23	0.39	3.72	3.72	5.91	2.60
1723/24	0.34	3.72	3.72	6.38	2.68
1724/25	0.36	3.72	3.72	7.63	2.81
1725/26	0.32	3.72	3.72	6.78	2.40
1726/27	0.33	3.72	3.72	6.80	2.39
1727/28	0.39	3.72	3.72	7.13	2.50
1728/29	0.55	3.72	3.72	6.62	2.59
1729/30	0.46	3.72	3.72	6.95	2.47
1730/31	0.37	3.69	3.69	6.56	2.55
1731/32	0.48	3.68	3.68	6.16	2.53
1732/33	0.55	3.68	3.68	5.86	2.45
1733/34	0.55	3.68	3.68	5.91	2.42
1734/35	0.55	3.68	3.68	6.08	2.42
1735/36	0.50	3.68	3.68	6.15	2.59
1736/37	0.51	3.68	3.68	6.05	2.47
1737/38	0.50	3.68	3.68	5.88	2.37

* See below p. 300 concerning these prices.

Table V (continued)

	Persian Silk	Bengali Silk	Chinese Silk	Japanese Copper
	fl. per pond	fl. per pond	fl. per pond	fl. per 100 ponds
1649/50	—	—	—	42.54
1650/51	—	—	—	—
1651/52	—	—	—	36.99
1652/53	—	—	—	36.44
1653/54	7.59	8.92	11.44*	—
1654/55	—	—	—	—
1655/56	—	—	—	—
1656/57	—	—	—	—
1657/58	—	—	—	—
1658/59	—	—	—	50.18
1659/60	—	—	—	56.20
1660/61	—	—	—	56.69
1661/62	—	—	—	53.63
1662/63	—	—	—	51.57
1663/64	—	—	—	50.96
1664/65	—	—	—	63.93
1665/66	—	—	—	60.59
1666/67	—	—	—	61.29
1667/68	—	—	—	58.04
1668/69	5.19	—	—	54.98
1669/70	—	—	—	58.65
1670/71	—	—	—	60.82
1671/72	—	—	—	61.77
1672/73	5.21	5.23	—	56.15
1673/74	—	7.00	—	58.43
1674/75	—	8.03	—	56.24
1675/76	5.34	—	—	55.36
1676/77	5.18	6.89	—	62.01
1677/78	6.41	—	—	—
1678/79	5.49	6.46	—	—
1679/80	5.00	—	7.82	51.57
1680/81	4.75	6.00	7.00	55.03
1681/82	4.72	6.51	—	—
1682/83	4.19	5.63	—	—
1683/84	—	5.87	—	—
1684/85	3.98	6.02	—	—
1685/86	3.95	5.54	—	—
1686/87	—	7.15	—	—
1687/88	4.99	6.60	8.56	—
1688/89	—	6.29	6.32	—
1689/90	—	—	6.50	57.05
1690/91	—	7.79	7.00	53.83
1691/92	—	8.32	8.22	59.64
1692/93	4.73	7.49	—	60.51

* Tongkingese silk.

Table V (continued)

	Persian Silk	Bengali Silk	Chinese Silk	Japanese Copper
	fl. per pond	fl. per pond	fl. per pond	fl. per 100 ponds
1693/94	4.90	8.78	9.94	58.04
1694/95	—	8.95	8.52	53.83
1695/96	—	8.14	8.00	55.70
1696/97	—	11.06	11.15	59.82
1697/98	—	9.97	10.91	60.35
1698/99	To be continued in the following Table VI			62.73
1699/00				66.27
1700/01				62.47
1701/02				62.32
1702/03				60.96
1703/04				55.31
1704/05				55.66
1705/06				51.93
1706/07				49.35
1707/08				52.75
1708/09				55.97
1709/10				49.05
1710/11				54.26
1711/12				61.38
1712/13				—
1713/14				58.07
1714/15				65.57
1715/16				71.97
1716/17				67.17
1717/18				74.98
1718/19				—
1719/20				56.91
1720/21				50.61
1721/22				51.91
1722/23				57.51
1723/24				55.87
1724/25				—
1725/26				—
1726/27				—
1727/28				—
1728/29				—
1729/30				—
1730/31				—
1731/32				—
1732/33				—
1733/34				—
1734/35				58.03
1735/36				55.87
1736/37				—
1737/38				61.10

Table VI. *Estimated Averages, All Chambers, 1698–1740.*

	Persian Silk	Bengali Silk	Chinese Silk	*Armozijnen*	*Salempouris*
	fl. per pond	fl. per pond	fl. per pond	fl. per piece	fl. per piece
1698, Autumn .	8.45	11.89	14.90	21.00	8.66
1699, - .	—	10.37	11.95	21.40	8.70
1700, - .	—	7.97	9.30	22.38	8.20
1701, - .	—	9.02	9.53	17.00	7.30
1702, - .	—	8.25	7.85	19.20	5.80
1703, - .	5.60	7.10	7.13	19.66	8.20
1704, - .	6.20	8.93	7.85	20.66	7.80
1705, - .	—	7.03	6.62	20.25	8.66
1706, - .	5.30	7.93	7.05	23.20	8.50
1707, - .	—	6.60	6.38	22.50	9.50
1708, - .	—	6.05	5.80	18.70	10.00
1709, - .	—	6.50	5.95	15.70	8.70
1710, - .	—	6.00	—	15.17	8.44
1711, - .	—	6.73	7.65	13.90	8.00
1712, - .	6.00	6.53	—	14.50	8.10
1713, - .	5.95	7.45	—	17.17	8.70
1714, - .	8.15	10.70	—	20.00	9.90
1715, - .	7.00	8.63	10.03	17.25	7.70
1716, - .	6.00	7.20	—	16.70	8.38
1717, - .	—	7.60	6.50	17.50	8.40
1718, - .	—	6.56	—	17.50	8.80
1719, - .	—	6.21	—	16.00	7.70
1720, - .	—	5.50	—	14.37	6.15
1721, - .	—	5.83	—	14.13	6.06
1722, - .	—	6.77	—	14.25	7.06
1723, - .	—	6.05	6.80	14.25	7.25
1724, - .	—	6.28	7.05	17.25	7.75
1725, - .	—	6.60	7.85	16.33	7.38
1726, Spring . .	—	6.34	—	16.20	8.38
- , Autumn .	—	5.95	—	13.75	7.63
1727, - .	—	5.55	6.43	13.00	6.50
1728, - .	—	5.35	—	13.60	7.75
1729, Nov.-Dec.	—	5.78	—	15.17	8.13
1730, Oct.-Nov.	—	5.79	—	14.75	8.25
1731, May-June	—	5.85*	—	14.25	7.75
- , Oct.-Nov.	—	5.50*	5.40	13.88	8.88
1732, Nov.-Dec.	—	5.64*	—	14.81	10.17
1733, Apr.-May	—	6.20*	—	14.40	9.75
- , Nov.-Dec.	—	5.86*	—	14.40	7.70
1734, Apr.-May	—	6.00*	—	14.13	—
- , Nov.-Dec.	—	5.43*	—	14.80	7.00
1735, Oct.-Nov.	—	5.05*	—	13.00	6.56
1736, Oct.-Nov.	—	5.60*	—	12.94	6.81
1737, Apr.-May	—	—	—	—	6.75
- , Oct.-Nov.	—	5.64*	—	12.19	5.88
1738, Oct.-Nov.	—	5.96*	—	12.60	6.05
1739, Oct.-Nov.	—	6.50*	—	12.60	6.33
1740, Nov.-Dec.	—	6.20*	—	13.50	6.38

* *Tanny.*

Table VI (continued)

	Guinees	Bohea Tea	Green Tea	Mocha Coffee	Java Coffee
	fl. per piece	fl. per pond	fl. per pond	fl. per pond	fl. per pond
1698, Autumn .	21.20	7.75	—	1.09	
1699, - .	22.00	5.38	—	0.96	
1700, - .	21.40	3.50	—	0.80	
1701, - .	17.50	2.32	—	—	
1702, - .	13.60	4.06	—	1.19	
1703, - .	18.66	—	—	1.14	
1704, - .	17.88	7.13	—	—	
1705, - .	19.25	7.20	—	—	
1706, - .	19.13	8.13	—	1.78	
1707, - .	20.90	7.40	—	1.91	
1708, - .	21.38	—	—	2.46	
1709, - .	19.00	8.13	4.70	1.87	
1710, - .	18.38	—	—	1.56	
1711, - .	18.13	6.90	3.21	—	
1712, - .	17.63	—	—	1.41	1.16
1713, - .	19.38	5.70	4.10	—	1.36
1714, - .	22.00	4.60	4.20	1.21	1.24
1715, - .	17.70	4.75	4.13	1.18	1.18
1716, - .	18.40	8.44	4.06	1.60	1.36
1717, - .	18.10	6.20	3.60	1.28	1.16
1718, - .	19.13	6.20	5.00	1.20	0.93
1719, - .	17.90	4.66	3.25	1.46	1.33
1720, - .	14.80	2.29	2.20	1.39	1.36
1721, - .	14.00	2.18	1.55	1.29	1.04
1722, - .	15.88	2.70	1.33	1.23	1.20
1723, Apr.	—	2.66	1.32	—	—
- , Aug.	—	2.32	1.21	1.08	0.88
- , Autumn .	16.00	—	—	—	1.04
1724, July-Aug.	—	2.09	1.66	—	0.83
- , Autumn .	18.25	—	—	1.24	1.00
1725, Febr.	—	2.19	1.34	—	1.00
- , July-Aug.	—	3.01	1.21	1.01	0.88
1725, Oct.-Dec.	16.13	3.18	1.52	—	0.89
1726, Apr.-May	17.00	—	—	—	—
- , Aug.-Sept.	—	3.43	2.27	1.20	0.86
- , Nov.-Dec.	15.75	3.12	2.18	—	—
1727, Aug.-Sept.	—	3.78	—	1.21	0.87
- , Oct.-Dec.	14.38	3.40	3.39	—	0.85
1728, Aug.-Sept.	—	3.69	4.11	0.97	0.70
- , Oct.-Nov.	16.63	—	—	—	0.71
- , Dec.	15.33	3.58	—	—	—
1729, Nov.-Dec.	18.17	2.40	—	—	0.84
1730, Apr.	—	2.28	3.56	—	—
- , Oct.-Nov.	18.19	1.69&2.13*	2.21	0.94	0.93

* Tea directly from China.

Table VI (continued)

	Guinees	Bohea Tea	Green Tea	Mocha Coffee	Java Coffee
	fl. per piece	fl. per pond	fl. per pond	fl. per pond	fl. per pond
1731, May-June	16.50	1.64	1.83	—	—
- , Oct......	—	1.40*	1.41*	—	—
- , Oct.-Nov.	19.56	1.18	—	1.03	0.99
- , Dec.	—	1.36*&1.44*	1.55*	—	—
1732, Nov.-Dec.	21.50	1.24&1.50*	1.23&1.34*	—	0.85
1733, Apr.-May	19.00	1.53	1.35	—	—
- , Nov.	—	1.63*	1.29*	—	—
- , Nov.-Dec.	16.80	1.43	1.36	—	0.77
1734, Apr.-May	14.83	—	—	—	—
- , Nov.-Dec.	16.63	1.63&1.66*	1.41&1.65*	—	0.76
1735, Oct......	—	1.59*	1.93*	—	—
- , Oct.-Nov.	14.66	1.63	—	—	0.62
1736, Oct.-Nov.	13.38	1.41&1.48*	1.76&1.81*	—	0.55
1737, Apr.-May	14.56	—	—	—	0.41
- , Oct.-Nov.	12.50	1.14	2.51	0.63	0.34
- , Nov.	—	1.67*	—	—	—
1738, Oct.-Nov.	12.75	1.19&1.48*	2.61	0.50	0.44
1739, Oct.-Nov.	13.07	0.86&1.29*	2.06&1.99*	—	0.50
1740, Nov.-Dec.	13.31	1.07&1.32*	1.92&1.83*	—	0.50

* Tea directly from China.

APPENDIX D

Bullion and Money

Quantities, Sorts, and Prices in the 18th Century

Every year the Heeren XVII decided how much gold and silver the Company was to send from Nederland to the East. The basis of their decision was the demands sent home by the Batavian Government in the General Letters. In the first third of the 18th century the practice was that the Heeren XVII in the autumn drew up a table of distribution among the chambers for the portion which was to be dispatched by the first shipments to the East, after which the Court of Directors in the following February or March decided on the supplementary material of bullion and specie, which amongst other things was adapted according to the bulletins last received from Batavia. Simultaneously a statement was made of the extent to which the various chambers had realized the autumn programme. These tables are found entered in the Court Minutes. If they are compared with the accounts of the chambers, which generally were balanced per the middle of May – exceptionally per the middle of June – we have a possibility of estimating the extent of the equipments of silver and gold from Nederland. Below (Table VII), such a comparison has been made in the case of Kamer Amsterdam for the period 1717–25.

Table VII. *Silver and Gold Shipped from Kamer Amsterdam, 1717/18–1725/26. Fl.*

Seasons	The Heeren XVII's resolutions	Shipped at the statement in Feb.–March	Shipped in all at the balancing of the accounts in the middle of May
1717/18	1,800,000	1,258,574	1,946,598
1718/19	2,000,000	1,598,385	2,000,000
1719/20	2,562,500	2,011,888	2,562,500
1720/21	2,000,000	1,877,527	2,000,000
1721/22	3,412,500	2,214,512	3,257,035
1722/23	3,487,500	2,070,698	3,377,757
1723/24	3,446,745	2,230,719	3,449,557
1724/25	3,709,500	3,251,738	3,722,501
1725/26	3,612,500	2,953,339	3,908,261

The normal ratio of the distribution was that Amsterdam was to provide ½, Zeeland $^1/_4$, and each of the other four chambers $^1/_{16}$. From the analysis above it appears that Kamer Amsterdam generally fulfilled its obligations and that the greater part had been sent at the February–March statement. In February–March the smaller chambers might very well be at some distance from the journey's end, as appears from Table VIII.

Table VIII. *Silver and Gold Shipped from the Chambers Hoorn and Enkhuizen 1718/19–1719/20. Fl.*

Seasons	Chambers	The Heeren XVII's resolutions	Shipped at the statement in Feb.-March	Shipped in all at the balancing of the accounts in the middle of May
1718/19	Hoorn	250,000	137,500	250,000
	Enkhuizen	250,000	118,760	220,407
1719/20	Hoorn	320,312	95,312	320,312
	Enkhuizen	320,312	116,894	349,852

This example also shows that Enkhuizen in 1719/20 shipped the amount by which the chamber was below its quota in the preceding season. This was one way of regulating possible failing equipments. Another way was that of having one of the other chambers taking over the obligations. In general it may be said that the chambers on the whole provided what the Company's Directors had decided to ship to the East.

If, therefore, we want a quick and approximate survey of the amounts shipped, we may obtain it through the Heeren XVII's resolutions as to the equipments of bullion and money. But the exact figures are found in the accounts – which, however, are not extant in their entirety – and in the material of invoices, which is an enormously heavy material to work up and which is not complete, either. Of course we find the cash in the accounts from Batavia entered as commodities received. The accounts of Batavia, however, are also incomplete and furthermore, the accounting year runs from the 1st of September to the end of August, for which reason the shipments sent from Nederland in one season of equipment are distributed on two of the accounting seasons of Batavia, apart from the fact that the bullion and money which might be lost during the transport of course were not entered in the accounts of Batavia. The same applies to the – indeed modest – part of the cash destined for Ceylon.

Klerk de Reus in his work on the Dutch Company's administration and finances has communicated a statistical material concerning the amounts of money sent to the East.[1] Like so much else of the author's material this is also devoid of heuristic comments, but it seems evident that the figures communicated by him down to 1719 inclusive are directly or indirectly based on the Heeren XVII's resolutions. As to the 17th century Klerk de Reus is presumably indebted to Pieter van Dam's surveys.[2] Unfortunately mostly only the Seventeen's resolution from the autumn was compiled by Klerk de Reus or his source, whereas in a number of cases the supplementary distribution of February–March was overlooked. This means that many of the figures are too small. The figures rendered by de Reus from 1720 on represent the balance of the amounts shipped so far, as found in the statement of February–March, and thus are misleading. Under 1720 the figure from the statement on 28 February 1720 is placed, this figure, as mentioned above, showing how much of the distribution plan from the autumn of 1719 had been implemented. Thus it is actually figures from the same season which were rendered by Klerk de Reus in 1719 and 1720, respectively, viz. under the year 1719, the plan of distribution for the season 1719/20 – the supplementary plan in that year was exceptionally drawn up as early as September, only about a fortnight after the main plan had been formed – and under the year 1720, the statement of February 1720 of the extent to which the distribution had been carried into effect. The comparison presented in Table IX shows how glaring the deviations may be.

The comparison shows that the Company's shipments of cash as early as the season of 1721/22 increased highly, not, as appears from Klerk de Reus' figures, only in 1725/26. The decreasing trend which may be traced from 1728/29, is weakened by the Company's incipient trade to China, which does not appear from the above-mentioned figures from the Heeren XVII's resolutions. In December 1728 Kamer Amsterdam shipped about 300,000 fl. in silver by the "Coxhorn" to Canton, in the season of 1729/30 about 250,000 fl. in silver by the "Duyfje", in the season of 1730/31 about 550,000 fl. in silver by the "Leyduyn" and the "Coxhorn", in the season of 1731/32 about 600,000 fl. by the "Knappenhof" and the "Ypenrode", and in 1732/33 about 440,000 fl. by the "Leyduyn" and the "Voorduyn". To these should be added the equipments from Kamer Zeeland, which are unknown.[3]

[1] Beilage V, the column headed "Baares Geld".

[2] *Pieter van Dam* 1:I, p. 364, Appendix II.

[3] The Amsterdam figures have been taken from the accounts.

Table IX. *Amounts of Money Sent to the East.*

Years		Cash shipped (fl.) according to	
Klerk de Reus	Season of equipment	Klerk de Reus	The Heeren XVII's resolution
1714	1714/15	3,750,000	3,700,000
1715	1715/16	4,225,000	4,225,000
1716	1716/17	3,800,000	4,200,000
1717	1717/18	3,600,000	3,600,000
1718	1718/19	4,000,000	4,000,000
1719	1719/20	5,125,000	5,125,000
1720		3,204,791	
1721	1720/21	3,072,401	4,125,000
1722	1721/22	4,086,003	6,825,000
1723	1722/23	3,539,764	6,975,000
1724	1723/24	4,225,383	6,887,500
1725	1724/25	5,431,435	7,419,000
1726	1725/26	5,914,454	7,415,964
1727	1726/27	6,156,603	7,681,000
1728	1727/28	6,034,163	7,968,500
1729	1728/29	3,727,729	5,558,500
1730	1729/30	3,373,568	4,525,000
1731	1730/31	2,600,333	4,242,663
1732	1731/32	2,726,351	3,800,000
1733	1732/33	2,346,452	4,250,000

The schemes of distribution in the Court Minutes also indicate the composition of the bullion and money. As a couple of examples it may be mentioned that the Heeren XVII at the meeting on 28 September 1714 decided that gold and silver to a value of 3.25 mill. fl. should be shipped to the East. On 9 March 1715 they further decided to send 0.4 mill. fl. as a supplement, the whole value thus amounting to 3.65 mill. fl. Of this amount only 0.25 mill. fl. was destined for Ceylon, the rest was intended for "Indië", i.e. headquarters in Batavia. The composition of the various sorts appears from Table X.

Table X. *Composition Scheme 1714/15.*

Gold:	ducats, gold in bars	0.6 mill. fl.
Silver:	mark rials	1.4 - -
	dukatons	1.0 - -
	silver in bars	0.3 - -
	payement	0.4 - -

The portion of Ceylon comprised 0.25 mill. fl. gold in bars or coins. The shipment of the following year was composed as stated in Table XI.

Table XI. *Composition Scheme 1715/16.*

Gold:	ducats gold in bars	0.725	mill. fl.
Silver:	mark rials	1.1	- -
	dukatons	1.1	- -
	silver in bars	0.5	- -
	payement	0.8	- -

This was a total of 4.225 mill. fl., of which Ceylon was to have only 0.225 mill. fl. in gold in bullion or specie. It applied to both schemes that the silver in bars should be of the same standard as rupees, that the rials should be supplemented by *dukatons* or bar silver and that the *payement* should consist of good Dutch or Zeeland *schellingen* and double *stuivers*, but no "Westfriesse, half dubbeltjes en half schellingen".

As to the actual composition of the shipments of gold and silver we must, however, go to the General Commerce Ledgers of Batavia for information. Below (Table XII), we shall render an analysis of theDutch silver and gold shipped to Batavia in the years 1713/14–1726/27 according to the accounts of the Head Office.

Table XII. *Analysis of Silver and Gold Shipped to Batavia, 1713/14–1726/27. In 1,000 Fl.*

		1713/14	1715/16	1718/19	1721/22	1723/24	1724/25	1726/27
Gold:	ducats	322	212	579	—	—	79	1,052
	gold in bars	285	—	—	—	—	—	694
Silver:	mark rials	1,255	555	574	1,943	1,644	2,197	941
	dukatons	1,853	2,108	947	228	319	556	517
	kruysdaalders	1	1	2	2	1	—	1
	silver in bars	669	114	119	4,218	3,539	6,697	3,397
	payement	827	177	423	1,597	738	1,522	1,180

The analysis shows that there was often a considerable difference between the schemes of the Heeren XVII and what was executed. Thus the mark rials during the first half of the period to a wide extent were supplemented by *dukatons*, while the bar silver later actually dominated more than in the distributions. The Batavian accounts for that matter also give information of the distribution of the quantities of bullion and money received at the various factories in Asia, and of the quantities of precious metals received by the Company from the Asiatic areas. The share of Nederland in the total supplies of bullion and money in Batavia during those years was much greater than in the 17th century. Normally more than three fourths of the silver and gold came from Holland, even though there were a few seasons, e.g. 1718/19, when the Dutch shipments amounted to only about half of the supplies. The distribution to the factories shows that Bengal received more than half of the bullion and money from Batavia, immediately followed by the archipelago and then, in the third place, by the Coromandel Coast.[4]

On one point the Company material leaves us in the lurch, viz. as regards the cost prices of the silver and gold. In the text it was mentioned that the chambers should keep each other posted as to the cost prices of the equipment goods in general. For this purpose the Heeren XVII had forms printed which show that the prices of bullion and money were also included in the duty of report, which in the 18th century was to be sent in every month. However, no comprehensive set of reports is extant. Nor do the accounts offer any details. On the other hand, an average price may be calculated on the basis of the accounts of Batavia, but in this case the difference between "light" and "heavy" coins enters as a disturbing element. This may be illustrated by Table XIII comprising the prices of bar silver and rials of eight in the years 1719–1727, in which for want of Company prices we have taken the silver prices of the Amsterdam price lists and compared them with the prices booked in Batavia.[5]

Table XIII. *Silver Prices.*

Amsterdam Price Lists				Prices Booked In Batavia		
Year	Bar silver	Rials of eight: Pillars	Rials of eight: Mexicans	Season	Bar silver	Mark rials
	fl. banco per mark	fl. banco per mark	fl. banco per mark		fl. per mark	fl. per mark
1719 Sept....	25.44	23.12	22.75	1718/19 ...	32.01	29.70
1720 May ...	25.50	23.65	22.85			
- June ...	25.45	23.75	22.93			
1721 June ...	25.31	23.60	22.80			
1722 May ...	24.20	22.55	22.73	1721/22 ...	32.13	30.04
1723 May ...	24.25	22.36	22.50			
1724 May ...	24.35	22.45	22.45	1723/24 ...	32.26	29.00
1725 May ...	24.30	22.50	22.35	1724/25 ...	32.13	
1726 June ...	24.55	22.95	22.85			
1727 May ...	24.25	22.55	22.55	1726/27 ...	32.58	

[4] The Batavian General Commerce Ledgers are Kol. Arch. Nos. 10,813–10,819 from the years quoted.

[5] The Amsterdam quotations derive from a collection of original price lists found in Rigsarkivet, Copenhagen, Amsterdamske Faktorregnskaber, as N. W. Posthumus, *Nederlandsche Prijsgeschiedenis* (Leiden, 1943) offers very little information for these years.

At the estimate of the difference between Nederland and Batavia the expenses in Nederland must be taken into consideration. They appear from an example from 1728. In that year Kamer Zeeland amongst other things bought 20 chests of silver at 50 rods, i.e. 1000 rods in all, each rod weighing 8 marks. The standard of the silver was 11 penn. 20 grein, i.e. that the lot converted into Cologne marks of fine silver amounted to 7888:10:16. The price was 24.30 fl. per mark of fine silver. To this should be added $^1/_4$ per cent. "verstaangelt" and 4 per cent. agio on *bankgelt* (banco) and 5 st. per mark of fine silver in payment for refining and smelting. In this way the average cost price per mark became 25.60 fl.[6]

[6] Kol. Arch No. 10,331, 1 April 1728.

APPENDIX E

Pepper

Quantities and Prices

The necessity of distinguishing between the various stages of the trade at the drawing up of quantitative statistics of the Company's annual arrivals and sales of pepper in Nederland clearly appears from the draft for a description of the history of the trade in pepper made by the Dutch historian W. A. Horst.[1] Although it is difficult in detail to follow the author's various sources, he mentions himself the Court Minutes, Pieter van Dam, and some special auction and sales books from Kamer Amsterdam, which must be identical with Kol. Arch. No. 10,228. On this basis Horst drew up statistics with quantities and prices at the sales in Nederland during the long period of 1600–1794.[2] The result is confusing, first of all because the author has neglected to determine his sources critically.

As to the quantities we must distinguish between four stages: (i) What was shipped, (ii) What was received, (iii) What was offered, and (iv) What was sold. The differences between these figures may occasionally be great. In what follows we shall consider them in more detail for the years 1715–32, from which period an almost complete basis of sources is available. During this period brown pepper was shipped from year to year in very varying quantities ranging from a minimum of about 3.2 mill. ponds to a maximum of about 9.5 mill. ponds. During the long transport from Batavia and Ceylon to Nederland the pepper dwindled (leakage, etc.) and one of the first things done in Nederland at the reception was weighing the lots and ascertaining the magnitude of the shrinkage. The statements to this effect were reported to the Heeren XVII and entered in their minutes as "Bijeenbrenging van de specerijen". The percentage of shrinkage ranged between about 2 and well over 10, in the later years

[1] W. A. Horst, "De peperhandel van de Vereenigde Oost-Indische Compagnie", *Bijdragen voor Vaderlandsche Geschiedenis en Oudheidkunde*, VIII:3 ('s-Gravenhage, 1941), pp. 95–103.

[2] About the first three years of this period the author offers no information at all and the statements of quantities down to 1668 are very sporadic.

of the period mainly being 8. There was, however, a further shrinkage of the stocks in Nederland dependent on the time in which the pepper was stored in the warehouses and the extent to which it was necessary to rid it of impurities. From a calculation dated at October 1728 from Kamer Amsterdam it is seen that the *bewindhebbers* reduced the Indian export figures by 15 per cent. in order to attain to the European sales figures.[3] This comparatively great total shrinkage also appears if we follow the individual crop of pepper on its way from the East to the sales in Europe.

Because of the time factor the crop of pepper did not reach the market in Nederland until the following year. The pepper was normally sold at the Company's spring sales, which took place in the period of April–May. These sales were recorded in the accounts, which were balanced in the middle of May. Thus on the days 9th, 18th, 23rd, and 25th of April and 1st and 3rd of May 1725 a total of about 5.56 mill. ponds of brown pepper was sold from the six chambers. We shall refer these sales to the calendar year 1725 and it is found to have been entered under the accounting year 1724/25. Later in the year 1725 no pepper was sold. The pepper had arrived in Nederland towards the end of 1724 and in the beginning of 1725, and on 26 February 1725 the survey of the cargoes received was submitted to the Heeren XVII. From this survey it appeared that about 6.28 mill. ponds of pepper had been shipped from the East, which thus was the share of Nederland in the 1724 crop of pepper. During the transport this quantity had dwindled by barely 7 per cent. to about 5.87 mill. ponds. If we consider the stocks at the beginning and the end of the accounting season 1724/25, we obtain by a calculation the result that the total shrinkage was about 15 per cent.

The pepper was ordered in bales, but sold at a price per pond. In the text it was mentioned that the Company long – Horst says down to 1668 – followed the old tradition from the spice market in Antwerp not to inform the buyers of the quantities arrived. It was also on the model of selling conditions in Antwerp that the price of pepper throughout the period was quoted in Flemish *grooten*. However, in order to facilitate the comparisons in the text, we have converted the price into fl. per pond. During the 17th century the bale of pepper grew larger, and the following are the rates of conversion used where in the text we have stated the quantities of the demand in ponds: the orders during the first decades

[3] Kol. Arch. No. 314, "Verbalen van de Haagse Besoignes en andere commissien", 1727–1731. Calculation of the quantities received during the accounting period from 15 May 1724 to 15 May 1728 made in connexion with the drawing up of the balance-sheet after the 21st four-year period.

of the Company's history were expressed either in sacks of 60 ponds[4] or in bales of 350 ponds. From 1640 on it must be considered that the bale was estimated at 400 ponds, and after 1668 the Heeren XVII meant 430 ponds when ordering a bale of pepper.[5] An average for the years 1714–1720 of the weight of the bales sold at Kamer Amsterdam calculated on the basis of the information offered by the accounts about the quantities of pepper sold gives 432.61 ponds per bale. This weight is net, just as the price per pond in the tables, as the buyer was given a tare of 4 ½ ponds per bale for the packing. In 1718 the tare was increased to 5 ponds, because the canvas for the bales was made thicker for the better protection of the pepper.[6]

Disregarding the quantity shipped, we may then draw up Table XIV for the years 1715–1732 of (1) the quantities of pepper received, with indication of the year of the crop, (2) the quantities offered for sale, calculated from the Heeren XVII's estimate at 430 ponds per bale, (3) the quantities sold according to the accounts, and (4) Horst's information about the sales. All quantities are placed after the calendar year and for the sake of clearness given in mill. ponds.

As appears from this table, the Company actually had insignificant stocks of pepper on hand. Allowing for the established shrinkage in Nederland the greater part of the pepper received was generally sold immediately at the sales. Furthermore, we may establish a very close agreement between the quantities offered and those sold. This also applies to the connexion as regards prices, which shows a simple inverse ratio between the quantity offered/sold and the price. Cf. the following diagram.

We have not succeeded in explaining all deviations in Horst's statistics; but for the years 1715 and 1719–1721 (incl.) it is evident that he lists the pepper shipped from the East in 1714 and 1718–20 (incl.), respectively, while in the other years he mainly keeps to the quantities offered in Nederland. Thus it is not in agreement with the facts when Horst appoints the year 1721 to being the record year for the Company's sales of brown pepper. The peak was in 1722 with a sale of 8.63 mill. ponds of pepper, to which corresponds the lowest price in the first three decades of the 18th century, viz. 31 fl. per 100 ponds.

[4] The Company's communication to the Admiralty in 1639 with reference to the convoy duty, that the Bantam sack of pepper "ten respecte van de leccagie ende het indroogen" ought not to be put at more than 48 ponds, does not alter this fact. Kol. Arch. No. 250, 29 September 1639.

[5] The transition was hardly very abrupt.

[6] Kol. Arch. No. 198, 10 March 1718.

Table XIV. *Amounts of Pepper.*

Calendar year	Received from the East	Crop	Offered	Sold	Horst's figures for sales	Horst's deviations from actual sales
	Mill. ponds		Mill. ponds	Mill. ponds	Mill. ponds	Mill. ponds
1715	3.05	1714	2.86	2.84	5.33	+ 2.49
1716	5.13	1715	4.90	4.90	4.02	— 0.88
1717	4.34	1716	4.05	4.07	5.26	+ 1.19
1718	4.86	1717	4.53	4.52	4.08	— 0,44
1719	4.34	1718	4.13	4.12	6.68	+ 2.56
1720	6.42	1719	6.01	6.00	6.13	— 0.13
1721	5.82	1720	5.44	5.43	9.55	+ 4.12
1722	9.05	1721	8.57	8.63	6.13	— 2.50
1723	4.72	1722	4.27	4.29	4.25	— 0.04
1724	7.92	1723	7.31	7.37	7.40	+ 0.03
1725	5.87	1724	5.60	5.56	5.59	— 0.03
1726	8.31	1725	7.97	7.96	8.00	+ 0.04
1727	6.01	1726	5.63	5.62	5.64	+ 0.02
1728	4.74	1728	4.26	4.25	4.28	+ 0.03
1729	3.91	1728	3.61	3.60	3.71	+ 0.11
1730	4.45	1729	4.18	4.20	6.43	+ 2.23
1731	6.87	1730	6.43	6.43	4.20	+ 2.23
1732	3.49	1731	3.25	3.38	3.27	— 0.11

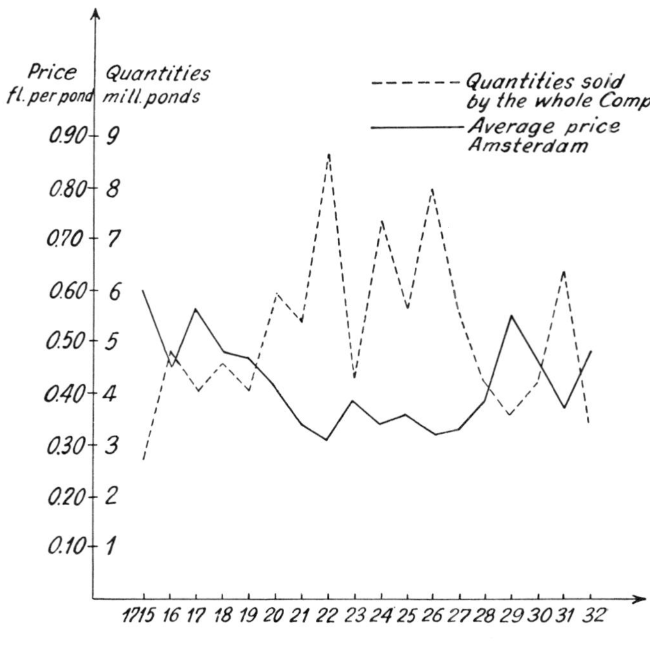

If we pass from the 18th to the 17th century, it is more difficult to determine the quantities as the material is far from being so comprehensive. The difficulties especially concern the quantities offered and those sold, which are only known in the case of the second half of the century. Horst mainly bases his statistics on Pieter van Dam's information in Book I, Chapter 35, of his *Beschryvinge van de Oostindische Compagnie*. Van Dam's main source was the Heeren XVII's resolutions on the sales, and the same basis – but in its compilations more thoroughly than van Dam and Horst – includes a survey in the Collectie van Ghesel No. 199, which runs from 1660 to 1708, and a similar survey in the Collectie Radermacher No. 140, which runs from 1690 to 1748.[7] The Heeren XVII's resolutions concerning the sales, however, are not exhaustive, partly because it was sometimes omitted entering the quantities which were to be offered, partly because the quantities offered were not always sold. As an example we may adduce the year 1679. In October of that year the Heeren XVII decided to sell 6,000 bales of brown pepper, half of it to be offered at the auctions in the same autumn, the second half to be sold at the spring auctions in 1680.[8] It was decided that the pepper should be kept at a minimum price of 35 fl. per 100 ponds. The quantities that could not be sold at that price should be held back. In February 1680 the Heeren XVII found that the Company had only succeeded in selling 840 bales on the terms mentioned, the rest, 2,160 bales, having been held back. The Court of Directors still demanded a minimum price of 35 fl. per 100 ponds and offered the second half on these terms.[9] After the arrival of the returning fleet the minimum limit, however, was given up, and in September 1680 the Heeren XVII decided to sell 6,000 bales of pepper "sonder limitatie van prijs."[10] Horst in his statistics enters 6,000 bales of pepper as being sold in 1679 and another 6,000 bales in 1680, while the Collectie van Ghesel No. 199 reckons with 1,050 bales and 6,000 bales. Even though it may be said in advance that neither Horst's figures nor the figures in the Collectie van Ghesel correspond to the offer – we have no knowledge of any spring sales of pepper in 1679 – it is impossible on the existing basis to estimate the actual sales. The extant surveys of the sales from Kamer Amsterdam, however, may give a hint, it being remembered that roughly half of the commodities were sold at this Head Chamber of the Company. Converted into ponds according to the standard of 1 bale = 400 ponds and compared with the quantities

[7] There are several other "anonymous" lists in the archives of the Company as well as in the various collections comprising *bewindhebber* papers. Those mentioned here are only a few typical examples.

[8] *Pieter van Dam* 1:II, p. 242. [9] *Ibid.* p. 243. [10] *Ibid.* p. 244.

of pepper actually sold at Kamer Amsterdam, we shall get the following figures for offer and sales:

	Total offer Horst	Total offer Collectie van Ghesel	Sale at Kamer Amsterdam
1679......	2,400,000	420,000	445,237
1680......	2,400,000	2,400,000	840,932

The accounts of Amsterdam run from the first of June to the end of May, i.e. that the mentioned sale in 1679 covered the share of the chamber of 840 bales or 336,000 ponds sold in the autumn of 1679 according to the Heeren XVII quoted above, and the corresponding share of the part sold out of the 3,000 bales or 1,200,000 ponds offered in the spring of 1680. Assuming that the share of Amsterdam at both sales was half of the total sales, just under half of the 1.2 mill. ponds of pepper offered in the spring of 1680 were sold. From this and similar analyses we have based our account of the Company's total sale on the sales figures of Amsterdam available from 1649/50 on. On the other hand the statements of quantity from the former half of the 17th century mainly comprise only the shipped quantities in the invoice material. It should be added that whereas pepper in the 18th century as a rule exclusively was sold at the spring sales together with the other spices, it was in the 17th century sold both in the spring and in the autumn, the main stress, however, being laid on the autumn sale. The change is connected with the fact that the returning fleet, as the equipments increased in volume, but also because of the wars between the maritime powers, arrived later and later in the year from Batavia, so that most of the pepper simply did not arrive early enough for the autumn sales. The turning-point must have been in 1698, when the Heeren XVII in the month of March decided to sell 7,300 bales of pepper "vermits de ... late aankomste van de retourvloot in 't jaar te voren."[11] Although this new practice according to the same decision was not supposed to involve consequences for the future, it did so all the same, as, at the same time, out of consideration for the buyers, the Heeren XVII made a statement to the effect that the next sale of pepper would not take place until after 1 March 1699. This displacement of the point of gravity from the autumn to the spring means that we cannot read the price of pepper in the calendar year 1697 from the accounting surveys of Kamer Amsterdam. The accounts 1696/97 (the middle of May) show an average price of 51 fl. per 100 ponds. This average is based on the sale in the

[11] *Ibid.* p. 283.

autumn of 1696, since, to our knowledge, no pepper was sold at the spring sale of 1697. The accounting year 1697/98 (end of May) shows the average of 63 fl. per 100 ponds, but as the sale in the autumn of 1697 was modest,[12] this price must mainly refer to the spring sale of 1698. We have therefore taken the price of the calendar year 1697 – the price at the modest sale at the autumn auction – from the Collectie van Ghesel No. 199. A comparison between the averages in the accounts from Kamer Amsterdam and the Collectie van Ghesel No. 199, the average of which covers all the chambers, gives the following result (Table XV) for this transitional period.

Table XV. *Prices of Pepper, 1696–1699.*

	Collectie van Ghesel Price per 100 ponds	Kamer Amsterdam Price per 100 ponds
Autumn	1696: 48 fl.	1696/97: 51 fl.
Autumn	1697: 53 -	
Spring	1698: 63 -	1697/98: 63 -
Spring	1699: 54 -	1698/99: 54 -

As a consequence of the dominant character of Kamer Amsterdam there is nothing surprising in the fact that its calculated average prices are near the average of all chambers. Altogether brown pepper is a commodity of rather a uniform quality – the Company mixed the pepper from the various areas in order by this means to make the quality the same – for which reason any wide range of prices is out of the question, both at the single auction and from chamber to chamber. The way in which the averages of the chambers might occur, may be illustrated by the example of Table XVI from the spring sales of 1670:[13]

Table XVI. *The Company's Pepper Prices, Spring 1670.*

Amsterdam	18 *groot* per pond	Rotterdam	17 ¼ *groot* per pond
Middelburg	17 ³/₈ - - -	Hoorn	17 ⁵/₈ - - -
Delft	17 ¼ - - -	Enkhuizen	18 - - -

As mentioned above, the account of the price development in Nederland given in the text is mainly built on the averages for the period after 1649/50 calculated on the basis of the Amsterdam material. For the first half of the 17th century we have – similar to W. A. Horst – mainly taken the prices from the Court Minutes of the Heeren XVII. Down to 1639 pepper was sold in whole lots by contract with one or more buyers. The price development from 1642 to 1649 is estimated on the basis of the material published in N.W. Posthumus, *Nederlandsche Prijsgeschiedenis.*

[12] *Ibid.* p. 282. [13] Kol. Arch. No. 255, 17 May 1670, "Vercoop, ende rendement van de peper, mitsgaders salpeter".

APPENDIX F

Table XVII. *Sales of Cloves at Surat, 1641–1698.*

Years	Amounts	Prices	
	ponds	rupees per *man* at 36.25 ponds	"light" st. per pond
1641	60,015	33.50–35.75	22.11–23.67
1642	43,534	39.00–39.50	25.66–26.21
1643	28,919	40.00–46.00	26.48–30.46
1644	—	—	—
1645	98,459	40.00	26.48
1646	54,791	40.00	26.48
1647	25,233	40.00	26.48
1648	76,491	41.50	27.48
1649	60,545	41.00	27.41
1650	62,187	50.00	33.10
1651	92,094	52.00	34.43
1652	62,957	52.00	34.43
1653	117,586	52.00	34.43
1654	119,734	76.00	50.32
1655	30,631	77.25	51.14
1656	45,458	73.00	48.33
1657	53,915	74.25–80.00	51.14–52.97
1658	19,085	110.00	72.83
1659	80,085	90.00–116.00	59.59–76.81
1660	53,650	122.00	80.77
1661	55,708	105.00	69.52
1662	27,575	109.00	72.17
1663	56,369	126.00	80.66
1664	14,138	120.00	79.45
1665	56,550	121.00	80.11
1666	23,245	123.00	81.43
1667	75,146	122.00	94.23
1668	50,424	125.00	96.55
1669	41,216	129.50	99.48
1670	61,417	126.00	97.39
1671	68,032	117.00	90.37
1672	70,791	122.00	94.23
1673	65,506	125.00	96.55

Table XVII (continued).

Years	Amounts	Prices	
	ponds	rupees per *man* at 36.25 ponds	"light" st. per pond
1674	123,531	120.00	92.69
1675	74,875	116.00	89.60
1676	46,051	113.00	87.28
1677	95,464	113.00	87.28
1678	52,055	112.00	86.51
1679	96,715	114.00	88.06
1680	71,376	119.25	92.11
1681	76,815	120.00	92.69
1682	95,703	122.00	94.23
1683	70,252	122.50	101.38
1684	76,635	120.00	99.31
1685	95,383	109.00	90.21
1686	—	—	—
1687	100,000	109.00	90.21
1688	57,335	109.00	90.21
1689	77,549	118.00–125.00	97.65–103.45
1690	194,371	121.00–122.00	100.14–100.96
1691	—	—	—
1692	12,688	117.00–120.00	96.83–99.28
1693	81,329	108.50	89.79
1694	115,252	109.00–110.00	90.83–91.03
1695	92,578	105.50–107.00	89.17–90.93
1696	100,780	110.00–112.25	91.02–93.33
1697	96,321	108.50	89.95
1698	100,956	110.50–114.25	91.45–95.16

SOURCES: The years 1641–1684, Kol. Arch. No. 1297, fo. 810 *et seq.*; the years 1685–1698, *Pieter van Dam* 2:III, p. 131.

APPENDIX G

Dutch and English Purchases of Coffee at Mocha

1713–1727

I. Chronology. While the Dutch material, viz. the Ceylon invoices and the Mocha missives, does not give rise to any appreciable problems as regards chronology, things are slightly different in the case of the English material. In the accounts of the English East India Company the invoices of arriving ships are normally entered comparatively near the date of arrival and with the date of the invoice entered in the text of the account. The invoices are dated either at Mocha or at Bombay, but the Old Style was not carried through consistently in the indication of the year. Where exceptionally no date of the invoice is indicated, the placing of the cargoes in the seasons at Mocha was made only according to the date of arrival. This applies to the "Nathaniel", arrival in August 1716, which was placed under the season of 1715, and the "British Merchant", arrival in August 1717, which was placed under the season of 1716. Furthermore, the "Sommers", arrival in April 1715, with the invoice being dated at Bombay 1 May 1714, was entered under the season of 1713.

II. Rates of Conversion. With one exception, the "British Merchant" mentioned, the English accounts always quote the value of the cargo of coffee in Spanish rials or in rupees. 1 Spanish rial was reckoned as equal to 2 rupees or 5 shillings. These rates of conversion were fixed. The same applies to the Dutch invoices or missives, in which 1 Spanish rial was put equal to 66 "light" *stuivers*. As the purchases in Arabia were made in Spanish rials, the Arabian cost-prices thus are reflected in the Company material either direct or by a re-conversion by way of the fixed rates of exchange.

III. Weights. The English as well as the Dutch material states the cargoes of coffee in bales and lbs. avd. and ponds, respectively. As the bales were of too uncertain a size for a calculation of averages (cf. below) lbs. avd. and ponds have been used as a basis, with 1 lb. avd. = 453.59 grammes and 1 pond = 494.09 grammes, the English average prices then being converted into Dutch ponds. For an easier comparison with observations of prices in diaries, letters, etc., the average prices finally are calculated per bahar at 735 ponds. The bahar was the commonest weight in which the prices of coffee were quoted, but the bahar denoted several weights, so that a few remarks on the weights in Yemen are needed. The Arabian weights caused great difficulties to the Europeans, a fact which for that matter was not changed. As late as the beginning of the 19th century Milburn wrote about weights and measures at Mocha: "The custom-house weights are only stones sewed up in gunnies. The weights are seldom exact, and the smaller they are, the greater the difference, though they annually rectify them by the weights of the Imaum's shroff, whose business is to examine them, under which cover he has an opportunity to add something to the money weights, for which he is well paid by the Banians, who are the principal exporters of silver."[1] This characterization also applies to the period treated here. Three different weights can be distinguished in the notes about prices of coffee entered by the European traders in their diaries, letters, etc. The smallest unit corresponds to 100 ponds and occurs in the communications, mostly through Turkish merchants, about the market prices at Jidda. Next follows the bahar of Mocha, which the Dutch reckoned at 393¾ ponds or 15 frazils at $26^1/_4$ ponds.[2] The English in 1723 put the bahar of Mocha at 444 lbs. avd. or 405 ponds Dutch.[3] The third and greatest unit was the bahar in the centre of the coffee trade, Beit-el-Faki. The Dutch counted this bahar as $1^{13}/_{15}$ of the bahar of Mocha or 28 frazils, i.e. 735 ponds,[4] while the English counted it as

[1] W. Milburn, *Oriental Commerce*, vol. 1 (London, 1825), p. 98.

[2] Handbook of "Measures and Weight" in Kol. Arch. No. 1307, fos. 511–61, later printed at Middelburg 1691. In this book 1 frazil is stated to be 26.50 ponds or 28 ponds. The weight of 26.25 ponds, however, is that occurring most frequently in the letters from Mocha and agrees with the 393.75 ponds per bahar of 15 frazils. See e.g. Kol. Arch. No. 1491, fo. 1811 *et seq.*, letter dated at Mocha 20 May 1699.

[3] C. R. O. London, Egypt & Red Sea, vol. I, 1644–1726, No. 85, 4 August 1723. On the basis of the above-mentioned rate of conversion of lb. avd. and pond into grammes, this gives respectively 201 kilos and 200 kilos to the Mocha bahar. It may be added that Carsten Niebuhr and Milburn put 1 Mocha bahar = 15 frazils = 450 lbs.

[4] Kol. Arch. No. 1491, fos. 1674 ff., letter dated at Mocha 23 August 1698. It should be mentioned that the Beit-el-Faki bahar may also be found to be put at only 27 frazils. Kol. Arch. No. 1810, "Daghregister Mocha", 24 January 1719.

[5] C. R. O. London, Egypt & Red Sea, vol. I, 1644–1726, letter from Mocha dated at 30 June 1720. While the English counted 20 lbs. avd. per frazil, the Dutch, as mentioned above, counted 26.25 ponds per frazil. The weight of the Beit-el-Faki bahar in both cases was exactly the same, viz. 363 kilos.

40 frazils or 807 lbs. avd., i.e. about 20 lbs. avd. per frazil.[5] – The difference in the two nations' statements of the frazil is undoubtedly connected with the way in which the coffee was packed. It was generally packed in large bales, each of which contained a number of smaller bales or frazils.[6] The bales actually were a kind of natural weights indicating how much coffee a camel could carry. A camel's load was reckoned to be 2 bales.[7] It appears from the accounts of the English company that the bales of coffee throughout the period on their arrival in Europe mainly counted 13–14 frazils. 14 frazils or 280 lbs. per bale is the weight occurring most frequently.[8] The average weight of the Dutch bales of coffee fluctuated between 252 ponds and 265 ponds with 261 ponds as the prevalent weight.[9] If we select 280 lbs. avd. and 261 ponds, respectively, as a kind of mean, we get bales of coffee of 127 kilos and 129 kilos, respectively. This good agreement[10] shows that the companies at the packing of the coffee had the varying Arabian camel measure, the bale, made fairly uniform.

IV. Net and Gross Prices. It is important to keep this agreement in mind when we are to decide whether the average prices per lb. and pond contained in the invoice material are gross or net prices. At the calculations of prices the tare must be considered. Fortunately the Dutch material in a few cases gives information of both gross and net purchases of coffee during the season. Thus in 1723, when 3,300 bales of coffee were entered by a gross weight of 913,477 ponds and 863,647 ponds net, i.e. with a tare of $15^1/_{10}$ ponds per bale.[11] Another example is the season of 1727, when 2,050 bales of coffee were entered at a gross weight of 568,395 ponds and 534,057 ponds net, with a tare of 16¾ ponds per bale.[12] It is evident from the letters from Mocha that the average price stated for the purchases during a season was a net price, and a comparison with the invoice material shows that it was always the net weight that was entered there. As the examination of the weights of the English and the Dutch bales gives an almost concordant result it seems probable that also the quantities in the English invoice material in the East India

[6] Milburn, *op. cit.* p. 104 *et seq.*

[7] la Roque, *Voyage de l'Arabie Heureuse* (Amsterdam, 1716), p. 104 *et seq.*

[8] A calculation of the cargoes adduced from the years 1711–1729, comprising a total of 37,584 bales of coffee, gives 274 lbs. avd. per bale.

[9] The Dutch material includes the years 1707–1727, with a total of 42,787 bales of coffee.

[10] It should be kept in mind that the English as well as the Dutch material contains an uncertain factor, some of the bales of coffee undoubtedly being half-bales or small bales, by the Dutch termed *baaltjens*. It has been tried to reduce this source of error by basing the calculation on the greatest material possible.

[11] Kol. Arch. No. 1884, fo. 1035 *et seq.* [12] Kol. Arch. No. 1954, fo. 3666.

Company's accounts are indicated in net weight. In spite of a certain scattering in the material fluctuations as a consequence of tare would be revealed when it appears from the Dutch tare mentioned above that the bale of coffee e.g. in 1727 had an average gross weight of 277 ponds and an average net weight of 261 ponds. The problem how tare and bales were regulated at the sales in Europe is a question apart, which does not concern the purchases.

V. Is the Material Representative? The answer is easiest as regards the Dutch material as it is actually complete. The Dutch averages are based on the total annual purchases. The English material is not complete, which amongst other things is conditioned by the fact that the bookkeepers did not in all cases take the trouble of entering the main quantities of the invoice in the text of the account.[13] The average prices are based upon annual quantities, which during the period range between a minimum of 757 bales or 238,043 lbs. (the season of 1719) and a maximum of 6,184 bales or 1,683,280 lbs. (the season of 1724). Through the 1720's it is a question of at least 2,500 bales or 700,000 lbs. a year of usable records. From the occasional information in the letters from Mocha about the exports of the European nations, it may be seen that the extant material of the English company is complete for the seasons of 1721 and 1725, probably also for 1724. From the season of 1718 2,007 of the 4,600 bales purchased are on record, and from the season of 1723 3,404 of the 7,100 bales purchased. Thus, to sum up, it may be said that in the case of the decisive years we have in the English sources a material which at least corresponds to about half of the presumed total purchases.

[13] Thus the cases in which the size of the cargo is exclusively stated in bales, have been discarded at the collection of the material.

APPENDIX H

Purchases of Tea in Batavia and Canton

I. Chronology. This is of current interest if we are to compare the cost-prices with the selling prices and if we want to compare the prices on the market in Canton with the purchases in Batavia.

The direct trade to China will cause no difficulties. In this case the tea was bought during the autumn and the ships left for Europe about the New Year. Thus the first Dutch ship, the "Coxhorn", arrived at Canton in the beginning of August 1729 and left at the beginning of January 1730. The tea loaded was tea from the season of 1729. It arrived in Europe in the middle of July 1730 and the greater part of it was sold at the auctions in October-November of that year. Consequently the Chinese cost-prices must be compared to the selling prices of the following year, i.e. at the autumn sales.

It is not quite so simple in the case of the purchases in Batavia from the Chinese junks. In order to get as full information as possible about prices in Batavia, we have chosen to calculate the average cost-prices on the basis of the total statements for the buying season which every year were drawn up during the months of August to November.[1] The junks as a rule arrived at Batavia in January, but they might also arrive singly as late as May and June. As the first of them left China in December, the tea entered in the Dutch surveys thus originated from the previous season. Some of this tea succeeded in being dispatched to Europe rather promptly, as the Company placed it onboard the so-called "after-ships", which as a rule left for Europe in February or March. They were also called the "book-ships", because they carried accounts and books from Batavia (now the bulky collections *Overgekomen papieren* and *In-*

[1] "Notitie der ingekogte en verkogte coopmanschappen van en aan vreemde handelaars tot Batavia" beginning in 1717 and collected until 1733 (incl.). These surveys may be found in the series *Overgekomen papieren*, Kol. Arch. Nos. 1780 (fo. 835 *et seq.*), 1793 (fo. 867), 1808 (fo. 1033 bis), 1825 (fo. 1151), 1843 (fo. 1125 *et seq.*), 1860 (fo. 1084), 1879 (fo. 1268 *et seq.*), 1895 (fo. 1534), 1912 (fo. 1179), 1928 (fo. 553 *et seq.*), 1950 (fo. 610), 1974 (fo. 394), 2003 (fo. 1546), 2036 (fo. 3337 *et seq.*), 2064 (fo. 1000 *et seq.*), 2103 (fo. 3765), and 2154 (fo. 2752 *et seq.*).

komende papieren overgekomen in the Hague). As the trade in tea was established, they were named the "tea-ships". The tea of these ships thus might reach the Dutch market for sale in November-December, only a couple of months later than the cargoes of the ships arriving direct from China. It was not, however, possible to place all tea in them, amongst other things because the purchases took some time, which, again, might be due to the fact that some of the junks did not arrive until some time in the spring (from a European point of view). Some of the tea of the buying season therefore was shipped by the first groups of ships of the ordinary homeward-bound fleet in the autumn and arrived in Europe in the summer of the following year, so that e.g. tea from the Canton season of 1720 bought in the buying season at Batavia in 1721 reached Nederland and was sold in the selling season of 1722/23 (the autumn sales of 1722, or perhaps the spring sales of 1723). The question then arises how much was dispatched promptly by the "tea-ships" and how much was shipped in the autumn by the returning fleet. This can be illustrated by a comparison of the buying statistics with the General Commerce Ledgers of Batavia.[2] We shall select the buying statistics dated at Batavia at the end of October 1721. They show a total purchase of Bohea tea from the junks of 170,427 ponds during the buying season of 1721. It appears from the accounts that on 19 February 1721 respectively 46,427 ponds and 46,141 ponds of Bohea tea were dispatched to the chambers of Amsterdam and Zeeland by a tea-ship, and at the balancing of the accounts by the end of August 1721 figures a rest of 92,568 ponds of Bohea tea, which was transferred to the following accounting period and which was the quantity from which the shipments of tea by the fleet returning in the autumn could be ordered. There was constantly a certain stock of tea at Batavia, so that it cannot be expected that the figures mentioned should add up to the 170,427 ponds bought in the buying season. They add up to 185,136 ponds, which would seem to indicate that some of the cargo of the "tea-ship" was Bohea tea from the preceding buying season. We have no possibility of fixing this part exactly. Therefore we shall venture the following rough estimate: the buying season of 1721 at Batavia gave the Company well over 170,000 ponds of Bohea tea at an average cost price of 59 "light" st. per pond. Half of the lot was promptly sent to Europe and therefore the prices must be compared with the prices at the autumn sales in 1721, which were about 43½ st., while the second half must be considered in relation to

[2] Kol. Arch. Nos. 10,813–10,822.

the autumn sales in 1722, when the average price was about 54 st. According to this and similar estimates the valuation of the Company's profit on tea has been made. It applies to the latter half of the period that the greater part of the quantities of the buying season as a rule was shipped to Europe by the returning fleet in the autumn.

II. Weights. There is not much to discuss here, as the unit at the sales of tea was 1 picul = 100 catties. The English put 1 picul at $133^1/_3$ lbs. avd.,[3] which corresponds to a weight in grammes of 60,477 or about 60.5 kilos. The Dutch reckoned 1 picul to be equal to 125 ponds at the purchases from the Chinese junks at Batavia, i.e. equal to 61,761 grammes or about 61.8 kilos, but it is mentioned about 1730 in "Stukken concernerende de directe vaart in China"[4] that 1 picul at Canton often weighed only 120–122 ponds. In Batavia they were not sure, either, that the picul always was equal to 125 ponds; for which reason we have everywhere reckoned 1 picul as equal to 122½ ponds or 60,526 grammes.

III. Rates of Conversion. The *tael* in China was a term common to a weight unit and a monetary unit. The weight tael was $^1/_{16}$ catty, and its subdivisions – *maas, condrin,* and *kas* – were simple decimals of it. The monetary unit of the tael had corresponding decimals; 1 tael Chinese current actually was a term for 1 weight tael of silver at a fineness of 94 *toets*, i.e. 14 *lod* 12 *gren* of fine silver, 100 *toets* corresponding to the 16 *lod* of the silver weight of Cologne. The conversion of European bar silver and silver coins took place on a pure basis of weight, so that the Company won or lost in relation to the Chinese monetary standard.

When the Dutch sent the "Coxhorn" to Canton, it carried silver to a European invoice value of just under 300,000 fl. The greater part was *dukatons*, the fineness of which in China was put at 96 *toets*, while the rest consisted of pillar dollars and mexicans with a fineness of 95 and 94 *toets*, respectively. In the first period during the Dutch purchases at Canton 1 tael was counted to be about 72 st. From a large report from the 1750's concerning the trade to China it appears that the Batavian Government gradually increased the value of the Chinese tael from 72 st. to 80 and from 80 to 88 st. This was done with a view to the export of pepper from Batavia to China, the rate of conversion of 72 st. being a "heavy" rate

[3] See H. B. Morse, *Chronicles of the East India Company Trading to China*, 1635–1834, vol. I (Oxford, 1926). [4] Collectie Radermacher No. 495.

– as compared with the Dutch price of silver – while Batavia as mentioned above, operated with "light" money.[5]

Actually it is at the calculation of the prices at Batavia that the rate of conversion of the tael is of current interest. But the prices at Canton are not difficult to determine, for both the Dutch and the English purchases were quoted in taels in the sources. The statements of purchases from Batavia, on the other hand, were made in rixdollars, while the General Commerce Ledgers of Batavia were kept in fl. In the table in the text we have reckoned 1 rixdollar as equal to 60 st., as it was done at Batavia, and then made a conversion into taels according to the rate of conversion of 1 tael = 72 st. This is a conversion to a kind of "light" taels. If we put the rixdollar at 50 st., we get the cost-prices in "heavy" taels; cf. Table XVIII.

Table XVIII. *Cost-Prices of Bohea Tea at Batavia 1717–1733. Taels per Picul.*

	"Light" taels	"Heavy" taels		"Light" taels	"Heavy" taels
1717......	56.90	47.42	1726......	43.23	36.02
1718......	97.54	81.28	1727......	45.96	38.30
1719......	70.31	58.59	1728......	47.61	39.68
1720......	70.00	58.34	1729......	43.61	36.34
1721......	100.45	83.71	1730......	42.02	35.02
1722......	37.44	31.20	1731......	19.90	16.58
1723......	32.44	27.03	1732......	12.89	10.75
1724......	59.75	49.79	1733......	13.23	11.02
1725......	40.67	33.89			

IV. The Material. The annual statistics of purchases from Batavia were mentioned above and need no further comments. Nor do the General Commerce Ledgers of Batavia, but some remarks on the Canton material are required. The Dutch cost-prices have been calculated from the account-books of the ships.[6] The ships in question are the "Coxhorn" (the season of 1729), the "Duyfje" (the season of 1730), the "Leyduyn" and the "Coxhorn" (the season of 1731), the "Knappenhof" and the "Ypenrode" (the season of 1732), and finally the "Voorduyn" and the "Leyduyn" (the season of 1733); but the "Nieuwvliet" from the season of 1731 and the "Anna Catherina" and the "Nieuwvliet" from the season of 1733 are missing,[7] i.e. that the Dutch material in the case of the three

[5] According to the books of the ships trading direct to China 100 marks of pillar dollars were equalled to 654.5 taels, to which should be added 1 per 94 for greater fineness. At a Dutch price of about 23 fl. per Cologne mark of fine silver for the pillar dollars this corresponds to just under 70 st. per tael. *Dukatons* were put at 86.5 taels per 100 pieces. If the *dukaton* is counted as equal to 63–66 st., the tael will be 72–76 st. Kol. Arch. Nos. 3889–93.

[6] Kol. Arch. Nos. 3889–93, *grootboeken* and *journalen.*

[7] The "Noord Wolfsbergen" from the season of 1734 is also missing.

seasons is complete, while in the case of one season it includes about two thirds and in the case of another season about half of the purchases. The English material originates from the East India Company's accounts,[8] which are considered a more reliable material on which to build than the *Chronicles* edited by H. B. Morse. For the period 1729–1733 the English traffic to Canton was as follows: four ships, viz. the "Houghton", the "Monmouth", the "Enfield", and the "Lynn", made purchases in 1729. They all returned to England and are found in the Company's accounts. In 1730 there were five English ships, viz. the "Princess of Wales", the "Lyell", the "Devonshire", the "Prince Augustus", and the "King George". The first four of them returned to England, while the "King George" went to Madras, for which reason its possible purchases of tea are not found in the accounts used. The English Canton ships of the following year, the "Hartford", the "Macclesfield", the "Caesar", and the "Harrison", were all in the direct trade, while only two of the four company ships of the season 1732, viz. the "Lynn" and the "Richmond", returned to England, the other two going to Bombay and Madras, respectively. The cargo of the Bombay ship is known from Morse's edition. It did not include any tea. Furthermore, there were in 1732 two English "country" ships at Canton. In 1733 there were in all five English ships at Canton, two of them company ships returning to Europe, viz. the "Wyndham" and the "Compton". The English material thus is complete as regards the direct returning company ships. The same applies to the material for the table of the purchases at Canton in 1716–1722.

[8] C.R.O. London, East India Company, The General Commerce Journals.

APPENDIX I

On the Financial Figures

Klerk de Reus in his great work also treated the Company's financial circumstances and although – as said by Mansvelt[1] – compelled more by the wording of the prize subject proposed than by a desire voluntarily to make his way into what the author himself called "moles indigesta", Klerk de Reus in his appendices conscientiously communicated a large material of tables concerning his subject. This material has later been used by practically everybody who has inquired into the Company's finances. Pieter van Dam and van der Oudermeulen also adduced financial material, which probably to a higher degree than that of de Reus was based on primary sources. Klerk de Reus' tables, however, have been those most easily accessible and those ranging over the longest term of years.

It is outside the scope of the present work to discuss the Company's finances as an independent sphere, but it has been necessary to have recourse to the Company's balances[2] in order to re-examine de Reus' figures for equipments, sales, etc. The re-examination revealed some bewildering errors. The first time when in the set of balances used we find a statement of the equipments – the total *equipagien* – is in the balance per 15 April 1648. The *equipagien* are there recorded to be 3,319,187 fl. This figure was by Pieter van Dam placed in his Appendix II (vol. 1:I, p. 364) under the year 1647, but van Dam in the heading of the column expressly states that in the original balances the figure is found under the following year, i.e. 1648. Pieter van Dam also has an abridged balance survey in the text itself (*op. cit.* p. 352), where the figures for the *equipagie* are placed correctly, i.e. as in the originals. De Reus must have followed van Dam's Appendix II and entered all the figures for *equipagie* one year too early. Furthermore, de Reus was of opinion that both the figures of *equipagie*

[1] W. M. F. Mansvelt, *Rechtsvorm en geldelijk beheer bij de Oost-Indische Compagnie* (Amsterdam, 1922).

[2] Kol. Arch. Nos. 10,234–10,242 F.

and the figures for the monthly wages down to 1702 only apply to Kamer Amsterdam, for which reason the Company's total figures must be twice as high. It is true that the monthly wages only apply to Kamer Amsterdam, but the figures of *equipagie* are certainly total, and we have rendered them as such in the table in the text above. That de Reus did not draw up his surveys on the basis of the original material of balances, also appears from the fact that he records no monthly wages for the period after 1702.

In his edition of Pieter van Dam's work Dr. Stapel calls attention to the fact that van Dam's statement of the item of "Uitstaande schulden" down to 1683 inclusive is smaller than that in the actual balances.[3] The "actual balances" probably mean de Reus' tables, and indeed it is true that there is occasionally a great difference, especially down to the beginning of the 1670's. It should, however, be pointed out that van Dam's "Uitstaande schulden" agree with those in the original balances, but that the Company had other outstanding claims than those, both the so-called "desperate" ones mentioned by Dr. Stapel and – as appeared – more hopeful ones, such as outstanding debts owed by the States General for assistance rendered during the wars. From 1654 to 1668 the debts of the States General figure separately in the balances. If these figures are added to the "Uitstaande schulden", the amounts approach nearly to de Reus' figures.

Finally the confrontation of de Reus' tables with the balances have revealed a number of inaccuracies which in our cases are less important, as they to a higher degree concern the estimate of the single years than the development on the long view. Thus the credit amount per 15 May 1691 is 12,683,946 fl. and not 13,859,979 fl., the surplus balance in the same year was 1,176,932 fl. and not 1,436,482 fl., the amount of unpaid bills of exchange per 31 May 1698 was 172,797 fl. and not 127,797 fl., "Uitstaande schulden" per 15 May 1707 was 592,516 fl. and not 392,516 fl., the Company's bonded debt per 15 May 1715 was 4,603,254 fl. + 1,874,909 fl. and not 3,910,858 fl. + 1,874,909 fl., etc.

[3] *Pieter van Dam* 1:I, p. 351, Note 1.

APPENDIX J

Dansk Resumé

Afhandlingens emne er givet med bogens titel: »Nederlandsk-Asiatisk Handel, 1620–1740«. Hovedpersonen er det hollandske ostindiske kompagni i den florissante handelsperiode. Allerførst en kort præsentation. Oprettet i 1602 er kompagniet politisk nøje knyttet til selve det nederlandske statssamfunds genesis; det aftegner sig så at sige som en stat i staten. Anderledes i Asien, hvor det hurtigt fremtræder som en suveræn på ondt og godt, en stat udenfor staten med egen jurisdiktion, eget flag, egne krige og traktater. Forretningsmæssig set var »De Vereenigde Nederlandtsche Geoctroyeerde Oost-Indische Compagnie« med sine mere end 8,000 mand årlig sejlende på havene, sine mandskaber og anlæg i det omfattende net af stationer over hele det maritime Asien fra Japan i øst, via Tonkin, Siam, Malacca, Indonesien, Indien, Ceylon, Persien, til Arabien og Kap-kolonien i vest, med sine skibsværfter, magasiner og kontorer i Amsterdam, Middelburg, Rotterdam, Delft, Hoorn og Enkhuizen formentlig den tids største enkeltforetagende. Igennem mange år anså man Europa over selskabets aktier for at være guldrandede papirer. Kulturelt stod det som en formidler af Asiens kunst og smag. Dets auktioner var internationale begivenheder, kundekredsen strakte sig – direkte eller indirekte – fra hoffet i Versailles til jævne hollandske borgerhjem. Også socialt satte det sine spor. I byerne var dets agenter virksomme med at presse mandskab til den hårde tørn om bord på skibene og Jan Compagnie's skæbne var ofte ubarmhjertig. Det er en broget, sammenløben skare, der kommer en i møde fra kompagniets mønsterruller, man træffer også danske bønderkarle iblandt. Der er endnu flere facetter af kompagniets virke: missionen, arbejdet med de fremmede sprog, naturvidenskaben, rejseskildringerne . . .

I introduktionen redegøres for forfatterens tese. Undersøgelsen, der i vid udstrækning bygger på utrykt materiale – emnet har ikke tidligere været gjort til genstand for et samlet studium – er foretaget ud fra den generelle betragtning, at man ved bedømmelsen af kompagniet qua handelsforetagende må se det som en helhed og fra et centralt punkt. Selskabets egenartede organisatoriske struktur er i denne sammenhæng underordnet, interessen gælder først og fremmest den levende, arbejdende virksomhed. Som udgangspunkt er valgt faktoriet Nederland, der var sædet for kompagniets ledelse, de såkaldte Sytten Herrer (»Heeren XVII«). Når selskabets europæiske afdeling er blevet anskuet som eet stort faktori på linie med de asiatiske er dette afledet af helhedsbetragtningen. Kompagniet er en organisme, hvis europæiske og asiatiske organer ikke lader sig skille ad. Samspillet mellem de to store områder udgør en af fremstillingens ledetråde. Det økonomiske – respektive driftsøkonomiske – aspekt åbner for nye perspektiver i diskussionen om kompagniets fallit i slutningen af det 18. århundrede og berører i endnu videre sammenhæng det aktuelle verdenshistoriske spørgsmål om europæernes ekspansion i Asien. Den gængse opfattelse af kompagniets monopolagtige karakter anfægtes, idet det blandt andet hævdes, at kompagniets aktivitet i Europa må ses i relation til de konkurrerende nordvesteuropæiske selskaber, først og fremmest det engelske. Afhandlingen rummer i konsekvens heraf et større komparativt materiale vedrørende de andre ostindiske kompagnier, især det engelske, men også aktstykkerne fra det belgiske Ostende-kompagni, fra det franske, det svenske og det danske kompagni er der lejlighedsvis øst af. Den anvendte metode er selektiv-kritisk. Det kritiske og delvis det statistiske apparat er af fremstillingsmæssige grunde anbragt som appendiks.

Kapitlet om faktoriet Nederland indledes med en række analyser af kompagniets import til Europa i det 17. og 18. århundrede. Analyserne afkræfter myten om den ostindiske handels stabile og »historieløse« karakter. Den viser, at der især er grund til at hæfte opmærksomheden ved de sidste decennier af det 17. århundrede og de første decennier af det 18. århundrede, hvor forskydningerne i handelen er slående. Skiftet i interessen for de enkelte varegrupper og væksten i handelens omfang involverer ændrede indkøbs- og salgsmæssige kår, som senere i afhandlingens kapitler om de enkelte handelsvarer følges mere detailleret. Førend dette kan ske må rammerne om faktoriet Nederlands virksomhed trækkes op. De vigtigste størrelser blandt dets indtægter og udgifter beskrives. Problemerne i forbindelse med salget diskuteres, ligeså udredningerne. Ledelsens forhold til kompagniets kunder belyses. Man kan i denne forbindelse nævne, at ikke mindst kompagnimaterialets specielle oplysninger om kontrakter og salg i det 17. århundredes første halvdel giver interessante og konkrete bidrag til den amsterdamske kapitalismes historie.

Det samme gælder i øvrigt også hele komplekset af kilder omkring kompagniets regnskabsvæsen.

I kapitlet om ædelmetallerne behandles kompagniets vigtigste eksport»vare« til Østen, medens kapitlerne om peber, krydderier, silke, bomulds- og silkestoffer, sukker, japansk kobber, kaffe og the rummer et udvalg af importen til Nederland dækkende mere end 85% af denne. Disse kapitler af varehandelens historie er skrevet ud fra aspektet: udbud/efterspørgsel og med vekselvirkningen mellem det asiatiske og det europæiske marked som et gennemgående tema. Et fremtrædende træk er også konkurrencen mellem de europæiske kompagnier såvel i Europa som i Asien.

De fremdragne resultater sættes til slut i kapitlet om gevinst og tab i relation til kompagniets finanser og til årsagsforklaringerne om kompagniets undergang. Finansielt set er de meget aktive årtier omkring 1700 præget af store udbytter, som på et tidligt tidspunkt har skaffet Heeren XVII ry for letsindighed og dermed for adskillige forklaret en væsentlig del af tilbagegangen. Som allerede påvist af van der Oudermeulen i 1770'erne og senere af dr. Mansvelt i en afhandling fra 1922 turde udbytterne dog ikke være uforsvarlige, når de sammenholdes med kompagniets reserver i Nederland og Asien. Det er derfor næppe sandsynligt, at man i udbyttepolitikken kan finde hovedårsagen til kompagniets deroute. Dr. Mansvelt opstillede i stedet for en på en analyse af kompagniets regnskabsvæsen baseret »administrativ« forklaring. Kompagniets ledelse begik den fejl, at den anskuede hele handelsvirksomheden fra et nederlandsk import-stade. Herved mistede man overblikket og kontrollen. Man sammenlignede indtægterne og udgifterne i Nederland uden at tænke på, at disse størrelser havde relation til vidt forskellige spørgsmål. Det var en gevinstberegning af allerprimitiveste art, ganske utilstrækkelig for et selskab af det hollandske kompagnis dimensioner. Ingen kostprisberegning, ingen deling af udgifterne i kapitaludgifter og omkostninger. Man undlod også at påføre de enkelte varer specifike omkostninger som f. eks. fragt, rente og assurance. Dette til trods for at man selv betalte rente af lånte penge, og til trods for at de udsendte kapitalers omløbstid var yderst forskellig på de forskellige kontorer. At man ikke beregnede fragt, hang sammen med, at man selv byggede og ejede skibene, modsat det engelske kompagni, der overvejende sejlede med hyrede skibe, hvilket bl. a. ansporede til at forkorte sejltiden. Sådan set afskrev det hollandske selskab direkte sine skibe, men det skete ikke ud fra soliditetsgrunde. Det var simpelthen et udslag af manglende administrativ eller bogholderimæssig formåen. Kompagniet blev i årevis ved med at handle på pladser og med varer, som længe havde givet tab, og omvendt forsømte det at tage handelen i nye varer på nye pladser op. Direktionen i Nederland foretrak at betale det voksende indiske underskud, d.v.s. en del af de indiske driftsomkostninger, i stedet for at holde den indiske administration adskilt fra Nederland og f. eks. tillade Batavia at indregne en gevinst på 20 à 30 % på de til Europa afsendte varer. De store gevinster i Nederland i begyndelsen af det 18. århundrede tilslørede i virkeligheden billedet. Først da provenuet af returerne i anden halvdel af det 18. århundrede tog af – fra 1700 til o. 1780 kan man konstatere, at udredningsomkostningerne steg med 100 %, medens provenuet af salget af returerne kun steg med 50 % – blev skavanken åbenlys. Slige skævheder kunne selv den største reserve i det lange løb ikke bøde på.

Det er rigtigt, at det hollandske kompagni blev hængende i en regnskabsform, som allerede i løbet af det 17. århundrede viste sig utilfredsstillende, og som i det 18. århundrede var forældet i sammenligning med de mønsterværdige regnskaber, som f. eks. dets lille danske konkurrent førte. På den anden side opstillede det ved forskellige lejligheder beregninger og kalkulationer efter mere hensigtsmæssige principper; endvidere foretog man regelmæssigt udenfor regnskaberne bruttogevinstudregninger, hvorpå dispositionerne baseredes. Ligeledes var man på det rene med overskud og tab fra sæson til sæson på hver enkelt plads i Asien. Det er derfor næppe urimeligt at antage, at Heeren XVII ret hurtigt registrerede frem- og tilbagegange på de forskellige områder. Gennemgangen af deres ønsker om returvarer vidner om et vågent blik for ændringerne i handelen. Her var ikke tale om, at man frivilligt fortsatte handel i ikke-kurante varer. Ikke mindst den florissante periode i årtierne omkring 1700 afgiver adskillige beviser på Heeren XVII's agtpågivenhed og ustandselige kritik af returerne, baseret på gevinstprocenterne, konkurrenternes udbytter, omkostningerne og de asiatiske kontorers tilstand. Man var klar over svaghederne. Det skortede ej heller på reformforslag. De store faste omkostninger til forter, militær, patruljeskibe m. v. føltes hæmmende. Man kritiserede hele apparatets placering i Batavia, forskellige kontorer blev med mellemrum dømt til lukning, men kun få af dem virkelig ophævet, sejltiden var genstand for den største interesse, og kommissioner arbejdede med forslag til dens nedsættelse. Så var der embedsmisbrug i forbindelse med privat handel. En gang afsløret sprang disse misbrug særlig i øjnene, og korruptionen har siden stået som den måske tiest fremhævede årsag til kompagniets undergang, indtil dr. Mansvelt med sin inciterende analyse føjede de administrative skavanker til. Korruptionen er ubestridelig. Den er nøje forbundet med den private handels udvikling i årene omkring 1700, ikke mindst den engelske »interloping«, som er et af de vigtigste nye træk i den asiatiske handel.

Men der er andre, handelsmæssige årsager, som man ikke tidligere har gjort sig klart, simpelthen fordi man ikke har studeret det hollandske kompagni som det, det først og fremmest var: et handelsselskab. Trods sit i løbet af det 17. århundrede udbyggede monopol på krydderierne kan man ikke betegne kompagniet som et i økonomisk henseende monopoliseret foretagende. Det havde ganske vist et nationalt monopol på den asiatiske handel, men betragter man det nordvesteuropæiske marked som en helhed – og dette kunne en nederlænder med god grund gøre på grund af sit lands frihandelsvenlige politik – var der flere selskaber om at bestemme udbuddet. Sammenlignende prisstudier viser, at der var en tydelig sammenhæng mellem de nationale markeder for ostindiske produkter, hvilket ikke kan overraske i betragtning af re-eksportens store rolle. I for høj grad har man hæftet sig ved oktrojernes bestemmelse om enehandel øst for Kap det Gode Håb og ved de store bruttofortjenester på krydderierne, hvorved man har overset, at også på markeder, hvor der kun var få konkurrenter, kunne priskonkurrence og anden form for konkurrence bryde løs, ligesom man har glemt, at krydderierne ikke dominerede importen fra Asien, og at bruttofortjenester var eet, nettofortjenester noget andet. En betydelig del af det ostindiske kompagnis import omfattede varer, som på det europæiske marked måtte konkurrere med beslægtede produkter fra Europa eller fra andre oversøiske lande. Dette gjaldt f. eks. silke og bomuld, tekstilerne, salpeter, indigo, sukker, kobber og kaffe. I adskillige tilfælde var det disse beslægtede produkters priser, som bestemte, hvorvidt en import fra Asien var lønnende eller ej. Det nordvesteuropæiske marked for asiatiske varer var langt fra stabilt. Bedst aflæses ændringerne i den europæiske efterspørgsel i Heeren XVII's ønsker og i salgsanalyserne. Det er tydeligt, at den 40-årige periode omkring 1700 vender op og ned på meget. De ostindiske tekstiler, samt kaffen og theen omkalfatrer de vante former. Nye områder dukker op og skaber ændrede vilkår for indkøbene. Hertil føjer sig en udtalt konkurrence fra de nye eller genoplivede selskaber i Ostende, Göteborg og København. Henvisningen til »vore konkurrenter« bliver en stående vending i Heeren XVII's missiver til Batavia.

Vender man sig mod de asiatiske markeder, er konkurrencemomentet endnu mere tydeligt. Her gælder konkurrencen ikke blot de europæiske selskaber, men først og fremmest de asiatiske handlende. Der er lang vej tilbage, førend vi har tilstrækkelig klarhed over den asiatiske handels og økonomis karakter i disse mange år. Man tør håbe på, at ikke mindst de asiatiske historikere vil fortsætte de undersøgelser, som allerede er begyndt, og således bidrage til at klargøre os de asiatiske forudsætninger. Fra et kompagnihistorisk synspunkt vil ikke mindst en redegørelse for forholdene i Bengalen i årene efter 1680 være af stor betydning. Kompagniets asiatiske handel var ikke blot en aktivitet i bestemte områder, men også en trafik fra land til land, en international affære, som i Asien strakte sig over distancer af næsten samme størrelsesorden som vejen over havet fra Nordsøen til Ceylon og Batavia. Ved behandlingen af et enkelt områdes forhold vil derfor de handelsmæssige indslag fra andre asiatiske lande i mange tilfælde være ligeså afgørende som de europæiske indslag. Af de særlig tydelige ændringer i det hollandske kompagnis asiatiske handel, som er konstateret i den foreliggende afhandling, kan der være grund til her at fremdrage de kinesiske og især de japanske ædelmetallers vekslende strøm mod vest. Den kinesiske strøm af guld til Koromandelkysten løber frem til Koxinga's erobring af Taiwan. Den japanske sølvstrøm flyder frem til 1668, hvor den afløses af en guldstrøm, der dog ret hurtigt tager kendelig af og dirigeres over i en kobberstrøm. Også fra det persiske område er kompagniet i stand til at trække ædle metaller, og dette træk bliver stærkere, alt som eksporten af silke mister terræn, og forsyningerne af guld og sølv fra Kina og Japan vanskeliggøres. De persiske leverancer formår dog ikke at opveje tabet af leverancerne fra Kina og Japan, hvorfor man i slutningen af det 17. århundrede oplever et stort behov for europæiske forsendelser af sølv og guld. Dette er så meget mere afgørende som ændringerne i den europæiske efterspørgsel nogenlunde samtidig stimulerer behovet for ædle metaller ved at forlange varer fra sølv- og guldfortærende områder. Et andet iøjnefaldende træk er Koromandelkystens op- og undergang – for at bruge Daniel Havart's ord. Med de indiske borgerkriges ødelæggelse af kysten mistede kompagniet sit tag i et stort område, som det fra det 17. århundredes begyndelse af havde helliget den største opmærksomhed. Kompagniets »venstre arm« visnede, og selvom nederlænderne tog initiativet til en handel i Bengalen, lykkedes det dog ikke her at sikre sig et forspring fremfor den nærmeste europæiske konkurrent, englænderne, af lignende karakter som på kysten. Hertil kom, at hollænderne indirekte gennem deres initiativ på andre felter var med til at skabe nye forbindelser i den inter-asiatiske handel, først og fremmest den direkte fart mellem Bengalen og Kina, med tiden aksen i den engelske handelsmekanisme. Det hollandske eksportfremstød i Suratområdet og Persien for den nye javanske sukkerkulturs produkter medvirkede til at overskære den gamle forbindelse mellem Bengalen og

Surat baseret på bengalsk sukker, råsilke og suratsk bomuld. Også tilførslerne til Nordvestindien af kinesisk silke og sukker virkede i samme retning. I løbet af det 18. århundrede dirigeredes den bengalske handel mod øst, mod Kina, og en indirekte såkaldt »country trade« udvikledes mellem Bombay og Kina baseret på bomuld. De engelske »country traders« var ledende i disse bevægelser. De nye veje havde den stigende europæiske efterspørgsel efter the som sin baggrund, hvortil kom det som en følge heraf opståede voldsomme pres på de europæiske resourcer af sølv med deraf følgende bestræbelser for i Indien at finde en anvendelig erstatningsvare for sølv til Kina. Erstatningsvaren fandtes. Den hed opium, og med den overførtes også betydelige dele af den tidligere fra Koromandelkysten på Indonesien drevne private handel til de engelske besiddelser. Kina-handelen, der omtrent samtidig åbnedes direkte fra Europa, bragte det nederlandske selskab i et dilemma. I begyndelsen undervurderede man utvivlsomt denne handel. Senere da dens succes stod alle klart, vaklede man mellem direkte fart fra Nederland og indirekte kontakt via Batavia. Den sidste mulighed sparede kontanter, idet den kinesiske the kunne betales med peber, krydderier og andre varer. Den repræsenterede en udbygning af den gamle asiatiske rute mellem Kanton og Bantam, som havde været så iøjnefaldende for hollandske iagttagere ved deres ankomst til Indonesien omkring 1600, endnu førend kompagniet fik hovedparten af den indonesiske pebereksport omlagt fra Kina til Europa, og førend den kinesiske handel i de indiske farvande trak sig tilbage som følge af dynastiernes kampe i Kina. Som talsmænd for denne rute stod Batavia-regeringen, hvis position var styrket ved den heldige overførsel af kaffekulturen til Java. Det var en gentagelse af successen med sukkeret og betød, at et nyt planter-moment dukkede op ved siden af handelshensynene. Heller ikke projekter om overførelse til Java af en thekultur savnes. Den direkte forbindelse anbefaledes derimod af Nederland. Motiveringen herfor var konkurrencen, som nødvendiggjorde opkøb på stedet og hurtig transport til Europa. Det engelske handelsfremstød i Kina banede vejen for andre europæiske nationer og gjorde den hollandske kontrol med sejladsen omkring krydderiøerne desto mere påkrævet. Men dette betød vedvarende store omkostninger til opretholdelsen af monopolet på varer, som kun gav kompagniet $^1/_4$ af indtægterne ved det mest gevinstgivende faktori, Nederland. Frygten for, at englænderne (og andre) ville trænge videre frem, førte til en hårdnakket håndhævelse af handelen med Japan, skønt denne efterhånden gav et beskedent udbytte. Det lykkedes at holde englænderne ude, men alligevel blev Japan-kobberet, som spillede så stor en rolle i kompagniets asiatiske handel, i det 18. århundredes løb truet, da briterne begyndte at importere engelsk kobber til Indien.

Konkurrence og omskiftelighed snarere end monopol og konstans var det, som karakteriserede det hollandske ostindiske kompagni som handelsforetagende. Set fra et europæisk synspunkt er der netop i det handelsmæssige adskilligt, som indicerer, at perioden o. 1680 – o. 1740 bød på en række forskydninger, som forringede kompagniets indtil da så fordelagtige position i Asien. Disse afgørende år ændrede den europæisk-asiatiske samhandels karakter. Handelens volumen tog et stort opsving med basis i de efterspurgte bomulds- og silketøjer. Et par nye artikler, kaffe og the, udviklede sig til store varer, hvis fordelagtighed snart kom til at bestå i større omsætning til mindre fortjenester og i hurtig transport. Forskydningerne i det europæiske markeds behov, mode og smag, ændrede asiatiske forudsætninger og et stigende antal konkurrerende selskaber belastede kompagniformen og undergravede den. Man har tidligere anset kompagniet for i handelsmæssig henseende at være noget nær et stedsegrønt pagodetræ, hvis guldfrugter direktionen havde monopol på med passende mellemrum at ryste ned i sin turban og kun til slut hindredes deri af svigagtige, dovne og uduelige embedsmænd. Det hollandske selskab bør snarere betegnes som et hårdt arbejdende foretagende i til tider skarp konkurrence med de andre europæiske kompagnier og med de asiatiske købmænd. En gang engageret i den asiatiske handel måtte det blive ved, ekspandere, finde nye markeder for køb og salg. Aldrig i ro. Kompagniets historie rummer mange træk: krige, undertrykkelse, handel, mission, administration, plantagedrift, videnskab, etc. Det er altsammen sider af nederlændernes forhold til de asiatiske folkeslag. For det 17. og 18. århundrede er ikke mindst de handelsmæssige vilkår afgørende for forståelsen af det europæiske initiativ.

APPENDIX K

Main Manuscript Sources

ALGEMEEN RIJKSARCHIEF, 's-Gravenhage.

Koloniale Archieven Oost-Indië en de Kaap: Archieven van de Vereenigde Oost-Indische Compagnie, 1602–1796. Abbr. "Kol. Arch."

Resolutien Heeren XVII.
Verbalen van de Haagsche Besognes en andere commissiës.
Extract ordinaire en secret resolutien van de Staten General etc.
Brieven Heeren XVII aan Indië.
Copie-Resolutien van Gouverneur-Generaal en Raden van Indië.
Overgekomen papieren.
Inkomende papieren overgekomen.
Overgekomen brieven en papieren uit China.
Bijeenbrenging van verkoopingen.
Generale staten van verhandelde goederen, uitstaande schulden en onverkochte goederen van de verschillende kamers.
Negotie grootboeken en journalen, Kamer Amsterdam.
Negotie grootboeken en journalen, Batavia.

Further: Manuscripts in connexion with the Kol. Arch. such as the Aanwinsten, the Collectie van Ghesel, the Collectie Radermacher, the Collectie van Vredenburch, etc.

ARCHIVES DÉPARTEMENTALES DE LA LOIRE-INFÉRIEURE, Nantes.

Chambre de Commerce de Nantes: Compagnie des Indes.

ARCHIVES MUNICIPALES DE NANTES, Nantes.

Procès-verbaux de vente de cargaisons de la Compagnie des Indes.

ARCHIVES NATIONALES, Paris.

Archives de la Marine, Serie B^1 - Decisions.

COMMONWEALTH RELATIONS OFFICE, London.

East India Company records. Abbr. "C. R. O. London, E. I. C."

Court Minutes.
Committee of Correspondance: Memoranda.
Miscellaneous Letters Received.
Letter Books.
Home Miscellaneous.
General Ledgers and Journals.

GEMEENTE-ARCHIEF AMSTERDAM, Amsterdam.

Notarial Archief.
Archief Brants.
Verkoopingen van koopmanschappen.
The Library: collection of printed price lists.

RIGSARKIVET, København.

Rentekammeret, reviderede regnskaber: Amsterdamske faktorregnskaber.

RIKSARKIVET, Stockholm.

Handel och Sjöfart, Handelskompagnier: Ostindiska Kompagniet.

STADSARCHIEF ANTWERPEN, Antwerpen.

Archief der Generale Indische Compagnie (Compagnie d'Ostende) 1723–1777. Abbr. "Stadsarchief Antwerpen, G. I. C."
Venditieboeken.
Insolvente Boedelskamer No. LXII (de Pret).

APPENDIX L

Works Quoted

AECKERLE, H. W.: "Amsterdamer Börsenpreislisten 1624–1626", *Economisch-Historisch Jaarboek*, vol. XIII, 's-Gravenhage 1927.

BADDELEY, JOHN F.: *Russia, Mongolia, China*, London 1919.

BARBOUR, VIOLET: *Capitalism in Amsterdam in the Seventeenth Century*, Baltimore 1950 (The Johns Hopkins University Studies in Historical and Political Science, Series LXVII, No. 1).

Begin ende voortgang van de vereenigde Nederlandtsche geoctroyeerde Oost-Indische Compagnie, 1. deel, Amsterdam 1646.

BHATTACHARYA, SUKUMAR: *The East India Company and the Economy of Bengal*, From 1704 to 1740, London 1954.

Boletim da Filmoteca Ultramarina Portuguesa, No. 2, Lisboa 1955.

BRUGMANS, I. J.: "De Oost-Indische Compagnie en de weelvaart in de Republiek", *Tijdschrift voor Geschiedenis*, 61. jaargang (1948).

Calendar of the Court Minutes etc. of the East India Company 1635–79, A, ed. by Ethel Bruce Sainsbury. With an introduction and notes by William Foster a.o. I–XI, Oxford 1907–38.

CARON, FRANÇOIS, & SCHOUTEN, JOOST: *A True Description of the Mighty Kingdoms of Japan and Siam*, ed. C. R. Boxer, London 1935.

CARY, J.: *A Discourse Concerning the East India Trade*, London 1699.

VAN DER CHIJS, J. A.: *Realia, Register op de generale resolutiën van het Kasteel Batavia*, 1632–1805, vols. I–III, 's Hage-Batavia, 1882–1885.

CODRINGTON, H. W.: *Ceylon Coins and Currency*, Colombo 1924 (Memoirs of the Colombo Museum, Series A, No. 3).

COLENBRANDER, H. T., & COOLHAAS, W. PH.: *Jan Pietersz. Coen, Bescheiden omtrent zijn bedrijf in Indië*, deel 1–7, 's-Gravenhage 1919–1953.

Dagbog fra en Ostindiefart 1672–75 af J. P. Cortemünde, ed. Henning Henningsen, Handels- og Søfartsmuseet på Kronborg 1953 (Søhistoriske Skrifter, vol. V).

Dagh-Register gehouden int Casteel Batavia vant passerende daer ter plaetse als over geheel Nederlands-India, ed. J. E. Heeres o.a., 's-Gravenhage-Batavia 1896–1931.

VAN DAM, PIETER: *Beschryvinge van de Oostindische Compagnie*, 1. boek deel I–II, 2. boek deel I–III, 3. boek, Uitgegeven door Dr. F. W. Stapel, 's-Gravenhage 1927–43 (Rijks Geschiedkundige Publicatiën, Nos. 63, 68, 74, 76, 83, and 87).

DASÍ, TOMÁS: *Estudio De Los Reales De A Ocho*, tome 2, Valencia 1950.

VAN DILLEN, J. G.: "Amsterdam als wereldmarkt der edele metalen in de 17de en 18de eeuw", *De Economist*, jaargang 1923, 's-Gravenhage.

VAN DILLEN, J. G.: "Amsterdamsche notarieele acten betreffende den koperhandel en de uitoefening van mijnbouw en metaalindustrie in Zweden", *Bijdragen en Mededeelingen van het Historisch Genootschap* (Utrecht), deel 58, 1937.

Documentos Remettidos da India, vol. I, Lisboa 1853.

DOWELL, STEPHEN: *A History of Taxation and Taxes in England*, vol. IV: Taxes on Articles of Consumption, London 1888.

DUNLOP, H.: *Bronnen to de geschiedenis der Oostindische Compagnie in Perzië*, 1. deel, 1611–1638, 's-Gravenhage 1930 (Rijks Geschiedkundige Publicatiën, No. 72).

Early English Tracts on Commerce ed. by J. R. McCulloch, Cambridge 1952 (Reprinted for The Economic History Society).

ELIAS, J. E.: *De vroedschap van Amsterdam*, Haarlem 1903–1905.

Encyclopaedie van Nederlandsch-Indië, 2. ed., 's-Gravenhage-Leiden 1917–1939.

English Factories in India 1630–1633, The, by William Foster, Oxford 1910.

FRIIS, ASTRID: "Forbindelsen mellem det europæiske og asiatiske Kobbermarked", *Scandia* XII: 1, Stockholm-København-Oslo 1939.

FURBER, HOLDEN: *John Company at Work*, A Study of European Expansion in India in the Late Eighteenth Century, Cambridge Mass. 1948 (Harvard Historical Studies, vol. LV).

VAN GELDER, H. E.: "Gegevens omtrent den porceleinhandel der O.-I. Compagnie", *Economisch-Historisch Jaarboek*, vol. X, 's-Gravenhage 1924.

GLAMANN, KRISTOF: "En ostindisk Rejse eller Thomas Thomson på Galejen", *Sjöhistorisk Årsbok* 1953–54, Stockholm 1954.

GLAMANN, KRISTOF: "Hollandske Indberetninger om Altona-projektet 1728–29", *Danske Magazin*, 7 rk. bd. V, København 1953.

GLAMANN, KRISTOF: "Studie i Asiatisk Kompagnis økonomiske Historie, 1732–1772", *Historisk Tidsskrift*, 11 rk. bd. II, København 1949.

GLAMANN, KRISTOF: "The Dutch East India Company's Trade in Japanese Copper, 1645–1736", *The Scandinavian Economic History Review*, vol. I, Copenhagen 1953.

GONGGRIJP, G.: *Schets eener economische geschiedenis van Nederlandsch-Indië*, Haarlem 1928.

GREENBERG, MICHAEL: *British Trade and the Opening of China*, 1800–42, Cambridge 1951.

GROENEVELDT, W. P.: "De Nederlanders in China", *Bijdragen tot de Taal-, Land- en Volkenkunde van Nederlandsch-Indië*, 6. volgreeks 4. deel, 's-Gravenhage 1898.

DE HAAN, F.: *Priangan, De Preanger-regentschappen onder het Nederl. Bestuur tot 1811*, 4 vols, Batavia 1910–12.

HEATON, HERBERT: *Economic History of Europe*, New York 1948.

DU HALGOUET, H.: "Pages coloniales – Relations maritimes de la Bretagne et de la Chine au XVIIIe siècle", *Memoire de la Société d'Histoire et d'Archéologie de Bretagne*, tome XV: 2, 1934.

HALL, D. G. E.: *A History of South East Asia*, London 1955.

HAMILTON, EARL J.: *War and Prices in Spain 1651–1800*, Cambridge Mass. 1947 (Harvard Economic Studies, vol. LXXXI).

HAMILTON, H.: *The English Brass and Copper Industries to 1800*, London 1926.

HAUSER, HENRI: *Recherches et Documents sur l'Histoire des Prix en France de 1500 à 1800*, Paris 1936.

HAVART, D.: *Op- en ondergang van Coromandel*, Amsterdam 1693.

HECKSCHER, ELI F.: "Den europäiske kopparmarknaden under 1600-talet", *Scandia* XI: 2, Stockholm-København-Oslo 1938.

DE HEER, CORNELIS: *Bijdrage tot de financieele geschiedenis der O.-I. Compagnie*, 's-Gravenhage 1929.

HEERINGA, K.: *Bronnen tot de geschiedenis van den Levantschen handel*, 2. deel, 's-Gravenhage 1917 (Rijks Geschiedkundige Publicatien, No. 34).

Hobson-Jobson, A Glossary of Colloquial Anglo-Indian Words and Phrases, and of kindred terms, etymological, historical, geographical and discursive, by H. Yule & A. C. Burnell (W. Crooke), London 1903.

VAN HOGENDORP, DIRK: *Stukken rakende den tegenwoordigen toestand der Bataafsche bezittingen in Oost-Indië*, Den Haag-Delft 1801 (in which the report of B. van der Oudermeulen).

Hollantse Mercurius.

HOLLINGWORTH: "List of the principal tea districts in China, etc.", *Journal of the North China Branch of the Royal Asiatic Society*, New Series, no. X.

HORST, W. A.: "De peperhandel van de vereenigde Oostindische Compagnie", *Bijdragen voor Vaderlandsche Geschiedenis en Oudheidkunde*, 8:III, 's-Gravenhage 1941.

DE HULLU, J.: "De instelling van de commissie voor den handel der Oost-Indische Compagnie op China in 1756", *Bijdragen tot de Taal-, Land- en Volkenkunde van Nederlandsch-Indië*, deel 79, 's-Gravenhage 1923.

DE HULLU, J.: "De matrozen en soldaten op de schepen der Oost-Indische Compagnie", *Bijdragen voor de Taal-, Land- en Volkenkunde van Nederlandsch-Indië*, deel 69, 's-Gravenhage 1914.

DE HULLU, J.: "Over den Chinaschen handel der Oost-Indische Compagnie in de eerste dertig jaar van de 18e eeuw", *Bijdragen tot de Taal-, Land- en Volkenkunde van Nederlandsch-Indië*, deel 73, 's-Gravenhage 1917.

VAN IMHOFF, G. W.: "Consideratiën over den Jappanschen handel", *Tijdschrift van Nederlandsch-Indië* 1853.

VAN IMHOFF, G. W.: "Consideratiën over den tegenwoordigen staat van de Nederlandsche Oost Indische Maatschappij", ed. J. E. Heeres, *Bijdragen tot de Taal-, Land- en Volkenkunde van Nederlandsch-Indië*, deel 66, 's-Gravenhage 1912.

DE JONGE, J. K. J., a. o.: *De opkomst van het Nederlandsch gezag in Oost-Indië*, vols. 1–17, 's-Gravenhage-Amsterdam 1862–1909.

JUSTICE, ALEXANDER: "A Treatise of the Weights of Holland and of their Conformity with those of other Countries", *General Treatise of Monies and Exchanges*, London 1707.

KHAN, S. A.: *The East India Trade in the 17th Century*, Oxford 1923.

KRISHNA, BAL: *Commercial Relations between India and England* (1601 to 1757), London 1924 (Studies in Economics and Political Science, No. 67).

KUIPER, J. FEENSTRA: *Japan en de buitenwereld in de achttiende eeuw*, 's-Gravenhage 1921 (Werken uitgegeven door de vereeniging Het Nederlandsch Economisch-Historisch Archief, No. 3).

DE LANNOY, CHARLES, & VAN DER LINDEN, HERMAN: *Histoire de L'Expansion Coloniale des Peuples Européens*, vol. Néerlande et Danemark, Bruxelles 1911.

LEUPE, P. A.: "Invoering der koffijkultuur op Java, 1700–1750", *Bijdragen tot de Taal-, Land- en Volkenkunde van Nederlandsch-Indië*, Amsterdam 1859.

VAN LEUR, J. C.: *Indonesian Trade and Society*, Essays in Asian Social and Economic History, The Hague-Bandung 1955 (Selected Studies on Indonesia by Dutch Scholars, vol. I).

MANSVELT, W. M. F.: *Rechtsvorm en geldelijk beheer bij de Oost-Indische Compagnie*, Amsterdam 1922.

MARTIN, GASTON, *Nantes et la Compagnie des Indes 1664–1769*, Paris 1926.

Memorie boek van pakhuismeesteren van de thee te Amsterdam 1818–1918 en de Nederlandsche theehandel in den loop der tijden, Amsterdam n. d.

MILBURN, W., & THORNTON, *Oriental Commerce*, vol. I, London 1825.

MORELAND, W. H., & CHATTERJEE, ATUL CHANDRA: *A Short History of India*, London 1936.

MORELAND, W. H.: *From Akbar to Aurangzeb*, A Study in Indian Economic History, London 1923.

MORSE, H. B.: *The Chronicles of the East India Company Trading to China*, 1635–1834, vol. I, Oxford 1926.

NACHOD, OSKAR: *Die Beziehungen der Niederländischen Ostindischen Kompagnie zu Japan im siebzehnten Jahrhundert*, Leipzig 1897.

NETSCHER, E., & VAN DER CHIJS, J. A.: *De munten van Nederlandsch Indië, beschreven en afgebeeld*, Batavia 1863.

NIEBUHR, CARSTEN: *Reisebeschreibung nach Arabien und andere umliegenden Ländern*, København 1774.

OLÁN, ESKIL: *Ostindiska Compagniets Saga, Historien om Sveriges märkligaste handelsföretag*, Göteborg 1923.

OLSEN, ALBERT: "Kobberpolitik i den svenske stormagtstid", *Scandia* X: 1, Stockholm-København-Oslo 1937.

VAN DER OUDERMEULEN, B.; *vide* DIRK VAN HOGENDORP.

PARKINSON, C. NORTHCOTE: *Trade in the Eastern Seas 1793–1813*, Cambridge 1937.

POSTHUMUS, N. W.: *Nederlandsche Prijsgeschiedenis*, Leiden 1943.

PRITCHARD, EARL H.: *The Crucial Years of Early Anglo-Chinese Relations*, 1750–1800, Washington 1936 (Research Studies of the State College of Washington, vol. IV).

RASCH, AAGE, & SVEISTRUP, P. P.: *Asiatisk Kompagni i den florissante periode*, 1772–1792, København 1948.

REESSE, J. J.: *De suikerhandel van Amsterdam*, Haarlem 1908.

Reports from Committees of the House of Commons, vol. I, London 1803.

VAN RESANDT, W. WIJNAENDTS: *De Gezaghebbers der Oost-Indische Compagnie op hare Buiten-Comptoiren in Azië*, Amsterdam 1944 (Genealogische Bibliotheek, vol. II).

DE REUS, G. C. KLERCK: *Geschichtlicher Überblick der administrativen, rechtlichen und finanziellen Entwicklung der Niederländisch-Ostindischen Compagnie*, Batavia -'s Hage 1894 (Verhandelingen van het Bataviaasch Genootschap van Kunsten en Wetenschappen, deel 47).

RING, VIKTOR: *Asiatische Handlungscompagnien Friederichs des Grossen*, Berlin 1890.

ROELOFSZ, M. A. P.: *De vestiging der Nederlanders ter kuste Malabar*, 's-Gravenhage 1943 (Verhandelingen van het Koninklijk Instituut voor de Taal-, Land- en Volkenkunde van Nederlandsch-Indië, deel 4).

LA ROQUE, *Voyage de l'Arabie Heureuse*, Amsterdam 1716.

SAVARY, JACQUES: *Dictionnaire Universel de Commerce*, vols. I–III, Amsterdam 1726–1732.

SCHLEGEL, G.: "First Introduction of Tea into Holland", *T'oung Pao*, serie II, vol. I, Leiden 1900.

SCHRIEKE, B.: *Indonesian Sociological Studies*, Selected Writings of B. Schrieke, Part I, The Hague-Bandung 1955 (Selected Studies on Indonesia by Dutch Scholars, vol. 2).

SÉE, H., & VIGNOLS, L.: "Les ventes de la Compagnie des Indes à Nantes 1723–1733", *Revue de l'Historie des Colonies*, 1925.

SLOMANN, VILH.: *Bizarre Designs in Silks*, Trade and Traditions, Published for the Ny Carlsberg Foundation, Copenhagen 1953.

STAPEL, F. W.: *De Vereenigde Oostindische Compagnie in de groote oorlogen der XVII[de] eeuw*, Den Haag-Batavia 1932.

STAPEL, F. W.: "Johannes Hudde over de balansen van de Oostindische Compagnie", *Economisch-Historisch Jaarboek*, vol. XIII, 's-Gravenhage 1927.

TAVERNIER, JEAN BAPTISTE: *Les six voyages*, 2. partie, Paris 1678.

TERPSTRA, H.: *De factorij der Oostindische Compagnie te Patani*, 's-Gravenhage 1938 (Verhandelingen van het Koninklijk Instituut voor de Taal-, Land- en Volkenkunde van Nederlandsch-Indië, deel 1).

TERPSTRA, H.: *De Nederlanders in Voor-Indië*, Amsterdam 1947, (Patria, Vaderlandsche cultuurgeschiedenis in monografieën, deel 39).

TERPSTRA, H.: *De opkomst der Westerkwartieren van de Oost-Indische Compagnie* (Suratte, Arabië, Perzië), 's-Gravenhage 1918.

TERPSTRA, H.: *De vestiging der Nederlanders aan de kust van Koromandel*, Groningen 1911.

TERPSTRA, H.: "Enige opmerkingen over het bedrijf der Oostindische Compagnie", *Tijdschrift voor Geschiedenis*, 57. jaargang, 1942.

Uytrekening van de goude en silvere muntswaardye, inhout der maten en swaarte der gewigten in de respective gewesten van Indiën, Middelburg 1691.

VALENTIJN, FRANÇOIS: *Oud en Nieuw Oost-Indiën*, Dordrecht-Amsterdam 1724-26.

VLEKKE, B.: *Geschiedenis van den Indischen Archipel*, 1947.

WILBUR, M. E.: *The East India Company and the British Empire in the Far East*, New York 1945.

WILLIAMSON, J. A.: *The Ocean in English History*, Oxford 1941.

YAMEY, B. S.: "Scientific Bookkeeping and the Rise of Capitalism", *The Economic History Review*, Sec. Ser., vol. I, 1949.

Index